AF822799

Contributions to Economics

More information about this series at http://www.springer.com/series/1262

Vladimir M. Filippov • Alexander A. Chursin •
Julia V. Ragulina • Elena G. Popkova
Editors

The Cyber Economy

Opportunities and Challenges for Artificial Intelligence in the Digital Workplace

Springer

Editors
Vladimir M. Filippov
Peoples' Friendship University of Russia
Moscow, Russia

Alexander A. Chursin
Center of Management of Industrial Spheres
Peoples' Friendship University of Russia
Moscow, Russia

Julia V. Ragulina
Peoples' Friendship University of Russia
Moscow, Russia

Elena G. Popkova
Plekhanov Russian University of Economics
Moscow, Russia

ISSN 1431-1933 ISSN 2197-7178 (electronic)
Contributions to Economics
ISBN 978-3-030-31565-8 ISBN 978-3-030-31566-5 (eBook)
https://doi.org/10.1007/978-3-030-31566-5

© Springer Nature Switzerland AG 2019
This work is subject to copyright. All rights are reserved by the Publisher, whether the whole or part of the material is concerned, specifically the rights of translation, reprinting, reuse of illustrations, recitation, broadcasting, reproduction on microfilms or in any other physical way, and transmission or information storage and retrieval, electronic adaptation, computer software, or by similar or dissimilar methodology now known or hereafter developed.
The use of general descriptive names, registered names, trademarks, service marks, etc. in this publication does not imply, even in the absence of a specific statement, that such names are exempt from the relevant protective laws and regulations and therefore free for general use.
The publisher, the authors, and the editors are safe to assume that the advice and information in this book are believed to be true and accurate at the date of publication. Neither the publisher nor the authors or the editors give a warranty, expressed or implied, with respect to the material contained herein or for any errors or omissions that may have been made. The publisher remains neutral with regard to jurisdictional claims in published maps and institutional affiliations.

This Springer imprint is published by the registered company Springer Nature Switzerland AG.
The registered company address is: Gewerbestrasse 11, 6330 Cham, Switzerland

Acknowledgments

The publication has been prepared with the support of the "RUDN University Program 5-100."

About the Book

Breakthrough inventions in science and technology in recent years have started the Fourth Industrial Revolution (Industry 4.0). This is expected to lead to radical changes in economic activity, encompassing the production, distribution, consumption, and management of all goods and services, and forming new types of economic systems. The consequences of these changes are important topics for current scientific research and are widely studied in modern economic literature.

However, the underdevelopment of a categorical set of tools to study these new economic systems has resulted in multiple terms and interpretations, which will replace each other over the course of this revolution. Certain scholars use the term "e-economy," backing up their position with the fact that new technologies have enabled the creation of electronic goods and services that can be sold online, stimulating the globalization of societies and economies. This term has been used since the early 2000s in the works of, for example, Avila et al. (2014), Chun-Phuoc (2008), and De Jong et al. (2006). Also, new market sectors can be distinguished in the e-economy, e.g., e-commerce and e-government.

Other experts stress the fact that Internet technologies are ubiquitous nowadays and still possess large potential for further development. Based on this, they prefer using the term "Internet economy" to denote the new type of economic systems that form in the process of Industry 4.0. Examples can be found in the publications of Sukhodolov et al. (2018) and Carayannis et al. (2018), which focus on the Internet of Things as a vector of growth in the modern Internet economy. These works state that the subject of the Internet economy is Internet business, which, in turn, is based on utilizing Internet technologies in its activities.

The latest studies prefer the term "digital economy." Obviously, the growing usage in academic circles is predetermined by the normative and legal meaning of the term in certain countries of the world. For example, the Russian national program for the formation of new types of economic systems, which form in the process of the Fourth Industrial Revolution, is called "Digital Economy of the Russian Federation" (adopted in 2017).

The logic of the usage of this term consists in the fact that the new vector of growth in the modern economy lies in the sphere of digital technologies (DigiTech) and hi-tech segments in various sectors of economy: the financial sector (FinTech), educational sector (EdTech), etc. The term "digital economy" is used in the works of Mueller and Grindal (2019) and Bogoviz et al. (2019). However, this term is not always used in the proper context, which undermines its scientific foundation. For example, White (2019) uses a contradictory formulation in his paper: "A Universal Basic Income in the Superstar (Digital) Economy."

The term "Industry 4.0" is now often seen in works devoted to studying a new type of economic system that forms in the process of the Fourth Industrial Revolution. The basis for its usage is the fact that the modern digital and technological industrial revolution is the Fourth Industrial Revolution we have seen. This term is used in the works of Lopes de Sousa Jabbour et al. (2018), Popkova (2019), and Ragulina (2019). It is also used in the national program for the modernization of the German economy under the title "Industrie 4.0." From the scientific point of view, the use of this term is valid for the segments of industrial sectors in which breakthrough technologies are used.

The various terms used for new types of economic systems which form in the process of the Fourth Industrial Revolution complicate the formation of a unified system of knowledge on this topic and hinder the development of a comprehensive scientific and economic concept within which such systems are studied. That is why it is necessary to have a universal term for denoting this new type of economic system that would reflect all of its manifestations and would unify all previous scientific studies on the topic.

In this book, we offer the term "cyber economy" to achieve this aim. We believe that this brings together the truly revolutionary features of the modern economy, acquired under the influence of the Fourth Industrial Revolution: the integration of electronic devices, physical objects, and living organisms (primarily humans) into cyber-physical systems utilizing the Internet of Things, AI, and other technologies of the fourth mode. This has been studied in the works of Cottey (2018) and Seo et al. (2017).

One of the most serious problems of the cyber economy will be social adaptation to the changes that it portends. These will include the need for the workforce to master digital competencies and to become "digital personnel"—employees who have skills with digital technologies and use them during the production of goods and provision of services, and for intelligent machines—digital devices under the control of AI—to be socialized as new participants in the cyber economy. The purpose of this book is to study the relationship between intelligent machines and digital personnel from a number of perspectives and develop recommendations for managing it in the interests of a crisis-free and sustainable transition from the modern socioeconomic system to the cyber economy.

In Part I, the authors substantiate the application of the term "cyber economy" for denoting the new type of economic system that forms in the process of the Fourth Industrial Revolution. Part II aims to determine the place and role of intelligent machines in the cyber economy. Part III analyzes the process of training digital personnel for the cyber economy. In Part IV, the authors study the relationship between intelligent machines and digital personnel in the cyber economy. Finally, Part V is devoted to issues relating to how best to manage the competitiveness of the cyber economy.

Contents

List of Contributors

Arsen S. Abdulkadyrov Federal State Institution of Science "Institute of Social and Political Research" of the Russian Academy of Sciences, Moscow, Russia

Olga E. Akimova Volgograd State Technical University, Volgograd, Russia

Anna V. Bodiako Federal State-Funded Educational Institution of Higher Education "Financial University under the Government of the Russian Federation", Moscow, Russia

Alexander A. Chursin Peoples' Friendship University of Russia (RUDN University), Moscow, Russia

Polina Yu. Grosheva RUDN University, Moscow, Russia

Karine S. Khachaturyan Federal State Military Educational Institution of Higher Education "Military University" of the Ministry of Defense of the Russian Federation, Moscow, Russia

Tatiana V. Kokuytseva Peoples' Friendship University of Russia (RUDN University), Moscow, Russia

Mikhail A. Kovazhenkov Volgograd State Technical University, Volgograd, Russia

Elena S. Kutukova Financial University under the Government of the Russian Federation, Moscow, Russia

Nikita A. Lebedev Institute of Economics of the Russian Academy of Sciences, Moscow, Russia

Svetlana V. Lobova Altai State University, Barnaul, Russia
Ural State University of Economics, Ekaterinburg, Russia

Vera I. Menshchikova Tambov State Technical University, Tambov, Russia

Irina A. Morozova Volgograd State Technical University, Volgograd, Russia

Svetlana Yu. Murtuzalieva RUDN University, Moscow, Russia

Leyla A. Mytareva Volgograd State University, Volgograd, Russia

Evgeny A. Nesterov Joint Stock Company "Russian Space Systems, Moscow, Russia

Vladimir S. Osipov MGIMO University, Moscow, Russia

Anna A. Ostrovskaya RUDN University, Moscow, Russia

Elena S. Petrenko Plekhanov Russian University of Economics, Moscow, Russia

Stanislav E. Prokofyev Financial University under the Government of the RF, Moscow, Russia

Julia V. Ragulina Peoples' Friendship University of Russia (RUDN University), Moscow, Russia

Tatiana M. Rogulenko Federal State Budgetary Educational Institution for Higher Professional Education "State University of Management", Moscow, Russia

Inna N. Rykova Federal State Budgetary Institution "Financial Research Institute of the Ministry of Finance of the Russian Federation", Moscow, Russia

Roman V. Shamin MIREA – Russian Technological University, Moscow, Russia
RUDN University, Moscow, Russia

Marina I. Suganova Orel State University, Orel, Russia

Valery A. Tsvetkov Market Economy Institute (MEI RAS), Moscow, Russia

Alexander S. Tulupov Market Economy Institute of the Russian Academy of Sciences, Moscow, Russia

Andrey E. Tyulin Joint Stock Company "Russian Space Systems", Moscow, Russia

Alexander V. Yudin Peoples' Friendship University of Russia (RUDN University), Moscow, Russia

Natalia A. Zavalko Financial University under the Government of the Russian Federation, Moscow, Russia

Nabi S. Ziyadullaev Market Economy Institute (MEI RAS), Moscow, Russia

Part I
The Cyber Economy as a New Type of Economic System Under the Conditions of Industry 4.0

The Cyber Economy as an Outcome of Digital Modernization Based on the Breakthrough Technologies of Industry 4.0

Elena G. Popkova and Lubinda Haabazoka

Abstract *Purpose*: The purpose of this chapter is to provide a critical analysis of the initial results of digital modernization in the modern economy based on the breakthrough technologies of Industry 4.0. The chapter also introduces the concept of the 'Cyber Economy' as a new type of economic system. The chapter illustrates that the cyber economy is a product of digital modernization, provides a definition of the cyber economy and also scientifically substantiates the logic and sequence of the birth of the cyber economy.

Design/methodology/approach: Because the expected result of any country's modernization is to enhance the livelihoods of its citizens, an assessment of the effect of the level of an economy's digital competitiveness on the population's living standards was conducted. The assessment was done with the help of regression analysis using statistical data from the IMD World Competitiveness Center and Numbeo. The research was conducted on countries with the highest level of digital competitiveness in 2018, including Russia. The rationale behind the selection of countries was that they are the only ones where there is a statistically significant influence of digital modernization on the population's living standards.

Findings: As a result of studying the peculiarities of various technological modes, the stages of digital modernization for the economy based on the breakthrough technologies of Industry 4.0 were characterized as follows: the information economy, the digital economy, and, ultimately, the cyber economy. A conceptual model of the cyber economy was built reflecting its technological mode, objectives and means of management, criterion for measuring the effectiveness of management, new subjects of economic relations, and new spheres of the economy.

Originality/value: It is substantiated that the digital modernization of the economy based on the breakthrough technologies of Industry 4.0 will lead to the formation of the cyber economy that will involve the close interaction of humans

E. G. Popkova (✉)
Plekhanov Russian University of Economics, Moscow, Russia

L. Haabazoka
Graduate School of Business, University of Zambia, Lusaka, Zambia

© Springer Nature Switzerland AG 2019

V. M. Filippov et al. (eds.), *The Cyber Economy*, Contributions to Economics,
https://doi.org/10.1007/978-3-030-31566-5_1

and fully autonomous machines within cyber-physical systems that are transparent, predictable, and manageable.

1 Introduction

The rapid development of breakthrough digital technologies at the beginning of the twenty-first century initiated an active search for their practical application for increasing the effectiveness and accelerating the rates of growth and development in modern socioeconomic systems. In most progressive countries of the world, programs aimed at the formation of an information society and digital modernization of the economy based on the breakthrough technologies of Industry 4.0 has already started. The end result of this digital modernization should be the increased global competitiveness of domestic entrepreneurship and improvements in the level of citizens' livelihoods.

From a scientific point of view, the result of the digital modernization of the economy should see a transition to a new type of economic system, which will ensure the above advantages. The tools that will enable this process are not yet completely defined. Information and communication technologies, digital technologies, and technologies of Industry 4.0 (cyber technologies) belong to different technological modes. This is why we believe that the digital economy should be based not on information, but on a digital society. The technologies of Industry 4.0 should be applied not for its formation but for its modernization.

Underdevelopment of the foundations of digital modernization in modern economies is the main reason why there exist different approaches to implementing digital modernization programs. For example, in Germany, which was the first country to adopt a digital modernization program for its economy based on the breakthrough technologies of Industry 4.0 (2012), this program is called "Industrie 4.0" (Federal Ministry of Germany for Economic Affairs and Energy, Federal Ministry of Germany of Education and Research 2019); and in Russia, which adopted its program after most of the other developed countries (2017), the program is called "Digital Economy" (Government of the Russian Federation 2019).

The contradictions inherent in various national initiatives in the sphere of digital modernization of the economy is a scientific and practical problem of modern times. Current disparate approaches do not allow for the universal statistical accounting of progress in the implementation of these initiatives and causes uncertainty as to their results. This is because the programs focus on expected advantages with insufficient attention on possible risks and diverge on sequence of the process of modernization, which, from a scientific point of view, should have a universally clear logic and structure.

The purpose of this chapter is to critically analyze the initial results of digital modernization in the modern economy and the development of the concept of the cyber economy as a new type of economic system, which will develop as a product of digital modernization. The chapter also defines the concept of the cyber economy and scientifically substantiates the logic and sequence of the transition from one digital model to another.

2 Materials and Method

A review of similar studies in the area of digital modernization of the modern economy, based on the breakthrough technologies of Industry 4.0, showed that the existing work in this area is scattered and fragmented. Some scholars, including Cho et al. (2019), Crittenden et al. (2019), and Zaytsev et al. (2019), define the new type of economic system emerging from Industry 4.0 as an information economy. Other scholars define this new economic system as a digital economy: Moinuddin (2019), Mueller and Grindal (2019), Sanjuán et al. (2018), Bogoviz (2019), Popkova (2019), and Popkova et al. (2019). There are also several studies that have focused on the cyber economy, including Cottey (2018), Dutta and McCrohan (2002), Rohret and Vella (2018), Saiz-Álvarez (2011), Teoh and Mahmood (2017), and Walker (2012).

These varying interpretations of the new type of economic system we will see with Industry 4.0 leads to uncertainty as to the overall results of the digital modernization of the modern economy. We believe that there is a need to specify, reconsider, and systematize this accumulated knowledge, which we aim to do in this study.

As a key expected advantage of digital economic modernization is an improvement into the livelihoods of citizens, we evaluate the effect of the level of digital competitiveness of differing economies on the population's living standards using regression analysis based on statistical data from IMD World Competitiveness Center and Numbeo. The study focuses on countries with the highest level of digital competitiveness in 2018, including Russia. Table 1 outlines initial data from the countries studied.

A preliminary overview of data from Table 1 shows that countries with the highest living standards also have the highest level of digital competitiveness in their economies. This is explained by the fact that the most progressive countries were the first to implement programs for the digital modernization of their economies. The result of a regression analysis, which allows for a precise determination of the mutual dependencies of the studied indicators, is provided in Table 2.

From Table 2 we can see that the linear regression generated is $y = -10.2500 + 1.9937*x$. According to this model, a growth in the value of the digital competitiveness index by 1 point leads to an increase in the value of the index of quality of life by 1.9937 points. As significance F constitutes 0.0044 (and does not exceed 0.05) and according to the F-test, the regression equation is statistically significant at the level of significance $\alpha = 0.05$. An evaluation of the statistical significance of the regression parameter is performed with the help of t-test, as the R-value of coefficient b is below 0.05, coefficient b is statistically significant, and the confidence interval for this coefficient is $0.7411 \leq b \leq 3.2462$.

Table 1 Digital competitiveness and quality of life in countries with the highest rates of digital modernization in their economies, 2018

Country	Digital competitiveness index, points 1–100	Life quality index, points 1–200
USA	100.000	179.20
Singapore	99.422	156.91
Sweden	97.453	178.67
Denmark	96.764	198.57
Switzerland	95.851	195.53
Norway	95.724	181.86
Finland	95.246	194.01
Canada	95.201	170.32
Netherlands	93.886	188.91
UK	93.239	170.81
Israel	92.922	153.82
Australia	90.226	191.13
South Korea	87.983	149.53
Austria	84.770	191.05
Russia	65.204	104.94

Source: Compiled by the authors based on IMD World Competitiveness Center (2019), Numbeo (2019)

Table 2 Regression analysis of the influence of digital competitiveness on living standards in the countries that show the highest rate of digital modernization in their economies, 2018

Regression statistics						
Multiple R	0.6901					
R-square	0.4763					
Normed R-square	0.4360					
Standard error	18.4765					
Observations	15					
Dispersion analysis						
	Df	**SS**	**MS**	**F**	**Significance F**	
Regression	1	4036.3468	4036.3468	11.8236	0.0044	
Leftover	13	4437.9408	341.3801			
Total	14	8474.2876				
	Coefficients	**Standard error**	**t-statistics**	**R-value**	**Lower 95%**	**Upper 95%**
Y-crossing	−10.2500	53.7041	−0.1909	0.8516	−126.2706	105.7706
x	1.9937	0.5798	3.4385	0.0044	0.7411	3.2462

Source: Calculated and compiled by the authors

The correlation coefficient r equals 0.6901 ($\approx$0.7), which shows a strong linear positive (an increase in the digital competitiveness index stimulates an increase in the life quality index and vice versa) relationship. The coefficient of determination

R^2 has a value of 0.4763; the change of the life quality index by 47.63% is explained by the change of the digital competitiveness index (52.37% is explained by other factors).

The determined significant dependence of the studied indicators shows that the early years of digital modernization in the modern economy bring the expected advantages. This emphasizes the importance of further study of this tendency and the necessity for its deep elaboration.

3 Results

As a result of studying the unique features of various technological modes, the stages of digital modernization in the modern economy based on the breakthrough technologies of Industry 4.0 are determined in Table 3.

Table 3 Characteristics of the stages of digital modernization of the modern economy based on the breakthrough technologies of Industry 4.0

Characteristics of stages	Stages of digital modernization of the modern economy based on the breakthrough technologies of Industry 4.0		
	Information economy	Digital economy	Cyber economy
Approximate time frames	Late twentieth century—2010	2011–2024	Starting from 2025
Technological mode	Information and communication technologies (PC, mobile communications, the Internet)	Digital technologies (Big Data, blockchain technologies, cloud technologies)	Cyber technologies (Internet of Things, AI, virtual and alternate reality, ubiquitous computing)
Objective of management in the economy	Information in any form	Digital data	Cyber-physical systems
Methods of management	Stimulation of R&D, protection of intellectual property	Provision of digital security	Provision of cybersecurity
Criterion for the effectiveness of management in the economy	Protection of new, unique information	Preservation and integrity of digital data, their effective storing, transfer, and processing	Integrity and continuity of work of cyber-physical systems
New subjects of economic relations	Humans as the bearers of intellectual capital	Digital employees (digital personnel) as the bearers of digital thinking and digital competences	Machines with remote control, intelligent machines
New spheres of the economy	Information and communication technologies	Hi-tech	Hi-tech segments of all spheres of economy

Source: Compiled by the authors

Table 3 shows that the first stage in the digital modernization of the modern economy based on the breakthrough technologies of Industry 4.0 is the information economy. In the most progressive countries, this stage was passed in the late twentieth century—2010. It was dominated by information and communication technologies (PC, mobile communications, and the Internet). The management objective in the information economy was the creation of information in any form, with new, unique information having a special value.

The tools for the management of the information economy were the stimulation of R&D and protection of intellectual property. The criterion for the effectiveness of management was the protection of new, unique information. A new subject of economic relations in this mode was the human as a bearer of intellectual capital, replacing labor resources. The information and communication technologies sector appeared as a new sphere of economic activity in the information economy.

The second stage of digital modernization of the modern economy is the digital economy. In the most technologically advanced countries, this stage started in around 2011 and will last until around 2024, according to the national programs of modernization. This stage is dominated by digital technologies (Big Data, blockchain technologies, and cloud technologies). Digital data are the objective of management in the digital economy.

The means of management in the digital economy is the provision of digital security, and the criterion for its effectiveness is the preservation and integrity of digital data, its effective storage, transfer, and processing. A new subject of economic relations is the digital employee (digital personnel) as the bearer of digital thinking and digital competences. The sphere of hi-tech emerges and develops in the digital economy (across complete industry sectors—e.g., the pharmaceutical industry or machine building).

The third stage of digital modernization of the modern economy is the cyber economy. In the most advanced countries, transition to this stage will take place from 2025. The conceptual model of the cyber economy is shown in Fig. 1.

As is seen from Fig. 1, the cyber economy is the final stage (result) in the digital modernization of the modern economy. Cyber technologies (the Internet of Things, artificial intelligence, virtual and alternate reality, and ubiquitous computing) will dominate. The objectives of management in the cyber economy will be cyber-physical systems—the systems in which machines interact both with each other and with humans. The method of management of the cyber economy will be through the provision of cybersecurity, and the criterion for its effectiveness will be through maintaining the integrity and continuity of the work of such cyber-physical systems.

The new subjects of economic relations will be machines with remote control (e.g., manipulators and unmanned transport vehicles) and intelligent machines (e.g., robots). The cyber economy will see the development of hi-tech segments in all spheres of the economy, e.g., hi-tech education (EdTech), financial innovations (FinTech), "smart" networks (SmartGrid) in energy, digital literacy (Industrie 4.0) in the real sector, digital agriculture (Agriculture 4.0) in the agro-industrial complex, etc.

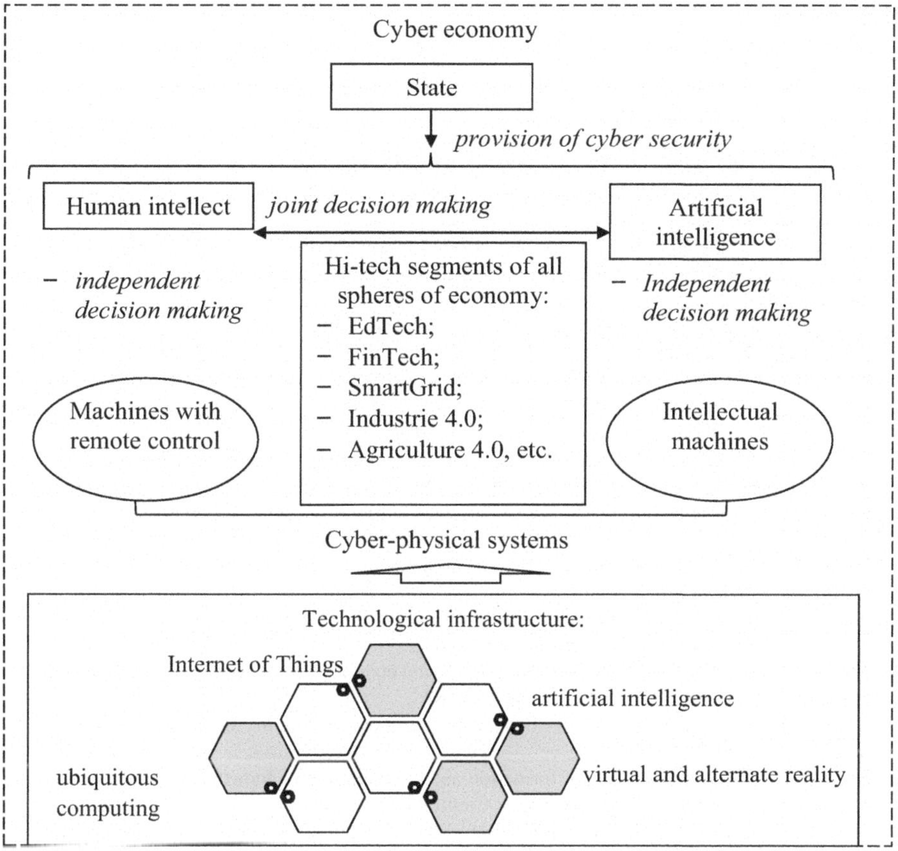

Fig. 1 The cyber economy as a result of digital modernization of the modern economy based on the breakthrough technologies of Industry 4.0 (Source: Compiled by the authors)

4 Conclusion

Following on from the information and digital economies, the cyber economy will be created as the final result of the digital modernization of the modern economy based on the breakthrough technologies of Industry 4.0. It will exhibit close interconnections and interactions between humans and intelligent (fully autonomous) machines within cyber-physical systems, with full transparency, predictability, and controllability of these systems.

Acknowledgments The reported study was funded by RFBR according to the research project No. 18-010-00103 A.

References

Bogoviz AV (2019) Industry 4.0 as a new vector of growth and development of knowledge economy. Stud Syst Decis Control 169:85–91

Cho S, Park C, Kim J (2019) Leveraging consumption intention with identity information on sharing economy platforms. J Comput Inf Syst 59(2):178–187

Cottey A (2018) Economic language and economy change: with implications for cyber-physical systems. AI Soc 33(3):323–333

Crittenden VL, Crittenden WF, Ajjan H (2019) Empowering women micro-entrepreneurs in emerging economies: the role of information communications technology. J Bus Res 98:191–203

Dutta A, McCrohan K (2002) Management's role in information security in a the cyber economy. Calif Manag Rev 45(1):67–87

Federal Ministry of Germany for Economic Affairs and Energy, Federal Ministry of Germany of Education and Research (2019) Platform Industrie 4.0. https://www.plattform-i40.de/I40/Navigation/EN/Home/home.html. Accessed 23 Feb 2019

Government of the Russian Federation (2019) Program "Digital economy of the Russian Federation", adopted by the Decree dated July 28, 2017, No. 1632-p. http://static.government.ru/media/files/9gFM4FHj4PsB79I5v7yLVuPgu4bvR7M0.pdf. Accessed 23 Feb 2019

IMD World Competitiveness Center (2019) World digital competitiveness ranking. https://www.imd.org/wcc/world-competitiveness-center-rankings/world-digital-competitiveness-rankings-2018/. Accessed 23 Feb 2019

Moinuddin S (2019) Digital political economy of India I. In: The political Twittersphere in India, Springer geography. Springer, Cham, pp 91–98

Mueller M, Grindal K (2019) Data flows and the digital economy: information as a mobile factor of production. Digit Policy Regul Gov 21(1):71–87

Numbeo (2019) Quality of life index. https://www.numbeo.com/quality-of-life/rankings_by_country.jsp. Accessed 23 Feb 2019

Popkova EG (2019) Preconditions of formation and development of Industry 4.0 in the conditions of knowledge economy. Stud Syst Decis Control 169:65–72

Popkova EG, Ragulina YV, Bogoviz AV (2019) Fundamental differences of transition to Industry 4.0 from previous industrial revolutions. Stud Syst Decis Control 169:21–29

Rohret D, Vella M (2018) Crypto currency: expanding the underground the cyber economy. In: Proceedings of the 13th international conference on cyber warfare and security, ICCWS 2018, March 2018, pp 645–650

Saiz-Álvarez J-M (2011) Social market economy and welfare state towards the formation of a new cybereconomy. In: International political economy. Nova Science Publishers, Hauppauge, NY, pp 219–232

Sanjuán CE, Cárdenas Garciá M, De Cañizares Arévalo J (2018) Architecture of a digital economy policy: a tool to achieve efficiency in the development of the local economy. J Phys Conf Ser 1126(1):012064

Teoh CS, Mahmood AK (2017) National cyber security strategies for digital economy. J Theor Appl Inf Technol 95(23):6510–6522

Walker S (2012) Economics and the cyber challenge. Inf Secur Tech Rep 17(1–2):9–18

Zaytsev AG, Plakhova LV, Legostaeva SA, Zakharkina NV, Zviagintceva YA (2019) Establishment of information economy under the influence of scientific and technical progress: new challenges and possibilities. Adv Int Syst Comput 726:3–10

Digital Business in the Cyber Economy: The Organization of Production and Distribution Based on the Breakthrough Technologies of Industry 4.0

Elena S. Petrenko, Stanislav Benčič, and Anna A. Koroleva

Abstract *Purpose*: The purpose of this chapter is to develop a conceptual model of the organization of production and distribution based on the breakthrough technologies of Industry 4.0 within the sphere of digital business.

Design/methodology/approach: The authors use the case method to perform an overview of the level of automatization in sales and purchases within the Russian economy in 2018 based on the statistical data of the National Research University "Higher School of Economics." It is determined that the automatization of only two business processes in modern Russia is frequent: purchases and sales. Digital business is becoming more prevalent in the service sector, but the pre-digital mode of business structure is still preserved in industry.

Findings: The sectoral specifics of the automatization of business processes are determined based on breakthrough technologies of Industry 4.0, which should be taken into account during the statistical accounting of digital business. The following essential differences of digital business from pre-digital business are determined: complex offers, automatic internal and external communications, the organization of information processing using Big Data technologies, and the increasingly complex demands on management.

Originality/value: It is shown that digital business is a complex system that consists of many interconnected elements that are integrated through the breakthrough technologies of Industry 4.0. A conceptual model for the organization of production and distribution based on the breakthrough technologies of Industry 4.0 within digital business is developed. The advantages of digital business are shown: high effectiveness, a reduction in resource use, holistic consideration of individual

---

E. S. Petrenko (✉)
Plekhanov Russian University of Economics, Moscow, Russia

S. Benčič
Pan-European University, Bratislava, Slovakia

A. A. Koroleva
Karaganda State Technical University, Karaganda, Russia

© Springer Nature Switzerland AG 2019

V. M. Filippov et al. (eds.), *The Cyber Economy*, Contributions to Economics,
https://doi.org/10.1007/978-3-030-31566-5_2

consumer preferences even in the case of mass offers, and sustainable development due to continuous automatic crisis management.

1 Introduction

The most important condition for the formation of the cyber economy and the expected advantages for all parties (state, business, and society) is the transition to a new technological mode. One of the most significant transformation processes in the economy through such modernization will be the emergence of digital business.

A serious barrier to the formation of digital business (for both developing and developed countries) is uncertainty surrounding the organizational and economic aspects of its implementation.

Firstly, it is not clear how the internal and external communications of businesses will change with the transition to digital information and communication technologies.

Secondly, it is necessary to organize the process of data processing by business structures. The move from paper-based systems to digital databases will expand the possibilities of how they are processed and used and also increase the needs of information provision for business activity. Thus, the volume of analyzed business data will grow, which will require completely new algorithms for their processing.

Thirdly, it is necessary to study the management of digital business, including its subjects and their interactions with each other. Underdevelopment of the concept of digital business hinders its practical application, despite the availability of technological infrastructure in most developed and emerging economies of the world, including Russia.

The purpose of this chapter is to solve this problem by developing a conceptual model for the organization of production and distribution based on the breakthrough technologies of Industry 4.0 within digital business.

2 Materials and Method

Perspectives on the creation of digital business are studied in the works of Ansong and Boateng (2019), Balocco et al. (2019), Bogoviz (2019), Flyverbom et al. (2019), Frank et al. (2019), Olaf and Hanser (2019), Popkova (2019), Popkova and Sergi (2019), Popkova et al. (2019), Senyo et al. (2019a, b), Sousa and Rocha (2019), Sukhodolov et al. (2018), and Venkatesh et al. (2019). However, despite the large number of publications on this topic, digital business is still poorly studied at the fundamental level due to insufficient elaboration of the organizational and managerial aspects and at the empirical level due to a deficit of statistical data.

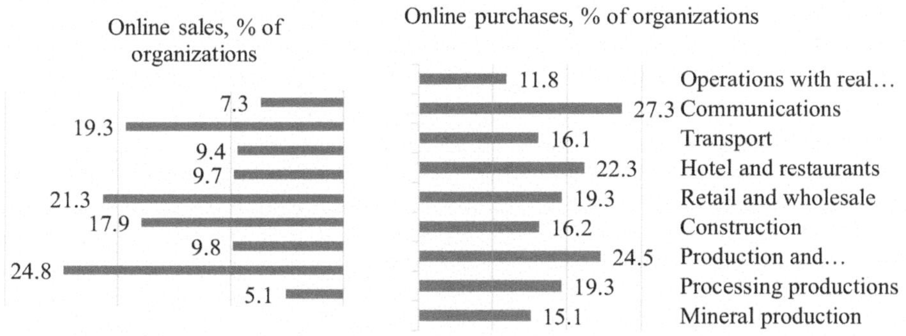

Fig. 1 The level of automatization of sales and purchases in key sectors of the Russian economy in 2018 (Source: Compiled by the authors based on National Research University "Higher School of Economics" (2019))

Here, we use the case method to perform an overview of the level of automatization in sales and purchases within the Russian economy in 2018 utilizing statistical data from the National Research University "Higher School of Economics" (Fig. 1).

Figure 1 shows that automatization of only two business processes is frequent in modern Russia: sales and purchases. The highest percentage of business entities that perform online sales are in the processing productions sector (24.8%), and the lowest are in mineral production (5.1%). The highest percentage of business structures that perform online purchases are in the communications sector (27.3%), and the lowest are in the sphere of real estate, rent, and provision of services (11.8%). According to the calculations of the National Research University "Higher School of Economics" (2019), the share of online sales as a proportion of all sales in the Russian economy is 12.6%, and the share of online purchases is 16.7% on average.

A further scientific and empirical analysis of the peculiarities of products and services allows us to determine the sectoral specifics of the automatization of business processes (Table 1).

Figure 1 shows that the scope for digital modernization is the greatest in the industrial sphere—all business processes could be automatized using the breakthrough technologies of Industry 4.0. In the service sphere, the important role of social interaction between business representatives and consumers means that only purchases and production could be automatized, while other business processes such as management, R&D, and sales cannot be modernized.

Such sectoral specifics must be taken into account during any statistical accounting of digital business. For example, according to the statistical data of National Research University "Higher School of Economics" (2019), digital business has already been formed in the service sphere in Russia, while the pre-digital mode of business structures is preserved in the industrial sphere. The determined contradiction of opportunities and achieved results of digital modernization of the modern Russian economy shows a "market gap" and the necessity for its overcoming with the help of state regulation. This regulation should be aimed at stimulation of digital modernization of the economy's industrial sphere.

Table 1 Sectoral specifics of the automatization of business processes based on the breakthrough technologies of Industry 4.0

Economic sector		Business processes that are accessible for automatization					Maximum level of automatization
		Management	R&D	Purchases	Production	Sales	
Industrial sphere	Minerals production	+	+	+	+	+	Full
	Processing productions						
	Production and distribution of electric energy, gas, and water						
	Construction						
Service sphere	Wholesale and retail trade	–	–	+	+	–	Partial
	Hotels and restaurants						
	Transport						
	Communications						
	Operations with real estate, rent, and provision of services						

Source: Compiled by the authors

3 Results

Figure 2 shows a conceptual model for the organization of production and distribution based on the breakthrough technologies of Industry 4.0 within digital business, in which the ratio of functions of digital personnel and AI (i.e., the level of automatization) could be different depending on the specific sector of a business, the socioeconomic context, and the current needs of the business structures.

As is seen in Fig. 2, digital business is a complex system consisting of many interconnected elements, the integration of which is achieved by using the breakthrough technologies of Industry 4.0. An essential difference of digital business from pre-digital business is the implementation of both mass (standardized) and individual (bespoke) offers in the market.

The target market for a digital company are consumers who use ubiquitous computing (digital devices in "smart" cities and "smart" homes) and products equipped with the Internet of Things (sensors connected to high-speed Internet). Digital business receives marketing information from consumers on a constant basis, e.g., reports on purchases, health, interests, and location, which allow them to determine consumer preferences and current needs.

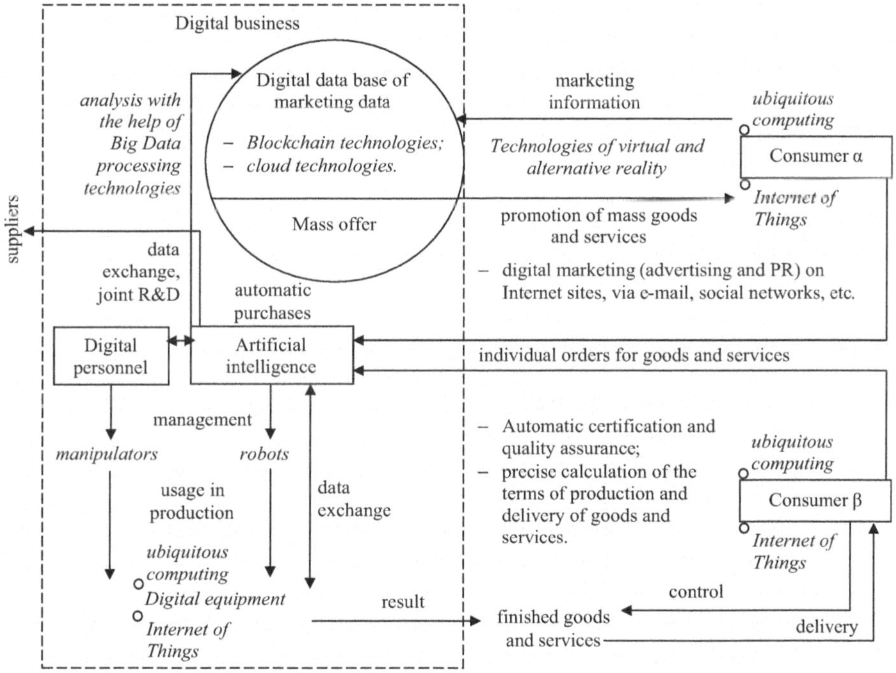

Fig. 2 A conceptual model for the organization of production and distribution based on the breakthrough technologies of Industry 4.0 within digital business (Source: Compiled by the authors)

Marketing information is downloaded into the digital database of the business, organized with the help of blockchain technologies and cloud technologies to ensure cybersecurity. This database also contains information on the mass offers of its digital business, which is promoted automatically in the sectoral market through digital marketing (advertising and PR) on websites, e-mail, through social networks, etc. Marketing communications are performed with consideration for known consumer preferences (e.g., convenient times for the consumer, addressing the consumer in the preferred form, and emphasis on the consumers' needs).

Artificial intelligence performs a key role in digital business through regular automatic analysis of the information contained in the digital database of marketing data using the technologies of Big Data processing. Artificial intelligence also collects individual orders from consumers using technologies of virtual and alternate reality and automatically evaluates the resource and material needs of the digital business and makes purchases from suppliers (suppliers do not necessarily have to have a digital business). Upon request, it exchanges data and conducts joint R&D with digitally competent personnel.

Artificial intelligence controls robots, and digital personnel control manipulators, which use digital equipment in production. Digital personnel are equipped with ubiquitous computing and the Internet of Things and constantly exchange data with artificial intelligence. As a result, finished goods and services appear on the market, and then are delivered to consumers. This high level of automatization allows companies to achieve automatic certification and quality assurance, as well as having precise control over production planning and the delivery of goods and services. Consumers can also access the whole process of production and delivery of goods, starting from the placement of an order.

4 Conclusion

As a result of this research, the following essential differences between digital and pre-digital business have been determined:

- Complex offers, which includes bulk (standard) products and services and the execution of consumers' individual orders;
- Automatic internal (AI's commands to robots and digital equipment) and external (purchases, marketing, and sales) communications;
- Organization of the process of information processing on the basis of Big Data technologies, which allows AI to take into account the whole set of factors and conditions, to assess the situation, and to make optimal decisions;
- The key subjects for the management of digital business will be digital personnel and AI, who will interact within R&D at the initiative of HR department.

The above differences should ensure that the advantages of digital business: high effectiveness due to the optimization of reserves, a reduction in the spending of resources, comprehensive consideration of individual consumer preferences even with mass offers and, secondly, to sustainable development due to continuous automatic crisis management.

It should be concluded that although this conceptual model for the organization of production and distribution based on the breakthrough technologies of Industry 4.0 provides a foundation for research into and the establishment of digital business, it requires further improvement and elaboration for its successful practical application in various sectors of the economy and in different countries of the world. This should be the subject of further research in the continuation of this work.

References

Ansong E, Boateng R (2019) Surviving in the digital era—business models of digital enterprises in a developing economy. Digit Policy Regul Gov 2(1):18–26

Balocco R, Cavallo A, Ghezzi A, Berbegal-Mirabent J (2019) Lean business models change process in digital entrepreneurship. Bus Process Manag J 2(1):47–53

Bogoviz AV (2019) Industry 4.0 as a new vector of growth and development of knowledge economy. Stud Syst Decis Control 169:85–91

Flyverbom M, Deibert R, Matten D (2019) The governance of digital technology, big data, and the internet: new roles and responsibilities for business. Bus Soc 58(1):3–19

Frank AG, Mendes GHS, Ayala NF, Ghezzi A (2019) Servitization and Industry 4.0 convergence in the digital transformation of product firms: a business model innovation perspective. Technol Forecast Soc Chang 2(1):34–45

National Research University "Higher School of Economics" (2019) Indicators of digital economy 2018: statistical collection. https://www.hse.ru/data/2018/08/20/1154812142/ICE2018.pdf.pdf. Accessed 25 June 2019

Olaf JM, Hanser E (2019) Manufacturing in times of digital business and Industry 4.0—the industrial internet of things not only changes the world of manufacturing. Lect Notes Mech Eng F9:11–17

Popkova EG (2019) Preconditions of formation and development of Industry 4.0 in the conditions of knowledge economy. Stud Syst Decis Control 169:65–72

Popkova EG, Sergi BS (2019) Will Industry 4.0 and other innovations impact Russia's development? In: Sergi BS (ed) Exploring the future of Russia's economy and markets. Emerald, Bingley, pp 34–42

Popkova EG, Ragulina YV, Bogoviz AV (2019) Fundamental differences of transition to Industry 4.0 from previous industrial revolutions. Stud Syst Decis Control 169:21–29

Senyo PK, Liu K, Effah J (2019a) Digital business ecosystem: literature review and a framework for future research. Int J Inf Manag 47:52–64

Senyo PK, Liu K, Effah J (2019b) Understanding behaviour patterns of multi-agents in digital business ecosystems: an organisational semiotics inspired framework. Adv Intell Syst Comput 783:206–217

Sousa MJ, Rocha Á (2019) Skills for disruptive digital business. J Bus Res 94:257–263

Sukhodolov AP, Popkova EG, Litvinova TN (2018) Models of modern information economy: conceptual contradictions and practical examples. Emerald, Bingley, pp 1–38

Venkatesh R, Mathew L, Singhal TK (2019) Imperatives of business models and digital transformation for digital services providers. Int J Bus Data Commun Netw 15(1):105–124

The Cyber Economy and Digitization: Impacts on the Quality of Life

Leyla A. Mytareva, Natalia V. Gorshkova, Ekaterina A. Shkarupa, and Rustam A. Yalmaev

Abstract *Purpose*: The purpose of the chapter is to study the influence that the digitization of national economies has on human living standards and quality of life.

Methodology: The methodology includes historical and logical analysis, systemic analysis, synthesis, induction, deduction, and graphic methods. The level of development of human capital and quality of life is studied through sociological surveys and expert methods.

Results: The authors determine the current characteristics of human capital and living standards before the full implementation of Industry 4.0; determine the specific features of the digital and cyber economy that influence human living standards; evaluate the current changes in human living standards under the influence of technological transformation; and outline the conditions under which the changes will have the most positive outcomes for the quality of life.

Recommendations: Governments should target regulation on the processes of digitization of the economy to increase the social protection for citizens who are at risk of losing employment. At the preliminary stages in the development of AI it is necessary to train the future work force from the preschool age, developing the key cognitive skills and supporting social entrepreneurship initiatives as an option to reduce pressures on the labor market due to robotization, automatization, and the digitization of economic activities.

1 Introduction

Many countries are already implementing Industry 4.0 as a strategic plan to develop their national economies and the global economy in general. Industry 4.0 connects industrial machinery and information systems into one space, which allows them to

L. A. Mytareva (✉) · N. V. Gorshkova · E. A. Shkarupa
Volgograd State University, Volgograd, Russia
e-mail: mytarevala@volsu.ru; gorshkovanv@volsu.ru; shkarupaea@volsu.ru

R. A. Yalmaev
Chechen State University, Grozny, Russia
e-mail: r.yalmaev@chesu.ru

© Springer Nature Switzerland AG 2019
V. M. Filippov et al. (eds.), *The Cyber Economy*, Contributions to Economics,
https://doi.org/10.1007/978-3-030-31566-5_3

interact with each other and the external environment without human participation (Korobenkov 2018).

The world is now at the threshold of a new technological revolution, the preparatory phase of which, in the form of the digitization of economy has commenced in many countries, including Russia. The emerging digital economy is already changing the world, and researchers now lead discussions concerning the likely impacts—both good and bad—on an average statistical resident of Earth (or, in our case, a Russian) in the decades to come.

There have been three waves of technological revolutions in the history of humankind:

1. In 1784—new technologies leading to the mechanization of production, and the replacement of manual labor by steam engines;
2. 1870—the electrification of production and implementation of factory conveyor production;
3. 1969—the implementation of automatized and robotized systems.

The fourth stage of the technological revolution—Industry 4.0—(based on the implementation of "smart production") has already begun. There are alternative approaches to the division of technological progress into stages, e.g., distinguishing three stages: the creation of mechanical technologies (Hard), the emergence of necessary information technologies (Soft), and the economic impact of technological progress (Quality of life).

2 Materials and Method

It is possible to measure the changes to the technological modes of the economy through four industrial revolutions. The First (late eighteenth–early nineteenth centuries) saw coal extraction lead to the development of water and steam engines, mechanization, rail transport, and advances in metallurgy leading to a transition from the agrarian economy to industrial production. The Second (late nineteenth–early twentieth centuries) was characterized by the appearance of electric energy, high-quality steel, oil and chemical industries, telephone and telegraph communications, stimulating the appearance of mass industrial production, electrification, railroads, and labor division. The Third (late twentieth century) saw digitization, development of electronics, ICTs, and software lead to growing automatization and robototronics. The Fourth (beginning in 2011 and ongoing) sees continuing advances in global industrial networks, the Internet of Things, renewable sources of energy, a transition from metallurgy to composite materials, food synthesis, neural networks, unmanned vehicles, genetic modification, biotechnologies, and AI.

In the past, each new wave of technological and scientific progress led to the following: an active transformation of production leading to a reduction of transaction costs; waves of change in all spheres of life, as greater efficiencies led to the qualitative growth of manufactured goods and services; step changes in the power and destructiveness of weapons (changing the balance of power in the world); and drastic changes to the requirements for natural resources and human capital. In the long-term, the first three technological revolutions led to an improvement of living standards and quality of life for the majority of the population of the Earth. However, in the short term, each wave of the technological revolution had significant negative impacts on the lives of certain people, countries, and territories. In addition, each wave of the technological revolution led to an increase in the gap between the socioeconomic development of rich and poor countries.

The current stage of the technological revolution has at least two specific features that are different from previous technological breakthrough periods: firstly, in the global community the main value, indicator, and tool of socioeconomic development, unlike all of the previous historical stages, is human, as developed countries, followed by emerging and developing states, largely use the socially oriented model of the market economy. In this system, human capital is the main basis of all economic development, both nationally and globally. Secondly, Internet technologies and automatized systems in management and production have become an inseparable part of modern human life, leading to the creation of a previously unseen platform for implementing AI and the technologies of Big Data.

Industry 4.0, therefore, threatens the basic foundation for human involvement in economic value. There are, today, three basic points of entry for human inclusion in the modern economic processes: entrepreneurship (people create businesses and earn entrepreneurial income, providing hired help with employment and labor income); labor activities as the basis of employment by public or private entities; and the system of public welfare (often government-funded) and/or family social protection and support systems for unemployable citizens (underaged, overaged, or handicapped). The financial equivalent of labor and entrepreneurial capability for able-bodied people and social protection for the unemployable or vulnerable kick starts the turnover of goods, works, and services—and, therefore, finances—in any country's economy (Fig. 1).

Humans and human economic activity are the centerpoint around which all other economic subjects of the economy—the state, business, financial, and credit institutions—function. Public and private economic activities are based on humans, or, in a wider sense, on human capital.

The "World Development Report 2019: The changing nature of work" notes that humans are afraid that "machines will take over their jobs" (World Bank 2019). In the labor market of Industry 4.0, robots replace humans in routine processes and oust the unskilled labor force. However, according to the World Bank, "the leading technologies open new opportunities, creating the conditions for the emergence of new and transformed jobs, increasing the efficiency and effectiveness of the provision of public services" (World Bank 2019). Experts say that present-day high school pupils will work in specialties that do not yet exist. The World Bank report focuses on the basic role of human capital in the age of robotization, digitization, and the cyber economy.

The current transformation to a knowledge economy is actually just a stage in the establishment of the cyber economy. As AI becomes an important rival for the

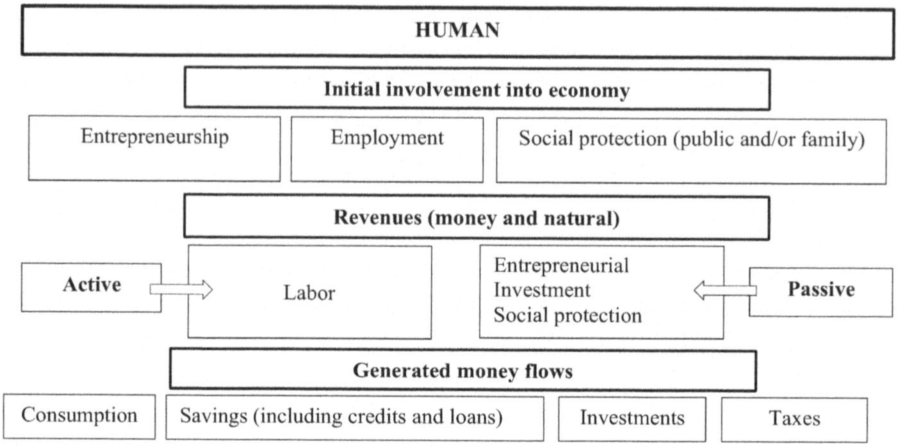

Fig. 1 The place for and role of humans in a national economy

human worker with its ability to accumulate, process, analyze, store, transfer, and produce knowledge, robots and the automatization of production compete with and make redundant human physical labor. In such conditions, the professions of physical and intellectual work become very important. Until now, humanity has not faced such aggressive competition to its economic dominance.

Concerns regarding the fate of humanity in the age of robotization are highlighted in the 2018 report by Deloitte, which is devoted to an analysis of international trends in the sphere of human capital (Deloitte 2018). Deloitte states the necessity for unifying the efforts of business in increasing its social role under the conditions of automatization, an aging workforce, and a growth in the needs for new skills to fill deficits in the labor markets. It suggests that one solution may be to foster the growth of social entrepreneurship.

As we can see, the problem of how to evaluate the influence and impact of the new technological revolution on the level and quality of life of an ordinary human is extremely important and acknowledged by the global expert community.

3 Results

In the modern world, all types of human activities and social roles have an economic (monetary) expression. The field of economics constantly changes its dominant vision of the place and role of the human in the economy (Fedotov 2008), which is primarily a discussion of the motivations behind human economic behavior.

Regardless of the human place in the economic model, a human (or group of humans: society) is the beneficiary owner of all resources in the economy: natural, human, and informational. Humans also produce and consume all goods, works, and services. In order to reduce transactional and other costs, humans join formal and informal groups and agree on common rules and norms of behavior in different spheres of their life activities. From this viewpoint, the state and companies could also be considered as various groups of people (whether they join such groups on a voluntary or forced basis). Each new generation either accepts the existing economic model and becomes the members of the existing state and business, or changes it completely, creating new states and business. In any case, each generation is either evolutionary or revolutionary, but during their lifetime they will have an impact on the socioeconomic picture of the world.

The modern state and development of human capital and the living standards and quality of life of people around the world could be evaluated through two groups of indicators: statistical indicators and index indicators. The first group includes statistical data on the number of people and their geographical, age, sex, and socioeconomic indicators. The second group is represented by the analytical rating evaluations of experts who perform specialized monitoring on the level and development of human capital, quality and cost of life, and well-being in different countries.

Statistical data show a quickly growing population with unequal distribution in the world and a strong polarization of countries depending on the level of socioeconomic development and population number. At present, most of the planetary population live in developing and Third World countries. Their current living standards and quality of life are lower than in developed countries, and they are less prepared for the new technological revolution.

Global statistics show that as of now the current population of the Earth constitutes 7.69 billion people, of which 50.4% are males (3.88 billion people) and 49.6% are females (3.81 billion people), with an average age of 30.4 (2018) and average expected life span of 70 years (Countrymeters 2019). More than 50% of the population live in cities. Population density (considering that 70% of Earth's 136 million km^2 are covered with water) is 56.3 per km^2 (Pewforum 2012). All around the world, people increasingly migrate from rural to urban centers, and this process is most active in developing countries (Helliwell et al. 2018).

As of early 2019, there were 251 countries, with 195 countries having the status of a sovereign state (Passportwiki 2019) (76% of the total number). The territorial distribution of people is unequal: 70% of the whole population (5.4 billion people) live in the 20 most densely populated countries. The five most densely populated countries are China (18.3%), India (17.9%), USA (4.3%), Indonesia (3.5%), and Brazil (2.8%). Russia is ranked ninth in the world (1.9% of the global population). The most popular religions are Christianity (32%), Islam (24.4%), Hinduism (15%), Buddhism (7%), with 15.4% of the global population identifying as atheists (Helliwell et al. 2018).

The socioeconomic indicators are not good. Most of the Earth's population live in very poor conditions (famine, no access to clean drinking water, little access to medicine, low-income levels, high unemployment, military conflicts, etc.). Only 43% of the population have access to clean water (Rozenberg and Fay 2019); 46% (3.4 billion people) fight to satisfy basic human needs and live on less than USD 5.5 per day (the poverty boundary in countries with an income level above average) and 26% of people live for less than USD 3.2 per day (the poverty boundary in countries with an income level below average). Most of these impoverished population live in Latin America (almost 30% of the poor people of the world) and Asia (80% of the residents of Asia) (RIA 2018). According to 2017 estimates, 11% of the world's population has a lack of food (821 million people; up from 795 million people in 2015). In addition, 38 million children and 12.5% of adults have obesity (FAO, IFAD, UNICEF, WFP and WHO 2018). According to the forecast of the Food and Agriculture Organization of the United Nations, in order to satisfy the needs of the growing population, agricultural production has to grow by 50% by 2050 (FAO, IFAD, UNICEF, WFP, and WHO 2018). The International Labor Organization notes that in 2018 (International Labour Office 2019):

1. 3.3 billion out of 5.8 billion people were employed, which accounts for 75% of able-bodied males and 48% of able-bodied females;
2. The increase of involvement of young people in education coupled with longer life expectancy in the last 25 years has led to an increase in the dependency ratio as the share of economically inactive people has grown;
3. 3.3 billion employed people have insufficient resources for their well-being, as their employment does not guarantee a living wage or decent life;
4. 61% of the global workforce is employed in informal sectors of economy;
5. Only 172 million people out of an estimated 2.2 billion unemployed people are officially unemployed (5% of the workforce) and 140 million people have the status of a potential labor force—they look for a job but cannot get one;
6. The distribution of employment is as follows: 34% work in their own business, 11% are employed in a family business; 52% work for employers hired work; 3% are employers.

The level of literacy in the adult population of the world is almost 90% (Countrymeters 2019).

The analytical indicators also show very large gaps in human capital, living standards, and quality of life. Based on the ranking of 71 countries in the Quality of Life Index Rate (Numbeo 2019)[1] (developed and assessed by the website Numbeo, the world largest database on cost and quality of life in cities and countries around the world) in 2019 showed that the highest quality of life is observed in Denmark (quality of life index, 198.57), Switzerland (195.93), Finland (194.01), and Australia (191.13). Russia is ranked 59th with an index of 104.94, between Indonesia (107.2) and Pakistan (104.63). The lowest quality of life measured was in Egypt (83.98), Iran (87.02), and Kazakhstan (87.17) (Numbeo 2019).

The rating of 189 countries (as of 2018) for the Human Development Index (HDI) is based on three main indicators: (1) the possibility to lead a long and healthy life is

[1]Quality of Life Index (higher is better) is an estimation of overall quality of life by using an empirical formula which takes into account purchasing power index (higher is better), pollution index (lower is better), house price to income ratio (lower is better), cost of living index (lower is better), safety index (higher is better), health care index (higher is better), traffic commute time index (lower is better), and climate index (higher is better) (Numbeo 2019).

measured by expected life span from birth; (2) the ability to acquire knowledge is measured by the average expected years schooling for school-age children and average years of schooling in the adult population; (3) the ability to achieve a decent level of life is measured by gross national income per capita. According to the HDI, 59 countries have a very high level of development in human capital, 39 have a medium level, and 38 have a low level. The five leading countries in the HDI are Norway (0.953), Switzerland (0.944), Australia (0.939), Ireland (0.938), and Germany (0.936). The lowest five are: Burundi (0.417), Chad (0.404), South Sudan (0.388), Central African Republic (0.367), and Niger (0.354). The HDI constituted 0.728 in 2017 (which is higher by 22% when compared to 1990) (Hackl 2019). In 2018, Russia was ranked 49th according to the HDI (Hackl 2019).

According to the data of the British analytical center The Legatum Institute, in the rating of 149 countries according to the Legatum Prosperity Index (LPI) (a combined indicator, which reflects the values of nine subindices: Economic Quality; Business Environment; Governance; Education; Health; Safety and Security; Personal Freedom; Social Capital; Natural Environment) in 2018: 2.4 billion people had difficulties and problems in getting enough food; 2 billion people did not have accommodation (in 2018, these numbers were 1.6 and 1.4 billion, accordingly) (Prosperity Style 2018). According to the 2018 rating of 149 countries, 40 were prospering, and 20 countries had significant problems in terms of their development. Almost 90 countries with an average level of prosperity accounted for 78% of the global population.

People evaluate their level of happiness in many different ways. According to the annual UN World Happiness Report (World Happiness Report 2018) (a rating of 156 countries as to the level of happiness of the population and immigrants that compares countries using six indicators: income, health and life expectancy, social support, freedom, trust, and generosity) in 2018, the citizens of Finland were the happiest people in the word (index, 7.632). Russia is ranked 59th out of 156 countries with an index of 5.810, between Northern Cyprus (5.875) and Kazakhstan (5.790). As to the level of happiness of immigrants, Russia is ranked 51st (5.548), between Uzbekistan (5.6) and Turkmenistan (5.547). The least happy people are those in Burundi (2.905), and the least happy immigrants are in Syria (3.516).

According to the data, as the population of the planet grows, the gap between rich and poor countries increases and the number of rich countries remains low. The problems of famine, security, and poverty increase each year. In such conditions, the commercialization of Industry 4.0 may become an accelerator for an even larger differentiation and polarization of economies and activate negative tendencies in both rich and poor countries.

The components of Industry 4.0 are the elements of the Internet of Things, AI, machine learning, robototronics, cloud calculations, Big Data, adaptive production systems, cybersecurity, integration systems, modeling, and alternate reality.

However, all of these elements remain very expensive to implement, exploit, and service; besides, due to low levels of development of such technologies (no common standards, harmonization, unification, etc.), the risk of an unsuccessful implementation and ineffective exploitation are high (Gorshkova et al. 2019).

At present, according to Venture Scanner, the market for solutions in the sphere of AI constitutes USD 4.8 billion (by 2024 it will constitute USD 11.1 billion), though revenues from sales are only USD 202.5 million (IOT 2018). AI is often used in advertising, finance, healthcare, and insurance—sectors where there is a need to discover hidden trends through Big Data analysis. The obvious leaders in the development of AI are the USA, the UK, Germany, France, and the Netherlands.

The components of Industry 4.0 will become more widely used and cheaper over the course of time (Korobenkov 2018): The Internet of Things; Big Data technology; cyber-physical systems; digitization and virtualization of human communications, and relations (personal, financial, administrative, etc.); systems of AI in production and nonproduction spheres and sectors.

Evaluations of the volume of the digital economy are different due to the differences in the approaches taken. According to one assessment, the share of the digital segment of the global economy accounts for 23% (USD 17 trillion), and it will reach 25% of global GDP and a value of USD 21 trillion by 2020. In the largest countries of the world, the share of the digital economy constitutes from 11% in China to 34% in the USA (in Russia, it is between 2.0 and 5.1% of GDP) (Apec-center 2018).

The performed analysis of the influence of technologies on human living standards coupled with statistical data and expert assessments allows us to state the following:

Firstly, the quality of life for people with access to new technological and digital innovation has grown, as their needs and desires are increasingly catered for. Previously complex transactions (transportation, consumption of financial services, medical treatment, and studying personal communications) become cheaper and simpler. However, the quality of life for those without access to such innovations is reduced. According to the forecasts, free price formation will lead to the "radical improvement" of humankind with the help of new technologies, when "rich and privileged people will receive access to expensive methods of improvement of quality long before the middle class and the poor, and then they will use these advantages for expanding the existing large gap between the rich and the poor" (Masci 2016).

In the countries with a high level of societal well-being there appears an innovative spiral where "development of society stimulates innovative technologies, and they raise quality of life to a higher level" (Arkhipova 2013). It is possible to state that the gap in accessibility to the results of innovations in poor countries leads to a reverse spiral—they consume obsolete technologies from developed countries, and the more they consume the less chance there is for their own innovative breakthroughs.

It should be noted that according to one position history shows that when people receive more control over their lives, they become more sensitive. The higher the health, intellect, and life span, the higher the sense of compassion and sensitiveness (Pinker 2011).

Secondly, even when new technologies become widely accessible, people are very careful with them and treat them with concern. There are many possibilities (and they will increase in the future) for improving the human being as a biological form. These will include a wide range of biomedical procedures in the form of implementing biochemical, surgical, or other changes, for the improvement of cognitive, psychological, and physical abilities, including changes aimed at the improvement of physical and mental health (Pewresearch 2016). However, the surveys performed in the USA in the last 6 years show that 70% of respondents are afraid of brain implants (which could provide humans with a better ability to concentrate and process information), 68% of respondents are afraid of genetic engineering (the possibility of changing genes to ensure that a child will live a life with a small risk of serious diseases), and 63% of respondents are afraid of synthesized blood (for higher speed, strength, and stamina) (Pewresearch 2016). It should also be noted that 73% of respondents were sure that these improvements would increase the gap between the rich and the poor, for if these technologies became available, only the rich would have initial access to them.

The survey shows that public opinion on the ethical nature of human improvement is closely connected to religious differences: with more religious respondents having more negative attitudes towards such medical innovation.

Despite the fact that technologies are developing very rapidly, there are still discussions on the ethical and moral aspects of these improvements (Masci 2016). There is not yet public support or a government position on the legality of a range of technological inventions.

Fourthly, new technologies are already changing the labor market, and they will lead to its fundamental change in the future. Automatization predicates increased demand for a workforce with cognitive skills of the highest level. The studies show that three types of skills become very important: developed cognitive skills (complex solution of problems), socio-behavioral skills (teamwork), and combinations of skills that predetermine the ability for adaptation (logical thinking and self-confidence). The formation of such skills is determined by the quality of human capital, investments into it, and its development in the course over human life. According to the recent survey of Eurobarometer, 75% of EU citizens are sure that new technologies are beneficial to their jobs, 64% believe that they are useful for society, and 67% that they improve quality of life (World Bank 2019).

Fifth, Internet technologies and digitization lead to the transformation of business models. Any regional company, with a minimum of materials, assets, or personnel could become a world leader through a digital platform. This model of "maximum scale with minimum mass" opens economic opportunities for millions of people who do not reside in industrially developed countries or leading industrial regions.

Sixth, all new technologies—especially the biomedical improvement of humans and AI—have a range of potential dangers. According to most respondents, AI is perceived as a very dangerous element of the cyber economy. According to most expert forecasts, AI will slowly move from its current specialized level to the general human level and then will make an instantaneous huge leap, turning into a superintelligence by 2040 (Urban 2017), becoming a quasi-god in the classical understanding as an all-seeing, all-knowing, and omnipotent entity (HABR 2018). Experts say that "intellect brings power," and this is a threat for all humankind. The danger of intelligent machines enslaving humanity has been noted by leading world scholars, including Stephen Hawking, Bill Gates, and others.

Digitization—especially in the monetary and credit sphere—is also potentially rather dangerous. The threats include the growth of cybercrimes, digital fraud, and personal data leaks. In addition, the increasing emergence of cryptocurrencies may threaten monetary and financial operations and the monopoly of central banks.

There is a position that while Industry 4.0 is generally perceived as a radical change to industrial production, it is actually a real transformation only in "financial and logistics provision" (Tadviser 2018). Some experts also think that the establishment of Industry 4.0 is only possible by dehumanization of the operational space, as it can only function effectively as a socially irresponsible mechanism. There are also suppositions that interest in Industry 4.0 has been increased artificially and it is aimed at preparing the world for the "global investment default" (Tadviser 2018).

To ally these concerns, the transition to Industry 4.0 should be controlled by at least two powers: governments and voluntary associations of private businesses. In the first case, there should be total control over the transparency, certification, and application of new technologies—especially in spheres where there are moral and ethical concerns. Such legal and administrative control could be accompanied by a system of state support for directions that are important for the development of human capital—in particular, for reducing prices and increasing the accessibility of new technologies in medicine and healthcare, education, entrepreneurship, and food and agricultural security. It will also be necessary to increase the levels of social security to compensate a workforce made redundant by the automatization and robotization of production.

Business groups are necessary in order to boost social entrepreneurship and consolidate efforts with society and state to increase the accessibility of hi-tech goods and services for wide swathes of the population.

The workforce (human capital) for the digital and cyber economy should be prepared from a young age and will require raising the quality of preschool and secondary education.

4 Conclusion

As this chapter has shown, the current transition of humanity to the cyber economy takes place in specific conditions: the dehumanization of economy and how that is dealt with by national policies, the morality of new technologies competing in the market with physical labor, high levels of development of Internet technologies, and new technologies such as AI as a real threat to humanity. An effective transition to the cyber economy is possible only with strict government control and the social initiatives of business.

The main conditions in which the cyber economy and digital economy increase quality of life and living standards are as follows: social entrepreneurship; national policies to compensate the workforce as machines replace human labor; a change in the paradigm of education to focus on the development of cognitive skills, starting from preschool education; and free price formation for technologies that contribute towards human improvement is inadmissible, because this will increase the gap between poor and rich countries.

References

Apec-center (2018) Digital economy: Russia and the world. http://apec-center.ru/wp-content/uploads/2018/02/Monitoring_5_RFTA_APEC_OECD.pdf. Accessed 22 June 2019

Arkhipova MY (2013) Innovations and population's living standards: a study of interconnection and the main tendencies of development. Issues Stat 4:45–53

Countrymeters (2019) World population. https://countrymeters.info/ru/World. Accessed 22 June 2019

Deloitte (2018) The rise of the social enterprise Deloitte Global Human Capital Trends 2018. https://www2.deloitte.com/content/dam/insights/us/articles/HCTrends2018/2018-HCtrends_Rise-of-the-social-enterprise.pdf. Accessed 22 June 2019

FAO, IFAD, UNICEF, WFP and WHO (2018) The state of food security and nutrition in the world—2018. http://www.fao.org/publications/sofi/ru/. Accessed 22 June 2019

Fedotov VG (ed) (2008) Human in economy and other social environment: a collective monograph. Russian Academy of Sciences, Institute of Philosophy, Moscow

Gorshkova NV, Mytareva LA, Shkarupa EA, Yalmaev RA (2019) The concept of tax stimulation of informatization of modern entrepreneurships studies in systems. Decis Control 182:179–188

HABR (2018) Revolution of AI—a path to super intellect. https://habr.com/ru/post/293156/. Accessed 22 June 2019

Hackl P (2019) A new generation of data for human development 2018. Background paper. UNDP Human Development Report Office. http://hdr.undp.org/sites/default/files/hackl_final_02.pdf. Accessed 22 June 2019

Helliwell JF, Layard R, Sachs JD (2018) World happiness report 2018. https://s3.amazonaws.com/happiness-report/2018/WHR_web.pdf. Accessed 22 June 2019

International Labour Office (2019) World employment social outlook. Trends 2019. https://www.ilo.org/wcmsp5/groups/public/%2D%2D-dgreports/%2D%2D-dcomm/%2D%2D-publ/documents/publication/wcms_670542.pdf. Accessed 22 June 2019

IOT (2018) AI. History of development and market overview. https://iot.ru/gadzhety/iskusstvennyy-intellekt-istoriya-razvitiya-i-obzor-rynka. Accessed 22 June 2019

Korobenkov A (2018) The digital system of production management—an important step towards Industry 4.0. https://controlengrussia.com/internet-veshhej/tsifrovaya-sistema-upravleniya-proizvodstvom-vazhny-j-shag-k-industrii-4-0/. Accessed 22 June 2019

Masci D (2016) Human enhancement: the scientific and ethical dimensions of striving for perfection. http://www.pewresearch.org/science/2016/07/26/human-enhancement-the-scientific-and-ethical-dimensions-of-striving-for-perfection/. Accessed 22 June 2019

Numbeo (2019) Quality of life index 2019. https://www.numbeo.com/quality-of-life/indices_explained.jsp. Accessed 22 June 2019

Passportwiki (2019) Number of countries in the world in 2019. http://passportwiki.ru/skolko-vsego-v-mire-stran/. Accessed 22 June 2019

Pewforum (2012) The global religious landscape. http://www.pewforum.org/2012/12/18/global-religious-landscape-exec/. Accessed 22 June 2019

Pewresearch (2016) U.S. public wary of biomedical technologies to 'enhance' human abilities. http://www.pewresearch.org/science/2016/07/26/u-s-public-wary-of-biomedical-technologies-to-enhance-human-abilities/. Accessed 22 June 2019

Pinker S (2011) The better angels of our nature: why violence has declined. https://www.ted.com/talks/steven_pinker_on_the_myth_of_violence. Accessed 22 June 2019

Prosperity Style (2018) The Legatum Prosperity Index™ 2018, 12th edn. https://prosperitysite.s3-accelerate.amazonaws.com/2515/4321/8072/2018_Prosperity_Index.pdf. Accessed 22 June 2019

RIA (2018) The World Bank learned how many people live for less than $5.5 per day. https://ria.ru/20181017/1530821422.html. Accessed 22 June 2019

Rozenberg J, Fay M (2019) Beyond the gap: how countries can afford the infrastructure they need while protecting the planet. Sustainable infrastructure. Washington, DC: World Bank. https://openknowledge.worldbank.org/handle/10986/31291. Accessed 22 June 2019

Tadviser (2018) The fourth industrial revolution. Popular story of the main technological trend of the 21st century. http://www.tadviser.ru/index.php/%D0%A1%D1%82%D0%B0%D1%82%D1%8C%D1%8F:%D0%A7%D0%B5%D1%82%. Accessed 22 June 2019

Urban T (2017) Neuralink and the brain's magical future. 20 April 2017. https://waitbutwhy.com/2017/04/neuralink.html. Accessed 22 June 2019

World Bank (2019) The world development report 2019: the changing nature of work. http://documents.worldbank.org/curated/en/923251543930325486/pdf/WDR2019-Overview-Russian.pdf. Accessed 22 June 2019

State Regulation of the Cyber Economy Based on the Breakthrough Technologies of Industry 4.0

Julia V. Ragulina, Alexander Settles, and Olga A. Shilkina

Abstract *Purpose*: The purpose of this chapter is to determine the perspectives and to develop recommendations for the digital modernization of state regulation of the economy in Russia, using the breakthrough technologies of Industry 4.0.

Design/methodology/approach: The authors perform a statistical overview of the modern Russian practice of obtaining state services by economic subject using materials from "Indicators of the digital economy 2018," which was compiled by the National Research University "Higher School of Economics."

Findings: It is determined that in modern Russia, digital modernization of the practice of state regulation of the economy does not conform to the current needs of the cyber economy, as it is limited by its focus on only one direction (provision of state services) and it is based on traditional digital technologies (Internet).

Originality/value: A conceptual model for state regulation of the cyber economy based on the breakthrough technologies of Industry 4.0 is offered, according to which the digital modernization of regulatory practices also covers other areas (monitoring of economic activities, management of economic activities, and support for a favorable economic climate) through the utilization of digital technologies including blockchain, cloud technologies, the Internet of things, AI, quantum technologies, etc. Practical implementation of the developed model will satisfy the current and future needs of the cyber economy, which is currently forming in Russia, for hi-tech state regulation.

J. V. Ragulina (✉)
Peoples' Friendship University of Russia (RUDN University), Moscow, Russia

A. Settles
Entrepreneurship & Innovation Center, Florida University, Gainesville, FL, USA
e-mail: Alex.Settles@warrington.ufl.edu

O. A. Shilkina
Moscow State University, Moscow, Russia

© Springer Nature Switzerland AG 2019

V. M. Filippov et al. (eds.), *The Cyber Economy*, Contributions to Economics,
https://doi.org/10.1007/978-3-030-31566-5_4

1 Introduction

A current scientific and practical problem, caused by the formation of the cyber economy, is how best to digitally modernize the practice of state regulation of the economy using the breakthrough technologies of Industry 4.0. Firstly, the emergence of the cyber economy presents new challenges and threats to economic activities (e.g., threats to cybersecurity), which require regulation within the new technological mode. Secondly, the formation of the cyber economy opens new opportunities for improving state regulation of economy that, if ignored, will lead to failure in implementing its effectiveness. Thirdly, given the emergence of the cyber economy, there is a demand for modern (hi-tech) state regulation of economy, to support systemic (comprehensive) digital modernization.

In order to practically implement the national program, "Digital economy of the Russian Federation," adopted by the Decree of the Government of the Russian Federation (2019) dated July 28, 2017, No. 1632-r, "setting the standards and regulating the digital economy" are envisaged. This presupposes the formation and development of a system of e-government through the digital modernization of state regulation of the economy.

"The Global Information Technology Report 2016," compiled by the World Economic Forum (2019), highlights that this is likely to be problematic for Russia. The total value of the Networked Readiness Index in Russia is 4.5 points out of 7, which puts it in 41st position out of 139 countries assessed. Russia was given a score of 3.6 points out of 7 for the indicator of the development of its e-government system in 2016, putting it 88th out of 139 countries. The political and regulatory environment lags leading nations.

Based on this, the following hypothesis is offered: State regulation of the Russian economy does satisfy the increased needs, for the formation of the cyber economy. Digital modernization is conducted fragmentarily and does not plan for the usage of the breakthrough technologies of Industry 4.0. The purpose of this research is to determine the reasons behind this problem and to develop clear recommendations for the digital modernization of state regulation of the Russian economy.

2 Materials and Method

Fundamental issues for the formation and development of e-government systems are studied in detail in the works Adjei-Bamfo et al. (2019), Bogoviz (2019), Butt et al. (2019), Khan and Krishnan (2019), Palaco et al. (2019), Popkova (2019), Popkova and Sergi (2019), Popkova et al. (2019), Rosenberg (2019), and Sukhodolov et al. (2018). The problem of state regulation of the cyber economy based on the breakthrough technologies of Industry 4.0 is poorly studied and requires further consideration.

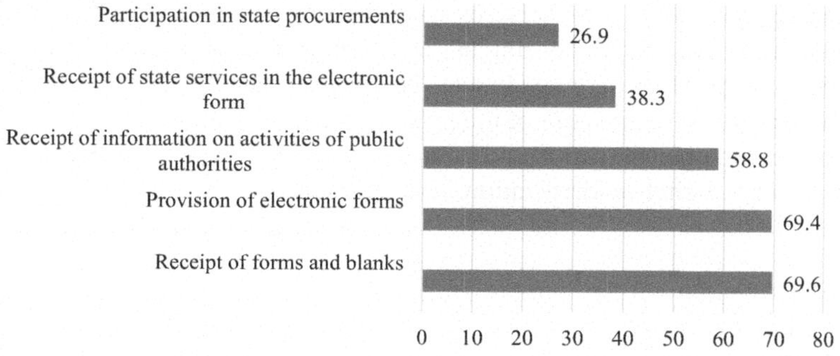

Fig. 1 Receipt of online state services by Russian businesses in 2018 [Source: Compiled by the authors based on the National Research University "Higher School of Economics" (2019)]

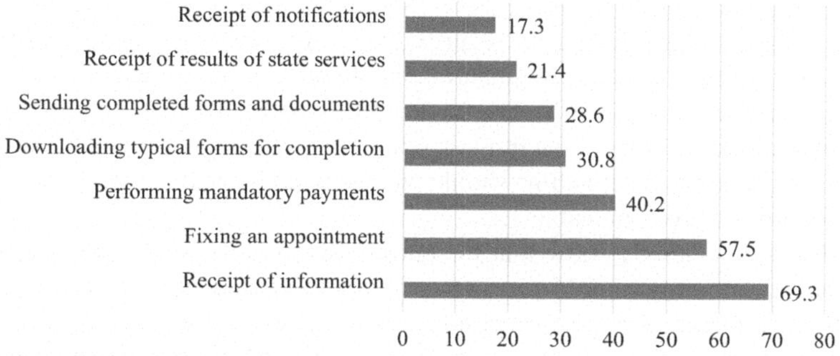

Fig. 2 Receipt of online state services by the Russian population, 2018 [Source: Compiled by the authors based on National Research University "Higher School of Economics" (2019)]

The methodology of the research is based on econometric analysis. According to the materials in the statistical collection "Indicators of the digital economy 2018," which was compiled by the National Research University "Higher School of Economics" (2019), the system of e-government in modern Russia is primarily used for the provision of state services. 42% of Russians obtain state services via the Internet. A more detailed statistical overview of online state services by economic subject is presented in Figs. 1 and 2.

As is seen in Fig. 1, the most popular use of online state services by businesses in Russia (as of 2018) was obtaining forms and blanks (69.6% of businesses), and the least popular use was participation in state procurement projects (26.9%).

As is seen from Fig. 2, the most popular use of online state services by the Russian populace (as of 2018) was to obtain information (69.3% of the population), and the least popular goal was to receive notifications (17.3%). The main reason for the low usage of online state services in Russia is their poor approval rates (many public officers who provide online services are poorly qualified) and weak infrastructural support (failures in the provision of online services due to bad Internet connections, badly designed software, and hardware).

By simply providing state services (ineffectively) online, the current Russian system does not cover the monitoring or management of economic activities, or offer support for a favorable economic climate. The low accessibility of the e-government system reduces the effectiveness of the process to digitally modernize. There is now a need for a comprehensive, root, and branch (covering all aspects of state regulation of the economy) digital modernization of this system.

3 Results

As a result of thorough expert research, we determined significant drawbacks in the modern practice of state regulation of the Russian economy, which are critical to address under the conditions of the cyber economy, as they will restrain its growth and development and threaten its security. These drawbacks include fragmentary rather than simultaneous analysis, insufficient attention to the threat of cyberattacks (due to an emphasis on the risks of globalization), and slow manual processing of data. Comparative analysis of the modern practice of state regulation of the economy and recommendations for how this should change to address the critical issues of the cyber economy is given in Table 1.

The data from Table 1 show that the current (as of early 2019) practice of state regulation of economy should receive new treatment and new technical support under the conditions of the cyber economy. This will overcome the existing drawbacks of the system while retaining its advantages. State regulation of the economy should be subject to systemic and continuous analysis on the basis of ubiquitous computing, the Internet of Things, and AI. Increased attention should be given to cyber risks utilizing quantum technologies, 5G communications, and high-speed Internet. There should be automatic processing of data that should be digital stored using blockchain technologies. Efforts should be made to develop "smart cities" and cloud technologies. Based on this, a conceptual model for state regulation of the cyber economy based on the breakthrough technologies of Industry 4.0 was developed (Fig. 3).

Figure 3 shows that under the conditions of the cyber economy, the management of economic activities and support for a favorable economic climate are conducted by public authorities (economic regulators) with intellectual support for decision-making. Other functions (namely, the monitoring of economic activities and provision of state services) are performed by AI, which conducts continuous analysis of the unified national digital databases, which are organized on the basis of blockchain and cloud technologies.

Due to the fact that both consumers and businesses have ready access to ubiquitous computing and the Internet of Things, it is possible to conduct continuous automatic collection of digital information and queries for state services. The identification and registration of economic operations are conducted automatically

Table 1 Comparative analysis of the modern practice of state regulation of the economy and recommendations for how this should change to address the critical issues of the cyber economy

Direction of state regulation of economy		Modern practice in Russia (2019)	In the cyber economy	
			Treatment	Technologies
Monitoring of economic activities	Statistical accounting	Survey of economic subjects	Automatic collection of data	Ubiquitous computing
	Tax administration and control	Manual inspection of reports	Automatic inspection of reports	Internet of things
	Analysis of sectoral markets	Manual fragmentary analysis	Automatic full analysis	AI
Provision of state services	Registration of economic operations	Manual registration in due time	Digital registration in real time	Blockchain (distributed ledger)
	Regulation of economic conflicts	Personal provision of documents in due time	Provision of documents in digital form	"Smart cities"
	Provision of documents and confirmations	Upon the request in due time	Upon the request in real time	Cloud technologies
Management of economic activities	Managing the situation in sectoral markets	Manual analysis	Intellectual support for making of managerial decisions	AI
	Support for business	Manual analysis, upon the request in due time	Automatically or upon the request in real time	
	Social support			
Support for favorable economic climate	Creation and development of infrastructure	Transport and logistics infrastructure	Telecommunications infrastructure	5G, high-speed Internet
	Provision of economic security	Positive balance of foreign trade	Cybersecurity	Quantum technologies
	Crisis management	Managing the threats to globalization and the shadow economy, determining the "market gaps"	Managing cyber threats and competitiveness (stimulation of innovative activities in economy)	AI

Source: Compiled by the authors

in real time, as well as the provision of most state services (e.g., issuing references and documents). Economic security is provided through the prism of cybersecurity on the basis of quantum technologies.

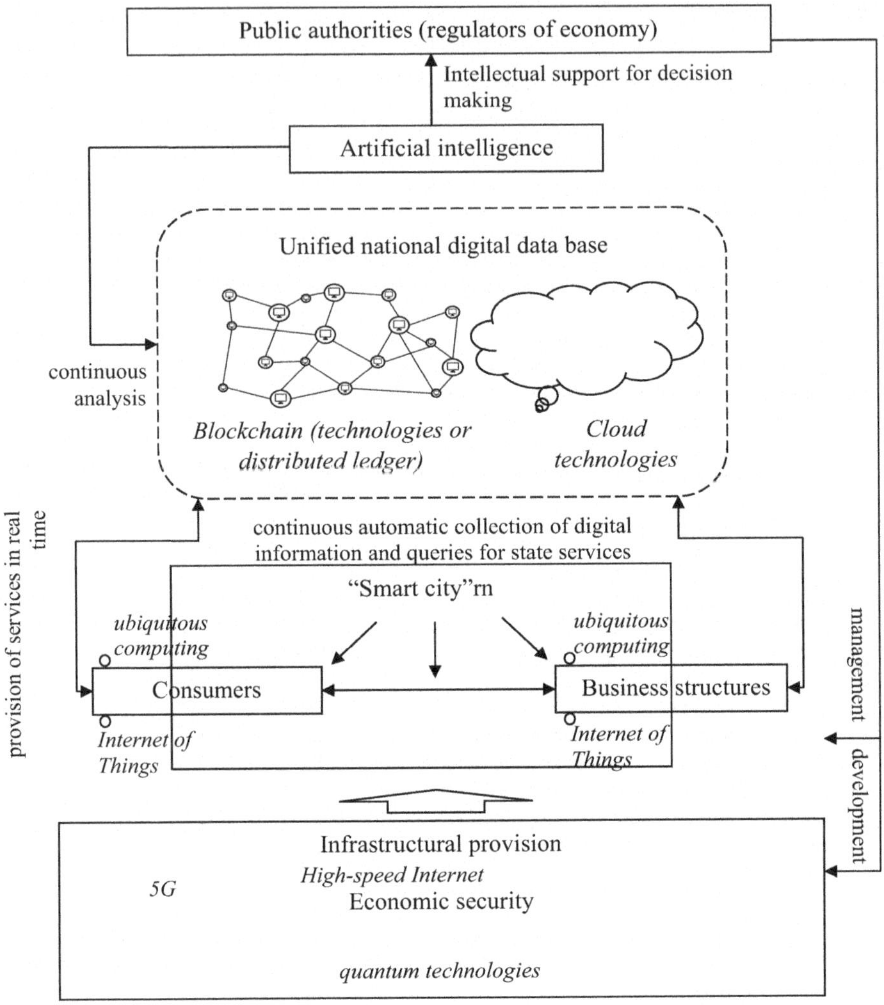

Fig. 3 Conceptual model for the state regulation of the cyber economy based on the breakthrough technologies of Industry 4.0 (Source: Compiled by the authors)

4 Conclusion

As a result of the research, it has been substantiated that digital modernization of the practice of state regulation of the economy in modern Russia does not support the current needs of the cyber economy, as it is limited by one direction (provision of state services) and is based on traditional digital technologies (Internet).

The conceptual model of state regulation of the cyber economy provided, in which digital modernization of regulatory practices also covers other areas (monitoring and management of economic activities, and support for a favorable economic climate) and is based on the breakthrough digital technologies (blockchain, cloud technologies, the Internet of Things, AI, quantum technologies, etc.) is recommended. Practical implementation of the developed model will allow for the satisfaction of the current and future needs of the cyber economy and for hi-tech state regulation in modern Russia.

Acknowledgments This chapter has been prepared with the support of the "RUDN University Program 5-100."

References

Adjei-Bamfo P, Maloreh-Nyamekye T, Ahenkan A (2019) The role of e-government in sustainable public procurement in developing countries: a systematic literature review. Resour Conserv Recycl 142:189–203

Bogoviz AV (2019) Industry 4.0 as a new vector of growth and development of knowledge economy. Stud Syst Decis Control 169:85–91

Butt N, Warraich NF, Tahira M (2019) Development level of electronic government services: an empirical study of e-government websites in Pakistan. Glob Knowl Mem Commun 68 (1–2):33–46

Government of the Russian Federation (2019) Program "Digital economy of the Russian Federation", adopted by the Decree dated July 28, 2017, No. 1632-r. http://static.government.ru/media/files/9gFM4FHj4PsB79I5v7yLVuPgu4bvR7M0.pdf. Accessed 28 Feb 2019

Khan A, Krishnan S (2019) Conceptualizing the impact of corruption in national institutions and national stakeholder service systems on e-government maturity. Int J Inf Manag 46:23–36

National Research University "Higher School of Economics" (2019) Indicators of digital economy 2018: statistical collection. https://www.hse.ru/data/2018/08/20/1154812142/ICE2018.pdf.pdf. Accessed 28 Feb 2019

Palaco I, Park MJ, Kim SK, Rho JJ (2019) Public–private partnerships for e-government in developing countries: an early stage assessment framework. Eval Program Plann 72:205–218

Popkova EG (2019) Preconditions of formation and development of Industry 4.0 in the conditions of knowledge economy. Stud Syst Decis Control 169:65–72

Popkova EG, Sergi BS (2019) Will Industry 4.0 and other innovations impact Russia's development? In: Sergi BS (ed) Exploring the future of Russia's economy and markets. Emerald Publishing, Bingley, pp 34–42

Popkova EG, Ragulina YV, Bogoviz AV (2019) Fundamental differences of transition to Industry 4.0 from previous industrial revolutions. Stud Syst Decis Control 169:21–29

Rosenberg D (2019) Use of e-government services in a deeply divided society: a test and an extension of the social inequality hypotheses. New Media Soc 21(2):464–482

Sukhodolov AP, Popkova EG, Litvinova TN (2018) Models of modern information economy: conceptual contradictions and practical examples. Emerald Publishing, Bingley, pp 1–38

World Economic Forum (2019) The Global Information Technology Report 2016. http://www3.weforum.org/docs/GITR2016/WEF_GITR_Full_Report.pdf. Accessed 28 Feb 2019

Diversification of Issued Goods as the Basis for Stable Economic Development Under the Conditions of the Cyber Economy

Alexander A. Chursin

Abstract This chapter focuses on the role of diversification in providing stable economic development for organizations under the modern conditions of the cyber economy. The author identifies the main directions in which diversification of the activities of science-driven companies should be supported by the government.

The first direction includes a complex set of measures to improve the mechanisms of state regulation, which stimulate the intensive development and implementation of innovative solutions by industrial companies. The second direction proposes the development of national projects for the development and manufacture of industrial science-driven innovative products that conform to the requirements of the sixth and seventh technological modes. The third direction includes state measures to stimulate investment into various sectors of the economy to support the sustainability of innovative development, the creation of systemic elements for the Russian innovative system, and mechanisms to attract assets from nongovernmental sources into the Russian innovative ecosystem to activate new business.

In order to evaluate the optimality of these directions for company diversification and their economic effects, proprietary mathematical tools are used, which allow cyber systems to make the corresponding conclusions and evaluations.

The chapter illustrates the key role of cyber economic systems. In current conditions, only the effective usage of cyber economic and flexible production systems can ensure a company's continuing competitiveness and sustainable economic development.

1 Introduction

One of the main directions of research in economic science is studying the ties and interconnections between the subjects and objects of economic relations during the production, exchange, and redistribution of material goods. The system for manag-

A. A. Chursin
RUDN University, Moscow, Russia
e-mail: chursin-aa@rudn.ru

© Springer Nature Switzerland AG 2019
V. M. Filippov et al. (eds.), *The Cyber Economy*, Contributions to Economics,
https://doi.org/10.1007/978-3-030-31566-5_5

ing such interactions is called the cyber economy. The cyber economy consists of systemic resources, which raise the effectiveness of economic processes through the optimal management of the connection and interaction between the subsystems of the subjects and objects of economic relations. The most important systemic process that ensures the sustainable economic development of an industrial company is diversification of manufactured goods. When dealing with issues related to the diversification of industrial production, we should use the possibilities of the cyber economy aimed at optimizing the resource provision of economic processes. The systems of the cyber economy allow for the effective control and management of various business processes in real time. Such systems are not designed for strict directive planning, but they provide a dynamic system of feedback in real time.

The purpose of the diversification of goods is to achieve a sustainable economic state and further supports it through the timely update of product offerings based on consumer demand and creation of value for the buyer. Depending on a company's specifics, the goals of diversification could be clearly defined. Thus, diversification for companies that primarily manufacture defense industry products would comprise developing other products for the consumer market. For many companies, the necessity for diversification is driven by the fact not all types of products can be guaranteed to provide profits or even breakeven, perhaps because of a lack of sufficient demand in the market. To address this, the product range should be supplemented by offerings with new consumer features and high-qualitative, technical, and economic characteristics. Done well, diversification creates the necessary conditions for a company to attain a leading position in the market.

2 Methods

The theoretical and applied issues of provision of sustainable development of the modern economic systems are studied in the works Chursin et al. (2017), Chursin and Tyulin (2017), Chursin and Makarov (2015), Golodnov (2018), Fudina et al. (2018), Trifonov and Trifonov (2019), Makarov et al. (2019), Li and Lo (2017), Hutzchenreuter and Horstkotte (2013), and Heisenberg and Belyakov (2014).

In modern market conditions, a company has to achieve sustainable economic development. Using the tools of the cyber economy, the company can develop an effective ecosystem for the optimal management of innovative potential and resource provision. The sustainable economic development of any company is directly connected to the effective solution of the following tasks:

1. Provision of sustainable economic development through increasing production volumes, reducing product costs, and competitive pricing in key sales markets.
2. Creation of new highly competitive products through investment assets generated from the revenues received from product sales.
3. Replenishment of the capital funds of the company by means of allocations from profits generated from the realization of products.

4. Maximization of profits from the realization of products in both the short and long term through adapting or changing the structure of the issued products based on mathematical modeling and the forecasting of prices, and developing, based on these forecasts, measures that ensure cost reductions in all types of the organization's activities.
5. Achievement of victory in the competitive struggle in the sales markets, which is based on the well-known fact of setting the optimal price at which consumer features of the product ensure its competitiveness in the market.

At the same time, the sustainable economic development of a company is connected to the necessity to consider the following aspects of effectiveness:

- Effectiveness of development of new products with characteristics that ensure competitive advantages in the sales markets;
- Effectiveness of production, where all necessary goods and services are manufactured with minimum costs;
- Effectiveness of distribution and optimization of resources and all business processes that support the organization's activities;
- Effectiveness of managing the organization through the use of modern information and innovative technologies.

Successful solution of the above tasks allows the company to form the necessary conditions for achieving rapid development, either through the creation of new markets for highly competitive products or obtaining a large share in their existing market.

Thus, if all of the above tasks are solved at the same time, it is possible to achieve a synergetic effect that stimulates sustainable innovative development of organization, which then transforms into rapid development.

Under the conditions of globalization, the structure of the economy has become more complex. An important subject of economic relations is complex integrated structures that conduct diversified activities and are created through the unification of the financial and industrial capital. The activities of a diversified company are aimed at various sectors of the economy, which requires moving internal consolidated capital to support the necessary level of profitability to ensure the development and application of innovative technologies that create competitive advantages for the issued products. The use of the technologies of the cyber economy and the digital economy, based on the intelligent analysis of Big Data and wide application of IT technologies, stimulates the development of a rational policy for company diversification.

There are three main directions of diversification. The first direction envisages the usage of the company's production potential. Here it is necessary to analyze the load of the production capacities on the whole and the load of the parts on hi-tech equipment (processing centers, robotized complexes, etc.). It is necessary to analyze the company's labor resources and to determine the effectiveness of the company's implementation of this labor potential. In doing this, the company's production and labor capacity to issue new types of products are also determined. Also, it is necessary to perform an analysis of the financial and economic indicators of the company's activities (net profits, revenues, cost of goods sold, operating expenses, etc.) for the purpose of forecasting the dynamics of these indicators during the execution of a diversification plan. Diversification of production should ensure the issue of products that are in high demand in various consumer markets that may be in disparate sectoral and geographical locations. For this, it is necessary to study consumer expectations and to determine the most optimal directions of diversification. Among popular types of products, it is necessary to select those that are feasible to manufacture at the company—i.e., the types of products whose manufacture will require little or no modernization of production facilities and therefore cause minimum additional financial expenditure. Thus, evaluations of the cost of preparation of production plants for the manufacture of new products are required.

Having studied the market and determined consumer expectations, it is necessary to understand whether the manufacture of the identified products could be facilitated at the production capacities of the diversified company. It is necessary to assess financial expenditures for the preparation of manufacture of new items and to form a production preparation plan. However, it is also important to understand that not all production areas can be used to produce new products without significant changes to technological planning. It may also become apparent that there is a need for new production facilities, which will mean a large financial expenditure.

The next direction to be tackled in the diversification of a company's activities is connected to mergers with adjacent production companies and the optimization of their production capacities. It should be noted that a lot of Western companies chose this direction during their diversification.

The third direction for diversification requires a concentration of competences and technology transfers for the creation of new competitive products. Japanese companies widely use this strategy.

For Russian companies, diversification is primarily connected to the need to issue competitive civil goods as a result of a reduction in state defense orders. The levels of diversification and commercialization of activities of corporations and companies of Russia remain very low when compared to their Western rivals.

High levels of diversification in the leading aerospace companies create conditions for the transfer of internal capital and technologies from one production sector to another to provide intensive innovative development in the latter. Diversified production also ensures the necessary level of profitability, which provides sustainable economic development for corporations on the basis of development and application of innovative technologies that create competitive advantages for the issued products—which, in its turn, ensures its promotion in the internal and external markets.

The most important issue during the implementation of a diversification strategy is resource provision. In terms of labor, diversification of a company responding to reductions in military orders may play a social role. If the production load on a company decreases, there will be no necessity for the corresponding volume of labor resources. Thus, if assets are used for the modernization of production and diversification, new products might bring profit and preserve jobs—and the investments will be returned. In this sense, the system of managing a company's diversification could be viewed as a large cyber system, with financial, material, personnel, and other resources.

Another source of resource provision for diversification could be government tax subsidies in the form of allowable deductions from profit. The freed financial resources could be used for implementing the diversification program. The successful issue of new products will allow companies to obtain additional revenues, from which taxes will be returned to the state budget. Financial resources for diversification may also come from private investments. In order to create attractive conditions for private investors tax subsidies from the government would again be useful.

In Russia, the diversification of activities in science-driven companies should be supported by the government in a number of ways to ensure a transition to an innovative path of development.

Firstly, it is necessary to introduce a complex set of measures to improve the mechanisms of state regulation, which will stimulate the intensive development and implementation of innovative solutions by industrial companies. These are critical in order to ensure the competitiveness of industrial science-driven products with high added value both for sale in the global market and to support the program of import substitution. These measures include the following:

- Improvement of the system of state regulation and support for science-driven spheres that issue competitive products for the global market;
- Creation of a system for the coordination and management of science-driven spheres in view of developments in the modern global economy;
- Improvement of the methodology for forecasting the competitiveness of science-driven spheres of industry, organizations, and the issued goods;
- Creation of legislative advantages, tax vacations, and financial subsidies for organizations that develop and implement innovative technologies into production.
- Development of the system of state protectionism and regulation of the processes for the country's transition to the innovative path of development to increase the country's competitiveness.

Secondly, there is a need for the development of national projects to support the development and issue of industrial science-driven innovative products which conform to the requirements of the sixth and seventh technological modes and assist in the modernization of the whole technical and technological basis of Russia to meet the challenges and requirements of the twenty-first century. The placement of government orders for the development and production of science-driven goods in large volumes will indirectly stimulate these spheres of the economy.

Thirdly, there is a need to develop regulatory and managerial approaches and measures for the state stimulation of investments into various spheres of the economy to create systemic elements to support the Russian innovation ecosystem. In order to sustain innovative development mechanisms that can attract private investment into the Russian Federation are required.

Given sanctions on Russia, there remains a need to implement programs of import substitution and innovative development. The scientific and technological expertise of science-driven companies could be better leveraged in this effort by encouraging diversification into consumer products. An important task is the organization of the production of components and assemblies for trains, airplanes, cars, and other complex items that have previously been imported. For example, a current task is the need for the full provision of domestic components for the SSJ-100 aircraft.

Companies following this path will need to master the production of new types of products. They will need to evaluate existing production possibilities and the level and load on capacity and the implications for human resources to ensure that such diversification will support their competitiveness. They may choose to update existing products or launch new ones. Either way, the likelihood is that they will need to modernize production and invest in new machinery. Business (particularly in Russia) is not always ready for such large expenditures, as the risks of non-return on finance are rather high. Such decisions will require a thorough analysis of the viability of expenditures for the issue of new products and evaluation of the impact on competitiveness and growth such activities will have.

Hi-tech companies have to observe a balance between diversification and concentration. This is due to the fact that the company has to focus all of its resources in one-specific direction to achieve large competitive advantages. This is especially important in the science-driven spheres that have high entrance barriers for rivals and high requirements for the manufactured products. Supporting hard-won competitive advantages; the company reduces its risks and thus increases economic sustainability.

Let us consider several forms of a company's activities and use mathematical modeling to show the procedure for determining the optimal share of issue for each type of product. From the point of view of resource provision of an organization's activities, diversification is expressed in the distribution of resources among several types of activities instead of a concentration of resources in one of them. The positive effect of diversification comes through a reduction of possible losses that may appear as the result of a negative manifestation of risk factors through a focus on just one direction of activity. Conducting several types of activities allows minimizing the losses from a concentration on just one type of product. The principle of diversification states that it is necessary to perform diverse operations in order to reach average effectiveness and low risk. This is one of the most effective mechanisms for the reduction of market and credit risks. Finding the right direction for diversification of a product range can be greatly aided by modern cyber economic systems that can, through the analysis of Big Data, forecast consumer expectations for new products. Such cyber systems are based on the methods of imitation modeling to assist the process of diversification and evaluate the likely economic effects.

Let us now describe the basic mathematical tools that allow cyber systems to make conclusions on the optimal directions for a company's diversification based on an evaluation of the economic effect with the help of economic indicators.

The quantitative indicator that characterizes the change of economic sustainability of a company due to diversification is economic indicator *NOP* designating the operational profit of company (%).

This indicator is calculated in the following way:

$$NOP = TR - VC - FC,$$

where *TR*—revenues from selling products, *VC*—Fixed expenses of production, and *FC*—variable expenses of production. Fixed expenses do not change with an increase in the volume of production. Of course, diversification may lead to certain fluctuations of this indicator, but, as per issued item, they change in an inverse ratio to the volume of production. Variable expenses do not change per production item, but they change by total issued item in an inverse ration to production volume.

Diversification leads to change in the volume of the realization of products. A quantitative evaluation of the change of profit depending on the change of sales volumes is enabled by the production tool *DOL*, which is calculated in the following way:

$$DOL = \frac{TR - VC}{TR - VC - FC}.$$

Indicator DOL shows the percentage change of operational profit of a company with a revenue change of 1%.

Let us show the economic effect as a result of a company's diversification of production. Let us suppose that diversification takes place in several stages, at each of which new types of products are issued. At each stage, we evaluate indicators *NOP* and *DOL* (Table 1).

Increasing production volumes and, therefore, sales volumes, as a result of diversification leads to increase of the company's operational profit (Fig. 1):

Indicator DOL, which is calculated for each stage, shows the increase of operational profit with the change of revenue of 1%. For example, at the third stage, DOL = 2. This means that the change of revenue at this stage of 5% leads to a change of operational profit by 5% × 2 = 10%. Operating leverage (DOL) has a direct connection to the level of risk of operational activities; the larger the operating

Table 1 Evaluation of the diversification of production

Stage	Sales volume, pcs	Revenue TR	VC	FC	NOP (%)	DOL
0	70	420	280	100	9.52	3.5
1	80	480	320	100	12.5	2.7
2	90	540	360	100	14.81	2.25
3	100	600	400	100	16.67	2
4	110	660	440	100	18.18	1.83
5	120	720	480	100	19.44	1.71
6	130	780	520	100	20.51	1.63

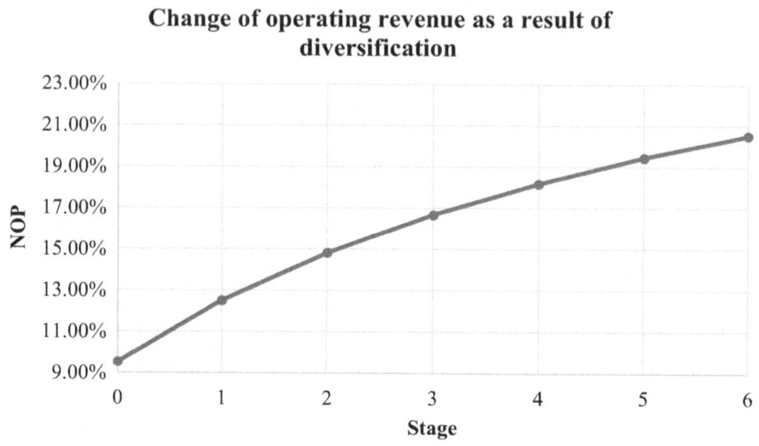

Fig. 1 Change of operational profit due to diversification

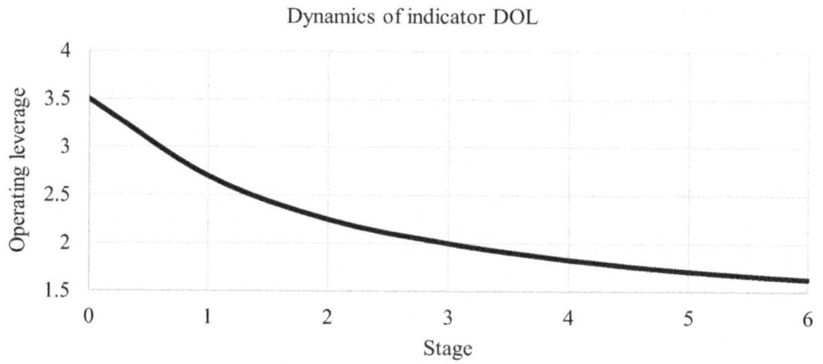

Fig. 2 Decrease of the indicator DOL shows an increase in a company's economic sustainability

leverage, the higher the risk. Thus, a reduction in the operating leverage from one stage to another shows an increase in the economic sustainability of the company (Fig. 2).

Thus, we have shown that an increase in the effectiveness of a company's functioning and, therefore, an increase in its economic sustainability can be achieved as a result of diversification.

Let further consider the increase of economic sustainability of companies due to diversification from the perspective of evaluating aggregate risks as a result of conducting several types of activities. It was shown that it is possible to minimize losses and increase a company's economic sustainability through diversification. As a result, the number and type of risks that need to be controlled also grows.

For example, the economic indicator VaR is one of the most convenient and important tools for indicating companies' risks. Each indicator can reflect maximum losses that might appear in the operational activities of the company in a set period.

Table 2 Characteristics of the profitability and risk of activities

Type of activities	Share in total volume of activities (%)	M (%)	σ (%)	Correlation between types of activities
Activity 1	30	12	3.5	−0.6
Activity 2	70	14.6	4.2	

The value of risk is the price of loss for the company or of the performed project as to a mathematically expected value; the probability of losses is set at 1–5%. Confidence interval equals 99–95%.

Let us assume a company conducts two types of activities, and each of these is characterized by the following values of profitability and risk (mathematical expectation M and standard deviation of profitability σ) (Table 2):

X and Y—profitability from the first and second types of activities, accordingly.

Then, joint profitability could be calculated with the following formula:

$$R = \omega_1 X + \omega_2 Y,$$

where ω_1, ω_2—shares of the corresponding types of activities.

Let us use this formula for calculating the probable characteristics of aggregate activities. Mathematical expectation equals:

$$M_R = \omega_1 M_X + \omega_2 M_Y = 13.82\%,$$

where M_X, M_Y—mathematical expectations of revenues of the corresponding types of activities.

Dispersion of profitability of aggregate activities could be calculated in the following way:

$$\sigma_R^2 = \omega_1^2 \sigma_X^2 + \omega_2^2 \sigma_Y^2 + 2\omega_1 \omega_2 \rho_{XY} \sigma_X \sigma_Y = (2.46\%)^2,$$

where $\sigma_X^2, \sigma_Y^2, \rho_{XY}$—the dispersion of profitability for each type of activity and the correlation between profitability from two types of activities.

Coefficient VaR, which shows the volume of losses, for correlation coefficient −0.6 and the significance level 0.05 shall constitute:

$$VaR_{-0.6} = 2.46\% \cdot 1.64 = 4.03\%$$

Let us consider how this correlation of the indicators of the types of activities influences the indicator of the risk of joint activities on the whole. To do this, we should calculate VaR for the values of correlation coefficient 0.0 and +0.6. The results of the calculations are given in Table 3.

Table 3 Dependence of VaR on the correlation coefficient

ρ	−0.06	0	0.6
VaR	4.03%	5.12%	6.01%

Thus, an increase in the value of the correlation coefficient between the types of activities leads to an increase in the risk of aggregate activities and VaR. In order to minimize the risk, it is necessary to form a portfolio of activities from negatively correlated types, or those that do not depend on each other (correlation coefficient equals zero).

3 Results

A reduction of the coefficient VaR as a result of implementing the independent or poorly correlating types of activities shows an increase in the company's sustainability. Additional types of activities, which do not depend on the existing ones or have a negative correlation, increase the company's economic sustainability and can ensure that it is taking the trajectory of rapid development. At the same time, the high competitiveness of the products and the company that manufactures them are the indicators of high innovative potential, which allow taking new competitive products to the market. Therefore, the notion of a company's innovative potential as applied to the conditions of sustainable economic development should be treated in a comprehensive manner—as a totality of all resources used for development in view of their interconnections and dynamics of change.

Such mathematical methods, which are fundamental within the tools of cyber economic systems for diversification management, allow evaluations of the effectiveness of a company's resource provision and the optimal conditions that are necessary for its sustainable economic development. They also allow the possibility of achieving rapid development through the formation of a new market for competitive products or the opportunity to capture a large share of an existing market. With sufficient resource provision, cyber economic systems can provide significant support for decision-making on the formation of a new products' image.

4 Conclusions

Cyber economic systems use modern information methods and technologies to manage the economic development of a company and support its economic sustainability. In fact, rather than simply diversifying production, the implementation of cyber economic systems allows for the creation of flexible production systems. In this case, the effective usage of cyber economic systems, based on information technologies and neural networks for the processing and analysis of Big Data, will allow for the monitoring of dynamics in various markets, analysis of prospective needs, determination of a company's production possibilities to issue new competitive products, creation of completely new sales markets, and management of product updates.

At the same time, the application of flexible production systems—comprised of different combinations of CNC machines, robotized technological complexes, and flexible production complexes—have the feature of automatized rearrangement during the manufacture of the items of selectable nomenclature in set limits of their characteristics. In other words, the coordinated interaction of the company's cyber economic system and a flexible production system allows for rapid reaction to market changes, forecasting future potential market niches, reducing the time spent mastering new products in the production cycle, and increasing labor efficiency, thus ensuring high competitiveness and economic sustainability for the company.

References

Chursin A, Makarov Y (2015) Management of competitiveness: theory and practice. Springer, Heidelberg

Chursin A, Tyulin A (2017) Competence management and competitive product development: concept and implications for practice. Springer, Heidelberg

Chursin A, Vlasov Y, Makarov Y (2017) Innovation as a basis for competitiveness: theory and practice. Springer, Heidelberg

Fudina E, Tumanova N, Kurmaeva I (2018) Features of diversification of production. In: Regional characteristics of the market socio-economic systems (structures) and their legal support of the IX international scientific and practical conference in Penza, Russian Federation, 2018, Moscow University named after S. Yu. Witte, Moscow, pp 235–239

Golodnov V (2018) Diversification of production of goods, products and services of enterprises. In: Advanced science proceedings of the II international practical conference in Penza, Russian Federation, 2018, Science and Education, Penza, pp 72–77

Heisenberg H, Belyakov N (2014) Methodical approaches to company's industrial diversification management. In: The role commerce and marketing in the development of promising directions in the educational environment of the XXI century proceedings of the international scientific and practical conference, Yelm, Science Book Publishing House LLC, Yelm, pp 78–90

Hutzchenreuter T, Horstkotte J (2013) Performance effects of top management team demographic faultlines in the process of product diversification. Working paper, Strategic Management Journal, Proquest ABI/INFORM, USA, issue 34, № 6, pp 704–726

Li P-Y, Lo F-Y (2017) Top management teams' managerial resources and international diversification: the evidence under an uncertain environment. Working paper, management decision. Emerald Group Publishing, Bingley

Makarov A, Ryabova E, Khvostova I (2019) Problems of improving financial methods and models of sustainable development of the company. INFRA-M Publishing House, Moscow

Trifonov Yu, Trifonov V (2019) Formation of the strategies for sustainable competitive development of the enterprises and firms. In: Economics and management in XXI century: strategy of sustainable development of the V international scientific-practical conference in Penza, Russian Federation, Science and Education, Penza, pp 87–90

Preconditions for the Transition of Developed and Developing Countries to the Cyber Economy Through the Process of Digital Modernization

Tatiana V. Kokuytseva , Irina A. Rodionova, and Vesna Damnjanovic

Abstract The development of the cyber economy is becoming a guarantor for the national competitiveness of countries. However, many developing and emerging economies do not possess the corresponding preconditions for its formation.

The purpose of this chapter is to describe the necessary conditions for the transition of developed and developing countries to the cyber economy and to determine factors that assist or hinder the development of this process. Economic and mathematical analysis is used in conjunction with data from global rating surveys that characterize the development of the cyber economy to determine interconnections with a range of macroeconomic indicators. The results of the mathematical calculations indicate that, on the one hand, development of the cyber economy is predetermined by the high level of a countries' well-being, and, on the other hand, stimulates an increase in the effectiveness of business processes in the country's economy on the whole.

1 Introduction

Development of the global economy in the twentieth and twenty-first centuries is notable for high dynamics of structural shifts at the national and regional levels (Rodionova 2014). At present, one of the key drivers in economic development is the emergence of information and communication technologies (ICT), which play a very important role in the effective implementation of business processes, the creation and implementation of innovations, and increases in labor efficiency and competitiveness. ICTs stimulate the diversification of the economy and business activity, thus ensuring an increase in the population's living standards.

T. V. Kokuytseva (✉) · I. A. Rodionova
RUDN University, Moscow, Russia
e-mail: kokuytseva-tv@rudn.ru

V. Damnjanovic
University of Belgrade, Belgrade, Serbia

© Springer Nature Switzerland AG 2019

V. M. Filippov et al. (eds.), *The Cyber Economy*, Contributions to Economics,
https://doi.org/10.1007/978-3-030-31566-5_6

According to our calculations of structural shifts, development of global industry—especially science-driven industry—has been irregular since 1980, both in its speed and proportion (Rodionova et al. 2016). The tendency for an increase in the speed of structural shifts and intensity from the base year of 1980 is evident for the period 1990–2000 (Rodionova et al. 2016).

The late 1990s marked the start of the IT revolution, being a period of rapid development of hi-tech and investment coupled with a consumer boom. The USA experienced a large growth in efficiency due to large investments in IT (Official web-site of the federal government of the USA). The consumer boom of the late 1990s saw a huge increase in the sale of consumer goods, especially those of Chinese origin. As for China and the "new industrial countries" of Asia, the highest rates of growth of fixed assets there were also observed in the late 1990s.

Accumulation of capital is the main driving force of economic development, according to A. Glyn (2004). Growth of investments is a more dynamic component in the growth of aggregate demand, especially at the global scale, where one country's export means another country's import. The growth of fixed capital is a precondition for a growth in production and investments in new technologies, through which they pass back into the system of production and increase profits. In the late 1990s, accumulation of capital in industrial countries was slower (1–3%) that in the world as the whole, while in developing countries, it was faster (China, 10.9%, South Korea, 9.6%, and India, 6.2%) (Kokuytseva 2014). All of this led to the fact that in 1995–2000 structural shifts became quicker and more intensive with an emphasis on the development of hi-tech industries, especially ICTs.

This period marked the emergence of a new term to characterize the tendencies that were taking place in the global economy: "the digital economy." The term appeared in the scientific and entrepreneurial community due to the Don Tapscott book, "The Digital Economy" (Tapscott 1999; Mamedyarov n.d.) and the American scholar Nicholas Negroponte from MIT, who had first introduced the term in 1995 (Negroponte 1996).

However, there is still no widely recognized definition of this term. There are many synonyms of the term "digital economy," such as "network economy," "electronic economy," "post-industrial economy," "API economy," "Internet economy," "economy of applications," "programmed economy," "creative economy," etc. The term "digital economy" became popular in Europe, while in American business society (due to Deloitte, IBM, and some other companies) it is often called the "API economy" (Strelkova 2018).

A popular definition of digital economy is that certain types of economic relations are mediated through the use of the Internet and other ICTs, with specification of a special technological context of economic relations—which determines their specific character.

Experts from the World Bank note that the development of the digital economy stimulates and increases the rate of economic growth. Their definition is "the digital economy is a new paradigm of quick economic development" (Strelkova 2018).

However, this rather narrow definition should really be wider than just a focus on development and the implementation of ICTs—which is also the position of many researchers. If this issue is considered in such a narrow way, everything will be reduced simply to the development of only one sector of the global economy—ICTs. Instead, the digital economy is a result of general technological progress, which influences the general development of economy on the whole. It influences all spheres of the economy and brings such "digital dividends" as economic growth, a reduction of production costs, additional jobs, and new and better services (Portal of selection of technologies and suppliers TAdviser).

The preconditions for the digital economy in modern conditions are "*the necessity for progressive development of innovative science-driven production, changes of organizational structures on the basis of integration of business processes of economic subjects, and the necessity for accelerating these business processes and providing sustainable growth and an increase of the effectiveness of economic development*" (Melnik and Salin 2018). In the dynamic of modern economic development, the appearance of new hi-tech production systems and new types of products and services, allied with an increasing complication in business processes requires an improvement to the approaches and technologies to manage and organize production, through the processing of Big Data, and effective and efficient activities to separate the subject of the economy and the country on the whole (Chursin and Tyulin 2018). All of this is impossible without ICTs.

According to V.P. Kolesov (2019), there are historical causes for the irregular course and differences between probable paths of digitization in various countries. However, these should not be overstated, as the speed of dissemination of digital innovations levels the playing field, reducing differences between the rates and trajectories of digitization. On the other hand, a precondition for the success of digitization requires a correctly formulated interconnection between the tasks of digitization and the topical problems of economic development for a particular national economy and how digitization aims to solve them. Such preconditions exist in Germany, the UK, the USA, Singapore, Japan, China, and other countries, where digitization programs are aligned with current problems of national economic development. Unfortunately, the situation in Russia is somewhat different, and the emphasis in the national program of digitization is made on quantitative indicators, not on the creation of a corresponding supportive environment or an interaction between the digital economy and the real economy.

It should be noted that these new technologies expand opportunities for the market participants and stimulate the increase of flexibility and speed of management by providing an ability to forecast financial, economic, and production indicators, to react to changes and manage risks, and, therefore, to ensure the possibility for increased competitiveness at all levels—company, sectoral, and national.

2 Materials and Method

In order for us to determine key factors for the transition of modern developed and developing countries to the cyber economy through the process of digital modernization, let us perform an analysis of the main modern indices and indicators that characterize the development of the digital economy. For this, we use the methods of comparative analysis and economic and mathematical methods (correlation analysis).

The initial data are the following statistical indicators: Digital Economy and Society Index, Digital Evolution Index, Networked Readiness Index (NRI), and ICT Development Index (IDI) (Measuring the Information Society Report 2017; Rating of countries as to the level of development of information and communication technologies), Global Competitiveness Index (The Global Competitiveness Report 2017–2018).

3 Results

We calculated the coefficients of correlation and determined direct dependence between such indices as the Knowledge Economy Index, Knowledge Index, Networked Readiness Index, Informational Society Index, and Global Innovation Index (The Global Innovation Index 2018), and such indicators as GDP per capita (correlation dependence 0.86–0.93), real GDP per employee (0.8–0.85), and volume of production of hi-tech spheres per capita (correlations 0.57–0.67) (Rodionova et al. 2010; 2018).

The obtained positive coefficients of correlation show, firstly, a high representation of integral indices, which characterize the level of an economy's development, which is based on knowledge. Secondly, only the countries with the highest level of socioeconomic development are ready for the development of the cyber economy. Thirdly, leaders in the manufacture of hi-tech products are countries that align knowledge management and ICTs to the service of their economy and thus achieve leading positions in the global economy and markets.

Analysis of the leading countries regarding the indicators that characterize innovative development and readiness for the cyber economy show that the leaders often include small (as to population) Scandinavian countries, as well as Singapore, Germany, Switzerland, and South Korea (The most innovative economies of the

Table 1 World leaders in innovative development

Global Innovation Index (2018) (126 countries)		Networked Readiness Index (2016) (139 countries)		ICT Development Index-IDI (2017) (176 countries)		Global Competitiveness Index (2017–2018) (137 countries)	
1	Switzerland	1	Singapore	1	Iceland	1	Switzerland
2	The Netherlands	2	Finland	2	South Korea	2	USA
3	Sweden	3	Sweden	3	Switzerland	3	Singapore
4	UK	4	Norway	4	Denmark	4	Netherlands
5	Singapore	5	USA	5	UK	5	Germany

world). The USA and Japan do not always make it into the top 10, though the level of innovative development in these countries is also very high (Table 1).

Let us now study the positions of countries in the Digital Economy and Society Index (DESI). This index is prepared by the European Commission to evaluate the state of digitization and digital competitiveness of the European economy and society on the basis of five groups of indicators of development for a digital Europe (Official website of the European Union). These are communication (quality and access), human capital (the level of the population's skills for digitization), usage of the Internet, integration of digital technologies (through an assessment of the digitization of business and usage of online sales channels), and digital state services (e-Government) (Digital Europe 2016).

According to the most recent statistical data of DESI (2018), Denmark, Sweden, Finland, and the Netherlands have the most developed digital economies in the EU, followed by Luxembourg, Ireland, the UK, Belgium, and Estonia. Romania, Greece, Bulgaria, Italy, Poland, and Hungary have the lowest scores. In 2017, all countries improved their indicators in the rating. Ireland and Spain gained 5 points (3.2 points is the average for the EU). On the other hand, Denmark and Portugal's growth were low (below 2 points) (DESI 2018).

Of course, coverage of countries by the DESI index is rather limited and is calculated only for developed countries and certain countries with developing or transitional economies within the EU. Unsurprisingly, among the analyzed countries, developed countries have the highest results from the point of view of having the most advanced rates of the digitization of economy and society.

The Digital Evolution Index (DEI) is calculated by the company Mastercard and Fletcher School of Law and Diplomacy at Tufts University in the US to evaluate the level of development of the digital economy in many more countries of the world. It aims to measure the integration of the digitization into daily life on the basis of summing up four groups of indicators for the development of the digital economy. These are the level of offer (access to the Internet and the level of development of infrastructure); consumer demand for digital technologies; the institutional environment (government policy, law, resources); and the innovative climate (investments into R&D and digital startups).

According to the 2017 statistical data, the following countries had the most developed digital economies: Norway, Sweden, Switzerland, Denmark, Finland, Singapore, South Korea, the UK, Hong Kong, and the USA.

Based on the calculated indices, four groups of countries are distinguished (The Digital Evolution Index 2017; Top 10 countries with the most developed digital economy):

1. *Stand Out*. A group of countries dubbed the digital elite. They are very developed in terms of digitization and developing very quickly. This group includes Singapore, the UK, New Zealand, the UAE, Estonia, Hong Kong, Japan, and Israel. These are primarily developed countries of the world. They show high rates of digital development and are leaders in the dissemination of innovation.

2. *Stall Out*. This group of countries has achieved a high level of digital evolution but might still lag behind due to slower rates of progress and the development of innovation. This group includes South Korea, Australia, some countries of Western Europe, and Scandinavian countries. Without the implementation of further innovations, these countries might continue to lag behind the leaders in digitization.
3. *Watch Out*. This group of countries has low ratings. They require development of their digital infrastructure and the implementation of new innovations. This group includes South Africa, Peru, Egypt, Greece, and Pakistan. They face serious challenges due to the low level of digital development and slow growth rates.
4. *Break Out*. This group of countries has good results in relation to innovative development or consumer demand. However, their development is restrained by having weak infrastructure and institutions. These are primarily poorly developed countries (Kenya, Bolivia, etc.) and the following countries: China, Russia, India, Brazil, Colombia, Chile, and Mexico along with the new industrial countries of Asia (Malaysia, Philippines, Indonesia, etc.). Despite current problems, they have potential that might allow them to reach the leading positions.

Next, we study country positions according to the Networked Readiness Index (NRI) (The Networked Readiness Index 2016). This index is calculated by the World Economic Forum and INSEAD and is an integral indicator that characterizes the level of development of ICTs in countries of the world on the basis of three groups of indicators (there are 53 sub-indicators in total): conditions for development of ICTs, readiness of citizens, business circles, and government bodies for the usage of ICTs, and the level of usage of ICTs in public, commercial, and government sectors. The initial data for the NRI come from statistical reports from international organizations such as the UN, the International Telecommunication Union, World Bank, etc.

As of 2016 (Networked Readiness Index 2016), the leaders were Singapore, Finland, Sweden, Norway, the USA, the Netherlands, Switzerland, the UK, Luxembourg, and Japan. Developing countries do not have the right conditions for ICTs, their business circles and government bodies are not ready for the usage of ICTs, and the level of usage of ICTs in the public, commercial, and government sectors is very low.

The ratio of positions for the ICT Development Index is similar. This index characterizes the achievements of countries of the world from the point of view of the development of ICTs and is calculated according to the methodology of the International Telecommunication Union, which determines global standards in the sphere of ICTs based on 11 indicators. These indicators cover access to ICTs, usage of ICTs, and practical skills with ICTs within the population. The authors of the research emphasize that the level of development of ICTs is one of the most important indicators of economic and social well-being of a country (ICT Development Index 2017). According to the 2017 data, the leaders are developed countries and newly industrialized Asian countries: Iceland, South Korea, Switzerland, Denmark, the UK, Hong Kong, the Netherlands, Norway, Luxembourg, and Japan.

4 Discussion

Through our analysis of the positions of countries in various world ratings that characterize the level of development of ICTs and the digitization, it is possible to distinguish the following preconditions for a country's transition to the cyber economy.

Firstly, the development of the cyber economy requires large financial investments, for the creation of the corresponding digital infrastructure and development and implementation of innovations in the sphere of ICTs. Therefore, a key precondition (confirmed in the course of mathematical calculations) is that the country firstly requires a thriving economy.

Secondly, the corresponding development of government institutions and supportive government policies, aimed at digital transformation and transition to the cyber economy, are necessary.

Thirdly, a serious precondition for development of the cyber economy is development of international cooperation in this sphere. Countries with high levels of development in the cyber economy could translate their knowledge into a new stage of economic growth, while providing developing countries with valuable experience as a result of such cooperation.

Fourthly, there is a need to increase the level of so-called digital trust, as well as advancing the development of access to the Internet through mobile devices.

5 Conclusion

It should be concluded that the modern transition to the cyber economy is far more advanced and dynamic in developed countries, which have all the necessary preconditions to support it. At the same time, developing economies, many of which have the necessary potential, lag behind due to the fragmentary character of the required preconditions.

However, without the transformation of national economies, their digital modernization, and a global transition to the cyber economy, the effective functioning of business processes in a globalized world will be impossible (Ereshko and Kokuytseva 2017). Structural shifts in the placement of the hi-tech production of goods and services will be determined not so much by the presence of skilled personnel and competencies (accumulated knowledge and technologies) as by the development of functioning digital infrastructures—in other words, the development of the cyber economy.

Acknowledgments The research was carried out within the framework of the state task of the Ministry of Science and Higher Education of the Russian Federation No. 730000F.99.1.BV16AA02001 "Scientific and methodological, analytical and regulatory support for the implementation of the Set of Measures for 2018–2020 for the implementation of the Interstate Program for Innovative Cooperation of the CIS countries until 2020...".

The publication has been prepared with the support of the "RUDN University Program 5-100."

References

Chursin A, Tyulin A (2018) Competence management and competitive product development: concept and implications for practice. Springer International Publishing, Cham, 241 p

Digital Europe: the present-day state 2016. https://evercare.ru/DESI-2016

Ereshko A, Kokuytseva T (2017) Computable models of the cooperation of digital economies. In: Proceedings of 10th international conference management of large-scale system development (MLSD)

Glyn A (2004) Marxist economics. In: Eatwell J, Milgate M, Newman P (eds) The world of economics. INFRA-M, Moscow

ICT Development Index (2017). https://www.itu.int/net4/ITU-D/idi/2017/index.html

Kokuytseva T (2014) Managing innovative development of a region. Lap Lambert Academic Publishing, 312 p

Kolesov V (2019) "Similarity of the issues of digitization of national economies and differences in approaches to solving them", International scientific conference "Digitization of Eurasia": new perspective of economic cooperation and development: conference proceedings, November 28, 2018, Moscow

Mamedyarov Z (n.d.) Digital economy and ways of its development. http://www.webeconomy.ru/index.php?page=cat&newsid=3957&type=news

Measuring the Information Society Report (2017). https://www.itu.int/net4/ITU-D/idi/2017/index.html

Melnik M, Salin V (2018) Preconditions of effective development of digital economy. Accounting. Analysis. Audit, No. 6. https://cyberleninka.ru/article/n/predposylki-effektivnogo-razvitiya-tsifrovoy-ekonomiki.

Negroponte N (1996) Being digital. Random House, New York, NY

Networked Readiness Index (2016). http://reports.weforum.org/global-information-technology-report-2016/networked-readiness-index/

Official website of the European Union. https://ec.europa.eu/commission/index

Official web-site of the federal government of the USA. https://www.usa.gov/features

Portal of selection of technologies and suppliers TAdviser. http://www.tadviser.ru/index.php/Статья%3AЦифровая_экономика_России#cite_note-qpcmsfdret 6

Rating of countries as to the level of development of information and communication technologies (2017-2018). https://gtmarket.ru/ratings/ict-development-index/ict-development-index-info

Rodionova I (2014) World industry in post-industrial society: tendencies and regional shifts. Miscellanea Geographica 18(1):31–36

Rodionova I, Gordeeva A, Kokuytseva T (2010) New technologies: the growing role in competitiveness of countries of the world. Bull Ural State Univ Econ 5(31):119–126. https://elibrary.ru/download/elibrary_16547672_27380044.pdf

Rodionova I, Kokuytseva T, Semenov A (2016) Features of migration processes in different world industries in the second half of the XX century. J Appl Econ Sci 11(8):1769–1780

Rodionova I, Kokuytseva T, Semenov A (2018) Mathematical model of the influence of innovative development factors on the economy of leading countries and Russia. Int J Eng Technol 7 (4):406–411

Strelkova I (2018) The digital economy: new opportunities and threats for development of the world economy. Economics Taxes Law, No. 2. https://cyberleninka.ru/article/n/tsifrovaya-ekonomika-novye-vozmozhnosti-i-ugrozy-dlya-razvitiya-mirovogo-hozyaystva

Tapscott D (1999) The digital economy: promise and peril in the age of networked intelligence. Kyiv, 403 p

The Digital Economy and Society Index (DESI) (2018). https://ec.europa.eu/digital-single-market/en/desi

The Digital Evolution Index (2017). https://globalrisk.mastercard.com/wp-content/uploads/2017/07/Mastercard_DigitalTrust_PDFPrint_FINAL_AG.pdf

The Global Competitiveness Report (2017–2018) World Economic Forum. Geneva, Switzerland 2018. https://www.weforum.org/reports/the-global-competitiveness-report-2017-2018
The Global Innovation Index (2018) Energizing the world with innovation. INSEAD (The Business School for the World) and the World Intellectual Property Organization (WIPO). https://www.wipo.int/edocs/pubdocs/en/wipo_pub_gii_2018.pdf
The most innovative economies of the world: Scandinavian countries in the top, South Korea the leader. http://theworldonly.org/rejting-innovatsionnyh-ekonomik/
The Networked Readiness Index (2016) The Global Information Technology Report 2016. World Economic Forum. https://www.wsj.com/public/resources/documents/GITR2016.pdf
Top 10 countries with the most developed digital economy. http://web-payment.ru/article/250/top-10-cifrovaya-/

Part II
The Role of Intelligent Machines in the Cyber Economy

Managing the Provision of Resources for the Creation of Products to Rapidly Develop the Cyber Economy

Evgeny A. Nesterov

Abstract In this chapter, the connection between the digital economy and the cyber economy is determined, and the global development trends for information technologies are analyzed.

The author substantiates the need to integrate production and economic processes into a unified cyber economic system to accelerate the development and manufacture of products with competitive consumer qualities, which could occupy the dominant positions and satisfy demand in existing markets. He also advocates that rapid development products with innovative qualities and unique consumer characteristics should be launched to create new markets and satisfy new needs in society.

The author formulates and solves the important task of determining the necessary level of resource provision, for the creation of both types of products with the usage of methodological tools.

Management of resource provision is aimed at creating an optimal balance for all types of an organization's resources in the global information space, which, as a result of their realization in the form of finished products, create the potential for acquiring either a large market share or satisfying market demand in new markets. The task of creating this optimal balance for all types of resources, through the optimization of business processes and organizational models is a very important element in the process of the creation of cyber economic systems.

1 Introduction

The modern global economy is experiencing increasingly rapid changes due to the appearance of new scientific innovations, the dynamic development of equipment and technologies, and the emergence of the global information space. All these changes are accompanied by the global digital transformation of almost every aspect of life, which should eventually lead to the creation of the cyber economy.

E. A. Nesterov
Joint Stock Company "Russian Space Systems", Moscow, Russian Federation
e-mail: nesterov@spacecorp.ru

© Springer Nature Switzerland AG 2019
V. M. Filippov et al. (eds.), *The Cyber Economy*, Contributions to Economics,
https://doi.org/10.1007/978-3-030-31566-5_7

The cyber economy—according to the existing notions—is a complex system, the functioning of which is assured by formation of the optimal ties and interactions between the subjects and objects of economic relations during the production, exchange, and distribution of material goods.

A cyber economic system envisages that the management of all economic processes takes place within the organized information space. This is created through the usage of digital and neural machine algorithms, which allow for the processing and analysis of large arrays of heterogeneous data to solve economic tasks through directive or alternative offers that are formed by intelligent information systems (cyber systems, neural networks, etc.).

Though digitization started nearly 50 years ago, digital technologies have not yet spread through the whole global economy. However, more than 65% of people in the world use personal mobile and stationary digital equipment and have access to information and communication networks. Over the last year, the number of unique mobile users grew by more than 4% worldwide—though in Central America this number remains below 50%.

The number of Internet users grows every year, and the speed of this growth continues to increase. This is shown in Fig. 1.

At the same time, there is rapid progress in science and innovation, the modern methods and technologies of machine learning, and wide usage of Big Data, complex algorithms, and network calculations. The results of these developments have already been implemented in many spheres of the global economy.

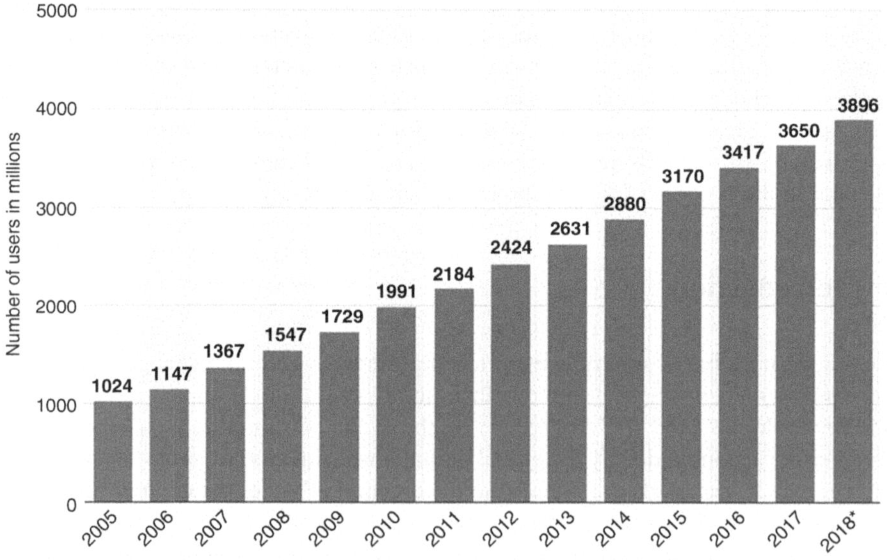

Fig. 1 Dynamics of the number of Internet users in the world (Source: https://www.statista.com/statistics/273018/number-of-internet-users-worldwide/)

For example, 30% of inventions that are used for medical diagnostics (e.g., vision testing or general medical examinations) include built-in components that are connected to AI, which emphasizes the potential of its application in medicine.

Digital transformation covers all activities of industrial companies. Over recent decades, companies' access to digital technologies has expanded profoundly. Companies use digital tools to become part of the cyber economic system and digitize their business processes with the planning of resources not only through the application of an Enterprise Resource Planning (ERP) system but also through the adaptive management of all company resources—even in the conditions of uncertainty during the creation of new hi-tech products. The objects of intellectual management and planning are now also seen just as much of a resource as new production equipment, materials, components, elements, and technical processes, which are all connected in the start-up of the production of unique items, new production areas, new unique specialists, and auxiliary companies.

The organizational management of such companies and corporations is built on the basis of cloud technologies and the service model. The industrial system is built on the creation of innovative products through the application of the technologies of processing and analyzing Big Data, using AI methods and the formation and organization of interrelationships with consumers and suppliers on the basis of information models and cyber systems. Production processes transform with the implementation of flexible production systems with adaptive schedules and distribution of resources, robotized complexes, and cyber-physical systems.

Full-scale application of cyber-physical systems in production, logistics, and urban life will help to manage the growing complexity of supply chains for high-quality products with minimum transaction costs. One of the key issues here is the organization of joint work for many cyber-physical systems around the planet within a unified cyber economic system.

However, digital transformation is not just about the implementation of digital algorithms into production processes. We must also speak to the transformation within society and business that is necessary for converting new technologies into economic and social value.

All of these processes require investments, unique competencies, organizational changes, new business models, new forms of intellectual assets, new technologies, and technological modes. All of this should allow for the creation of a product or service that has high value for the consumer and integrates production and economic processes into a unified cyber economic system.

All of these measures are implemented for the purpose of accelerating the processes of development to manufacture products with competitive consumer qualities, to take the dominating position and satisfy the need in the existing market, and rapid development products, which, due to their innovative qualities and unique consumer characteristics could create new markets and satisfy new needs in society.

Thus, the task of determining the optimal level of resource provision necessary for the creation of products that are market dominant, as well as rapid development products, appears.

2 Literature Review

In the modern economic literature, there are different methods for the evaluation of resource provision for an organization, to implement projects.

For example, methodologies developed by L.F. Berdnikova, V.V. Kovalev, O.V. Barashkova, and V.N. Ostretsov have a range of significant drawbacks.

The method of assessment of company's resource potential, offered by L.F. Berdnikova (2009), contains a rather wide range of indicators that characterize the usage of fixed production funds, while most of the indicators that characterize the effectiveness of material resources use and the personnel potential of the company are very limited. This complicates making optimal managerial decisions for the provision of a rational usage of resource potential.

The method of complex assessment of the effectiveness of a company's usage of resource potential, proposed by V.V. Kovalev (2016), considers the indicators that characterize separate elements of resource provision, without detailed calculations on the effectiveness of the usage of material, labor, and financial resources of the company.

The method of assessment of a company's resource potential, developed by O.V. Barashkova and V.N. Ostretsov (2012), includes calculations of the indicators of integral quantitative assessment with methods that show the level of deviation of real indicators of the studied object from the virtual model. However, this method does not include many of the main indicators of assessment of elements of resource potential that characterize the personnel, financial, property, material, and technological potential of the company (Chursin and Makarov 2015; Chursin and Tyulin 2018).

Thus, the existing methodologies, while all contributing to the development of methods of assessment for resource provision, do not assist in determining the sufficiency of resource provision that is necessary for the creation of rapid development products.

As a result, I offer the following methodological tool for solving this task.

3 Methods

The key problem in planning resource provision for a high-tech corporation lies in the complexity of precisely planning the volumes and type of resource provision required for the development and manufacture of rapid development products.

Expenditures for the development and manufacture of rapid development products depend on a range of factors, all of which require innovativeness, connected to the usage of:

- New equipment;
- New materials;
- New element basis;

- New technological processes, connected to starting production of a new product;
- New production areas;
- New specialists;
- New auxiliary companies.

In addition to these factors, very often during the development of a new hi-tech product, there is a need to correct construction or technological documents. This impacts the process as a change of construction or technological design is likely to result in repeated purchases of components and materials, readjustment of equipment, correction of technological processes, etc.

The most important factors in the process could be supplemented by others that become apparent in specific test productions.

The minimum production item required during the planning of resource provision is a work center.

The work center shall be treated as the totality of the following components that are necessary for performing a specific production operation:

- Production equipment;
- Employee (or group of employees);
- Production logistics (for this operation);
- Necessary material resources;
- Auxiliary processes and necessary operative managerial decisions.

The list of components of a work center could be modified and expanded in view of the peculiarities of the specific production.

A hi-tech corporation consists of N work centers. Then, the volume of i-th resource R_i, necessary for the corporation's functioning, could be calculated as a simple sum of the volumes of this resource that are necessary for the functioning of j work centers of the corporation:

$$R_i = \sum_{j=1}^{N} R_i^j,$$

where R_i^j—necessary volume of resource provision for the work center j.

Within the offered methodological tool the factors of innovativeness will be considered during the planning of the work center's resource provision.

To apply the necessary tools for the planning of resource provision for a hi-tech corporation, the following data are necessary:

- Planned value of resource provision for the main works that are performed by the work centers of the corporation;
- A statistical database that contains historical information on the resource provision of the hi-tech corporation;
- The necessary volume of resources for implementing the program of rapid development.

The tool for planning the optimal resource provision for the hi-tech corporation envisages the execution of four consecutive stages.

1. Assessment of the necessary resource provision for work centers of a hi-tech corporation according to the classical method.
2. Correction of the indicators of resource provision for work centers of a hi-tech corporation in view of the factors of innovativeness.
3. Forecasting of resource provision for the work centers of a hi-tech corporation based on the adaptive economic and mathematical model.
4. Evaluation of the sufficiency of the resources for rapid product development.

Stage 1 *Assessment of the necessary resource provision of work centers for a high-tech corporation according to the classical method.*

Classical formulas for calculating the resource expenditures for each type of resource are written down in the following form (the volumes of resources are assessed in monetary value whenever possible):

1. Financial resources

$$R_{fin} = \sum_{j=1}^{m} I_j,$$

where R_{fin}—volume of financial resources that are necessary for the functioning of a work center; *m*—number of stages of planning; I_j—volume of financial assets necessary for the functioning of a work center at the *j*-th stage of the planned period;

2. Time resources (timescale could also be the basis for measuring non-material resources—e.g., competencies)

$$R_{time} = \sum_{j=1}^{m} \left(t_j^K - t_j^H\right),$$

where R_{time}—time resources that are necessary for the execution of all works of a work center; t_j^K, t_j^H—planned dates for the start and ending of each type of the work center's activities;

3. Labor resources (expressed in cost)

$$R_{labor} = \sum_{j=1}^{m} \left(R_{time_j} \cdot \overline{C}_{p_j} \cdot P_j\right),$$

where R_{labor}—labor resources that are necessary for the functioning of the work center; R_{time_j}—expenditures of time resources in the studied planned period; $\overline{C}_{p_j}$—

average cost of work time in the planned period; P_j—number of personnel involved in the activities of the work center at the j-th stage of the planned period;

4. Material resources

$$R_{mat} = \sum_{j=1}^{m} E_j,$$

where R_{mat}—material resources that are necessary for the functioning of the work center; E_j—expenditures of material resources (equipment, materials, energy, etc.) at the j-th stage of the planned period;

5. Information resources

$$R_{inf} = E_{comp} + E_{ir},$$

where R_{inf}—information resources that are necessary for the functioning of the work center; E_{comp}—expenditures for attracting unique expert knowledge/competencies for functioning of the work center; E_{ir}—expenditures for accessing unique global information resources.

The result of the execution of this stage is seen in the following table outlining the basic level of resource provision for the work centers of a hi-tech corporation (Table 1).

Stage 2 *Correction of the indicators of resource provision for work centers of a hi-tech corporation in view of the factors of innovativeness*

For each i-th factor of innovativeness, such as:

- Usage of new equipment in production;
- New materials;
- New components;
- New technological process;
- New premises;
- New specialists,
- Other factors (hereinafter—n);

We shall determine probability P_i^j for correction of resource provision of j-th work center as statistical expectation (E) of the ratio of factual deviation of resource

Table 1 The basic level of resource provision of the work centers of a high-tech corporation

Work center	Resource 1, volume	Resource 2, volume	...	Resource N, volume
...	...	...	...	...
J	K_1^j	K_2^j	...	K_N^j
...	...	...	...	...

Source: Compiled by the author

provision from the planned expectation, which is necessary for executing the work center's operation, to the planned value:

$$P_i^j = E\left(\frac{K_j^0 - K_j^1}{K_j^0}\right),$$

where K_j^0—planned value of resource provision of the operation of the production center; K_j^1—factual resource provision for the execution of the operation of the production center.

Values of probability could be calculated on the basis of statistics of execution of production operations of the work center as an average value of the ratio that emerges as a result of the action of the studied factor of deviation from the planned resource provision of the work center's operation from the factual resource provision to the normative value.

With known values of probabilities P_i^j of correction of resource provision of operation j of the work center as a result of the influence of the factors of innovativeness, the factual value of resource provision for the execution of the production operation K_j could be calculated with the following formula:

$$K_j = K_j^0 \cdot \prod_{i=0}^{n} \left(1 + P_i^j\right), \tag{1}$$

where K_j^0—planned value of resource provision for the execution of the operation of the production center; n—number of factors of innovativeness.

After the exercise of the factors of innovativeness during several operational (or production) cycles of the work center, the probabilities for the correction of resource provision of operation of j-th work center could be reset to zero as a result of the manifestation of other factors of innovativeness. These effects are taken into account in formula (1).

Stage 3 *Forecasting of resource provision for the work centers of a hi-tech corporation based on the adaptive economic and mathematical model.*

At the third stage, it is necessary to use the statistical basis of the work centers' resource provision of hi-tech corporation, which has been compiled for the previous period of planning. For a specific work center such a database could be presented in the form of a table (Table 2).

Based on the presented statistical data, linear regression valuations for the resource provision of a work center from the start of the planned period to the moment of time t could be built:

$$\lambda_t^i = a_0 + b_0 t. \tag{2}$$

Table 2 Statistical database of resource provision of work centers of a hi-tech corporation

Moment of time	Resource			
	Resource 1	Resource 2	...	Resource N
1	λ_1^1	λ_1^2	...	λ_1^N
2	λ_2^1	λ_2^2	...	λ_2^N
...	...	...	...	...
T	λ_t^1	λ_t^2	...	λ_t^N

Note: λ_t^i—volume of i-th resource in the moment of time t
Source: Compiled by the author

Such valuations could be obtained automatically in various systems and software apps.

Due to the influence of a large number of factors in planning the resource provision of a hi-tech corporation, it is necessary to use adaptive models to forecast the resource provision of work centers, because there are no reasons to believe that all of the retrospective initial data of the time row are equally valid in the formation of the future values of the regression model.

The factors that influence the necessary resource provision of the work centers often have a strong seasonal character. This means that the volume of resource provision of work centers at various stages of the forecast period depend on the factors and processes that are peculiar to the whole economy (e.g., fewer workdays in January) and on sectoral specifics (e.g., inequality of the inflow of budget assets during a year). The applied models have to reflect these circumstances. For determining seasonal factors when forecasting resource provision, we would have to have a large statistical database (with more than 3 years of data). Then we would be able to use the popular Holt-Winters model. We shall instead use the multiplicative model with linear growth, which is based on the exponential scheme for a step of forecasting, which equals 1 (i.e., for $\tau = 1$, τ—step of forecasting), and has the form:

$$\begin{aligned} \widehat{\lambda}_{t+\tau} &= (a_t + b_t \times \tau) \times F_{t-L+\tau} \\ a_t &= \alpha_1 \times \frac{\lambda_t}{F_{t-L}} + (1-\alpha_1)(a_{t-\tau} + b_{t-\tau}) \\ b_t &= \alpha_3 \times (a_t - a_{t-\tau}) + (1-\alpha_3)b_{t-\tau} \\ F_t &= \alpha_2 \times \frac{\lambda_t}{a_t} + (1-\alpha_2)F_{t-L} \end{aligned},$$

where L—period of seasonality (thus, for quarter data $L = 4$, for monthly data $L = 12$); $\widehat{\lambda}_{t+\tau}$—forecasting value of the volume of resource in the moment of time $t + \tau$; $F_{t-L+\tau}$—value of coefficient of seasonality, ascribed to moment of time $t + \tau$, which is calculated for the season in the past, i.e., in the moment $(t - L + \tau)$; parameters a_t and b_t—parameters of the linear forecasting model, belonging to the moment of the compilation of the forecast t. The initial values of these parameters can be found through using regression models (2.2). The fourth equation sets the role

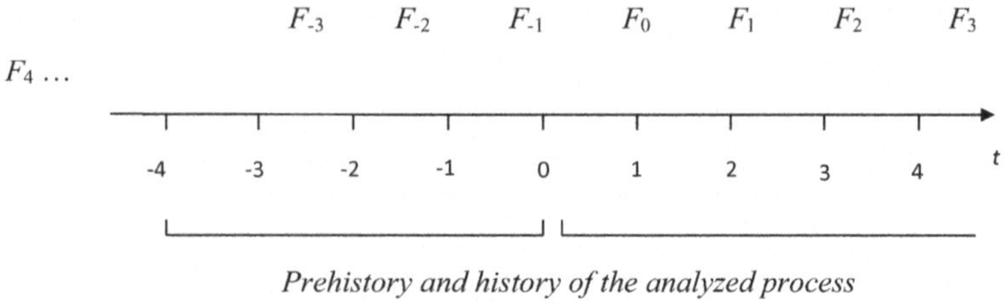

Fig. 2 Interpretation of the coefficients of seasonality with negative numbers of quarters (Source: Compiled by the author)

of update of the seasonality coefficient for the next season; a_1, $i = \{1; 2; 3\}$—parameters of leveling (take values from 0 to 1 and characterize the contribution of the seasonal component into formation of the forecast).

During calculation $\widehat{\lambda}_{t+\tau} = (a_t + b_t \times 1) \times F_{t-l+\tau}$, for the moment 1, i.e., with $t = 0$ and $\tau = 1$, we have to have $F_{0-4+1} = F_{-3}$. Obviously, F_{-3} should be treated as the seasonality coefficient, belonging to the first quarter of the year that precedes the first year of the range of observations (Fig. 2), i.e., a prehistory of the analyzed process. The initial coefficients of seasonality F_{-2}, F_{-1} and F_0 have the similar sense.

Assessment of the coefficients of seasonality "prehistory," which are necessary for the calculation of the coefficients of seasonality of the first year of "history," could be performed by dividing the first eight factual levels of the time row by their estimated values that are calculated according to the linear model of the regression model, with the following averaging for the same quarters (months).

Correction of the parameters could be performed with $\alpha_1 = 0.3$, $\alpha_2 = 0.6$ and $\alpha_3 = 0.3$.

The result of the third stage is a forecast of resource provision of the work centers of a high-tech corporation at each stage of the planned period.

***Stage* 4** *Evaluation of the sufficiency of the resources for rapid product development.*

As a result of completion of the previous stages, the aggregate volume of resource provision of the work centers of a high-tech corporation for each type of resource can be obtained.

Sufficiency of such resource provision for the implementation of the program of rapid development could be determined according to the following formula, the economic sense of which consists in determining the minimum value of resource provision for implementing measures for the rapid product development of a hi-tech corporation:

$$\gamma = \frac{\sum_{i=1}^{N} \widehat{\lambda}_i}{\sum_{j=1}^{n} \sum_{i=1}^{N} K_i^j},$$

where $\widehat{\lambda}_i$—forecasted volume of the resource of type i in view of statistically observed tendencies; K_i^j—necessary volume of the resource of the type i for the work center j in view of the factors of innovativeness; N—number of types of resources; n—number of work centers.

If $\gamma \geq 1$, the volume of resources could be deemed sufficient for the provision of a program of rapid product development of a hi-tech corporation.

4 Results

The offered methodological tool for planning the resource provision of a hi-tech corporation allows an evaluation of the necessary volume of resource provision of the work centers to create conditions for the development and manufacture of rapid development products (or products that could take a dominant position in the market).

Thus, the methodological tool enables the user to determine the sufficiency of resources for the creation of rapid development products. However, the next task—managing the processes for the formation of resource provision and creation of resource potential (including intellectual, competence-based, scientific, and technical) for an organization to create and manufacture highly competitive products—still remains.

Managing the processes for the formation of resource provision should be closely connected to solving the task of monitoring the external environment of organization and identifying new achievements in the sphere of science, new technologies and competencies, which have recently appeared in the global information space and which show promise as a potential resource base and source of competitive advantage for future rapid development products.

Thus, managing resource provision is aimed at creating an optimal balance of all types of the organization's resources in alignment with the global information space. This will, if the result is a finished product, create the possibility for the organization to capture a large market share or create a new market where demand can be satisfied. Solving the task of the formation of the optimal balance of all types of resources in the process of the optimization of the business processes and models of the organization is very important in creating cyber economic systems.

The creation of products with completely new consumer qualities that could attract additional sales markets, according to the formulated and mathematically substantiated economic law of management of competitiveness,[1] will lead to a sustainable competitive position in the market during the formation of a new economic system—the cyber economy.

The performed research allowed the author to define the cyber economy—a large organizational and economic system, which is based on the knowledge and

[1]Chursin A., Makarov Yu. Management of competitiveness: theory and practice. Springer, 2015.

technologies of intellectual systems, neural algorithms, and adaptive models and methods of processing and analyzing large arrays of data. This will allow building economic relations and ties between subjects on the basis of value criteria and forecasting interactions between subjects and objects of economic relations during the production, exchange, and distribution of material goods.

5 Conclusions

Optimal resource provision is important for any company considering the creation of a rapid product development program. It can be ensured through the implementation of the methods and principles of the cyber economy with the application of the mathematical tools, which have been offered in this chapter.

References

Barashkova OV, Ostretsov VN (2012) The methodology of evaluation of resource potential of an agricultural company. Econ Econ Sci 4(8):33

Berdnikova LF (2009) Methodological foundations of analysis of the resource potential of construction organizations. Ph.D. thesis, Tolyatti, 227 p

Chursin A, Makarov Y (2015) Management of competitiveness: theory and practice. Springer, Cham

Chursin A, Tyulin A (2018) Competence management and competitive product development: concept and implications for practice. Springer, p 241. https://doi.org/10.1007/978-3-319-75085-9

Kovalev VV (2016) The foundations of the theory of financial management. Infra-M, Moscow, 544 p

The Logic and Principles of Intelligent Machines' Decision-Making in the Cyber Economy

Alexander V. Yudin

Abstract This chapter focuses on the principles behind the functioning of intelligent systems and machines in the economic activities of the cyber economy. Using the example of an intelligent system for the management of the construction of a road, the author illustrates the possibilities for the automatization of business processes. It is shown that on the basis of data from remote probing of the Earth, processed with the help of AI methods, it is possible to determine the economic state of the subject of a space survey and solve the economic tasks connected to development, monitoring, and provision of the necessary resources for the subject without human participation. This allows for a reduction in the labor intensity of the processes and the likelihood of corruption, and connects the digitization of the Earth from space to the needs of the digital economy.

Mathematical tools are used to show the influence that the usage of intelligent systems and machines has on economic growth and labor efficiency.

1 Introduction

One of the most important shifts in the development of the cyber economy is the emergence of new forms of automatized, "intelligent" systems to manage the economy. Such systems enable huge gains in labor efficiency creating deep economic and, therefore, social changes. The current progress in the management of economic systems through advances in cybernetics allows for clear trajectories for economic development, creating an effective model of operative management of all economic processes, including the prediction and prevention of any crisis situation. The production system, built on the principles of the cyber economy, can continuously take into account even the smallest changes in societal need and adapt strategic and operative plans for the innovative development of an organization, sector, or the economy as a whole.

A. V. Yudin
RUDN University, Moscow, Russia
e-mail:

© Springer Nature Switzerland AG 2019
V. M. Filippov et al. (eds.), *The Cyber Economy*, Contributions to Economics,
https://doi.org/10.1007/978-3-030-31566-5_8

The innovative development of companies, harmonized with the evolution of technological shifts, allows for the transition of production to a higher level of efficiency with the creation of innovative scientific and production departments and centers of competencies. This process takes place on the basis of completely new production technologies for digital production. It is therefore necessary to consider adapting existing systems for the management of a company's business processes to the new economic reality. The cyber economy is based on adaptive production systems, in which any deviation from target indicators leads to qualitative analysis of the reasons for this deviation.

An adaptive production system is a system with feedback, which is an important condition for its stable functioning. On the one hand, the automatization of the management of business processes, which takes place within the production system, should lead to balancing the whole system and supporting the process within set limits. On the other hand, the presence of feedback opens the possibility for target development, so the system's balance is relative. Deviation of the technical and economic indicators from the planned trajectories (in both directions) leads to distortion of the system. In such a case it would be necessary to use a complex set of measures in order to return the system to its initial state of stable functioning. According to the general ideas behind cybernetics, which pass into the cyber economy, any system, including for economic production, is only stable in the case of the absence of strict restraining limits. The possibility of a fluctuation of certain elements within the set limits ensures the need for adaptability to the changing conditions.

In the process of organizing an adaptive intelligent cyber economic system for the management of business processes, it is necessary to take into account a number of subjective aspects. Management action is not always caused by a change of external conditions or a deviation from a set regime. If so, management would simply be a reaction to such deviations and only determined depending on changing circumstances. Rather, each new act of management takes place in view of the previous one. The task of management is to localize or neutralize the forces that impact negatively on the set order and to support its retention. Therefore, using the principle of adaptive management creates new perspectives for improving the system of management and simplifying the methodology for design of automatized systems at various levels.

The largest process occurring in the modern economy is digitization, which is underway globally. The Government of the Russian Federation adopted the program "Digital Economy of the Russian Federation," one of the tasks of which is to create a domestic digital platform for the collection, processing, storing, and distribution of data from remote probing of the Earth, which provides the needs of citizens, business, and public authorities ("Digital Earth"). The results of such space activities and their intellectual processing by modern methods of fundamental mathematics and informatics could become the first stage and foundation of the modern cyber economy. This requires a theory of the management of economic processes based on the information from space, which includes models describing the influence of space on processes in the economy, as well as the theoretical and practical foundations for utilizing the results of space activities to solve specific economic tasks on Earth.

2 Materials and Method

The scientific and methodological issues of intellectual decision support are studied in the works Chursin et al. (2017, 2019), Chursin and Tyulin (2017), Chursin and Makarov (2015), Kendal (2007), Popovich (2014), Voženilek (2009), Shamin et al. (2013, 2017), and Tyulin et al. (2017).

The digital economy offers wide opportunities for development of the system of managing economic processes at the company, sectoral, or national level. Modern technologies will create the environment for a hi-tech digital cyber economy, which will remove the human factor (and the accompanying corruption and mistakes) from many processes through the automatization of the collection of statistical, tax, and other data, and ensure that decision-making relies on analysis of the real situation. The tool for automatizing managerial decisions could be intelligent management systems and algorithms, included in various devices and machines. The main resource that ensures the functioning of intelligent systems is big data, created by amalgamating data collected from visual observations and measures (Earth remote sensing, GLONASS/GPS, and data exchanges in communication channels), and knowledge from the global information space. The processing of big data through AI methods and the formation of self-educating neural networks can produce information with a specific economic sense and ensure the presence of the digital economy in all spheres of the traditional economy, eventually leading to an increase in labor efficiency and a reduction of costs. The convergence of information from a wide range of sources includes economic knowledge data that enable conclusions to be reached on the direction for the automatized management of processes in various economic spheres.

For the further development of intelligent systems, improvements must be made to the methods for receiving the initial data and the mechanisms whereby they are processed, as the basis of any intelligent system is precise initial data. This directly determines the quality of the managerial decisions that are offered by the intelligent system.

Let us now consider the issue of the formation of such intelligent systems using the example of the system for managing the process of road construction. The technical basis of the intelligent system is space infrastructure, the information it provides, and the database containing different information (big data), relating to the project's life cycle and the management of assets in the course of implementing the project. The methodological basis is the intelligent algorithms used for the processing of information.

In order to implement the process of road construction, the database has to contain the machine-oriented documents (design, project, engineering, etc.) of the whole process of construction (for all stages and with the characteristics of all business processes), information on necessary materials, their suppliers, terms of delivery, information on workers, prices, and information on the economic state in the country of the project (customs fees, tax rates, etc.). The database is filled with this information in the automatic regime.

The system automatizes the processes of monitoring and management of the project implementation and its compliance, using the structured data of air and space systems from Earth remote surveys (satellites, laser scanning, drones, etc.), nonstructured—or poorly structured—data (Big Data) from networks, the technologies of AI for processing the data, and blockchain.

Intelligent space system data perform the following functions:

- Digital formation of the target parameters for the design based on the project documents;
- Automatization of the processes of receipt, processing, and storing of geometrical characteristics of the construction object, according to the requirements for precision and periodicity that are given in the project requirements, to the corresponding subsystem for the management of construction of the objects;
- Automatization of intellectual support for the project (including planning) and control of its current state according to three components of the project (nomenclature/terms, the budget of income/expenditure, and movement of financial assets) with the help of Earth remote probing, laser scanning, drones, etc.;
- Automatization of decision-making on the selection of personnel (designers, contractors, and suppliers of materials);
- Automatization of the process to initiation purchases according to the selection of the supplier;
- Automatization of document turnover (registration and certification of deals), protected from unsanctioned influence through the use of blockchain;
- Automatic connection of a data exchange with the BIM (Building Information Model) to design construction objects in view of their full life cycle.

The monitoring of the implementation of these projects starts from the receipt of the processed data from Earth remote probing, which pass into the subsystem of satellite Earth remote probing (resolution—1 m), drones (resolution—5–10 cm), laser scanning (resolution—2–3 mm), and on the basis of indirect methods for obtaining linear, space, volume, and other characteristics of the construction object (Fig. 1).

The measuring subsystem ensures the receipt of the necessary data with an allowable error (according to the official documents). It also ensures the receipt of the precise geometrical characteristics of the objects with periods set for each type of construction object according to the requirements of the corresponding subsystem. The measuring subsystem has a set of indirect methods for the approximate evaluation of characteristics of the construction object on the basis of an analysis of the volume of performed works and the quantity of materials used, as well as by a comparison of factual quantity and normative quantity.

Figure 2 shows a detailed scheme for the management of construction with the methods of the intelligent space system.

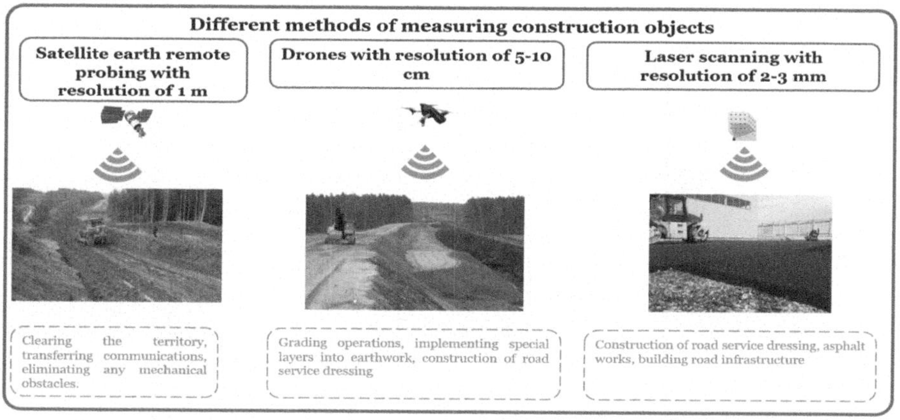

Fig. 1 Different methods of measuring construction objects (using the example of road construction)

This scheme is based on the principle of automatizing the processes for selecting the suppliers of materials and contractors based on the conclusions of an expert system and the data from Earth remote probing. The main goal of the presented scheme for the execution of the construction project with the usage of the data of Earth remote probing is to minimize the human factor at the stages of price formulation, determining suppliers and contractors, and evaluating the quality of project execution. The complex usage of remote probing (space surveys and drones) and AI methods (databases, Data Mining, and neural networks) allows for the building of a completely new system of objective analysis and monitoring of projects.

3 Results

As a result of an analysis of the data from Earth remote probing, the technical characteristics of the object are obtained. They are used for calculations of the normative quantity of materials for the works. The normative data determine the labor intensity of the works and automatize the selection of personnel that can perform all necessary works in view of time and logistics. The cost of the works is calculated, and the optimal performers are selected in the automatic regime. The system's report is given to the customer. After that, agreements with suppliers and performers/contractors are concluded.

The main peculiarity of the scheme is that all processes that are connected to the evaluation and construction of objects and spending of resources are controlled by the monitoring center. The following mechanism is used: After receiving data on the object, an automatized calculation of the necessary materials and human resources (through AI methods and 3D modeling) is performed. Then, the most acceptable

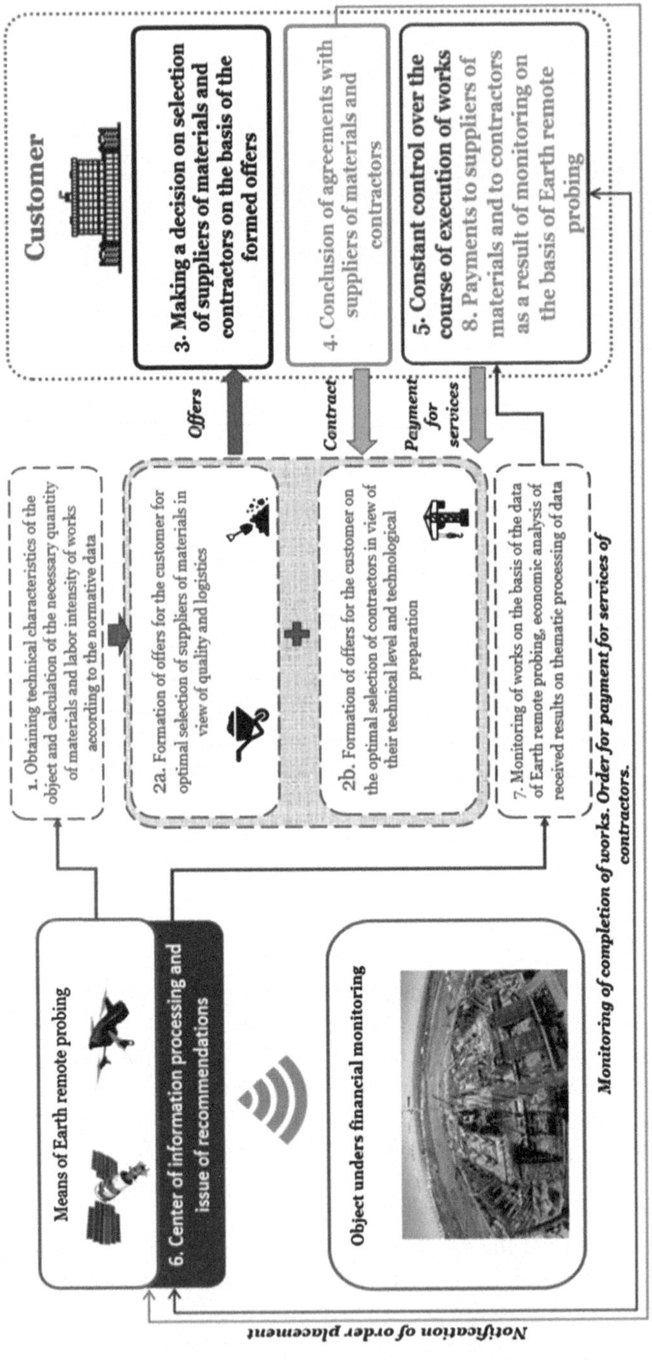

Fig. 2 The scheme for the execution of the construction project with the help of the data from Earth remote probing and AI

suppliers (who can deliver high-quality materials in the set time) are selected in the automatic regime. The conclusion of the monitoring is sent to the customer who then makes a decision on the start of the works. The monitoring of implementation of the project never stops.

Thus, the general scheme for the usage of intelligent space systems for the analysis and monitoring of projects using the example of road construction is the following:

1st step. Receipt of technical characteristics of the object in view of the project documents and with the application of space survey data.
2nd step. Calculation of the amount of necessary materials and the labor intensity of the works according to the normative data.
3rd step. Analysis of the adequacy of the necessary volume of materials and calculation of labor intensity with the usage of space survey data and intelligent data analysis.
4th step. Formation of offers for the optimal selection of contractors in view of their technical level and technological preparation on the basis of the information and analytical system.
5th step. Decision-making on the selection of suppliers of materials and contractors with the usage of the automatic expert system and provision of protocols to assist the calculations of the expert system.
6th step. Conclusion of agreements with suppliers of materials and contractors.
7th step. Continuous monitoring through the course of the execution of works and usage of the Earth remote probing data and reports.
8th step. Constant control over the results of monitoring based on the methods of Data Mining and intelligent data analysis.
9th step. Completion of the project and formation of a set of documents, confirmed by the results of the expert system.

The given scheme could be changed in view of the specifics of particular projects, but the main idea is that the traditional methods of analysis and monitoring of projects are supplemented by the modern tools of space technologies and AI methods. As a result, the intelligent space system provides significant added value.

The offered intelligent system solves the following tasks:

- Evaluation of the adequacy of the project's cost on the basis of the Earth remote probing data and knowledge database;
- Independent selection of contractors and suppliers without human participation (the intelligent system provides the best method for selection);
- Objective monitoring of the trajectory of the project's execution;
- Formation of justified protocols for automatic decisions.

Such intelligent systems are developed not only for construction management. They have become popular in forestry, agriculture, the management of water resources, ecological management, etc. In the agrarian sector, the usage of unmanned agricultural machinery with navigation systems is now common. The need for the timeliness of irrigation, fertilizing, and pest processing are controlled in real time by automatized intelligent systems, which use data from Earth remote probing as their main resource.

As space infrastructure—the most important component in the work of an intelligent system—is very difficult to repair, its innovative potential and reliability should ensure the possibility of solving many current economic tasks over the course of the next 10–15 years. As the modernization of technical components and devices in satellites is difficult, adaptation of the infrastructure to the changing needs of the economy should be ensured by means of management from the Earth.

The effectiveness of the work of the studied intelligent systems is determined by the quality of information they receive, as this dictates the decisions that are made and the level of development of space and Earth infrastructure. The infrastructure for intelligent systems has large flows of information, which circulate and connect separate segments to each other and the infrastructure on Earth.

The convergence of space data and knowledge from the global information environment could be a new source of economic growth. Thus, for example, the usage of this information in agriculture, geology, transport management, and cargo transportation is likely to increase the effectiveness of many economic processes. Development of space infrastructure stimulates the inclusion of useful information flows into the processes for management of the economy at the company, sectoral, and national level, and influences the innovative development of a country through the creation of new unique competencies, increases in the production of science-driven products with high added value, and transition of the national economy to a new technological mode. In this sense, space infrastructure and the information it provides are the basis of technical and economic cyber systems, which ensure rapid economic development, whether expressed as the growth of a company's income, gross regional products, or national GDP.

The economic growth, in this case, is connected to increased labor efficiency, which takes place as a result of the implementation of intelligent systems. To describe the cyber economic possibilities of intelligent systems on aggregate labor efficiency [i.e., to describe the growth of the total factor of efficiency $A(T)$], let us consider the Nelson-Phelps model. The growth of aggregate efficiency of factors under the influence of the opportunities of the intelligent systems could be expressed by the following ratio:

$$R(A(T)) = c(t)\left(\frac{T(t) - A(t)}{A(t)}\right).$$

where $T(t)$—the theoretically possible level of development of technologies able to use space information for the management of economic processes in case of timely development and implementation of all necessary technologies (i.e., in the conditions of absence of a time lag between the emergence of a technology and the start of its industrial usage) $c(t)$—function, depending on the level of development of competencies for the development and application of intelligent systems.

The growth of labor efficiency, which takes place as a result of digital technologies, is connected to the level of development of infrastructure, which ensures the actual application of digital technologies. Development of infrastructure in the modern world could be considered with the help of an indicator for the development of infrastructure $\gamma(t) \in [0, 1]$. The maximum value shows sufficient preparation of the infrastructure for the application of intelligent systems, and zero value shows a total absence of such infrastructure. The growth of aggregate efficiency of the factors under the influence of the cyber economic possibilities of intelligent systems as affected by the indicator of development of infrastructure is shown in the following form:

$$R(A(T)) = \gamma(t) \cdot c(t) \cdot \left(\frac{T(t) - A(t)}{A(t)} \right) \tag{1}$$

The gap between theoretical and actual levels of the development of technologies on which space services are based could be measured by entropy H information, which is necessary for the management of economic processes. In this sense, entropy is a measure not only of the quantitative evaluation of information but also a measure of development (innovativeness and progress) of the technologies for processing this information to receive economic knowledge. Entropy of information is a measure of its precision—i.e., it reflects the ability of intelligent systems to solve economic tasks. In our case, the maximum level of entropy conforms to an absence of information on the object's state. Minimum entropy (zero) conforms to having full information on the object's state.

Thus, formula (1) in view of entropy has the following form:

$$R(A(T)) - \gamma(t)c(t)F(1 - II), \tag{2}$$

where H—entropy of the information intelligent system, F—function that describes the influence of space information on the basis of measuring its entropy on the growth of labor efficiency.

The presented model allows us to make an evaluation on the growth of labor efficiency in a specific sphere of the economy, e.g., construction.

Formula (2) shows that labor efficiency grows with an increase in the level of competencies in the sphere of the usage of space information for the management of economic processes and an increase in the level of development of infrastructure for the usage of space information:

$$A(t) = \frac{\gamma(t)c(t)}{\gamma(t)c(t) + \lambda(H)} T_0 e^{\lambda(H)t}.$$

This level of competencies ensures growth in the short term, and a growth in labor efficiency with an increase of the rate $\lambda(H)$ by means of an increase of the volumes of space information, the quality of its economic processing, and development of technologies for its usage in the management of economic processes.

4 Conclusions

The rates of economic growth possible under the influence of cyber economic systems of management based on intelligent systems depend on a number of factors: the ability of companies to apply the results of space and other innovative activities, the intellectual potential of fundamental and applied sciences, the formation of unique competencies, and the speed of implementing innovative developments. In addition, effective interactions between the state, companies, and the scientific community are required for the purpose of economic development. The development of competencies to apply cyber economic systems to management is dependent on an increase in the quality of information and precision in measuring the various characteristics of the objects towards which management of intelligent systems are oriented.

References

Chursin A, Makarov Y (2015) Management of competitiveness: theory and practice [Text]. Springer, Heidelberg, p 378

Chursin A, Tyulin A (2017) Competence management and competitive product development: concept and implications for practice [Text]. Springer, Heidelberg, p 234

Chursin A, Vlasov Y, Makarov Y (2017) Innovation as a basis for competitiveness: theory and practice [Text]. Springer, Heidelberg, p 327

Chursin RA, Yudin AV, Grosheva PYu, Filippov PG, Butrova EV (2019) Tool for assessing the risks of R&D projects implementation in high-tech enterprises. In: IOP conference series: materials science and engineering, volume 476, 012005

Kendal SL (2007) An introduction to knowledge engineering. In: Kendal SL, Green M (eds) Springer, London, 287 p

Popovich V (2014) Intelligent GIS conceptualization. In: Popovich VV (ed) Information fusion and geographic information systems, Lecture notes in geoinformation and cartography, pp 17–44

Shamin RV, Gurevich PL, Tikhomirov SB (2013) Reaction-diffusion equations with spatially distributed hysteresis. SIAM J Math Anal 45(3):1328–1355

Shamin RV, Chursin AA, Fedorova LA (2017) The mathematical model of the law on the correlation of unique competencies with the emergence of new consumer markets. Eur Res Stud J XX(3 Part A):39–56

Tyulin A, Chursin A, Yudin A (2017) Production capacity optimization in cases of a new business line launching in a company. Espacios 38:20

Voženilek V (2009) Artificial intelligence and GIS: mutual meeting and passing. In: Voženilek V (ed) 2009 International conference on intelligent networking and collaborative systems, pp 279–284

Intelligent Machines as Participants in the Socioeconomic Relations of the Cyber Economy

Valery A. Tsvetkov and Mikhail N. Dudin

Abstract *Purpose*: The purpose of this chapter is to study the technical, sociocultural, and economic role of intelligent machines (also sometimes referred to as "intelligent agents") in the cyber economy. We present research results, conclusions, and recommendations on the systemic involvement of intelligent machines into the socioeconomic relations in the near future.

Design/methodology/approach: Not long ago it seemed that the usage of intelligent machines as an integral part of the economy would be many years away. However, the rapid technological shift in the second part of the twentieth century has enabled the intellectualization, automatization, and robotization of physical and virtual (digital) space. Intelligent machines now perform key roles in the socioeconomic relations of the cyber economy. In this chapter, the authors use content analysis of a wide range of publications, statistical analysis of the data on implementation of intelligent machines in the cyber economy, and futuristic forecasts regarding the midterm perspectives and limitations of using such agents in socioeconomic relations.

Findings: The research shows that the participation of intelligent machines in the cyber economy has already been established and has a positive influence on the development of global socioeconomic relations, stimulates the growth of national economies, and provides significant labor efficiencies. Conclusions regarding the performed study and future directions of research are offered.

Originality/value: It is substantiated that the benefits of using intelligent machines could be lost through economic and reputation losses. That is why there is a necessity for the institutionalization of the space of interaction between humans and intelligent machines under the condition that such intelligent agents have limited autonomy over their functioning and decision-making (i.e., they are controlled by humans), but they are also able to conduct monitoring of human activities and have the right to block human actions that are beyond their competences (through a system of controls and counterbalances).

V. A. Tsvetkov (✉) · M. N. Dudin
Market Economy Institute (MEI RAS), Moscow, Russia
e-mail: tsvetkov@ipr-ras.ru

© Springer Nature Switzerland AG 2019
V. M. Filippov et al. (eds.), *The Cyber Economy*, Contributions to Economics,
https://doi.org/10.1007/978-3-030-31566-5_9

1 Introduction

The fact that machines now routinely possess AI is no longer strange to us. We use such intelligent machines almost every day, even without noticing it. Voice support for search and operational systems, "smart" search boxes, virtual game characters, and "captcha" (A completely automated public Turing Test to validate that a human, rather than a computer, is accessing a website). Smart products such as "smart homes" or "smart household appliances" have become a part of everyday life. Intelligent machines are used in many spheres of science: technology and cybernetics, research in the sphere of NBICS convergence (integration of nano-, bio-, info-, and socio-technologies), etc.

AI is employed in a huge range of economic activities: medicine, recruiting, media and writing activities, music, technical support; and entertainment, games, management, and transport logistics, as well as other spheres of application (Kurzweil et al. 1990; Leenes et al. 2018).

AI continues to cause heated discussion among scholars from all over the world. The main questions include: Should AI be called real intelligence? Can a machine really think independently? AI and the implications for machines replacing humans is also a topic for popular culture. In the film, "Charlie and the Chocolate Factory" the main hero's father is fired due to the robotization of his job; "Terminator" envisages a future where war breaks out between intelligent machines and humans; "Robotropolis" sees human ambition as the cause of war with intelligent machines.

We view AI both positively—happy with its capability to create various benefits for humans—and, on the other hand, with trepidation—concerned over its potential to cause an apocalyptic scenario. There is a need for an objective study of the opportunities and limitations of using intelligent machines (AI) in social and economic relations—the day-to-day activities of modern society.

In view of the fact that the notion "artificial intelligence" has a stable negative connotation, and that the notion "intelligent machine" is considered in the narrow context of physical robotization/automatization, in this chapter we use the wider metaphor, "intelligent agents". The book "Artificial Intelligence: A Modern Approach" has a chapter devoted to intelligent agents (Russel and Norvig 2009).

2 Materials and Method

In this chapter, the authors use the following methods: content analysis of a wide range of publications, statistical analysis of data relevant to the implementation of intelligent machines in the cyber economy, and futuristic forecasts regarding mid-term perspectives and limitations on using such agents in socioeconomic relations.

Content analysis on the topic of the research allows us to state that an intelligent agent is an entity that functions in and can change the state of its surrounding

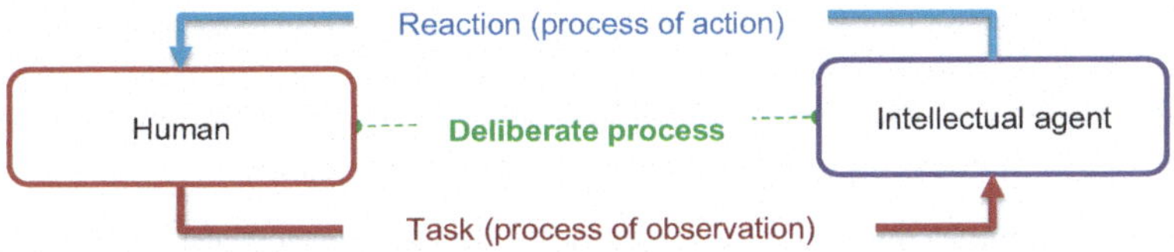

Fig. 1 Scheme of interaction between humans and intelligent agent [Source: Compiled by the authors based on Russel and Norvig (2009) and Yakovlev (2018)]

environment and can restore its state in the process its understanding of information (Russel and Norvig 2009). Intelligent agents can be divided into:

(a) Fully virtual (e.g., online game characters) that cannot influence the objective reality;
(b) Real (primarily, robot medics,[1] "smart products," and "smart homes") that can influence the objective reality;
(c) Virtual assistants (chatbots, etc.), which belong to a transitional state between the virtual world and objective reality (as a chatbot/voice assistant could be a search program or an application for a real specialist).

Until quite recently it was considered that the purpose of any machines/agents equipped with AI was defined by humans, i.e., the issue of targeted changes and self-training was not permissible. However, such intelligent agents are aimed only at one area/task/function and do not allow for the collection of data from other directions other than what they are applied to deal with. It has now become clear that intelligent agents become complicated due to deliberate processes, i.e., thinking appears in the intermediary stage of the traditional system "observation ⇒ result" (Yakovlev 2018) (Fig. 1).

Thus, from the methodological point of view, interactions between humans and intelligent agents in the context of socioeconomic relations are based on the concept of rationality. The concept of rationality consists of a lot of items, including specification, matrix tables of multilayer calculations, and careful formulations (Russel and Norvig 2009; Yakovlev 2018; Akerkar 2019), but the concept's axiom is a specification of the main categories of rationality and correctness, which intermediate the above interactions:

1. The correctness of the decision of an intelligent agent leads to the necessary sequence of its actions. If the sequence of actions conforms to the expected and required final result, the intelligent agent is deemed to have functioned correctly and rationally;
2. The indicators of the efficiency of the intelligent agent should conform to the objective result;

[1]For example, RIBA, the purpose of which is to move sick elderly people from their hospital bed to the operating room, etc. The robot was presented in Japan in 2009.

3. A rational intelligent agent strives to achieve the perfect result (idealization of expected and factual efficiency, without self-deceit or by deceiving its creator);
4. A rational intelligent agent should strive for autonomy and not wait for constant orders from the developer (though very often it is the same).

Intelligent agents must become not only the tools, but also participants in socioeconomic relations, which require their universality and ability to perform multiple tasks, which, in its turn, will lead to their active usage in the modern cyber economy.

3 Results

The cyber economy is a complex system, which provides the subjects and objects of socioeconomic relations with optimal connections for their better interaction. In the dominating process of globalization, the cyber economy has to consist of systemic resources, which also include intelligent agents.

The main spheres of application of intelligent agents in the cyber economy are in the analysis and forecasting of results, risks, and profits in the financial and real sectors. Intelligent agents are already widely used in the financial sector (Yakovlev 2018; Akerkar 2019; Faggella 2018; Arvizo 2017):

- Algorithmic trade. This application, which is sometimes called "Automatized trading systems," has been using complex intelligent agents since the 1970s. The systems of algorithmic trading perform 1000–1000,000 deals every day, which has led to the appearance of the term HFT (High-Frequency Trading).
- Management of personal finances and investment portfolios. As of now, a lot of companies use so-called "robot-consultants," though the presence of physical carrier means that they are not robots in the proper sense. Rather, these are algorithms that allow financial managers to incorporate corrections into their portfolios through an evaluation of an investments' risk. Based on the personal information of the user (age, financial assets, income, etc.), the intelligent agent offers the best investment schemes and, after the selection of a scheme, starts a calibration according to the changes of the user's demands and changes in the market situation in real time;
- Underwriting. For example, Zest Finance developed an intelligent agent, ZAML (Zest Automatized Machine Learning) based on Google-like algorithms, for evaluating the business solvency of a new generation (millennials), that, unlike the previous generation, do not have their own credit history (or it is too small). Unlike the traditional methods of underwriting, ZAML uses a system of machine learning to analyze tens of thousands of nontraditional and traditional variables, evaluating all categories of borrowers regardless of the completeness of their credit history.

In the economy, intelligent agents are used in various spheres—e.g., e-commerce and cloud services. The following are worthy of further consideration (Yakovlev 2018; Arvizo 2017):

- Intelligent databases for forecasting. These intelligent agents are specialized programs that analyze the search history of the customer and determine the keywords, links, an audit of websites visited and optimize webpages. This intelligent agent can also forecast the inflow and outflow of buyers for commercial digital platforms, review customers, and offer methods for attracting new customers and retaining existing ones;
- Hybrid Cloud Computing, HCC. The advantage of such intelligent agents is that they use local, private, and generally accessible data from cloud services, coordinated between several platforms, which can be applied by companies and private users. They ensure a more flexible usage of data and cannot be controlled by a single company. Such services work even in conditions of dynamic changes of the data or when faced with a critical workload.

These are several examples of usage of intelligent agents in the financial and real sectors of the cyber economy, which provide further insight into the development of intelligent-based technologies in socioeconomic relations.

As the institutes of state statistics (both in Russia and in developed countries) do not have unified data on the usage of intelligent agents in socioeconomic relations, we have to use corporate statistics, which are regularly published by Adobe Systems and the International Data Corporation. Thus, for example, as of 2018 (Adobe Systems 2018; International Data Corporation 2018):

(a) The number jobs, equipped with intelligent agents, grew by 4.5% in the period 2013–2017;
(b) The most popular skills that are required by specialists who develop intelligent agents are machine learning and linguistic programming;
(c) Average annual growth rates (distribution) of intelligent agents in the economy constitute 50%. Such large growth is ensured by investments into the intellectualization (automatization and robotization) of retail, banking business, healthcare, education, and industrial production.

Moreover, it seems that in the short- to midterm (1–7 years), the usage of intelligent agents in the physical and virtual robot ("robots-consultants" and chatbots) will double or triple as compared to 2010. Transition to unmanned technologies for the transportation of people and material goods is expected in the next 5–10 years.

It should be noted that intelligent agents provide not only benefits (social and economic) but also potential risks and disadvantages. Thus, for example, a small mistake in an intelligent algorithm, which is used in Sberbank, led to large financial and reputational losses (RBC 2019). Still, this major Russian financial institution has not stepped back from the use of intelligent agents, as new developments (directly financed from the revenues and profits of Sberbank) for the minimization of risks (e.g., biometric reading of a user's data to exclude the possibility for counterfeiting debit or credit cards) are conducted.

It is obvious that further studies on the development of technologies/algorithms for AI and its bearers (intelligent agents) are necessary. Despite the apocalyptic forecasts of futurologists and specialists in the sphere of neural sciences, the transition from the selective usage of intelligent agents to their systemic implementation into socioeconomic relations could be effective, and probable risks could be reduced by means of finding solutions that would avoid a loss of human control over intelligent agents; and solve the current problems around the ecologization and socialization of economic activities (connected primarily to production of material goods).

This is why intelligent agents are studied in the same context as the technologies of industrial metabolism. Industrial metabolism is the process of transforming industrial waste into secondary resources or biodegradable products, which will be decomposed by micro- and macroorganisms in the natural environment (Fan et al. 2017; Elia et al. 2017). The idea of a transformation of industrial and production processes from the linear model (from the creation of material product to its burial as waste) into a circular system that is based on the renewal of resources (partially achieved through energy savings) is increasingly popular. Therefore, from the social and ecological point of view, the cyber economy should also aim to become the economy of the closed cycle (Stahel 2016). The possibilities of the cyber economy in the context of social and environmental issues can be shown through the concept of "smart" eco-industrial parks (Gomez et al. 2018) and the use of intelligent agents in the production of material goods (Fig. 2).

By integrating these two concepts, we see the possibility to create a powerful artificial neural network, which will control (under human guidance) the functioning of an eco-industrial park, reducing social and ecological risks. Within such an artificial neural network, humans perform strategic management of the functioning and development of intelligent agents by means of integrating their informational and calculation processes to obtain social, economic, and ecological benefits (Gomez et al. 2018).

It should be mentioned that such networks of intelligent agents could be vulnerable to external cyber attacks that could change the target purpose of the operation as a result of opportunistic or objectively criminal behavior. Also, a human (or group of humans) who manages the training function of such a network on the basis of the accumulation and consideration (within its calculation capacities) of information could hijack such a system (Leenes et al. 2018; Martinez-Miranda et al. 2016). Various actions/operations of intelligent agents, modeled by a human, could be identified as specific crimes (King et al. 2018):

(a) Economic, financial, and commercial crimes (corporate fraud, deliberate bankruptcy, and the illegal takeover of assets);
(b) Socially dangerous crimes (production and distribution of drugs, document forgery, involvement into criminal and extremist activities);
(c) Crimes against individuals (blackmail, incitement to suicide, sexual crimes).

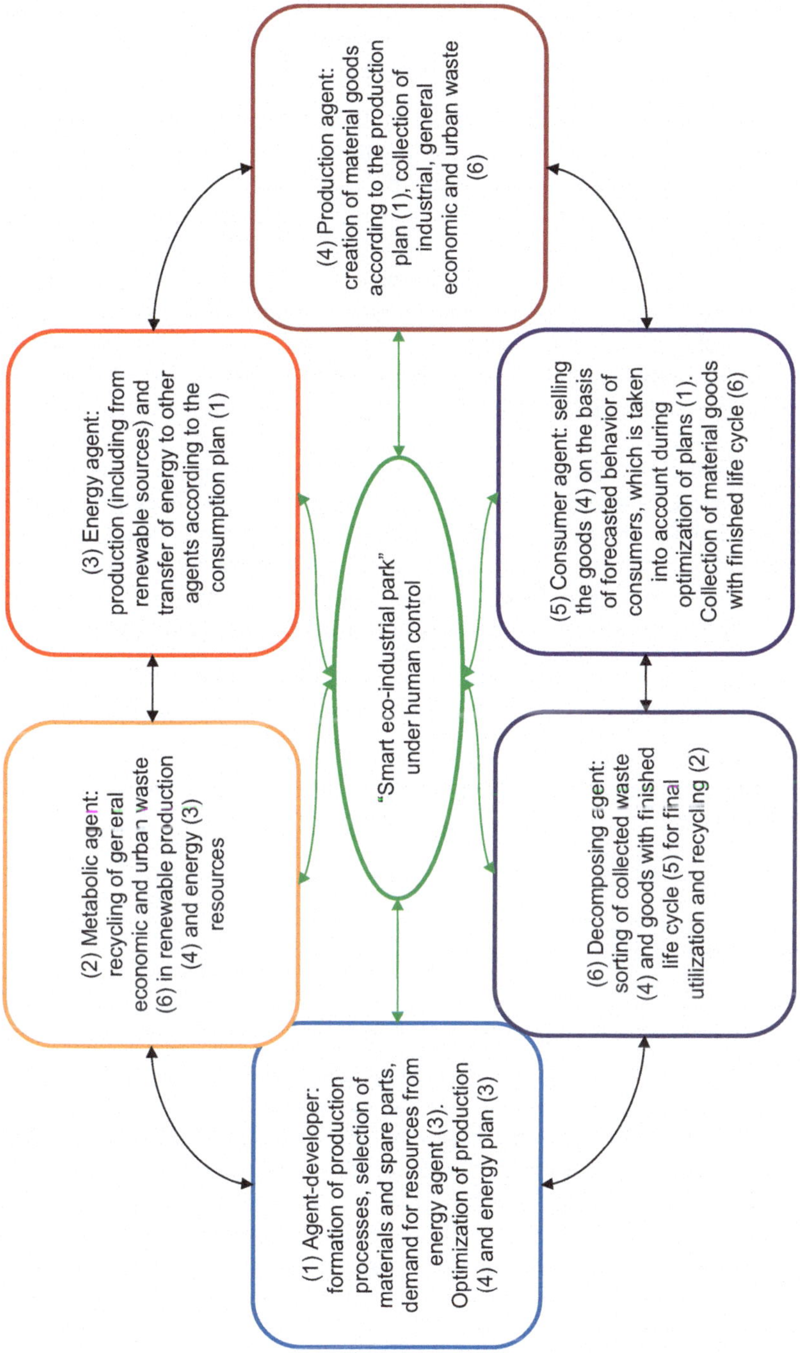

Fig. 2 Integration of the concepts of the "smart eco-industrial park" and "intelligent agents in material production" [Source: Compiled by the authors based on Stahel (2016) and Gomez et al. (2018)]

It is obvious that the problem of criminalizing the activities/operations of intelligent agents lies in the sphere of human responsibility, or, to be precise, in the sphere of the social responsibility of citizens, companies, and the state.

The possible solutions for all of the above could include:

1. Limitations on the autonomous work of intelligent agents to curtail their independence in making complex decisions. In other words, it is necessary to have a collection of formal and informal norms that determine the admissible level of autonomy of intelligent agents, which would avoid the apocalyptic scenarios that have been posited;
2. Diversification and securitization of the responsibilities shared by intelligent agents and humans. This means that humans should control the actions of intelligent agents (within the intelligent agent's competences), and intellectual agents should control human actions (within human competences). Both entities are assigned the right to block any action that goes beyond the set competences of the other;
3. Monitoring and collection of information for the formation of an open database on any deliberate or undeliberate actions of both human and intelligent agents, which could have led to a potentially apocalyptic scenario. Apart from the mathematical algorithms of AI, machine, and linguistic training, it is necessary to use neuropsychological models for scanning and behavioral forecasting, adapted for both the artificial neural network of intelligent agents and humans.

Thus, it is obvious that interrelations between human and intelligent agents require the development of a system of constraints and counterbalances so that:

- Intelligent agents remain under human control;
- Humans cannot change the targeted purpose of an intelligent agent and use it for criminal activities.

4 Conclusion

To summarize the above, it is possible to conclude that:

(a) The participation of intelligent agents (intelligent machines) in modern socio-economic relations is real and will increase in the future;
(b) Such participation allows for the mastering and development of new directions in human creative activities in the sphere of the global economic system;
(c) Statistical data show increasing growth rates of the usage of intelligent agents in the economy, which leads to growth of demand for specialists who know the "language" of these machines, can train them, and create a system of necessary restraints and counterbalances, which would exclude the possibility for criminal interference;

(d) Humans should not be excluded from these complex, but obviously mutually profitable relations, as the algorithms of intelligent agents could make errors that may lead to large-scale financial, economic, or reputation losses;
(e) The main problem in interactions between human and intelligent agents is that the latter could be used in both positive and negative ways. The positive include an increase of cybernetic and economic literacy, reductions in the use of polluting materials, and solving complex problems in the scientific sphere. The negative include cyber terrorism, the introduction of errors in the initial algorithmic code of the program/algorithm for the purpose of fraud, and socially dangerous processes.

In view of the above, we think that recommendations for further scientific research and practical systemic involvement of intelligent agents into socioeconomic relations going forward will consist of the following:

1. Although the autonomy and universal and multitasking character of intelligent agents are an obvious advantage, which simplify the task for its creator, it is impossible to fully recuse humans from the controlling role;
2. The algorithmic code of an intelligent agent should be very difficult to hack in order to prevent damage to socioeconomic relations at the industrial or even global scale. It is necessary to track even the least important notifications on errors and failures in the work of intelligent agents and eliminate them in due time;
3. The role of intelligent agents in the growth of environmentally friendly industrial production should be taken to a new qualitative and material level. Intelligent agents should be used not only in the programs of environment protection but also for work with hazardous waste and be utilized to deal with ecological catastrophes, e.g., explosions at nuclear power plants caused by human or other factors;
4. There is a need for a clear collection of formal and informal rules/norms for interactions between human and intelligent agents at all levels of usage from economic and legal to the everyday. A mechanism for the implementation of rules is also needed. In other words, it is necessary to create an institutionalized digital space for human creative activities in developing intelligent agents.

References

Adobe Systems (2018) Analytics. https://www.adobe.com/experience-cloud/topics/analytics.html?promoid=4JW79HWC&mv=other. Accessed 3 Mar 2019

Akerkar R (2019) Introduction to artificial intelligence. In: Artificial intelligence for business. Springer, Cham, pp 1–18

Arvizo S (2017) ZestFinance introduces machine learning platform to underwrite millennials and other consumers with limited credit history. https://www.businesswire.com/news/home/20170214005357/en/ZestFinance-Introduces-Machine-Learning-Platform-Underwrite-Millennials. Accessed 3 Mar 2019

Elia V, Gnoni MG, Tornese F (2017) Measuring circular economy strategies through index methods: a critical analysis. J Clean Prod 142:2741–2751

Faggella D (2018) Machine learning in finance–present and future applications. https://www.techemergence.com/machine-learning-in-finance/. Accessed 3 Mar 2019
Fan Y, Qiao Q, Fang L (2017) Network analysis of industrial metabolism in industrial park: a case study of Huai'an economic and technological development area. J Clean Prod 142:1552–1561
Gomez AMM, Gonzalez FA, Barcena MM (2018) Smart eco-industrial parks: a circular economy implementation based on industrial metabolism. Resour Conserv Recycl 135:58–69
International Data Corporation (2018) IDC investment research. https://www.idc.com/promo/investment-research. Accessed 3 Mar 2019
King T, Aggarwal N, Mariarosaria T, Floridi L (2018) Artificial intelligence crime: an interdisciplinary analysis of foreseeable threats and solutions (22 May 2018). https://ssrn.com/abstract=3183238. Accessed 3 Mar 2019
Kurzweil R, Richter R, Kurzweil R, Schneider ML (1990) The age of intelligent machines. MIT Press, Cambridge, p 579
Leenes R, Van Brakel R, Gutwirth S, De Hert P (2018) Data protection and privacy: the age of intelligent machines. Bloomsbury Publishing, New York, p 256
Martinez-Miranda E, McBurney P, Howard MJ (2016) Learning unfair trading: a market manipulation analysis from the reinforcement learning perspective. In: Proceedings of the 2016 IEEE conference on evolving and adaptive intelligent systems, EAIS, 103, p 9
RBC (2019) German Gref acknowledged the loss of a billion rubles due to AI. https://www.rbc.ru/finances/26/02/2019/5c74f4839a7947501397823f. Accessed 3 Mar 2019
Russel SJ, Norvig P (2009) Artificial intelligence: a modern approach, 3nd edn. Pearson Publishing, London, p 1152
Stahel WR (2016) The circular economy. Nat News 531(7595):435
Yakovlev K (2018) What is the difference between strong and weak AI? https://postnauka.ru/video/88720. Accessed 3 Mar 2019

Perspectives on the Potential Application of Intelligent Machines in the Cyber Economy

Stanislav E. Prokofyev, Tatyana V. Bratarchuk, and Irina I. Klimova

Abstract Intelligent machines have become important elements in modern economic development. This chapter studies potential directions for the application of intelligent machines in the cyber economy with a focus on industry, the development of cities, and healthcare. The opportunities and challenges of such applications are analyzed.

1 Introduction

Modern global economic processes are seeing the increasing implementation of innovative technologies. Many scholars believe that humanity is now at the threshold of a new age—the Fourth Industrial Revolution. It is characterized by a transition to comprehensive automatization, robotization in the production and service spheres, increases in labor efficiency, a growth of effectiveness, elimination of borders between spheres, a reduction of anthropogenic influence on the environment due to the implementation of energy-saving technologies, and increase in the demand for employees with competences in the IT sphere. The competitive advantages for countries that embrace these changes will include high quality of education, higher potential for innovation, rapidly developing infrastructure, and open government.

The global market for investments into robototronics, automatization, and accompanying technologies is growing very quickly; the 30 largest deals for purchase of hi-tech companies in 2016 totalled $18,870,000,000.

Intelligent machines are used in industry, the service sector, satellite navigation, research and development projects, and breakthrough inventions in various areas of science. China has a number of breakthrough achievements in this area: the first geosynchronous satellite for remote sensing of the Earth with high-definition Gaofen 1; the BeiDou Navigation Satellite System; the coupling of Shenzhou 11 and the space laboratory Tiangong-2; and the successful start of the first satellite for quantum

S. E. Prokofyev (✉) · T. V. Bratarchuk · I. I. Klimova
Financial University Under the Government of the RF, Moscow, Russia
e-mail: SEProkofev@fa.ru; tvbutova@fa.ru; iiklimova@fa.ru

© Springer Nature Switzerland AG 2019

V. M. Filippov et al. (eds.), *The Cyber Economy*, Contributions to Economics,
https://doi.org/10.1007/978-3-030-31566-5_10

communications. Within the program "Made in China 2025," China started a project of innovations for high-quality equipment and accelerated important technological projects: a high-quality CNC machine, new aviation engine, new gas turbines, etc. (Popkova and Ragulina 2018).

The unmanned submersible, Haidou-1, developed in China, allowed it to become the third country, after Japan and the USA, able to produce unmanned submersibles capable of descending down to 10,000 m. The high-speed multiple-unit trains of Chinese origin became a world symbol for the advances in China's production abilities (Ragulina et al. 2017).

The growing possibilities for the application of intelligent machines in the cyber economy may have a large influence on the transformation of markets, including railways, energy, transport, and automatization markets, and many more important production sectors. Experts have determined the following six key tendencies in Industry 4.0: modulation, identification, integration, setting, miniaturization, and digitization. These six tendencies represent various spheres for the development of hardware and software provision and open new directions for the future expansion of technological innovations.

2 Materials and Method

2.1 Industry

One important area for the application of intelligent machines in the cyber economy is industrial production (Ivanov et al. 2017). Thus, Magnitogorsk Metallurgical Plant PJSC—the world's largest manufacturer of steel—uses intelligent machines in five important processes (Table 1).

The usage of intelligent machines allows the plant to cooperate with and exchange information and documents online with all intermediaries. The company is notable for its integration with the information systems of key customers, primarily, pipe companies: Chelyabinsk Pipe Plant and Volzhsky Pipe Plant. It is able to transfer electronic certification for such products. Such informational interactions with suppliers of its main resources through online document systems are also considered. The type, quality, time of supply, form of transportation along the rail route, and time of shipment to the storage facility all add to the effectiveness of managing the technological process (Akhromeeva et al. 2017). The rapid solution of such issues supports the task of planning storage issues for resources at all stages of the technological chain, eliminating the influence of the human factor, reducing expenditure on the initial processing of information, and managing stock levels. The optimization of shipments increases the effectiveness of coke oven and blast furnace production, and it is important from the point of view of the spending of resources for cast iron.

Apart from electronic document turnover, the company offers to all intermediaries—customers and suppliers—the mobile apps "iCustomer" and "Plant supplier."

Table 1 The use of intelligent machines in the management of the Magnitogorsk Metallurgical Plant PJSC

No.	Area of usage	Result of implementation
1	Managing the product life cycle	Digital storage of finished and semifinished products, development of identification systems, and product tracking. Due to innovative technologies, the transition to digitization and improvement of business processes, connected to the planning and accounting of production, is possible
2	Smart factory	Increase of the intelligent component in personnel work, solving the tasks of modeling, optimization of technological processes, and the system of decision support in various aspects of activities. It is possible to use neurotechnologies and machine learning, as well as to develop and implement pilot projects with the usage of technologies of virtual and alternate reality (VR/AR), as well as optimize business processes with the usage of the technologies such as Robotic Process Automation (RPA) and chatbots
3	Industrial Internet of Things (IoT)	The ability to reduce the influence of the human factor and increase the quality of initial data. Innovation has led to a detailed assessment of the work of all production lines of the company. The obtained information is accessible to all departments and allows for cooperation between employees from different departments to quickly solve current problems. The technology has reduced the share of unexpected delays and the number of failures of the equipment IoT has also increased the social responsibility of the business in terms of care for personnel. Thus, within the workplace, it has enabled measuring air humidity, levels of pollution, and the structure of the atmosphere
4	Security	Intelligent machines have strengthened the company's security systems. Certain results were achieved in the sphere of cybersecurity and labor safety. It was possible to organize a complex set of measures that envisages execution of the requirements of federal law and the creation of a unified system for labor protection and industrial safety. In addition, it was possible to ensure the implementation of exoskeletal technologies and start a system of adaptive notification and registration of the parameters for the movement of pedestrians and car transport on railway crossings
5	HR engineering	The results here primarily relate to an increase in the effectiveness of personnel training. This is now conducted through usage of modern educational and practice-oriented technologies in the following directions: development of a training complex based on VR/AR technologies for training the plant's employees; application of a set of training programs for the transfer of "Industry 4.0" technologies into production; remote training; and development of a set of services using chatbot technology in various activities of the HR department (e.g., during the hiring or transfer of employees)

"iCustomer" provides information on the execution of an order online to ensure quick decision-making on managing the supply chain and optimizing costs.

In 2005, the plant was the first company in the sphere to transfer business processes into the ERP-system, "Oracle E-Business Suite". The large-scale program allows solving the tasks of Industry 4.0 in conjunction with all of the information flows of the company. The unified system includes the management of production (continuous and discrete production), reserves, purchases (including online trading platform), finance, personnel, projects, orders, and sales. It reflects the results of the plant's economic and financial activities and tracks the whole technological production chain, the state of operation of all large machines, and failures and maintenance of equipment. The data on the company's activities are checked in real time in the information system. The usage of intelligent technologies envisages changing the attitude of each manager and employee towards information (digital technologies) as a tool that increases the effectiveness of work (Sharkov et al. 2018). At the level of the system's formation architecture, this means that each built or modernized machine on the production platform (from the point of view of managing the technological process) should be viewed as a part of the unified information space and unified system of management. The company's management tries to stick to this ideology.

3 Results

The concept of "Industry 4.0" aims at the transformation of business. In practice, the plant has an automatized three-stage plan of production: volume, calendar, and operative planning.

The digital model of production used at the plant is illustrated in Fig. 1.

All information from the production departments goes to the technological database, which allows for the implementation of the corporate system of technology and quality management with integral assessment of execution according to customers, types of products, shops, and certain sets of any parameters. The system of statistics management SPM (shock pulse monitoring) shows a stability of the technological process and of the quality of the issued products. The plant also plans to implement the elements of predictive analysis.

A center of competence for the robotization of processes on the basis of RPA technology was created; mobile devices in technical servicing and repair are widely used; a project for robot-recruitment for HR is being developed; application of VR/AR technology during the training of personnel is used. A project on the creation of digital doubles of technological processes and machines with the use of industrial IoT is planned for 2019.

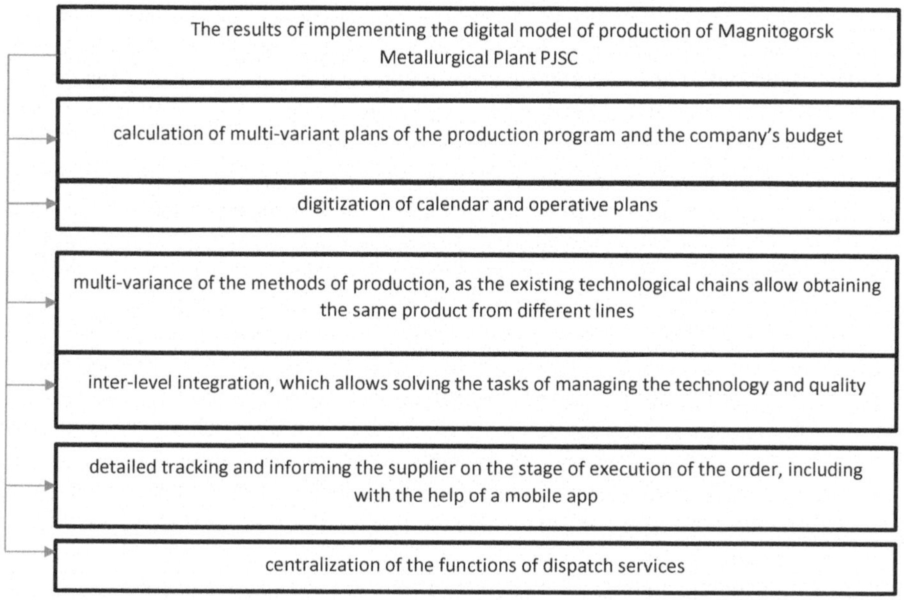

Fig. 1 The results of the digital model of production at Magnitogorsk Metallurgical Plant PJSC

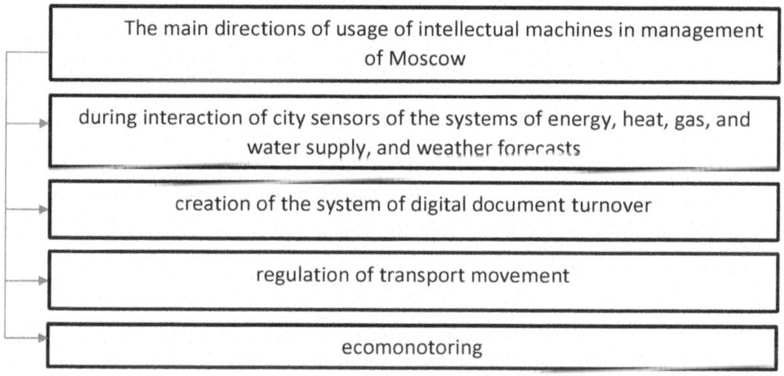

Fig. 2 The main directions for the use of intelligent machines in the management of Moscow

3.1 City Management

Large applications of intelligent machines are not necessarily expected for city management. However, by 2030, Moscow will become a data-driven city, with decision-making based on the automatic processing and analysis of accumulated Big Data (Fig. 2).

Digital technologies will allow expanding the horizons of openness in the functioning of public authorities during the provision of services to citizens and conducting control and monitoring of the financial flows of the territory, which, in in turn, will lead to an increase of effectiveness in spending budget assets and will reduce or exclude the number of transaction costs that accounts for a large share of the existing model of city's management of finances (Markina and Yakishina 2016).

It should be noted that Moscow has already made certain achievements in the digitization and openness of city processes. For example, the website Nash Gorod (*Our City*) published 839,200 reports on civic violations in 2017, of which 722,300 reports were acknowledged (95%), 710,800 violations were dealt with (98%), and 130,000 violations in the maintenance of yards, and roads were recorded and reports sent to those responsible. The website of open data (data.mos.ru) had 3.5 million visitors in 2017, with 75 new data collections and 16 bulletins published in 2017. The number of participants in the project "Active citizen" reached 2 million. The average number of voters on issues relevant to the management of the city is 220,000, with a high point of 337,500 (Official website of the Mayor of Moscow).

There are plans for implementation of an intelligent system that will provide real time access to information on city council decisions and opportunities on the website, mos.ru. This will allow the posting of full information on the city program of capital repairs, the terms of repairs in each house, the volume of allocated funds, and other data, thereby automatizing the full life cycle of city documents, implementing blockchain technologies for the provision of transparency in digital transactions for all sectors of the city economy and storing voting results, including on household management. Intelligent machines will also be used for the development of e-democracy in Moscow and is expected to increase accessibility to all tools of e-democracy in real time from any device, allowing participation in debates, voting, the collection of opinions, discussion of city issues, online voting, feedback, and crowdsourcing projects.

From the economic point of view, the usage of intelligent machines will allow reducing expenditures for document turnover and reducing the time for the provision of services, as well as evaluating the work of public officers by citizens in a real time regime. Intelligent platforms will enable the secure unification of all data of a citizen (domestic identification and passport, educational documents, electronic workbook, medical history, etc.) with a sufficient level of cybersecurity. This will allow for the automatization and personalization of all services that are provided to a citizen.

In the near future, all legal acts will be analyzed with the help of AI (expert systems and neural networks) to ensure the absence of contradiction and the need to harmonize the legal framework with the program "Digital economy of the Russian Federation," other federal programs and initiatives, the strategy of Moscow's "Smart city 2030" program, and other legal acts. The legal framework of Moscow will be changed on a constant basis to support the implementation and usage of digital technologies according to the requirements of the external and internal environment.

The application of intelligent machines will stimulate the formation of national programs based on automatized analysis of achieved indicators in regard to the demands and needs of citizens and the state, as a result of electronic voting, through the use of digital tools, including AI, Big Data, and predictive analysis.

Digital technologies such as blockchain and smart contracts will help create a city technological platform in the sphere of financing and state procurement, by means of unifying—within one ecosystem—manufacturers, suppliers of products and services, and representatives of new financial technologies. A system for smart contract execution is to be implemented allow the use of photos, videos, sensors, and AI for the automatic formation of typical sets of documents, tracking the inflow of purchased products, evaluating research work, and recording the execution of the contract. The system "Electronic storage" will provide constant monitoring of suppliers' leftovers to establish future need and evaluate supply. The platform will form an automatized, transparent, barrier-free, and highly competitive environment for purchases and will ensure a risk-oriented approach, ensuring synchronization and harmonization with federal programs and initiatives in the sphere of control and inspection.

4 Healthcare

Another important direction for the application of intelligent machines is in social processes. In the sphere of healthcare, the usage of innovative digital technologies is development priority. There are active processes for the development of telemedicine, which allows patients to receive medical services via special web services and mobile apps. This allows for an interaction between patient and doctor on an online regime, with possible monitoring of the patient's health and the issue of online prescriptions. Intelligent machines enable online medical histories and stimulate the development of the concept "connected patient," which provides monitoring of the provision of medical services with the help of connected intelligent devices.

Work in this direction has been performed in Russia since 2012. There is a unified medical information and analytical system in Moscow, which is to become a platform that connects the information systems of all medical organizations and profile departments. It will become the basis for the implementation of unified electronic medical history sheets and registers of people with certain diseases.

Among the existing problems for the development of intelligent machines is the insufficient development of high-speed Internet in Russia (Belyaeva 2013). This complicates access to the platform for both the professional community and patients.

5 Conclusions

The following conclusions can be made as follows:

1. As a result of the Fourth Industrial Revolution, fundamental changes will affect almost all spheres of life. These changes will stimulate the formation of a new technological model, which can transform economic sectors, markets, production processes, and methods for the provision of social services;

2. This new stage of development will determine the emergence of new knowledge and quality requirements for specialists and will lead to changes in the value of labor in favor of intellectual and creative abilities;
3. Digital technologies will allow greater inter-sectoral interaction and cooperation and will expand the horizons of analytical data processing;
4. The positive effects of this new stage of development will include an increase in labor efficiency, boosted added value in manufactured goods, a more customer-oriented approach, and market offers orientated at individual consumers;
5. Innovations will help to reduce risk and uncertainty to the minimum. However, the dependence of forecasting from digital technologies and AI will grow;
6. A positive characteristic of the development of the digital economy will be increased in the openness of data and, therefore, the possibility of more effective control over the usage of resources, including state resources.

The application of intelligent machines in production processes will stimulate an increase in labor efficiency, reduce risks, offer a more personalized approach to customers, offer new opportunities for increasing quality assurance, and offer employment to highly skilled personnel.

Intelligent machines show much promise in territory management. The possibility for the creation of unified digital platforms to assist in the functioning of cities and conglomerations; automatically assessing the quality of employees' work; and fully considering the opinions of citizens and representatives of business, as well as other groups of people via online communications. Intelligent technologies in this sphere can also solve financial tasks, in particular, billing for city and commercial services in all spheres of city life. The mechanism of automatized control over the usage of city infrastructure and consumption of resources will ensure fair billing, control, and the effectiveness of planning infrastructure development. Robototronics can automatize the provision of city services and processes.

Intelligent machines can change the way communication interactions occur in the field of social service provision, through remote technologies that allow for monitoring of the patients in real time on a constant basis. New equipment will reduce the number of medical errors and reduce the risk of low-quality medical services. Intelligent machines will lead to radically improved diagnostics, and diseases will be determined at an earlier stage.

The above innovations will change the whole approach to the provision of medical services, which will become accessible to a larger number of citizens.

References

Akhromeeva TS, Malinetsky GG, Posashkov SA (2017) Senses and values of the digital reality: the future. Wars. Synergy. Philos Sci

Belyaeva IY (2013) The problems of interaction between public authorities and the society on the Internet. Volume: The modern corporate strategies and technologies in Russia. Collection of scientific articles in three parts. Moscow, pp 27–33

Ivanov VV, Malinetsky GG, Kulba VV, Akhromeeva TS, Posashkov SA, Toropygina SA (2017) Digital economy of Russia. Risks. Threats. Perspectives. Volume: Problems of managing the security of complex systems. In: Proceedings of the 25th International scientific conference. Russian Academy of Science; Ministry of Education and Science of the Russian Federation; Russian State University for Humanities; Scientific council of the RAS on the theory of controlled processes and automatization; Institute of the problems of management of the RAS; Institute of applied mathematics named after M.V. Keldysh of the RAS; Ministry of the Russian Federation for Affairs for Civil Defence, Emergencies and Elimination of Consequences of Natural Disasters

Magnitogorsk Metallurgical Plant implements the concept "Industry 4.0" in strategic partnership with Oracle. Specialized scientific journal "Logistics". http://www.logistika-prim.ru/press-releases/mmk-realizuet-koncepciyu-industriya-40-v-strategicheskom-partnerstve-s-oracle. Accessed 22 June 2019

Markina EV, Yakishina TA (2016) Effectiveness of internal state financial control. Bull Financ Univ 5(95):73–86

Official web-site of Moscow Mayor. https://www.mos.ru/2030/n/n6/. Accessed 22 June 2019

Popkova EG, Ragulina YV (2018) The framework strategy of formation of Industry 4.0 in modern Russia/Bulletin of the Russian Fund of Fundamental Research. Humanit Soc Sci 3(92):45–52

Ragulina YV, Zavalko NA, Ragulin AD (2017) Financial regulation of innovative activities of industrial companies. Izdatelstvo Rusays, Moscow

Sharkov AV, Kilyachkov NA, Belobragin VV, Menshikova MA et al (2018) The concept of effective entrepreneurship in the sphere of new decisions, projects, and hypothesis, 2nd edn. Moscow

The Rise of Unemployment in the Cyber Economy

Vladimir S. Osipov

Abstract The goal of this chapter is to assess the impact of the transition to a digital economy on the labor force. To achieve this goal, the methods of analysis, synthesis, comparison, and statistic modeling have been used. Digital technologies are becoming increasingly ubiquitous and while raising labor efficiency, there are negative impacts on workers who lose employment. How to solve the problem of a redundant workforce is a critical issue as there is no strategy for this adaptation. Active and passive measures to combat technological unemployment, proposed by scientists and politicians, are ineffective and cannot realistically provide a livelihood for the huge number of workers released. Therefore, the question of the displacement of living objects by IT objects remains open. The results obtained in the course of this study can be used in further studies on structural (technological) unemployment and the problems of the labor market in the cyber economy.

1 Introduction

The policy of shaping the prerequisites for the transition to a cyber economy can increase a country's international competitiveness, but, at the same time, the issue of the impact of introducing information technologies into socioeconomic processes has not yet been deeply studied (Silvestrov et al. 2015; Schwab and Davis 2018). A particular concern is the continuous growth of structural unemployment arising under the influence of scientific and technological progress and the replacement of human labor by robots, machines, programs, and other IT objects. This topic continues to develop and requires deep scientific reflection.

Referring to the scientific literature devoted to structural (technological) unemployment, we find a number of authors dealing with this problem, including C.A. Pissarides, T.W. Schultz, R. Florida, A.B. Berberov, S.P. Zemtsov,

V. S. Osipov
MGIMO University, Moscow, Russia
e-mail: vs.ossipov@inno.mgimo.ru

© Springer Nature Switzerland AG 2019
V. M. Filippov et al. (eds.), *The Cyber Economy*, Contributions to Economics,
https://doi.org/10.1007/978-3-030-31566-5_11

R.I. Kapelyushnikov, V.K. Karpov, and D.S. Medovnikov. The selected authors indirectly or directly estimate unemployment rates as a result of scientific and technological progress, digital technologies and the emergence of the cyber economy. Other global implications for society and the economy were examined in the works of such researchers as E. Brynjolfsson, N. Davis, A. McAfee, M. Ford, K. Schwab, and S.Timberg.

The essence of Russia's current import substitution policy is to achieve the replacement of imported goods with domestic counterparts, as well as to encourage the reorganization of production of those goods that were previously imported from abroad. B. Onimode (1982) noted that "Import substitution is not only an industrialization strategy that is most often observed in developing countries: it probably represents the only way to move industrialization in general."

Erik S. Reinert offers a recipe for economic policy: "The Russian manufacturing sector is still not strong enough for free trade to be profitable for the country. The WTO and the OECD are sometimes called "clubs for the rich," but by joining this club, the country does not automatically get rich. History has proved that the only successful strategy is competition with rich countries in the sphere of production, and only by achieving success in it can a country get profit from free trade" (Reinert 2009). Albert Hirschman noted in this connection that "although the policy of import substitution may be caused by external difficulties, such as war, for example, the development of local import-substituting production nevertheless must be supported by the state besides these reasons. Import substitution can be applied as part of an industry development strategy."

As we noted earlier (Osipov 2013, 2017), the evolution of industrial policy, in countries that have implemented the policy of import substitution and successfully move into the category of highly developed countries, allows us to identify the characteristic stages of such a policy:

- Creation of an import-substituting industrial structure;
- Transition to the formation of export-oriented industries;
- Growth of technological and hi-tech potential of industry, the cultivation of "national champions"—firms capable of producing competitive products for the external market.

The reorientation of the process of implementing an import substitution policy from the production of goods for domestic consumption to the export of such goods requires a radical restructuring of industry. The change in the structure of industry is accompanied by a transition from manual production to hi-tech capital-intensive industries within the framework of the cyber economy. This gives impetus to the expansion and deepening of the quality of education at the national level, as new jobs require new skills and competencies. Such work adds economic value, and the welfare of the population grows in parallel with economic growth (Bogoviz et al. 2019; Stroiteleva et al. 2019). These are the general features of the economic development of the countries of South East Asia and China. The Russian version of the policy of import substitution was based on the same strategies and pursued the same goals, but it was caused by foreign policy events, and not as a conscious economic policy aimed at achieving high economic growth.

Relying on the achievements of modern scientists, we will estimate the impact of digitalization on the labor market, consider its features and development trends, and determine the advantages, disadvantages, and limitations of the use of intelligent machines the in cyber economy.

2 Materials and Method

The digitization of industry, the introduction of the Internet of things, and the expansion of robotization have created an insurmountable obstacle to the implementation of import substitution policies within the framework of previous successful recipes. It is now clear that the growth of industry due to robotization and digitalization is not accompanied by an increase in jobs, and hence an increase in the well-being of the population. In fact, the opposite is true as alarming tendencies of deepening inequality have appeared, with simultaneous high levels of economic growth and a decrease in the number of jobs available.

Modern studies (Ford 2015; Berberov 2017; Brynjolfsson and Mcafee 2014; Dorofeyev et al. 2018) show that in the very near future, due to robotization and digitalization, individual professions will become redundant. Thus, the introduction of online cash registers allows tax authorities to monitor the financial condition of firms, to plan the level of tax burden and the future amount of taxes collected. This raises a legitimate question: what will happen to the accountants? The widespread use of big data technologies makes it possible to make more informed decisions in a much shorter time. Thus, the machines have already learned how to diagnose a disease more quickly than a professional doctor or even a council of doctors. The ability of machines to process large amounts of information faster than humans increases the analytical function of bots, which means that this type of activity can replace human labor. The accuracy of the diagnosis made by the machine is more accurate than that of a person. Bots have learned to write related texts, which makes it possible to get ready-made journal articles when entering initial information. The widespread use of digital technology in education, the recording of lectures, the introduction of electronic testing, makes the presence of a teacher in the classroom almost unnecessary. Looking into the future, we can assume that a machine's normative legal acts will be written more qualitatively, and they will also learn how to make a more balanced (and therefore legal) court decision. The symptom of such a trend may be the fact that lawyers are dismissed from court cases as it turns out to be easier, faster, and more efficient to write lawsuits through the use of a bot. All activities that, one way or another, are associated with routine operations, repetitive actions, regularity, and ability to algorithmize, will be robotized. If we recall A. Smith's classic of economic science and his theory of the division of labor, then when his judgments are imposed on today's reality, a paradoxical situation arises where, as the degree of specialization increases, different types of activities or individual operations are more easily automated and, therefore, human labor is gradually being squeezed out of such operations.

Robotization and digitalization allow capital to abandon almost completely the labor factor, but at the same time achieve high profits from the production and sale of wealth. When introducing e-government technologies, the public administration system can also dispense with civil servants responsible for performing routine standardized operations—issuing documents, registering legally significant actions, making decisions regulated by the algorithm on certain issues in social and economic activities (Pissarides 1990; Schultz 1993; Osipov 2018; Karpov 2017).

These developments make it impossible to implement the policy of import substitution, since the goal of improving the welfare of the population is not achieved. It turns out that the achievement of technical progress, digitalization, and robotization prevents the creation of new jobs, and in fact, has made the labor factor much less important in the production function. Entrepreneurs, of course, agree to reduce labor costs and remove state regulation by reducing the use of labor in their industries (Medovnikov et al. 2017; Kapelushnikov 2017, 2018). However, what are the consequences for people? How can people earn an income if their work ceases to be a necessary factor in production?

Generally, the trend of widening income inequality in capitalist countries has been accompanied by an increase in labor productivity. This alarming trend leads to the fact that the share of labor in national income is steadily decreasing against the background of the increasing share of capital. Machines are becoming the main means of increasing productivity. Machines themselves become workers and squeeze out labor from the productive process. The forerunner of these trends lay in the consequences of recent economic recessions.

American economists (Jaimovich and Siu 2012) investigated the replacement of jobs, which were reduced during the economic crisis, with new jobs during the subsequent expansion of economic activity. They concluded that middle-class jobs are most at risk of extinction, while new jobs after the recovery of the economy are created in low-wage sectors and spheres of economic activity. Many jobs are created on a part-time basis. However, official statistics address only quantitative indicators, and do not reflect the qualitative parameters of the lost and newly formed jobs. C.B. Frey and M.A. Osborne from the University of Oxford and also R. Florida and S. Timberg point out that in the very near future, professions, which account for almost half of all those employed in the US economy, may become victims of automation and robotization (Frey and Osborne 2013; Florida 2011; Timberg 2013).

Some scientists (Standing 2008; Usman 2017; Bregman 2017), as well as politicians in some countries, particularly in Switzerland, Finland, and Canada, have offered a solution in the form of an unconditional fixed income—a Universal Basic Income (UBI)—paid from the state budget directly to citizens in the form of a gratuitous nonrefundable payment. The logic is that the taxation of entrepreneurs who robotize production and abandon the use of the labor should be enough to provide all citizens of the country with a UBI. However, there are risks of an international division of labor when the state may not be able to carry out industrial policy to ensure sufficient inflow of funds in the form of taxes to the state budget.

Then, social upheavals, similar to the Luddite movement of the industrial revolution, are inevitable, when citizens will turn on robotic production. Major political upheavals are also possible, since citizens who are incapable of improving their material well-being and driven to despair by poverty will demand radical changes (Kiseleva et al. 2018; Voronov et al. 2018).

Another way to solve the problem of releasing labor as a result of robotization and digitalization might be a model of forced incorporation of robotic industries with the transfer of part of the shares to the workers to be released. The payment of dividends, along with the UBI, will increase the material well-being of the released workers, but at the same time, provide them with a stake in robotic production. In our opinion, the formation of a new model of relations between capital and society, not only through UBI, but also deliberate action in favor of the released workers, will create the optimal balance between the interests of the state, business, and society, as well as extinguish possible social upheavals. The forced shareholding model certainly needs political support, since a business, using various lobbyist organizations and the direct bribing of politicians, will most likely resist such changes. However, it should be recognized that UBI will not be enough to maintain the delicate socioeconomic balance, and the violation of this is fraught with negative consequences not only for society and the state, but also for business. Political will becomes a decisive factor in the implementation of legislative initiatives on forced shareholding, that is, the mandatory free transfer of shares in a robotic enterprise to retiring employees. Institutionalization of such a political decision will open up the possibility for the technical reequipment of enterprises, while preserving the balance of social equilibrium (Dorskaia et al. 2016).

3 Results

Addressing the problem of structural unemployment arising from the introduction of new technologies, it is worth delving into history and examining precedents that have taken place, the most significant of which can be called the industrial revolution in England, which led to the release of a huge number of spinning workers; the "weaver as a profession" ceased to exist.

It seems obvious that the impending changes in the modern economy will have similar effects. M. Ford notes that massive unemployment, a sharp increase in inequality and, ultimately, a fall in the demand for goods and services amid a decrease in the purchasing power of consumers, will become a vicious circle out of which further economic growth is impossible (Ford 2015). In the coming era of ubiquitous digitalization, workers will compete with IT objects (robots, automata, software packages, artificial intelligence (AI), etc.) and inevitably lose. Unemployment will become widespread and the consequences are difficult to assess.

Let us consider in which sectors and spheres of life in Russian society the first signs of the pressure caused by the take-up of information technologies are already evident.

The digital economy is advancing on all fronts. In agriculture, in which working conditions are quite harsh, unmanned tractors (for example, a tractor from New Holland) and combine harvesters (for example, a combine harvester from Rostselmash) are being introduced, that will allow an increase in the production cycle from 8–10 to 24 h, because unmanned agricultural machines do not get tired and are not limited to only functioning in daylight.

All global car manufacturers are actively participating in the race to create unmanned vehicles, and legal frameworks are being developed for this. There are even projects to ban manual car driving in city conditions by 2025. The domestic Russian auto industry is also trying to deal, and Kamaz (the Russian engine and truck manufacturer) already has a prototype. The introduction of unmanned vehicles into daily life will lead to the mass ousting of truck drivers by automata and artificial intelligence, as well as all workers engaged in the role of driving within the transportation sector including bus drivers, taxi drivers, and drivers of agricultural machinery.

As noted in the UK's Guardian newspaper "...The potential saving to the freight transportation industry is estimated to be $168bn annually. The savings are expected to come from labor ($70bn), fuel efficiency ($35bn), productivity ($27bn) and accidents ($36bn), before including any estimates from non-truck freight modes like air and rail."

Despite the obvious benefits from the introduction of unmanned vehicles and the activities of a large number of IT companies involved in the development of hardware and software in this area, freight and passenger transportation will be among the first sectors to feel the pressure of technological progress on the labor market.

Unfortunately, the transition to the digital era will affect not only the working and intellectual professions, but also the arts. Jukedeck has created artificial intelligence capable of writing music (and this is not an isolated example), and it is obvious that this technology can be extended to painting (for example, a system created by researchers from Rutgers University in New Jersey and the AI laboratory in Los Angeles presented their own artistic style). There are also projects for teaching AI to generate prose, in particular. A project from Botnik and Calm generated/wrote a fairy tale "The Princess and the Fox" based on the works of The Brothers Grimm. Of course, these "works of art" are far from perfect, and at this stage of technological development they cannot compete with the human mind, but given the rapid development in this direction, we can predict successful implementations in the near future.

If we consider the military from the point of view of the number of people "employed," then they also will be affected by digitalization and robotization. Of course, it is difficult to estimate at what stage the development of combat robots capable of operating autonomously or in conjunction with an operator is, but there are already working prototypes, for example, the Mobile Robotic Complex of Izhevsk Radio Plant.

The same trend has emerged in the financial sector. On the website of any insurance company, you can apply and pay for insurance. In the banking sector, increasingly, operations are carried out online; in Russia, the example of Tinkoff Bank, which has a license to conduct banking operations, runs online, without any back-offices or traditional staff. The leading Russian financial institution, Sberbank, which actively promotes its online platform, is systematically reducing its staffing levels with the aim of cutting up to 2/3 of them.

Trends in the higher education system indicate that the future division of education will be offline (for a limited circle of consumers) and online (for a wide range of consumers). The transition to remote (distance) forms of learning will in the near future lead to audio/video lectures and the introduction of electronic testing, which will make the presence of a teacher in unnecessary, as a result of which their number will drastically decrease. It is estimated that up to 90% of teachers may become superfluous. Note that in the 2017/2018 academic year, the number of teaching staff in Russia was 245,000, leading to the possibility that up to 200,000 may be forced to retrain. In Russia, implemented projects in the field of online education include: Russian Internet University with the possibility of obtaining higher INTUIT (http://www.intuit.ru/), The world's first nonprofit accredited University Of the People (http://www.uopeople.edu/), and the Coursera educational platform (https://www.coursera.org/).

The public sector will also be digitized, and in this connection it is worth mentioning the online portal of public services, which is actively promoted by the Government of the Russian Federation, which, once it has digitized the entire planned list of services, will lead to a significant reduction in the number of public servants.

There are already multiple implemented projects in the daily lives of millions of citizens—ticket machines for subway tickets, machines for ordering fast (for example, Eatsa restaurant), self-service cash desks in grocery hypermarkets (for example, Magnit chain stores) (Sigarev et al. 2018).

The international corporation Amazon has gone even further and opened the world's first unmanned store. And, if we talk about the innovation of Amazon, then they already provide equipment for the organization of robotic warehouses.

The above examples clearly show that information technologies are changing the daily life of society and are beginning to force people out of their jobs. The problem of finding new employment for the released workforce is becoming more acute. Researchers have proposed a series of measures to reduce (or eliminate) this problem. Let us consider the realistic implementation of some of these measures in the Russian economy.

1. Reduction of the working day (or working week). Evidently, reducing the workday or week will inevitably lead to a reduction in wages, since employers will not pay as much for the smaller amount of work done. Accordingly, the proposed approach has a low probability of implementation without legally enshrining the rights of the employee.
2. Provide the workers, released from digitized companies with shares in these enterprises (but with lesser rights). There is a danger of repeating the history of privatization in Russia, when all citizens received vouchers as a form of

compensation. The low financial literacy of 90% of the population did not allow for these assets to be used effectively, and, as a result, national wealth was distributed among a narrow circle of people.

3. Payment of unemployment benefits to ensure a decent standard of living. To illustrate the utopian nature of such an idea, we will carry out rough calculations of the required amount of benefits, in the case that 50% of the workforce becomes unemployed. So, at the end of 2017 in Russia, there were about 76 million people capable of working. If the number of unemployed reached 38 million and were provided with an allowance amounting to the subsistence minimum of RUB 10,326/annum (legally fixed in 2018), about RUB 4.7 trillion would be needed annually. For context, the planned income of the federal budget of Russia for 2018 is RUB 15.2 trillion. Therefore, 30% of total revenue would go to the maintenance of this army of unemployed. Of course, we all understand that in any case, this subsistence minimum does not remotely provide an arbitrarily decent quality of life. If we instead use average per capita income for the calculation, which, at the end of 2017 was RUB 31,477, we get a figure of RUB 14.4 trillion, which is more than 90% of the revenue side of the budget.
4. There is only one real way out of this situation—the creation of new jobs. What professions will be needed in a digital economy? In this direction, nothing new can be invented for the manual worker; these are white- and blue-collar roles for only those, with a technical education. The former will produce highly intelligent products in the field of IT technologies (programs, algorithms, new technologies, etc.), and the latter will serve as assistants to robots and other IT infrastructure. But in this regard, the following question arises: how many jobs will these professions create? It seems evident that they will not be capable of absorbing the 30–40 million freed workers. Hence, the issue of solving the unemployment crisis in the digital economy remains open.

Advancing the theme of the new professions required by the digital economy, we turn to the Atlas of new professions (http://atlas100.ru/), which was developed by Skolkovo specialists. This analytical review indicates that by 2030 such intellectual professions as an accountant, statistician (most likely meaning a data collector), a loan manager, a journalist, a bank clerk, etc., will disappear from the market. Other nonintellectual professions such as call center operator, courier, security guard, and trainer will also be lost.

As to new areas of employment, Skolkovo predict that jobs such as an operator of medical robots, IT geneticist, environmental analyst in construction, designer of 3D printing in construction, designer of airships, curator of collective creativity, art appraiser, and intellectual property appraiser will emerge. Of course, when citing examples of future professions, it must be said that some of them already exist, some will be implemented, and some are utopian in nature, but in general, such professions are not able to solve the problem of technological unemployment, since few are designed for a mass replication of the current labor landscape and are mainly aimed at people with higher technical education.

To show the depth of the problem of the loss of labor under the influence of digitalization, let us turn to the recent history of Russia and consider agriculture. The causes of rural unemployment are different, but the consequences, in our opinion, are likely to be similar. Consider this process through the prism of historical events. In 1990, almost 10 million people were employed in agriculture. At the end of 2017, this figure was just over 5 million people. In the last 27 years the number of employees in the agricultural sector has decreased by 4.9 million people or 49%. The reason for this is a reduction in production, which is clearly expressed in the reduction of acreage. Thus, in the base period, the area under crops in farms of all categories was 117,705 thousand hectares, whereas in by 2017 it was down to 8048 thousand hectares, i.e., we have a reduction of 32%. Despite this significant decrease in cultivated areas, the gross grain harvest increased by 16%.

If we turn to animal husbandry, we see the same picture. The livestock of cattle in farms of all categories (at the end of the year) in 1990 was 57 million, whereas by 2017 it was 18.3 million, a decrease of 38.7 million. Despite this reduction, meat production during this period increased by 2%.

These figures clearly show that a 50% decrease in the number of people employed in agricultural production did not lead to the degradation of production, but, on the contrary, an increase was observed in key indicators.

What happened to the millions of people no longer working in this sector? There are several scenarios:

- Firstly, those workers who had the opportunity migrated to cities.
- Secondly, part of the population has replaced their formal work with substitutes, usually in the gray or shadow zone of the economy through self-employment in folk crafts, collection of natural bioresources, personal subsidiary farming, the collection of recyclable materials, etc.
- Thirdly, a pendulum of labor migration has arisen, in which workers go "to earn money" in a nearby city or region with high wages.
- Fourthly, citizens who could not follow any of the above scenarios have fallen into degradation.

As we can see from the above scenarios of the behavior of labor released from agricultural production, the state did not solve this problem in any way, shifting it onto the shoulders of the population.

It is very likely that events in other sectors will unfold in a similar way, since, as of 2018, the Government of the Russian Federation does not have a clear strategic plan for the adaptation or retraining of workers affected by digitization.

In some cases, it is quite problematic to find a valid alternative to current employment. As an example, let us consider truck drivers transporting goods over long distances. About 1.2 million trucks are registered in the PLATON system (an electronic toll collection **system** established in Russia in November 2015), meaning that approximately this number workers are at risk of becoming unemployed as a result of the introduction of unmanned vehicles. Given the specifics of this type of activity, the question remains open about the future employment of such a large number of citizens and (or) their conversion to other roles in the economy.

Table 1 Results of the evaluation of the econometric model on the impact of unemployment growth in the Russian economy

Indicators	Model's coefficients	Model's standard error	t-Statistics of student	p-Significance level
Free term equation	1.67	0.20	8.44	0.00
X	−0.54	0.20	−2.67	0.02

Note: Characteristics of the model $R = 0.63$; $R^2 = 0.39$; $F = 71{,}300$, $p < 0.02$
All calculations were carried out in the software package STATISTICA

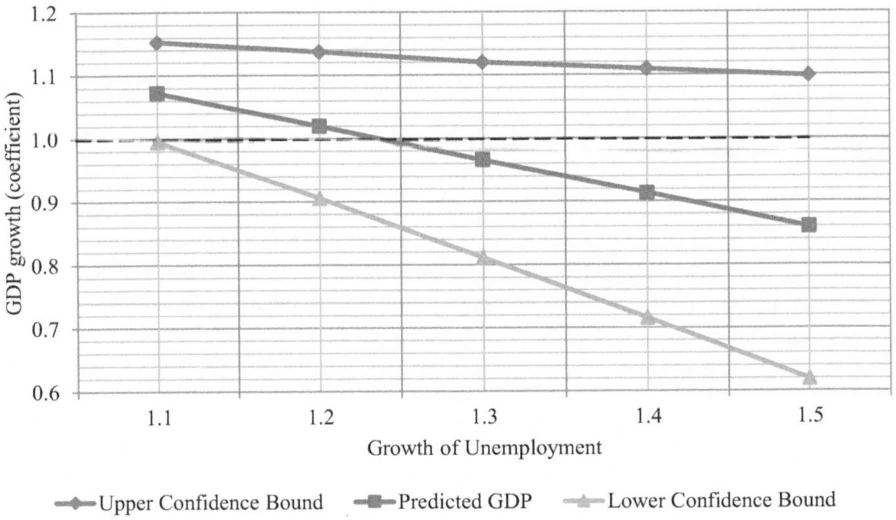

Fig. 1 Results of simulation modeling of the response of a dependent variable on the rate of unemployment growth

We should also consider one more key fact: The increase in the number of unemployed leads to an inevitable decrease in consumer demand, which in turn affects the general economic situation in the country. To illustrate this concept, let us estimate the relationship between the growth rate of GDP in the Russian Federation (denoted as Y in the model) and the unemployment rate (denoted as X) for the period 2005–2017 (Table 1).

The model parameters are statistically significant by the Student's t-test, the model itself is significant by Fisher's F-test. A low value of the multiple coefficient of determination (<0.5) indicates the existence of another (or series) variable not taken into account in the model.

The interpretation of the regression equation obtained is as follows: A rise in unemployment of 1% leads to a decrease in GDP by 0.54%.

In Fig. 1 we carry out simulation modeling based on the obtained model.

According to the above figure, growth in unemployment will invariably lead to a slowdown in GDP growth, and at a value of 25–30%, the economy stagnates, in general.

It is worth noting that this model does not claim to be highly accurate, since it is a significant simplification of macroeconomic relations, and the regression constructed should be taken only as an illustration of the negative impact of unemployment on the Russian economy. Nevertheless, it is an alarming trend amid growing tensions in the labor market.

4 Conclusion

Digitization and robotization will not result in a utopia, but for many workers a cruel reality in the near future. With no measures to mitigate the impact on the labor force, in Russia, it is possible to predict a future unemployment rate of up to 50%. If we take into account that at the end of 2018, 76 million people were employed in the economy, then we are at the risk of having 38 million people unemployed. According to the research of S.P. Zemtsov, the technological outlook for unemployment is 42.13 million people (Zemtsov 2018). If we assume that on average, there are three dependents per worker (children and elders), then we arrive at a figure of 108 million potential beggars (recall that in 2018 the population of the country is 147 million people). Therefore, the lack of a clear state program for the adaptation of workers displaced by IT objects is a significant threat to the national security of the country and the overall stability of society.

References

Berberov AB (2017) Robotization and technological unemployment of XXI century: revival of Luddizm? Mosc Econ J 3:20

Bogoviz AV et al (2019) Comparative analysis of formation of Industry 4.0 in developed and developing countries. Stud Syst Decis Control 169:155–164

Bregman R (2017) Utopian thinking: the easy way to eradicate poverty. The Guardian, 6 March

Brynjolfsson E, Mcafee A (2014) The second machine age: work, progress, and prosperity in a time of brilliant technologies. WW Norton & Company, New York

Dorofeyev MA et al (2018) Trends and prospects for the development of blockchain and cryptocurrencies in the digital economy. Eur Res Stud J 21(3):429–445

Dorskaia AA, Pashentsev DA et al (2016) Higher educational institutions of Russia as a subject of economic activity: innovations and their legal support. J Adv Res Law Econ 7(6):1338–1345

Florida R (2011) The great reset: how the post-crash economy will change the way we live and work. Harper Paperbacks, London

Ford M (2015) Rise of the robots: technology and the threat of a jobless future. Basic Books, New York

Frey CB, Osborne MA (2013) The future of employment: how susceptible are jobs to computerization? Working paper, Oxford Martin School

Jaimovich N, Siu HE (2012) The trend is the cycle: job polarization and jobless recoveries. Working paper # 18334, National Bureau of Economic Research, August
Kapelushnikov R (2017) Technological progress—workplaces eater? Preprint WP3/2017/03
Kapelushnikov R (2018) "Influence of the fourth industrial revolution on the labor market", stork on the roof. Demogr Mag 6(6):32–36
Karpov VK (2017) Robotization and its place in the digital economy. Russ Agrofood Policy 8 (68):32–39
Kiseleva IA et al (2018) Risk management in business: concept, types, evaluation criteria. Espacios 39(27):18
Medovnikov D et al (2017) Digital economics: global trends and practice of Russian business. High School of Economics, Moscow
Onimode B (1982) Imperialism and underdevelopment in Nigeria: the dialectics of mass poverty. Zed Press, London
Osipov VS (2013) The wheel of competition as a new instrument of strategic management. World Appl Sci J 27(8):1083–1086
Osipov VS (2017) The role of import substitution in forming the new model of development. Intellect Innov Invest 5:24–31
Osipov VS (2018) The policy of digitalization: necessary of live labor protection. Intellect Innov Invest 6:42–46
Pissarides CA (1990) Equilibrium unemployment theory. Basil Blackwell, Oxford
Reinert ES (2009) Spontant Kaos. Økonomi I en ulvetid. Forlaget Res Publica, Oslo
Schultz TW (1993) The economics of being poor. Blackwell Publishers, Cambridge, MA
Schwab K, Davis N (2018) Shaping the fourth industrial revolution. World Economic Forum, Geneva
Sigarev AV et al (2018) The role of chains in the Russian retail sector. Eur Res Stud J 21 (1):542–554
Silvestrov SN et al (2015) Introduction to the theory of economic dysfunction. Mediterr J Soc Sci 6 (3):394–399
Standing G (2008) How cash transfers promote the case for basic income. Basic Income Stud 3 (1):1–30
Stroiteleva TG et al (2019) Peculiarities and problems of formation of Industry 4.0 in modern Russia. Stud Syst Decis Control 169:145–153
Timberg S (2013) Jaron Lanier: the Internet destroyed the middle class. Salon.com. 12 May
Usman WCh (2017) "Universal basic income: a review", social science research network, 4 August. https://doi.org/10.2139/ssrn.3013634
Voronov AS et al (2018) Current issues in assessment of risks related to investment projects. Int J Eng Technol (UAE) 7(3.15):336–339
Zemtsov SP (2018) Can robots be able to replace people? Automation risk Assessment in the regions of Russia. Innovations 4:49–55

Machine Learning and Artificial Intelligence: The Basis of Intelligent Machines in the Cyber Economy

Roman V. Shamin and Natalia B. Brazhnikova

Abstract The chapter considers the issues of mathematical description and formalization of autonomous intelligent machines functioning in economic systems. A definition of intelligent machines in the cyber economy is given. It is shown that intelligent machines could be effectively used to solve various economic tasks. We employ the tools of finite-state machines and game theory to describe intelligent machines in the cyber economy and illustrate the importance of machine learning and the methods of AI. It is determined that the best AI method is conformation learning that fully corresponds to the architecture of intelligent machines in the cyber economy. The authors show the importance of the creation of unified standards for describing the interfaces of intelligent machines.

1 Introduction

The modern economy is being transformed into a digital and knowledge economy, in which information technologies and intellectual methods play a key role. Technologies connected to the Internet of Things (IoT) including household appliances that are connected to a global network and can perform intelligent tasks and work together are an important part of the transformation. This chapter focuses on the general principles for the functioning of intelligent machines in the cyber economy.

The usage of intelligent machines, based on machine learning and AI methods, could be improved if the economic environment was adapted for their mutual functioning.

R. V. Shamin (✉)
MIREA – Russian Technological University, Moscow, Russia

RUDN University, Moscow, Russia
e-mail: roman@shamin.ru

N. B. Brazhnikova
RUDN University, Moscow, Russia

© Springer Nature Switzerland AG 2019
V. M. Filippov et al. (eds.), *The Cyber Economy*, Contributions to Economics,
https://doi.org/10.1007/978-3-030-31566-5_12

In this chapter, the authors study the mathematical issues that appear during describing the role of intelligent machines in the cyber economy. Two methods are distinguished. Firstly, the tools of finite-state are employed and, secondly, the functioning of intelligent machines is described with the help of game theory. The two approaches supplement, rather than contradict each other.

As intelligent machines should be based on machine learning, this is considered for managing their behavior. It is shown that the most natural approach of machine learning for managing intelligent machines is with conformation.

The chapter also discusses using intelligent machines based on machine learning in economic processes, as well as the issues of standardizing the interfaces of intelligent machines between each other and with humans.

2 Materials and Method

An intelligent machine or intelligent agent is an autonomous agent that works in a certain environment. The agent can perceive external information, process this information, and perform possible actions based on that information, which change the state of an intelligent agent, and can change the external environment. The key aspect is the set goal of the intelligent machine. In addition, an intelligent machine (unlike an ordinary automaton) has to have memory, which facilitates learning and self-education.

The cyber economy envisages the presence of not only intelligent machines but also of a certain ecosystem in which they can exist, interact, and develop. To achieve this, it is necessary to develop certain standards and implement the technical possibilities for the creation of open systems, which include the population of intelligent machines (Shamin et al. 2017).

Groups of intelligent machines, e.g., a fleet of unmanned transport vehicles, can solve various technical tasks, but what we are interested in are the economic relations that emerge as a result of the interactions between intelligent machines in the common environment. Economic relations between machines appear when their owners delegate the function of making certain economic decisions. One example is mechanical trade systems in stock and currency markets. These systems compete in the world stock markets and change the ecosystem as the players process current information and make decisions (Shamin et al. 2013).

Intelligent machines could enter economic relations between each other and with humans. In the latter case, full competition between machines and humans, or their collaboration—when their purposes are aligned—is observed. For example, unmanned cars on highways try to avoid collision with other cars that are driven by humans.

It is possible to use different mathematical tools for a mathematical formalization of intelligent machines. The main mathematical constructions that are used to describe the functioning of intelligent machines in the economic realm are as follows:

- Finite-state machines;
- Game theory.

Let us consider these mathematical tools for the description of intelligent machines.

A finite-state machine is a model of calculations in which the incoming sequence of symbols transforms into outgoing sequences of symbols depending on the internal state of the machine, which is changing at each moment. A finite-state machine allows modeling the calculation processes with memory, as they are a convenient tool for modeling the dynamic processes in the economy. The theory of finite-state machines is studied in Gill (1962) and Ginsburg (1962).

A shall denote a finite set of incoming symbols. B shall denote a finite set of outgoing symbols (the results of the machine's work). Q shall denote a finite set of internal states of the machine. In set Q we shall distinguish the initial state—$q_0 \in Q$.

Finite-state machines work in discrete moments of time, which we shall measure in natural numbers. The sequence of incoming symbols (in moments of time $t = 1, 2, \ldots$) shall be denoted in the following way:

$$a(1), a(2), \ldots, a(k), \ldots.$$

The outgoing sequence is denoted through:

$$b(1), b(2), \ldots, b(k), \ldots.$$

Internal states, from the moment of time $t = 0$, shall be denoted as:

$$q(0), q(1), q(2), \ldots, q(k), \ldots.$$

and $q(0) = q_0$.

The outgoing sequence and succession of internal states are set with the help of the following recurrent equations:

$$b(k+1) = f(a(k), q(k)),$$
$$q(k+1) = g(a(k), q(k)),$$

where $k = 1, 2, \ldots$.

In economic processes, in calculations with the help of finite-state machines, sets A, B, Q shall be numbers or vectors from the numbers. In this case, these sets are not finite. However, in real economic tasks, one can consider only a finite set of numbers, so we shall consider finite-state machines.

Finite-state machines allow for the effective modeling of intelligent machines in economic situations, as they can perceive information and make decisions that are coded by the outgoing alphabet. Finite-state machines also have the necessary memory for decision-making. Most calculation devices could be presented in the form of a finite-state machine (Silva and Pereira 2017).

Another effective tool for description of the behavior of intelligent machines in economic situations is formalization with the help of game theory. The theory of games was initially developed for making effective decisions in the conditions of opposition, when different players have various goals (Ginsburg 1962).

Let us consider the setting for a finite noncooperative game of N persons. Each player with number n has S_n strategies. The game consists of the following: Each player—simultaneously and independently of each other—selects a strategy. Thus, a situation is formed, which is an N-dimensional vector.

$$\sigma = (s_1, s_2, \ldots, s_N), \text{where } s_n \in S_n.$$

After selecting the strategies, each player receives the gain according to the function H_n, which depends on the current situation.

$$H_n = H_n(\sigma), n = 1, 2, \ldots, N.$$

The theory of games considers a mixed expansion of the game, in which each player selects not one strategy but a distribution of probabilities on a set of strategies. If the strength of set S_n equals M_n, the mixed strategy of n-th vector is vector

$$P_n = (p_1, p_2, \ldots, p_{Mn}), p_i \geq 0, p_1 + p_2 + \ldots + p_{Mn} = 1.$$

The gain of i-th player is mathematical expectation from the gain function, in which the strategies of all players are random. The Nash theorem (Nash 1950) says that in mixed strategies there is always a situation of balance $\sigma*$. Situation is a balance situation if no player recuses from their well-balanced strategy. Thus, it is possible to calculate the gain of each player in a finite noncooperative game. This gain is denoted as V_i.

The studied mathematical methods—finite-state machines and game theory—allow for a description of the behavior of intelligent machines in solving economic tasks.

3 Results

The modern reality of using intelligent machines and autonomous agents envisages the application of self-learning machines, based on machine learning. Machine learning is the leading technology in IT. The recent achievements of algorithms that are based on machine learning and AI methods show that in a lot of spheres of activities machine intelligence rivals classical algorithms and human intellectual possibilities.

Deep machine learning could be based on various principles of AI, and real cyber-physical systems usually use various combinations of these methods. The main methods of machine learning that are used in intelligent machines are as follows:

- Neural networks;
- Bayesian machine learning;
- Reinforcement learning.

Neural networks are used primarily for solving the tasks of image recognition. Bayesian machine learning is used for taking decisions on statistical data. For describing the behavior of intelligent machines, it is also recommended to use formal models of learning with conformation.

Reinforcement learning is a method of machine learning on the basis of training an intelligent agent, which acts in the external environment. It is supposed that in each discrete moment of time the programmed agent is in a certain state s. Depending on this state, the agent has a choice of several possible actions. The agent selects a certain action, then passes to a new state and receives reinforcement, which depends on the previous state and selected action. It is expected that the agent will increase the sum of its reinforcements.

An essential aspect is the fact that the agent is not given any a priori information. It does not know the goal or the state it comes into during the selection of the action. It is given only the current state and possible variants of actions, and after the selection of an action, it is given the volume of reinforcement and the new state.

This allows for the effective creation of intelligent machines for solving universal tasks.

It is supposed that the agent can play the game many times during the learning process. It has memory and can change its strategy on the basis of this.

A significant advantage of reinforcement learning is a natural task setting, which conforms to most economic tasks.

The process of reinforcement learning consists in the fact that the agent selects its action on the basis of the function of assessing the result of the action in the current state. This function is traditionally shown in the following way:

$$Q = Q(s, a),$$

where s—current state, and a—possible action in state s. During reinforcement learning the agent is not supposed to be given the game rules. The agent should not know the future states and options for actions. That is why function (s,a) is readjusted in the moment of work.

Reinforcement learning envisages that the agent can play the game many times, and learning takes place through trial and error. The agent learns on the basis of the results of previous games.

There are several options of reinforcement learning, including the algorithms SARSA and Q-learning.

Confident learning usually requires a lot of iterations, as selection of the optimal strategy by the algorithm of reinforcement learning multiple attempts to find function Q(s,a). In this sense, information reinforcement learning has a small convergence order. The small convergence order is easily understood, as the algorithm is not given the rules of the game, so the agent has to understand these and then calculate the optimal strategy.

The usage of intelligent machines based on deep machine learning and AI could change the modern economy. For many years, the economy has been built on decisions taken by economically active players, both individuals and companies. At the same time, the psychology of making managerial decisions does not always conform to rational decision-making norms. In addition, the real economy requires decisions to be made very quickly, on the basis of analysis of multiple factors and large arrays of information. In these conditions, intelligent machines will be able to make more optimal and successful decisions.

In the future, many economic situations will rely only on automatic means of decision-making. This is why machine learning and AI are the basis for the formation of the cyber economy (Chursin et al. 2019).

The participation of intelligent machines in economic systems could include algorithms that make decisions in stock markets and various online trading platforms, or machines that take managerial decisions for corporate management. Recently, the cyber-physical systems of the Internet of Things, which could be also used in economic relations, have become popular. One might foresee the possibility of intelligent machines that can conduct economic negotiations with other intelligent machines.

Many economic situations could be described with the help of the game theory. For implementation of the successful strategy, it is necessary to use well-balanced states in the game. In balanced states, deviation will lead to aggravation of the game result. Theoretical balanced states are not achieved, as players cannot calculate and stick to optimal strategies. When intelligent machines participate in the game, these agents can make "agreements" with higher precision and reliability than humans (Tyulin et al. 2017).

As the cyber economy envisages the creation of a universal economic environment for the mutual functioning of intelligent machines, which belong to different economic actors, it is necessary to have unified standards for a mutual interface for these machines and with the environment in which they function.

These issues of standardization should focus on the following directions:

- Interfaces "machine–machine";
- Interfaces "machine–supervisor";
- Interfaces "machine–human";
- Standards for the possible actions of autonomous machines;
- Standards for legal definitions of the responsibility for the actions of autonomous machines.

These issues are critical in the spheres of modern robototronics and unmanned transport vehicles to ensure the sustainable economic development of the cyber economy.

4 Conclusions

It has been shown that intelligent machines that are based on deep machine learning and AI methods can be extremely effective in solving economic tasks.

For the mathematical formalization of behavior of intelligent machines, we have proposed using the methods of finite-state machines and the approach of game theory.

The main method of machine learning for intelligent machines should be reinforcement learning, which fully conforms to task setting during the formation of autonomous intelligent machines in economic systems.

The authors have also considered the issues surrounding the creation of unified standards for the interfaces of intelligent machines and the problems of the legal character of autonomous intelligent machines in economic relations.

References

Chursin RA, Yudin AV, Grosheva PYu, Filippov PG, Butrova EV (2019) Tool for assessing the risks of R&D projects implementation in high-tech enterprises. In: IOP conference series: materials science and engineering, vol 476, 012005

Gill A (1962) Introduction to the theory of finite-state machines. McGraw-Hill, New York

Ginsburg S (1962) An introduction to mathematical machine theory. Addison-Wesley, Reading, MA

Nash JF (1950) Equilibrium points in N-person games. Proc Natl Acad Sci U S A 36(1):48–49. https://doi.org/10.1073/pnas.36.1.48

Shamin RV, Gurevich PL, Tikhomirov SB (2013) Reaction-diffusion equations with spatially distributed hysteresis. SIAM J Math Anal 45(3):1328–1355

Shamin RV, Chursin AA, Fedorova LA (2017) The mathematical model of the law on the correlation of unique competencies with the emergence of new consumer markets. Eur Res Stud J XX(3 Part A):39–56

Silva JM, Pereira JA (2017) Finite state machine modelling of the macro-economy. J Adv Manag Sci 5(5):333–337. https://doi.org/10.18178/joams.5.5.333-337

Tyulin A, Chursin A, Yudin A (2017) Production capacity optimization in cases of a new business line launching in a company. Espacios 38:20

Part III
Training Digital Personnel for the Cyber Economy

The Role of Digital Personnel in the Cyber Economy

Karine S. Khachaturyan and Arutun A. Khachaturyan

Abstract *Purpose*: The purpose of this chapter is to specify the long-term consequences of a transition to the cyber economy for digital personnel, which are required and created for its formation, in the interests of preventing a social crisis through determining the place and role of digital personnel in the cyber economy.

Design/methodology/approach: The authors use regression analysis for determining the current value of digital personnel for the forming cyber economy (at the current stage of the digital economy) and for evaluating the influence of the share of specialists in the sphere of information and communication technologies (ICTs) at the level of digital competitiveness as an indicator of readiness for transition to the cyber economy. The research is performed using a selection of countries that show the best results in the sphere of digital modernization of economy (Top 30) in 2018. The information and analytical basis of the research is statistical data produced by the National Research University "Higher School of Economics" and the IMD.

Findings: It is determined that a high level of automatization (up to full automatization) can only be achieved at one of the four stages (the production stage) using the algorithm for the creation of added value in the conditions of the cyber economy. All other stages will require different types of digital personnel, including specialists in the spheres of ICT, machine building, and extremely specialized sectoral digital personnel, who will have the key role, performing essential functions with machine technical support.

Originality/value: It is established that there is a low level of risk of a social crisis in the labor market. It is shown that specialists with high levels of qualification will be in the highest demand. The main priority in the training and development of digital personnel should be paid not to quantitative (number of personnel trained) but qualitative indicators (the level of personnel qualification).

K. S. Khachaturyan (✉) · A. A. Khachaturyan
Federal State Military Educational Institution of Higher Education, "Military University" of the Ministry of Defense of the Russian Federation, Moscow, Russia

© Springer Nature Switzerland AG 2019
V. M. Filippov et al. (eds.), *The Cyber Economy*, Contributions to Economics,
https://doi.org/10.1007/978-3-030-31566-5_13

1 Introduction

Transition to the cyber economy as a result of the Fourth Industrial Revolution, similarly to the three previous industrial revolutions, will have systemic influence on economic systems, but will not be limited to a specific sphere (e.g., industry) or sphere of activities (e.g., the economic sphere). Because of this, in the process of planning the formation of the cyber economy state regulators should pay attention to complex short-term and long-term consequences.

At present, national programs of transition to the cyber economy such as the program "Digital economy of the Russian Federation," adopted by the Decree of the Government of the Russian Federation (2019) dated July 28, 2017, No. 1632-r, mostly focus on the expected economic advantages (growth of efficiency and increased competitiveness in entrepreneurship and the economy) and the short-term needs of the economic system for the transition (The need for digital personnel is the key issue here).

The long-term social consequences of the digital modernization of economy are studied primarily in relation to the effects on consumption: an increase in the accessibility of hi-tech goods and services and the growth of living standards. The consequences for the labor market have not been taken into account. A current trend in the labor markets of developed countries, including Russia, is the mass training of digital personnel for implementing breakthrough technologies for business process automatization. However, the risk of mass unemployment as a result of automatization and the elimination of the need for human labor resources (including increase in the usage of AI) has been overlooked.

Thus, there is a scientific and practical problem in specifying the long-term consequences of a transition to the cyber economy for digital personnel, which are required and must be trained for its formation, through the re-training of current digital personnel (who will have a secondary and smaller role in the cyber economy), or by their information and consultation support for future primary (large) role in the cyber economy. Here the authors try to solve the given problem by determining the place and role of digital personnel in the cyber economy.

2 Materials and Method

The place and role of digital personnel in the digital economy are studied in many works of modern scholars including Cominu (2018), Kissmer et al. (2018), Lampinen et al. (2018), and Wentrup et al. (2019). They agree that digital personnel are necessary for the formation of the cyber economy, as they occupy a central and key role in the process of R&D aimed at the automatization of business processes.

However, this is not proved empirically. Also, the long-term consequences on the labor market caused by a transition to the cyber economy, as well as the place and role of digital personnel are poorly studied. Certain issues related to this problem are

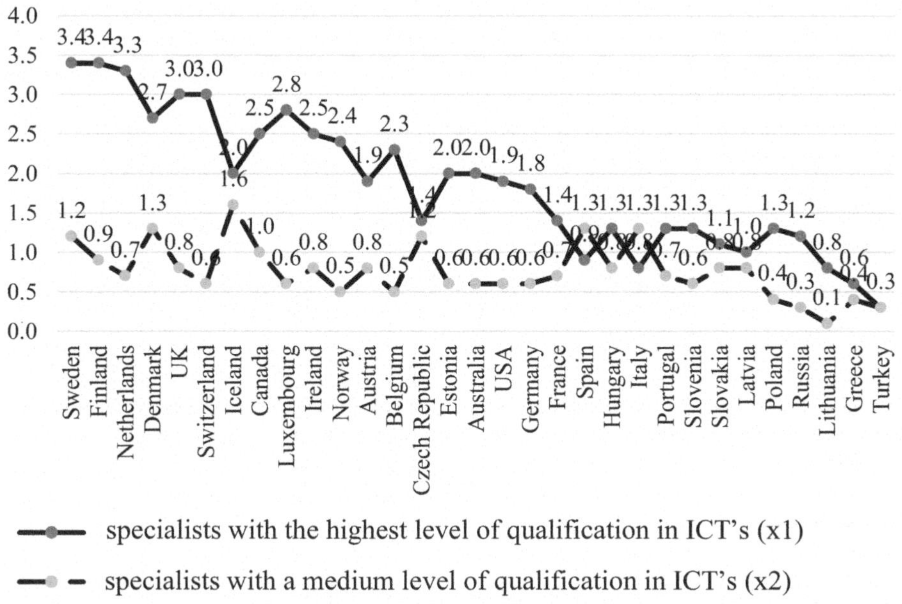

Fig. 1 Specialists in the sphere of ICTs according to their level of qualification and country (Top 30) in 2018, % of the total number of employed people [Source: Compiled by the authors based on National Research University "Higher School of Economics" (2019)]

studied in the publications of Bogoviz (2019), Popkova (2019), Popkova and Sergi (2019), Popkova et al. (2019), and Sukhodolov et al. (2018).

To determine the current role of digital personnel in the cyber economy (at the current stage of the digital economy), we use regression analysis. We evaluate the influence of the share of specialists in the sphere of information and communication technologies (ICTs) on the level of digital competitiveness of the economy as an indicator of readiness for transition to the cyber economy. The values of these indicators in the countries that show the most advanced results in terms of digital modernization (Top 30) in 2018 are given in Figs. 1 and 2.

As is seen from Figs. 1 and 2, the highest progress in the sphere of digital modernization of the economy (digital competitiveness index—95.046 points) has been achieved in Sweden, where the share of specialists in the sphere of ICTs with the highest level of qualification is 3.4%, and with a medium level of qualification, 1.2%. In Russia, the digital competitiveness index constitutes 67.179 points; the share of specialists in the sphere of ICTs with the highest level of qualification is 1.2%, and with a medium level of qualification, 0.3%.

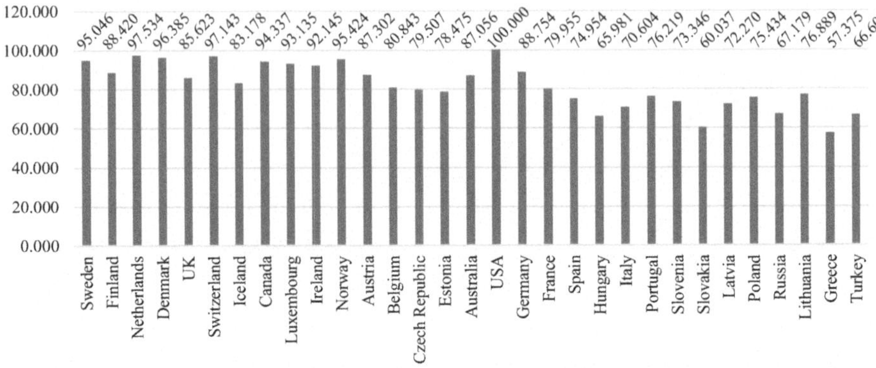

Fig. 2 Index of digital competitiveness of the economy (Top 30 countries as to the share of specialists in ICTs) in 2018 (y), points 1–100 [Source: Compiled by the authors based on IMD (2019)]

3 Results

The results of the regression analysis are given in Table 1.

According to the data of Table 1, an increase of the share of specialists with a medium level of qualification in ICTs by 1% leads to an increase in the digital competitiveness of the economy by 0.1228 points; an increase of the share of specialists with the highest level of qualification in the ICTs by 1% leads to an

Table 1 Regression analysis of the dependence of digital competitiveness of the economy on the share of specialists in ICTs

Regression statistics						
Multiple R	0.8251					
R-square	0.6807					
Adjusted R-square	0.6579					
Standard error	6.8901					
Observations	31					
Dispersion analysis						
	Df	**SS**	**MS**	**F**	**Significance F**	
Regression	2	2833.9391	1416.9695	29.8476	→0	
Residual	28	1329.2563	47.4734			
Total	30	4163.1954				
	Coefficients	**Standard error**	**t Statistics**	**P value**	**Lower 95%**	**Upper 95%**
Intercept	61.1454	3.6816	16.6084	→0	53.6040	68.6868
x_1	11.0899	1.4788	7.4992	→0	8.0607	14.1191
x_2	0.1228	3.7922	0.0324	0.9744	−7.6453	7.8908

Source: Calculated and compiled by the authors

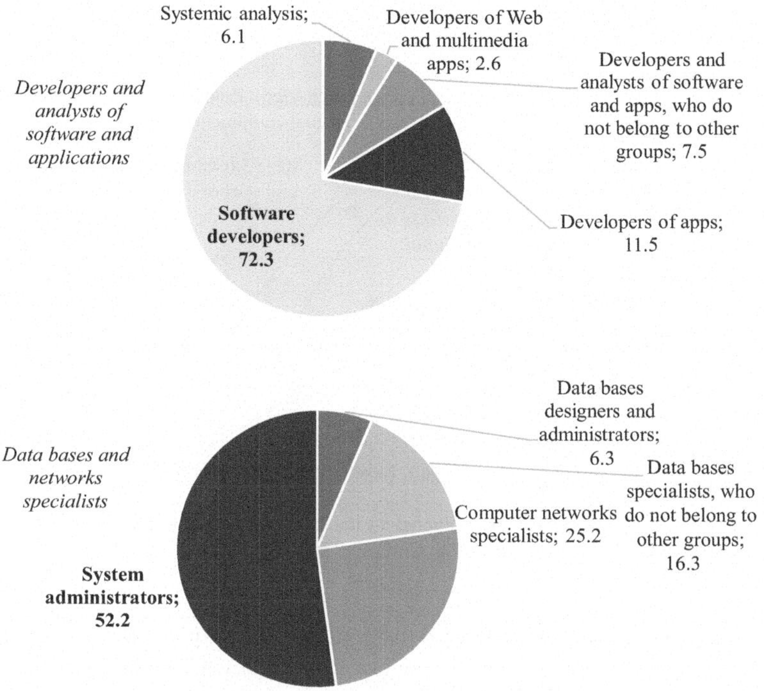

Fig. 3 The roles of specialists with the highest levels of qualification in ICTs in Russia in 2018, % of the number of the specialists [Source: Compiled by the authors based on National Research University "Higher School of Economics" (2019)]

increase in the digital competitiveness of the economy by 11.0899 points. Significance F $\rightarrow 0$ (striving to zero, constituting 0.0000001—i.e., does not exceed 0.05)—therefore, the set regression dependencies are correct at the significance level $\alpha = 0.05$.

However, R-value of x_1 (0.00000004) does not exceed 0.05—therefore, this independent variable is included in the regression equation. Multiple R constitutes 0.8251—therefore, the change of the dependent variable by 82.51% is explained by the change of the independent variables. Thus, the development of the digital economy (and transition to the cyber economy) depends on the share of specialists with the highest level of qualification in the sphere of ICTs, while specialists with medium levels of qualification have an insignificant (statistically small) role in this process.

We can therefore state that in the process of the formation of the cyber economy digital personnel are key intellectual resources with a central formative role. For a precise determination of their role in the formation of the cyber economy, let us perform logical analysis of the structure of specialists with the highest levels of qualification in ICTs (using the example of Russia, 2018) (Fig. 3).

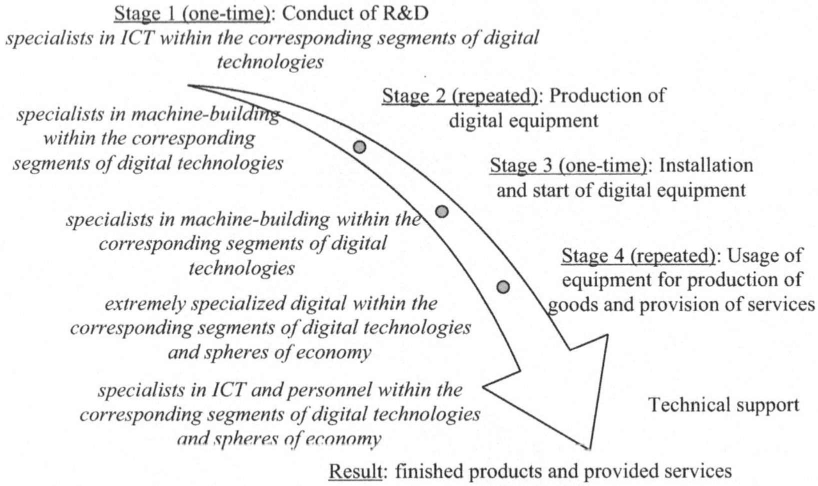

Fig. 4 The place and role of digital personnel in the cyber economy based on the stages of the algorithm for added value creation (Source: Compiled by the authors)

Figure 3 shows that specialists with the highest level of qualification in the sphere of ICTs perform two main roles in modern Russia: development of software, and system administration, i.e., R&D and technical maintenance of digital technologies and devices.

It should be noted that current specialists in ICTs are the first trained digital personnel, but they will not be the only ones. Transition to the cyber economy will also require other digital personnel: specialists in machine building and extremely specialized digital personnel within the corresponding segments of digital technologies and spheres of the economy. The place and role of digital personnel in the cyber economy in view of the stages of the algorithm for the creation of added value are shown in Fig. 4.

As is seen from Fig. 4, at each stage of the algorithm for added value creation different digital personnel are used, and they perform different roles. The first stage envisages R&D (one-time). The R&D specialists in ICTs within the corresponding segments of digital technologies are used.

In a classification of breakthrough digital technologies by the Government of the Russian Federation (2019) the following segments are distinguished: technologies of virtual and alternate reality, Wi-Fi, Big Data processing, distributed ledger (including blockchain), robototronics and sensors, the Internet of Things, neurotechnologies and AI, and quantum technologies.

The second stage includes the production of digital equipment (a repeated task). Specialists in the sphere of machine building within the corresponding segments of digital technologies are used here. The possibilities for automatization at this stage are rather wide, and the role of digital personnel may be secondary (maintenance of automatized conveyors, machines, and production units).

The third stage envisages the installation and start-up of digital equipment (one-time). Specialists in the sphere of machine building within the corresponding segments of digital technologies perform the primary role (direct assembly and the installation of equipment). The fourth stage envisages the usage of equipment for the manufacture of goods and the provision of services (repeatedly).

Extremely specialized digital personnel within the corresponding segments of digital technologies and economic sectors perform the primary role (the direct provision of services with digital equipment). Technical support is provided by specialists in the sphere of ICTs within the corresponding segments of digital technologies and economic sectors. As a result, products and services are supplied to the market.

Thus, digital personnel play a primary role at most stages of the algorithm for the creation of added value, and we can deduce that they will be central to the development of the cyber economy.

4 Conclusion

It has been determined that high levels of automatization (even full automatization) can be achieved at only one stage (production) out of four stages that make up the algorithm for the creation of added value in the cyber economy. The three other stages use different types of digital personnel, including specialists in ICTs and machine building and extremely specialized digital personnel who perform the primary role in machine technical support.

As a result, there will be no large-scale unemployment of digital personnel who are used in the process of digital modernization as a result of a transition to the cyber economy. However, it should be noted that specialists with a high level of qualification are likely to be in greater demand. Special attention should be paid during the training and development of digital personnel not to quantitative (the number of trained specialists) but qualitative indicators (the level of qualification).

References

Bogoviz AV (2019) Industry 4.0 as a new vector of growth and development of knowledge economy. Stud Syst Decis Control 169:85–91

Cominu S (2018) Are we all knowledge workers? Upskilling and deskilling at the time of digital [Tutti knowledge worker? Ricchezza e impoverimento dei lavori al tempo del digitale]. Sociologia del Lavoro 151:174–189

Government of the Russian Federation (2019) Program "Digital economy of the Russian Federation", adopted by the Decree dated July 28, 2017, No. 1632-p. http://static.government.ru/media/files/9gFM4FHj4PsB79I5v7yLVuPgu4bvR7M0.pdf. Accessed 1 Mar 2019

IMD (2019) World digital competitiveness rankings. https://www.imd.org/wcc/world-competitiveness-center-rankings/world-competitiveness-ranking-2018/. Accessed 1 Mar 2019

Kissmer T, Knoll J, Stieglitz S, Gross R (2018) 'Knowledge workers' expectations towards a digital workplace. Americas Conference on Information Systems 2018: Digital Disruption, AMCIS 2 (1):28–34

Lampinen A, Lutz C, Newlands G, Light A, Immorlica N (2018) Power struggles in the digital economy: platforms, workers, and markets. In: Proceedings of the ACM conference on computer supported cooperative work, CSCW, pp 417–423

National Research University "Higher School of Economics" (2019) Indicators of digital economy 2018: statistical collection. https://www.hse.ru/data/2018/08/20/1154812142/ICE2018.pdf.pdf. Accessed 1 Mar 2019

Popkova EG (2019) Preconditions of formation and development of Industry 4.0 in the conditions of knowledge economy. Stud Syst Decis Control 169:65–72

Popkova EG, Sergi BS (2019) Will Industry 4.0 and other innovations impact Russia's development? In: Sergi BS (ed) Exploring the future of Russia's economy and markets. Emerald Publishing, Bingley, pp 34–42

Popkova EG, Ragulina YV, Bogoviz AV (2019) Fundamental differences of transition to Industry 4.0 from previous industrial revolutions. Stud Syst Decis Control 169:21–29

Sukhodolov AP, Popkova EG, Litvinova TN (2018) Models of modern information economy: conceptual contradictions and practical examples. Emerald Publishing, Bingley, pp 1–38

Wentrup R, Nakamura HR, Ström P (2019) Uberization in Paris—the issue of trust between a digital platform and digital workers. Crit Perspect Int Bus 15(1):20–41

Current Problems in the Training of Digital Personnel for the Cyber Economy and How to Solve Them

Natalia A. Zavalko

Abstract *Purpose*: The purpose of this chapter is to study the current problems of training digital personnel for the cyber economy and to propose solutions.

Methodology: On July 28, 2017, the Government of the Russian Federation adopted a Decree on the implementation of a program of the digital economy in Russia. Its purpose is to form the infrastructure for a comprehensive information-based economy and to train personnel to develop the Russian digital economy. Thus, Russia plans to perform a qualitative transformation of the economy by 2024. This requires action in the following spheres: modernization of the digital infrastructure, implementation of digital practice into all key sectors of the economy, and the training of skilled personnel for the transitional period. In order to prepare skilled digital personnel, it is necessary to rebuild the conservative system of education and to stimulate graduates to work within the digital sphere. Universities have a key responsibility in this process, as they control the main concentrations of knowledge.

Results: By outlining the main problems surrounding the training of personnel for the digital economy, we determine ways to solve them: increased financing of education in the sphere of digital technologies, differentiating programs for the training of IT specialists, and involving large companies in the educational process through the organization of internships and further employment for graduates.

Conclusions: The current Russian system of education pays insufficient attention to the training of competent specialists in the sphere of information technologies. However, Russia has the resources to overcome this problem and train skilled personnel through the provision of attractive jobs with scope for professional growth.

N. A. Zavalko
Financial University Under the Government of the Russian Federation, Moscow, Russia

© Springer Nature Switzerland AG 2019

V. M. Filippov et al. (eds.), *The Cyber Economy*, Contributions to Economics,
https://doi.org/10.1007/978-3-030-31566-5_14

1 Introduction

Each day we create new digital assets: applications, functions, and ideas, which make us faster and more effective, and life more convenient and secure. This diversity of small digital steps forward has a larger impact on the economy on the whole.

The term "digital economy," first introduced during the digital revolution in 1995 by the IT specialist Nicholas Negroponte (Zavalko et al. 2018) is now part of everyday parlance.

The Decree of the President of the Russian Federation dated May 9, 2017, "Concerning the Strategy for the development of an information society in the Russian Federation for 2017–2030" introduced the following definition for the term: ". . .Digital economy is economic activities in which the key production factor is data in the digital form, processing and analysis of large volumes of which and usage of which, as compared to the traditional economic forms, allow increasing the effectiveness of various forms of production, technologies, storage, sales, and delivery of goods and services."

The importance of studying the training of digital personnel for the cyber economy and solving current problems with this task is predetermined by the fact that it is necessary to improve the Russian system of education, which has to provide the digital economy with competent and skilled personnel. It is also necessary to transform the labor market, which will need to conform to the main requirements of the digital economy. An important issue here is the creation of a system that stimulates the study and mastering of the main competencies needed for the development of the Russian digital economy.

2 Materials and Method

In Russia, special attention to the development of the digital economy was paid after Vladimir Putin's address to the Federal Assembly on December 1, 2016. He noted that "a country has no future without the digital economy." On July 28, 2017, the Government of the Russian Federation adopted the draft law on the implementation of a program to develop the digital economy in Russia.

The purpose of the program is to simplify and improve the lives of Russians by increasing the quality of goods and services that are manufactured through the help of modern information technologies. It aims to do this by developing a comprehensive informational environment and training digital personnel, to attain the goals of the Russian digital economy.

The program focuses on two main blocks: Establishing institutes for the training of skilled personnel for work in the digital economy; and key elements of the digital economy such as information infrastructure and security. The program has five main categories.

Specialty	Description
Digital technologies	Creation of a system of support for applied research in the sphere of the digital economy that ensures technical independence of the country for each direction of end-to-end digital technologies that are competitive at the global level
Digital state management	Provision of state services by implementing digital technologies and platform solutions in the sphere of state management
Information security	Protection of individuals, society, and the state from information threats (internal and external)
Information infrastructure	Implementation of digital platforms of work with data for provision of the needs of citizens and business
Personnel for digital cyber economy	Transformation of the educational system, which will provide the market with competent personnel, and transformation of the labor market, which has to conform to the requirements of the digital economy

By 2024, the Russian government aims for the following:

1. Russia will have at least 10 hi-tech companies that will manage digital technologies and platforms.
2. At least 500 small- and medium-sized companies will be involved in the functioning of the digital economy.
3. At least 120,000 graduates per year with a specialism in information and telecommunication technologies and at least 800,000 graduates per year in the sphere of IT.
4. At least 50% of the population will have digital skills.
5. At least 95% of the population will have access to high-speed Internet.
6. All cities with a population above 1 million people will have 5G.

The government is interested in a comprehensive implementation of the digital economy into everyday practice due to the following reasons:

1. Elimination of the current economic blockade. Through the development of the digital economy, Russia will ensure the inflow of capital for new projects.
2. Provision of security and elimination of anonymity (blockchain).
3. The digital economy is a source of potentially large tax revenues for the budget and the indicator of the independence of the country.

Russia's transition to the digital economy is inevitable, as this is a global process. The government pays close attention to such important issues such as cryptocurrencies, AI, and blockchain. Online technologies are very convenient, and as their global popularity grows annually, Russia is no exception. Contactless credit and debit cards, Wi-Fi on public transport, and online portals for state services are already widely used by Russians in everyday life. They are ready for the "digital revolution" (Matyunina et al. 2018).

However, such technological progress will influence many aspects of everyday life. It will directly influence 26 million jobs: 6 million jobs will disappear, and 20 million jobs will face new requirements under the conditions of digitization. New digital companies will have specific characteristics: usage of CRM systems, a high level of automatization, online databases, electronic internal turnover, etc. Properly utilizing labor resources and the provision of the proper level of security will be challenges for them.

Implementation of the digital economy will lead to the following new phenomena:

1. AI: It will allow using the tools and by the people with minimum technical knowledge due to intelligent automatization with convenient and simple (human-friendly) user interface.
2. Internet of Things: A network connecting the surrounding objects of the real and virtual world. Hundreds of millions of devices that are connected to the Internet of Things will disseminate the digital economy in all spheres of the economy.
3. Cloud technologies: Such storage solutions have multiple advantages including low cost, huge scale, secure, and reducing the possibility of loss or degradation. Cloud technologies also enable quick reactions to new opportunities and for the preservation of competitiveness.
4. 5G: The large-scale revolution of the telecommunications network will enable radical improvements in power and efficiency.
5. Information security: The security of information in an interconnected world has become a greater problem than ever before.

Together with the obvious positive effects of the digital economy, there will also be problems. Equipment and technologies will become obsolete, as will the employees that relied on them for a living. New skilled and competent personnel will be required. Today, Russian employers complain that the skills of even the best graduates from respected universities do not conform to market requirements (Zavalko 2013). Employers spend RUB 500 billion on the retraining of personnel, which is double the total expenditure of the federal budget for higher education.

The lack of qualified personnel in the Russian IT industry is a serious limitation on the development of this sphere. For example, the number of IT specialists in the USA is 4.5 million, in China, it is 2 million, and in Russia, just 400,000. In the last decade, there has been a tendency of seven vacancies for every qualified applicant.

The problem of this deficit in professional personnel is caused by an obsolete system for training IT specialists and the consequences of demographics.

The current problems with the training of digital personnel are as follows:

1. Existence of a conservative university system for the training of specialists in the IT industry.
2. Low level of knowledge of trained specialists in the sphere of digital technologies and the absence of the corresponding skills of doing digital business.
3. Insufficient financing of universities that train personnel in the IT sphere (According to the study by RBC, the financing of education by the government has decreased in the last 8 years. For example, the government spent RUB 3.9 trillion on education in 2013, and only RUB 3.1 trillion will be spent in 2019).

4. Insufficient differentiation of the programs for the training of digital specialists in universities (Even at prestigious universities, the number of courses does not exceed two or three).
5. Insufficient motivation and stimulation of high school graduates (There is a poor awareness of potential professions in the sphere of new technologies).
6. Insufficient number of state-funded slots at universities in IT specialties. For example, the educational portal GeekBrains.ru trained 450,000 specialists on its free basic online course "Basic programming," which is ten times as many as the number of students that entered universities to study IT-related courses, according to the state-funded program.
7. Unfavorable working conditions and limited options for further development in the Russian IT sector. There is a significant outflow of IT specialists abroad due to better conditions and higher wages in other countries.

Obviously, universities are the main institutes for the production and concentration of knowledge. For successful implementation of their functions in the twenty-first century, educational establishments of any type have to be able to adapt and react to changes in all spheres: information, technological, economic, etc. Universities have to master the new and most effective technologies in education. This will be impossible without a corresponding focus on equipping and training teachers to enable this (Ragulina and Zavalko 2013a).

The labor market requires specialists with a high level of knowledge in the IT sphere. Universities have to do more than teaching technical skills. Graduates also need skills related to project and teamwork. Graduates should also not only be guided toward roles with innovative hi-tech companies, but also have the entrepreneurial drive necessary to start their own companies (Ragulina and Zavalko 2013b).

The current absence of the necessary number of skilled specialists puts the development and manufacture of hi-tech products at risk. The results of a survey of employers (Do potential employees require work experience?) are presented in Fig. 1.

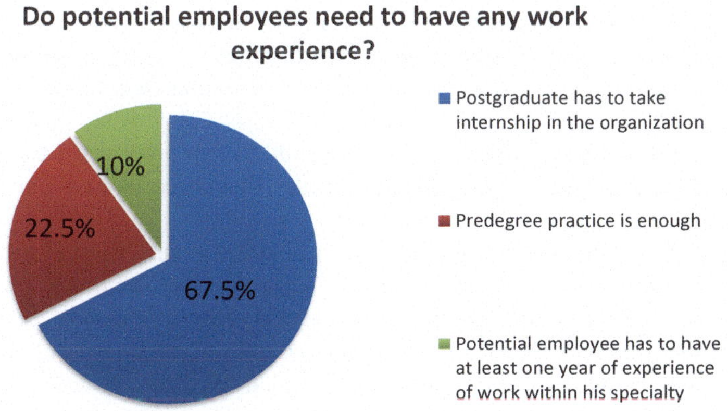

Fig. 1 Employer survey on the need for work experience

As is seen from Fig. 1, most (67.5%) employers acknowledge the necessity for work experience with potential employees. 22.5% of the respondents think that production practice is enough for employment by specialty and execution of professional responsibilities. Only 10% of the respondents think that a potential employee has to have at least 1 year of experience of work by the specialty to be considered a professional.

3 Results

Universities have to interact more proactively with the labor market. This will require a significant expansion of the responsibilities of universities, as the new conditions of the digital society require new strategies for the preparation of competitive personnel, who are digitally competent.

By outlining the main problems in the way that personnel are currently trained for the digital economy, it is possible to determine potential solutions, which might be implemented over the next 10 years:

(a) A qualitative transformation and reequipping of the conservative university system, which does not fully conform to the economy's requirements for personnel and cannot keep up with the speed of change in the labor market, particularly in the sphere of IT.
(b) Increases in the level and competences of digital literacy through a review of how they are taught and evaluated.
(c) Increases in the financing of education in the sphere of digital technologies (in the recent annual address to the Federal Assembly, Vladimir Putin noted that not all educational establishments had high-speed Internet and said that this problem had to be solved by 2021).
(d) Differentiation of programs for training IT specialists through more developed interactions with representatives of the IT sphere, who should be encouraged to open chairs, research centers, and laboratories in universities. Such programs should open the students' potential, which requires coverage of more scientific spheres: IT, economics, state regulation, business management, and fundamental and applied sciences).
(e) Organization of the educational process with the involvement of experts and practitioners from the best companies in the IT sphere to motivate and train students.
(f) Increase of state-financed scholarships to stimulate the provision of more opportunities for smart and motivated students (at present, limited finances hinder the attraction of the best applicants for training of digital personnel, due to complexity of employment and necessity for combining training and work—i.e., preferred character of extramural training, which does not allow for full mastering of digital competencies).

(g) Interactions between universities and such large market players as Yandex, Mail.ru, 1C, and Microsoft to offer training and internships with the further possibility for the provision of jobs on a competitive basis (more than 70% of universities offering IT-related courses confirm that partner companies provide jobs for their programs' graduates).

The IT sector is one of the most effective in the Russian economy. One skilled employee creates products valued at RUB 2 million per year (the data of the Ministry of Communications and Mass Media). This illustrates the economic value of adequate training for personnel to work in the digital economy.

We are in the era of the informational world, in which everything is interconnected. Society has already realized the value of network interaction. Two billion people have a connection to the Internet, and by 2020 more than half of the world's population will be online (Digital Economy, EU). The digital economy will become the most important driver of innovation, competitiveness, and economic growth in the world.

The digital economy has multiple advantages. It reduces the cost of payments and opens new sources of income. The cost of government and commercial services are lower than in the traditional economy and will become more accessible to more people. The digital economy provides more diverse information, educational, scientific, and entertaining content, with greater speed, quality, and convenience (Milner 2008). Further development of the digital economy in Russia is inevitable. However, without sufficient skilled personnel, this development may be slow and ineffective.

A new training platform may require creation by the institutes that will have to train skilled personnel able to adapt to the changing conditions of the future market.

How could this platform be established?

1. Transforming and reequipping the conservative university system, which does not conform to the economy's labor demands.
2. Development of a favorable business environment by the government to stimulate and support digital specialists and entrepreneurs and their initiatives.
3. Cooperation by the government with a wide circle of interested parties, including citizens, digital companies, educational establishments, suppliers of infrastructure, and infrastructural companies to ensure the most efficient usage of the effects of digitization.
4. Provision of high-speed Internet by the government to all educational establishments (At present, Russian universities obtain Internet access by common commercial terms, which leads to deficit and low speed of the Internet in Russian universities).

4 Conclusion

Thus, having studied the current problems of training of digital personnel for the cyber economy and having found possible ways of solving these problems, we can conclude that the benefits from an acceleration of digitization in the next decade will be significant if the government is able to create supportive conditions for training personnel and stimulating entrepreneurship. The system of education has to transform: typical knowledge should be replaced by information knowledge and realizing the creative potential of students. Otherwise, employers will have to continue to invest significant sums into retraining their employees (Metelev and Zavalko 2014).

The government has to accept responsibility for the labor shortage in the Russian IT sector and takes action.

References

Matyunina OE, Zavalko NA, Kozhina VO, Sokolov AA, Lebedeva OE (2018) Development of financial infrastructure in the system of state regulation of digital economy. Econ Entrep:26–29

Metelev SE, Zavalko NA (2014) Advancement in the aspect of regionalization of education. Life Sci J 11:129–132

Milner BZ (2008) "Knowledge economy" and new requirements to management. The issues of theory and practice of management, pp 108–120

Ragulina JV, Zavalko NA (2013a) Integration processes in the chain: science, higher vocational education and production, as a factor in increasing the competitiveness of the educational institution. Middle-East J Sci Res:161–166

Ragulina JV, Zavalko NA (2013b) Theoretical and methodical background of efficiency of educational services in the system of higher education. Life Sci J:199–204

Zavalko NA (2013) Formation of qualitative aspects of higher professional education in the conditions of market environment. Bull Acad:135–137

Zavalko NA, Matyunina OE, Kozhina VO, Sokolov AA, Lebedev KA (2018) Digital economy and its influence on state and municipal management. Econ Entrep:101–104

Digital Competence as a Measure of Employee Competitiveness in the Labor Market of the Cyber Economy

Polina Yu. Grosheva and Nataliya V. Bondarchuk

Abstract The authors show that in the conditions of the cyber economy digital competence is one of the key factors of employee competitiveness in the labor market. The authors determine interconnections between technical modernization and reequipping of organizations and the need for the development of employee competencies to create cyber-physical systems of management.

The importance of the task of diagnostics in order for managers to assess employee competencies according to the modern requirements of the cyber economy is substantiated. This task is important for all categories of a company's personnel: managers, specialists, and employees who are either involved in key scientific and production activities or have roles related to their organization and maintenance.

A methodology of diagnostics for employee competence is offered. It is used to determine the need for development of digital competencies in the conditions of the cyber economy and is based on the implementation of a three-stage algorithm, which contains the model of evaluation of the level of competency. The authors distinguish competencies that are the most important for development of personnel in the conditions of the cyber economy to support a high level of organizational competitiveness.

The diagnostic tool makes it possible to measure how closely employee competencies conform with the conditions of the cyber economy, and take decisions to plan improvements if they are deemed necessary.

1 Introduction

Recent decades have seen rapid growth in the number of computer and Internet technologies and the circle of tasks that they can solve. As new innovations appear (the cloud, neural networks, and AI) they become embedded in all spheres life stimulating the formation of the digital economy.

P. Y. Grosheva (✉)
RUDN University, Moscow, Russia

N. V. Bondarchuk
The Russian Presidential Academy of National Economy and Public Administration (RANEPA), Moscow, Russia

© Springer Nature Switzerland AG 2019
V. M. Filippov et al. (eds.), *The Cyber Economy*, Contributions to Economics,
https://doi.org/10.1007/978-3-030-31566-5_15

The digital economy is now one of the key drivers of global economic growth (Popkova 2019; Vinogradov et al. 2018). With the creation of an integrated digital system and the formation of the cyber economy, such growth will accelerate as companies will optimize and reduce expenditures, increase labor efficiency, and quicken the creation of new products with unique consumer qualities.

However, for the effective implementation of all these tasks employee competencies, which are connected to solving tasks in the development and application of digital solutions for new digital company, must be of the highest caliber (Chursin and Tyulin 2018; Chursin et al. 2017).

Ensuring the development of such competencies could be compared to the overall process of technical modernization and reequipping that will be necessary for the creation of cyber-physical systems, and the cyber economic systems needed to manage them.

Technical and technological reequipping will obviously require the initial training of personnel on new equipment with the usage of new digital technologies (Kleiner et al. 2018; Makogonchuk 2018). Thus, the need to analyze employee competencies (and digital competencies) in the context of cyber economy has become very important. Digital competence will be the key competitive advantage for employees in the labor market of the future (Dikopalova 2018; Popkova et al. 2019). Therefore, the need to create diagnostic tools to measure competencies, including digital competencies, has emerged. When an organization requires all of its personnel to exhibit digital competencies, such tools will be in urgent demand.

2 Materials and Method

The methodological diagnostic tool for employee competence, aimed at determining the need for the development of competencies in the sphere of digitization contains three stages (Fig. 1).

According to Fig. 1, the first stage envisages an external evaluation of the strategy and competence of the company's personnel on the basis of an analysis of the company's ability to develop according to its set strategic plan, which is aimed at the digitization of all business processes, with the optimal usage of the company's resource potential. If the strategy for a company's digitization cannot be implemented, a conclusion on the sufficiency of digital competence and top managers' ability or inability to form a high-quality strategic program for digitization is made. In the case of Result A (Fig. 1), it is necessary to create and implement a plan to increase the digital competence of top managers. If such digital competence is already sufficient for the implementation of the development strategy, it is necessary to move to the second stage of the methodology of diagnostics.

In the second stage, an internal evaluation of the correspondence between the company's competencies in applying digital solutions to its activities and current liabilities is performed to determine the level of the company's usage of digital solutions within the main profile of its activities. It is also determined whether the

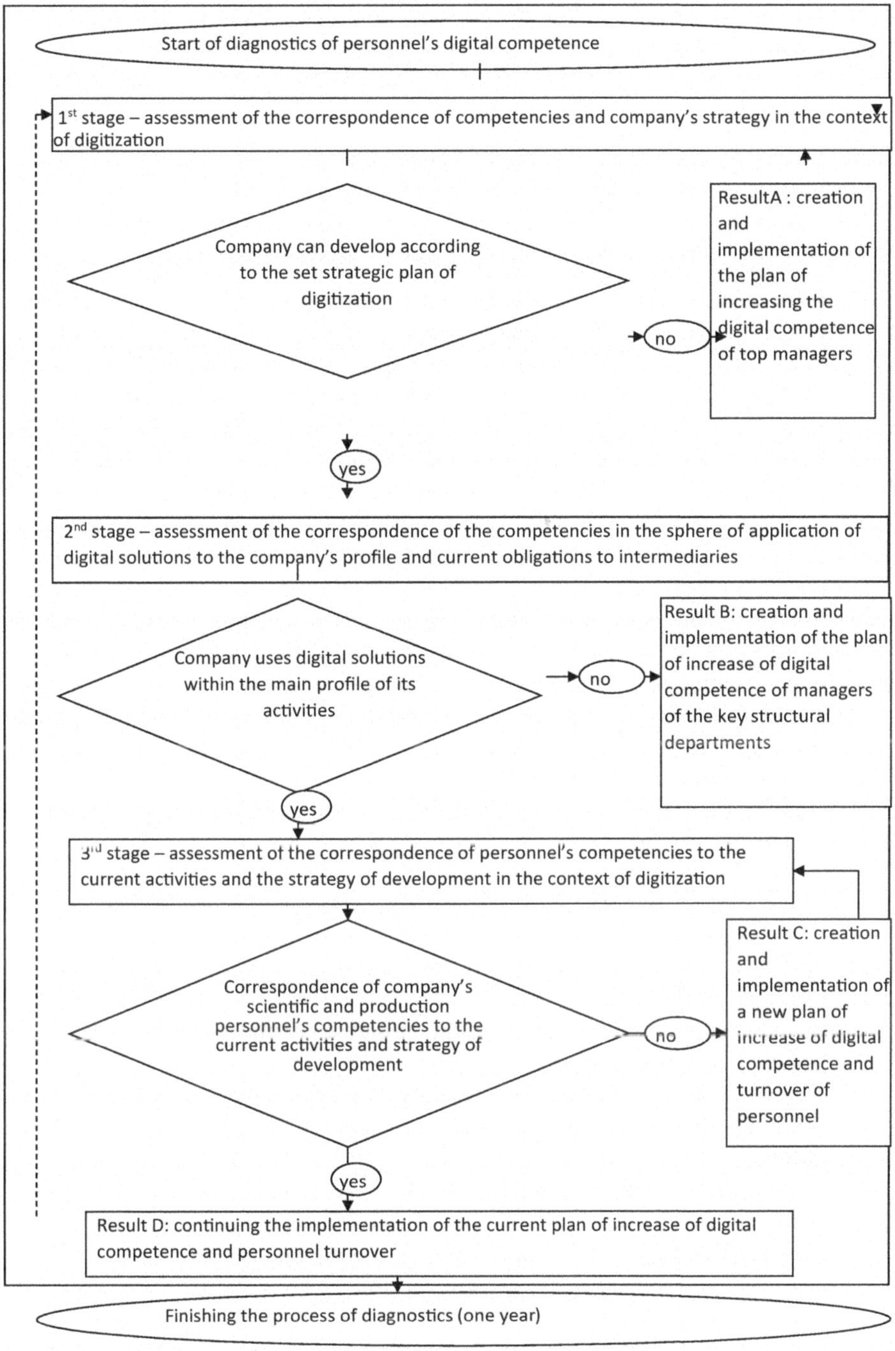

Fig. 1 The algorithm of diagnostics for employee digital competence

application of these digital solutions in production and management stimulates the improvement of financial and economic indicators:

- Growth of revenues from sales, which exceed the sectoral index of growth of prices.
- Absence of losses and achievement of planned profit.
- Sustainable growth of the indicators of profitability and sales.
- Normal financial state (Indicators of liquidity, payment capacity, and financial sustainability conform to the normative values, or are improving).

If the financial and economic activities of the company do not achieve stated targets, it is necessary to create and implement a plan to increase the digital competence, replacement, and advanced training of managers in key structural departments (Result B, Fig. 1). It is necessary to consider the replacement, or advanced training, of managers whose failures led to delays in the implementation of innovative projects for the creation of competitive products (impossible without implementation of the leading digital technologies), and those whose actions led to any negative economic consequences such as a reduction of profitability, unjustified pricing of goods or resources, etc (Chursin et al. 2019). If the company already meets its commitments to customers within the main profile of its activities and has indicators that characterize sustainable financial and economic activities, it is necessary to move to the third stage of diagnostics.

The third stage envisages an internal assessment of the correspondence of each specialist and employee competence with the key directions of current company activities and its development strategy in the context of digitization. It is expedient to use various quantitative criteria of correspondence for the main scientific and production, and supporting personnel.

For supporting personnel, it is expedient to use the following criterion of correspondence:

$$\mathrm{AMS_{ae}} < \mathrm{C_{ae}} * \mathrm{AMS_{mar}} / \mathrm{C_{mar}} \tag{1}$$

where $\mathrm{AMS_{ae}}$—average monthly salary of additional employee, accrued for all items;

$\mathrm{AMS_{mar}}$—average monthly salary of the employee of the given profession and qualification in the labor market;

$\mathrm{C_{ae}}$—number of significance—for execution of labor functions—competencies of the additional employee that he really has assessment of execution of labor responsibilities;

$\mathrm{C_{mar}}$—competencies that are required for the execution of professional liabilities according to described work duties, the presence of which can be seen in the CVs of job applicants according to the requirements of the digital economy.

Observation of the sign (1) ($<$) shows that despite the possibility of an incomplete correspondence to work duties due to an insufficient level of digital competence, determined as a result of attestation, the employee has a lower salary due to advanced training (digital competence), which is covered by the company, which will cause the employee to look for a better job in the labor market. Such training without a salary increase is inexpedient.

Employees, who are involved in the main activities—especially in jobs that require creative or sectoral competencies—require another approach, which is based on determining any missing competencies essential for the competitiveness of an employee in the cyber economy, and an evaluation of the cost for their creation. It is necessary to compile maps of competencies, with a description of each skill that is necessary for the execution of labor functions, and the coefficient that reflects the significance of this skill in the totality of all required competencies.

In this case, the normative model of the level of competencies will have the following form:

$$C_{norm} = a_1 * C_{1norm} + a_2 * C_{2norm} + a_3 * C_{3norm} + \ldots * a_n * C_{n\ norm} \quad (2)$$

where C_{norm}—normative level of competencies (including digital) for the employee of the main activities.

C_{1norm}, C_{2norm}, C_{3norm}, ... $C_{n\ norm}$—assessment of the necessary level of competencies (in the internal 1–10), with a description of the level of possession of competencies for each quantitative value (compiled by a specialist from the HR department).

a_1, a_2, a_3, ... a_n—numbers, in the interval 0–1 (determined on the basis of expert evaluation by the department manager), which reflect relative significance of the key competencies (including digital) in formation of the total value of competencies; their sum should equal:

$$a_1 + a_2 + a_3 + \ldots + a_n = 1{,}0 \quad (3)$$

The factual value of each employee's competencies should be calculated on the basis of this model, with a determination of the level of factual possession of the competencies:

$$C_{fact} = a_1 * C_{1fact} + a_2 * C_{2fact} + a_3 * C_{3fact} + \ldots * a_n * C_{n\ fact} \quad (4)$$

where C_{fact}—factual level of competencies (including digital) of the employee for the main activities.

a_1, a_2, a_3, ... a_n—numbers in interval 0–1, the same as with calculation of the normative level of the competencies of an employee of the main activities C_{norm} (for example, if the model has 10 competencies, the value of all the above indicators could equal 0.1; weight indicators could also change, based on the importance of a certain competency, especially competencies related to the application of digital solutions in production and managerial activities, for this job).

C_{1fact}, C_{2fact}, C_{3fact}, ... $C_{n\ fact}$—numerical evaluation of the factual level of competencies (in interval 1–10), evaluated according to the description of the normative level of possession of competencies for each quantitative value (performed by the department manager or assigned as a result of attestation).

Correspondence of the competencies of a competitive specialist to the competence-based requirements of the occupied position should be assessed by

Table 1 Analysis of deviation of competencies (including digital) of employees from the necessary level

Numerical order and title of competency	Numbers, in interval 0–1, which reflect the significance of each competency for the job	Normative level of competencies (in interval 1–10)	Factual level of competencies (in interval 1–10)	Deviations in the level of competencies If value Δ Ki > 0, the competency is excessive; if Ki < 0, the competency is deficit, and its increase is required
C_1–	a_1	C_{1norm}	C_{1fact}	$\Delta C_1 = (C_{1fact} - C_{1norm})$
C_2–	a_2	C_{2norm}	C_{2fact}	$\Delta C_2 = (C_{2fact} - C_{2norm})$
C_3–	a_3	C_{3norm}	C_{3fact}	$\Delta C_3 = (C_{3fact} - C_{3norm})$
...	...	...	...	...
C_n–	a_n	$C_{n\ norm}$	$C_{n\ fact}$	$\Delta C_n = (C_{n\ fact} - C_{n\ norm})$

completing the table of deviations of factual competencies of the employees of the main activities from the necessary level (Table 1).

To evaluate the total deviation for the totality of competencies of each employee, it is necessary to calculate the absolute deviation of factual possession of the totality of competencies from the level of the factual planned value of possession of competencies, especially digital competencies, for this job:

$$\Delta C = a_1 * (C_{1fact} - C_{1fact}) + a_2 * (C_{2fact} - C_{2fact}) + a_3(C_{3fact} - C_{3fact}) + *** + a_n(C_{n\ fact} - C_{n\ fact}) \tag{5}$$

If the value that is obtained during the assessment of a specific employee's competencies is below ($\Delta C < 0$), the totality of their competencies is in deficit, and serious additional training is required. If the value is $\Delta C > 0$, but certain $\Delta C_i < 0$, some advanced training is necessary, which should form or raise the level of deficit competencies, especially digital competencies.

For example, in the conditions of digitization and creation of the cyber economy, key importance should be placed on the following competencies:

- Ability to use information technologies in everyday scientific/production/managerial activities.
- Ability to form the directions of the development and implementation of the technologies of Industry 4.0 to increase the competitiveness of issued products.
- Ability to manage a mix of products to preserve leading positions in the market.
- Skills in digital design.
- Skills in the sphere of processing and analyzing Big Data.
- Skills in managing digital production and developing the functioning of a digital company.
- Skills with cyber-physical systems and intelligent machines and agents.

3 Results

As a result of running diagnostics on the level of digital competence of personnel with the described tools, it is possible to conclude that the current general level of employee competencies does not correspond to the conditions of the cyber economy. If an evaluation of the competencies of the scientific and production personnel of a company shows a mismatch of competencies of more than 5%, it is necessary to quickly implement a new plan to increase digital competencies through training, advanced training, and managed turnover of ineffective personnel. If the mismatch is less than 5%, it might be possible to realize a plan to digitize company operations.

After the described three stages have been undertaken and a need for additional competencies has been established, it is recommended to establish and enact a 1 year plan to raise digital skill levels and then repeat the diagnostic process to ensure that the necessary improvements have been achieved.

4 Conclusions

The transformation of the digital economy to the cyber economy will require the comprehensive development of employee competencies. Specialists will apply modern digital methods within everyday labor functions and will need to be periodically appraised to ensure that they have the necessary competencies for the changes in the production and the economic environment in which they work. There will be a need for continuous improvement in the digital competencies of such employees, especially in industrial organizations.

Companies will need to train and re-train specialists to ensure a reserve of digital personnel with unique competencies capable of contributing high-competitive advantages and satisfying new market demand.

References

Chursin A, Tyulin A (2018) Competence management and competitive product development: concept and implications for practice. Springer, Berlin

Chursin AA, Shamin RV, Fedorova LA (2017) The mathematical model of the law on the correlation of unique competencies with the emergence of new consumer markets. Eur Res Stud J 20(3):39–56

Chursin RA, Yudin AV, Grosheva PY, Filippov PG, Butrova EV (2019) Tool for assessing the risks of R&D projects implementation in high-tech enterprises. IOP Conf Ser Mater Sci Eng 476:012005

Dikopalova MS (2018) The main problem of preparing qualified personnel for the digital economy. Russian economy: goals, challenges and achievements, pp 57–59

Kleiner GB, Korablev YA, Shchepetova SE (2018) Human in digital economy. Econom Sci Mod Russ 2(1):169–175

Makogonchuk IA (2018) Preparing personnel for the Russian digital economy. Russian economy: goals, challenges and achievements, pp 156–158

Popkova EG (2019) Preconditions of formation and development of industry 4.0 in the conditions of knowledge economy. Stud Syst Decis Control 169:65–72

Popkova EG, Ragulina YV, Bogoviz AV (2019) Fundamental differences of transition to industry 4.0 from previous industrial revolutions. Stud Syst Decis Control 169:21–29

Vinogradov GP, Vinogradova NG, Shapel DA (2018) Building a specialist's knowledge model in the digital economy. Program Prod Syst 4(1):697–704

Key Competencies for Digital Personnel in the Cyber Economy and How to Master Them

Svetlana Yu. Murtuzalieva

Abstract The current formation of the cyber economy requires the development of new competencies in the labor force. In this chapter, the author considers the key competencies that need to be developed.

The increase of the role of information technologies in the modern economy presents new challenges for those who work in retail, the public sector, finance, and production. In order to achieve the expected increases in competitiveness, organizations must ensure that their management systems ensure the high levels of personnel training.

1 Introduction

The modern stage of economic development can be characterized as the age of digitization, in which the basis of economic transactions is information and knowledge, and transactions are performed via information technologies. Employees have to possess the knowledge and professional competencies that conform to the needs of this digital economy. Knowledge and competencies could be assigned to the category of cognitive resources, the usage of which forms the intellectual capital of society through the effect of multiplication. The transformation of cognitive resources into a final product with maximum added value is possible only through formation of professional competencies—i.e., knowledge, skills, and other personal characteristics that allow an individual to perform labor activities with maximum effectiveness.

S. Y. Murtuzalieva
RUDN University, Moscow, Russia
e-mail: murtuzalieva-syu@rudn.ru

© Springer Nature Switzerland AG 2019
V. M. Filippov et al. (eds.), *The Cyber Economy*, Contributions to Economics,
https://doi.org/10.1007/978-3-030-31566-5_16

2 Materials and Method

Before defining the competencies that are required for the cyber economy, it is necessary to dwell a little on its development. Starting from the second half of the twentieth century, technological revolutions have created huge potential for new knowledge and technologies in many spheres. However, the effective usage of these knowledge resources cannot be achieved without information technologies. The cyber economy as a science has deep roots. In Russia, the origin can be traced to cybernetics and the work of Nikolai I. Veduta.[1] His book, "Economic Cybernetics" was a bestseller in the 1970s. The cyber economy envisages the functioning of a complex system, which uses optimal connections and is built on interactions between the subjects and objects of economic relations during the production, exchange, and distribution of material goods. As a matter of fact, in the Soviet period, economists and cyberneticians were already attempting to solve how to build optimal connections and interactions between economic subjects. Today, the usage of IT technologies and the creation of the correct economic model are solving the task of optimality and effectiveness in the functioning of the economy. The cyber economy uses the transparency of the data, to build an effective system for the management of a company, sector, or national economy, or even the global economy.

Statistical data show that information technologies are now present in all areas of socioeconomic life and have an influence on the development of key sectors of the economy. As a result, information and intellectual rent appears as new form of value, which brings additional revenue to its owner. Thus, cognitive resources become the main factor for the development of modern society. A special place and role in this process belongs to intellectual capital (as a result of the usage of cognitive resources), which predetermines the structure of the national economy, the effectiveness of economic activities, and the level of competitiveness of economic subjects.

3 Results

In recent years, there have been multiple attempts by the Russian government to diversify the economy and perform a transition to an innovative trajectory of development. The current aim is to increase the number of university graduates in the sphere of IT technologies to establish a digitally competent workforce replete with specialists in key sectors.

[1]Nikolai I. Veduta (1913–1998)—Soviet and Belarusian economist and cybernetician, doctor of economics, professor, member of the National Academy of Sciences of Belarus, and founder of the Scientific School of Strategic Planning.

The following problems appear during the formation and usage of such competencies: (1) Not all knowledge and skills can be used in labor activities; (2) Knowledge important for the current level of development of the economic system will need to be constantly updated and multiplied to satisfy future levels of development; (3) The quality of knowledge could be variable, so it is important to ensure it is current and efficient. Knowledge as a characteristic of cognitive and labor potential should be transformed—via professional competencies—into organizational intellectual capital. It should be noted that intellectual labor and work with information and arrays of data are not the same thing. The formation of professional competencies requires wide knowledge—scientific and socially predetermined. According to the concept of H. Gardner, intellect is a multiple value. Humans possess several key competencies intellects, which different humans have in different proportions:

1. Abstract intellect: symbolic thinking and abilities in the sphere of mathematics and formal logic.
2. Social intellect: understanding social contexts and ability to communicate adequately with people.
3. Practical intellect: common sense.
4. Emotional intellect: self-conscience and self-management.
5. Esthetic intellect: a sense of form and abilities in the spheres of design, music, art, and literature.
6. Kinesthetic intellect: physical skills.

Sociological surveys show that 55% of any country's population is not ready to develop their cognitive complex of knowledge and skills and overcome the barriers to the formation of a competitive specialist. Only 30% of a population is ready for self-development through the formation of professional competencies, and only 15% of a population strives for the formation of intellectual capital.

What should be done with modern employee's competencies to form on the one hand a systemic and scientific basis to them and on the other hand, to orientate them toward the needs of the current stage of economic development? It is necessary to distinguish the role of universities in this process and outline the need to implement transformations that will lead to a more effective usage of cognitive resources. Thus, during formation of competencies, it is necessary to pass from convergent thinking (narrowing the circle of opportunities and searching for one correct answer) to divergent thinking (formation of complimentary thinking abilities that are connected to creative thinking, innovativeness, imagination, and inventiveness). Implementation of the Lifelong Learning paradigm can be successful only if it is the basis of the scientific platform of universities. This is possible through the implementation of programs of advanced training and business education. New requirements for the quantitative and qualitative elements of the system of advanced training, professional re-training, and business education constantly grow due to a number of reasons: (1) The number of employees who need knowledge not only in their professional sphere but also in adjacent spheres grows; (2) The multidisciplinary character of knowledge built from a good level of basic competencies provides an employee with a high level of personal competitiveness; (3) New spheres of knowledge, based on interdisciplinary interactions, appear.

The cyber economy sets new tasks for the education system and requires the formation of new competencies.

Human competencies should conform to the needs of modern society—especially as they relate to digital technologies. However, the problem of training specialists with corresponding levels of qualification and the required competencies is still unsolved.

According to one of the well-known definitions of the word, "Competency is an ability to use the results of training according to a certain context (education, work, personal, or professional development)" (Chursin and Makarov 2015). Different countries conduct active work on the formation of a list of skills that are necessary for any human in the twenty-first century. Figure 1 shows the map of professional skills of the future, formed by the independent commercial research group of "Institute for the Future."

The important competencies for the cyber economy include the following:

- Systemic thinking to stimulate the development of the skill to determine complex interactions that create a completely new quality, including simultaneous thinking and systemic engineering.
- Intersectoral communication: understanding technologies, processes, and economic situations in various spheres.
- Project management: the ability to construct, plan, and manage the completion of projects and processes.
- Programming IT solutions: the management of complex automatized processes, and work with AI.
- Client-oriented approach: the ability to adapt to consumer needs.
- Multilingualism and multiculturality: knowledge of English and at least one other language, understanding national and cultural differences of partner countries, and knowledge of the specifics of work in other spheres and countries.
- Working with people: the ability to work in a team and with other individuals.
- Work with uncertainty: the ability to make quick decisions, reacting to any changes in work conditions, ability to organize the distribution of resources, and good time management.
- Art skills: creativity and a developed sense of esthetics.

The basis of any economy is its labor resources. Their abilities determine the country's economic growth and its well-balanced development. This requires the development of a new understanding of work on the basis of the systemic approach to knowledge within innovative structures, which requires situational knowledge.

Development of digital skills and competencies, apart from development of digital infrastructure and digital skills, is a key condition for the successful development of the cyber economy.

Digital competence is a concept that describes the level of skill in relation to technologies. The process of digitization will result in 65% of all jobs in developing countries being automatized. In the countries of the OECD, automatization could

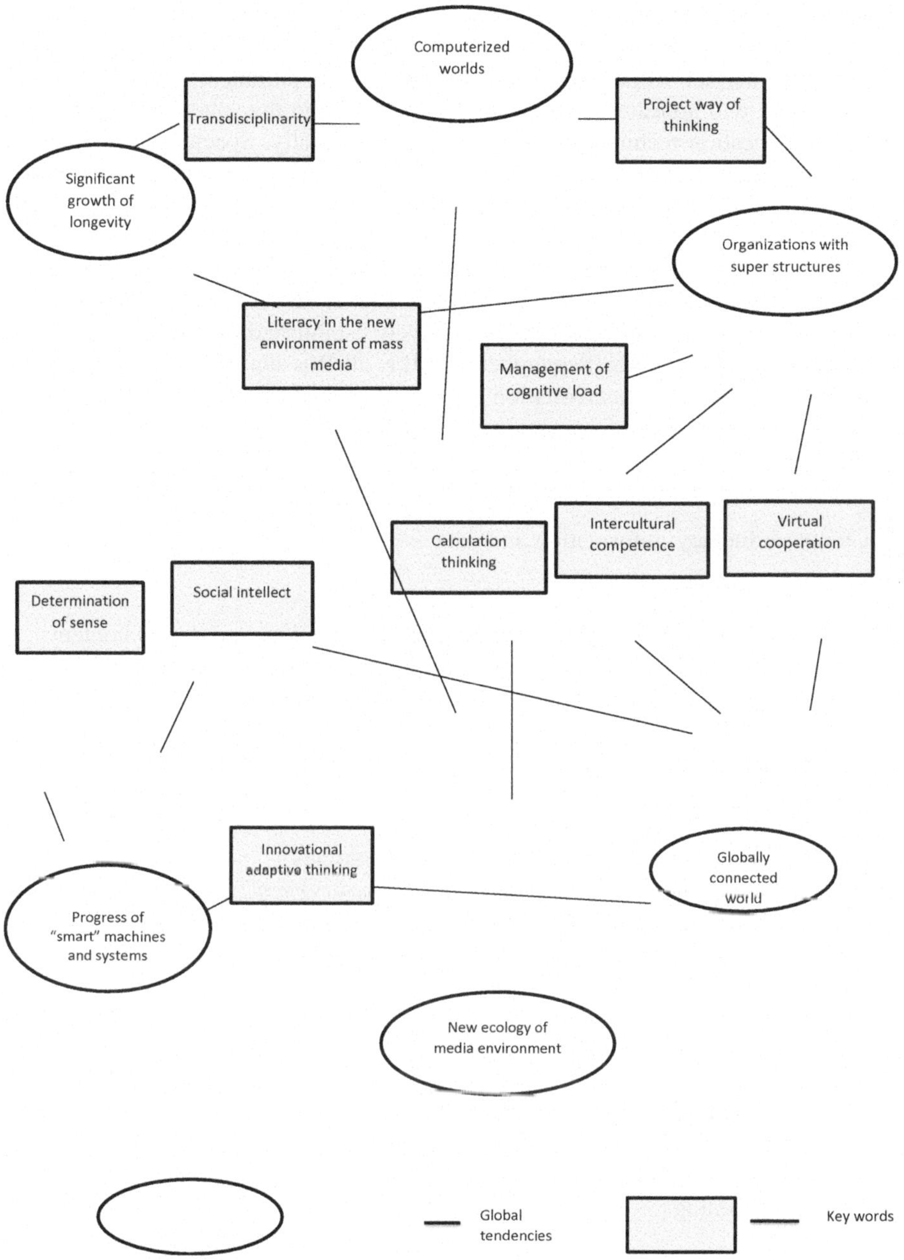

Fig. 1 The map of professional skills of the future

replace almost 60% of all jobs. Technologies could automatize activities that account for 1.2 billion qualified jobs and USD 14.6 trillion in wages. The structure of the employment market will change radically and new requirements for professional competencies will appear. The demand for specialists in the sphere of information and communication technologies will grow exponentially. Specialists involved in almost all spheres of the economy will need to be digitally literate and be comfortable in working with information, modern means of telecommunications, and software products.

The competency-based approach in most European countries (including Russia) is implemented at the level of national educational standards. The transition to competence-building education was legislatively established in Russia in the 2001 government program: since September 1, 2011, all Russian educational establishments with government accreditation passed to a new Federal State Educational Standard and the model of competencies in universities completely described the specialty and course.

The following end-to-end competencies are set:

1. Computer literacy: information and data

   Specific competencies:

   1.1. Overview, search, and filtering of data, information, and digital content
   1.2. Evaluation and analysis of data, information, and digital content
   1.3. Management of data, information, and digital content

2. Communication and cooperation

   Specific competencies:

   2.1. Interaction with the usage of digital technologies
   2.2. Exchange of digital technologies
   2.3. Participation in public life with the usage of digital technologies
   2.4. Cooperation with the usage of digital technologies
   2.5. Observation of network ethics
   2.6. Management of digital identifiers
   3. Creation of digital content
   3.1. Specific competencies:
   3.2. Development of digital content
   3.3. Integration and change of digital content
   3.4. Copyright and licenses
   3.5. Programming

4. Security

   Specific competencies;

   4.1. Protection devices
   4.2. Personal data protection and observation of confidentiality rules
   4.3. Protection of health
   4.4. Environment protection

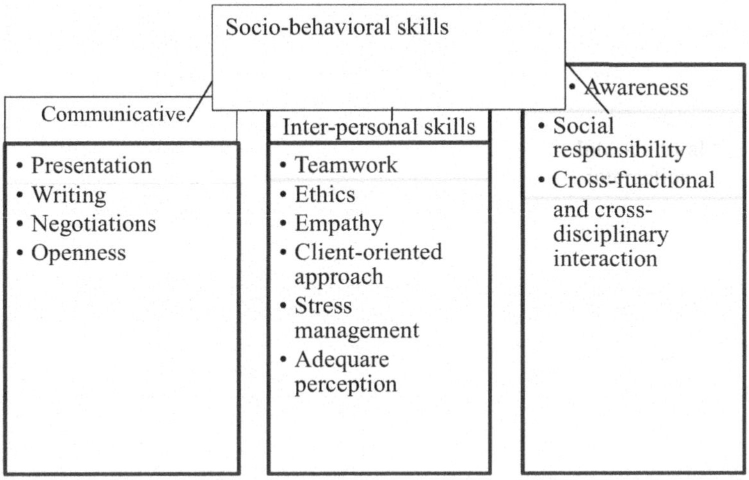

Fig. 2 Socio-behavioral skills

5. Solving problems

   Specific competencies;

   5.1 Solving technical problems
   5.2 Determining the needs and possible technological responses
   5.3 Creative usage of digital technologies
   5.4 Determining the gaps in digital literacy

6. Competencies that are connected to careers

   Specific competencies;

   6.1 Knowledge and skills for working with specialized hardware and software for a specific sphere
   6.2 Managing specialized digital technologies for a specific sphere
   6.3 Ability to select equipment (including peripheral devices), technologies, or interfaces for work—without mandatory practical experience of usage.

In order to increase the value of a young specialist for a modern company, it is necessary to add to senior courses skills in the adjustment of hardware and software and programming skills.

The target model of these competencies is that by 2025 they will have formed the necessary improvements to socio-behavioral, cognitive, and digital skills. Figure 2 shows such socio-behavioral skills that include communicative and interpersonal skills and skills of intercultural interaction. The processes of globalization and digitization and coming of the age of the cyber economy stimulate the freedom to attract labor resources from all over the world in order to ensure the optimal selection of employees according to competencies and the minimization of expenditures on wages.

Cognitive skills		
Self-development	**Organization**	**Managerial skills**
Self-awareness	Organization of own activities	Prioritization
Trainability	Resource management	Task setting
Perception of criticism and feedback		Formation of teams
Inquisitiveness		Development of others
		Motivation of others
		Delegation
Achievement of results	**Solving non-standard tasks**	**Adaptability**
Responsibility, acceptance of risk Perseverance in achievement of goals Initiative	Creativity, including the skill to see opportunities Critical thinking	Work in the conditions of uncertainty

Fig. 3 Cognitive skills

Digital skills	
Creation of systems	**Management of information**
Programming Development of apps Design of production systems	Processing and analysis of data

Fig. 4 Digital skills

Figure 3 shows cognitive skills such as self-development, organization, and managerial skills. The possession of cognitive skills is an important and decisive factor when selecting a specialist in the cyber economy for promotion.

Let us now characterize digital skills that include the following:

"Creation of a system": design of production systems and skills in programming and the development of apps. Their mandatory possession for all knowledge workers is not yet determined, but it is highly probable that at least a basic level of competence will be expected. For example, specialists may be charged with the independent adjustment of a company's IT system. Programmers often cannot see the mechanisms and reflect on all of the necessary elements of the work of a certain service and what its interactions with the software mean. Many managers now learn how to create chatbots.

"Information management": the skill of processing and analyzing data. In this context, we refer to the skill of using various systems for working with data (especially the skill to form queries for the processing of Big Data through an understanding of the specific features of working with certain systems). Data and information are sometimes referred to as the "oil of the twenty-first century," and possessing the necessary skills of working with them will be highly valuable (Fig. 4).

At present, more than 80% of the working population does not have the necessary competencies for working in the cyber economy.

In order to create competitive conditions of work for attracting and retaining professionals, it is necessary to implement the following complex series of measures:

(a) *Implementing goals for the optimization and digitization of key internal and external business processes.*
(b) *Transformation of the organizational culture to increase the flexibility and transparency of goals, and criteria for personnel assessment.*
(c) *Attraction of a critical mass of "change agents"—mid- and senior-level with competencies in and successful experience of implementing tasks in the commercial sector.*

It is also necessary to reduce ineffective "social employment" programs with the redistribution of labor compensation funds in favor of professionals.

(a) *Creation of a transparent mechanism that allows determining the approaches to optimize the number of staff needed.*
(b) *Optimization of ineffective staffing positions to target values with consideration of the principles of social responsibility.*
(c) *Aligning salaries at competitive levels.*

In addition, a system must be created for the re-training of digitally redundant workers at the national level:

(a) *Determining the areas of responsibility of the government, key employers, and private educational organizations within the created system of re-training.*

A favorable atmosphere for business must be fostered in Russia with a specific focus on stimulating the development of innovative small companies.

The Education system needs to prepare graduates far better for the job market:

(a) *Increasing the flexibility of the educational system through deregulating educational activities and ensuring the alignment of graduate skills with the labor market's requirements.*
(b) *Stimulation of better cooperation between educational organizations and employers, including an expansion of joint educational programs and the implementation of the practice of dual education.*
(c) *Supporting the development of the sector for private educational organizations. Shifting emphasis from educational programs that include the receipt of subject knowledge and memorizing of information to development of personal and meta-subject competencies.*

Stimulation of an influx of talent into the educational sector:

(a) *Real, not nominal, increase of wages in education.*
(b) *Transformation of the culture of educational organizations in favor of higher flexibility and openness to external ideas and personnel.*
(c) *Reformation of the system of training and advanced training for pedagogues in view of priority developments of target competencies.*

The creation of an environment that is favorable for the attraction and development of employees, through the promotion of the values of personal growth and professional development at the government level:

(a) *Systemic communication of "growth values," popularization of using professionals and entrepreneurs as role models.*
(b) *Popularization of the value of self-development and the concept of lifelong learning.*
(c) *Creation of a system to introduce key professions to high school students and undergraduates, with the involvement of employers.*

Transformation of corporate systems for the development of personnel incorporating the key element of lifelong learning:

(a) *Provision of top-priority training and development resources to personnel within the "knowledge" category.*
(b) *Increasing expenditures for the training and development of personnel by at least 3% of the labor compensation fund.*

A lot needs to be done to successfully train personnel for the demands of the cyber economy: Determining a mechanism to assess qualifications for separate competencies that together ensure the effective interaction of such economic actors as the labor market, business, and education for the digitization of economy; implementing independent assessments of qualification and separate competencies in the education system and labor market; and creation of norms for an individual to accumulate qualifications and separate competencies for the cyber economy.

Thus, it is expedient to distinguish the main social roles of citizens in the cyber economy: consumption, production, interaction, need for social protection, formation of public opinion, etc., and to systemize the tasks that are solved by a human to distinguish common (non-specific) tasks for all roles—basic tasks, and to distinguish the competencies that are necessary for solving them—basic competencies.

It is necessary to distinguish specific tasks, which are relevant for the given social role. These tasks could be treated as "keys" to this social role, and the competencies for solving them will be "key competencies."

Based on an analysis of the used strategies, it is necessary to formulate the titles of the determined competencies and to describe their contents, distinguishing the common "core" and variable component.

The basic model of competencies for the cyber economy.

The model of competencies is developed not on the basis of requirements for graduates but on the basis of the requirements of society, government, and the labor market for competencies of human (personality and employees) and digital society in view of realia of the Fourth Industrial Revolution. It is a foundation for the formation of successive Federal Educational Standards and educational programs of all levels and specialties. It should also be taken into account during development of professional standards. The basic model of competencies should have an advanced character.

Table 1 Components of the activities with the corresponding groups of competencies

Component of activities	Group of competencies
Motive	Competencies of value-based choice
Goal	Competencies of planning and organization of activities
Action (external)	Competency of implementation of activities
Self-development	Competency of self-management and self-development of the subject activities
Object	Competency of management of the results of activities
Consequences and effects	Competencies of evaluation and accounting of consequences and effects of activities

The basic model of competencies is a normative document that establishes a system of unified requirements for the formation and continual increase of competencies for the cyber economy during the whole life of a human.

The system of unified requirements includes the following:

- Requirements relating to the structure and description of the key and professional competencies;
- Requirements for the list and contents of the key competencies of the digital economy;
- Requirements for the conditions of constant update of the basic competencies;
- Requirements for the conditions of coordination of the basic and professional competencies.

The basic model of competencies sets the unified structure for key professional competencies based on the general theory of activities: values—goal (object)—actions.

The necessity for the establishment of the value and motivational basis of competencies (activities for solving problems) is the Fourth Industrial Revolution and the coming cyber economy. A competency (form of activities) always has the object at which it is aimed. The actions to achieve the goal include knowledge, skills, abilities, and experience.

The list of key competencies has been established based on analysis of the structure of activities in a complex digital world:

Motives—goals—actions (external)—self-development (internal actions and subjective results of activities)—object (objective results)—remote results (consequences and effects of activities). The components of the macrostructure of activities determined the groups of basic competencies are outlined in Table 1.

Any organization, from a school to large government corporation, where the evaluation and development of people is recorded, should create their own models of competencies. The main task is to use the principles of the formation and development of the basic model of competencies for the design and implementation of technological, communication, and methodological protocols of data exchange between the existing and created models of competencies.

During the change of the objective conditions, the following aspects could be changed and specified: titles of key competencies, values (on which the competencies are based), goals of activities, and sample generalized actions and their contexts.

The list of models ensures constant dialog between different social subjects and their coordinated activities for timely provision of competent personnel for the cyber economy.

The basic model of competencies established the levels of formation of the key competencies that are coordinated with the existing levels of qualification as end-to-end competencies of the cyber economy.

At each level of the key competencies, the following aspects are specified: knowledge, skills, abilities, and experience that are necessary for possession of a certain competency at the given level of its determined formation.

4 Conclusions/Recommendations

The succession and consistency of the development of key competencies and the possibility of their coordination with levels of qualification and professional competencies are ensured.

Educational organizations and employers can use the basic model of competencies for determining the list and levels of formation of key competencies for certain types of professional activities.

Acknowledgments The publication has been prepared with the support of the "RUDN University Program 5-100."

Reference

Chursin A, Makarov Y (2015) Management of competitiveness: theory and practice. Springer, Berlin, p 378

EdTech: The Scientific and Educational Platform for Training Digital Personnel for the Cyber Economy

Arsen S. Abdulkadyrov, Rasul M. Aliyev, and Gasan B. Badavov

Abstract *Purpose*: The purpose of this chapter is to develop a conceptual model for a university based on EdTech and a scientific and educational platform to train digital personnel for the cyber economy.

Design/methodology/approach: The authors use the case method to analyze Russia's experience to date with the EdTech sector. In addition, through the use of the statistical data of the World Economic Forum for 2016 and the IMD for 2018 the authors assess the efficiency of the scientific and educational platform for training digital personnel for the cyber economy.

Findings: It is substantiated that the existing paradigm for training digital personnel for the cyber economy does not offer universal practical solutions. The generally accepted theory on the division of scientific and educational functions for EdTech subjects do not conform to the needs of modern Russia and instead of stimulating the development of digital personnel restrain digital modernization due to a deficit of competencies and the low effectiveness of the scientific and educational infrastructure for digital business.

Originality/value: The authors specify the conceptual foundations of the process for the formation of EdTech—which is to become a scientific and educational platform to train digital personnel for the cyber economy. The developed conceptual model of a hi-tech university using EdTech and a scientific and educational platform to train digital personnel reduces uncertainty and provides solutions to current training problems.

A. S. Abdulkadyrov (✉)
Federal State Institution of Science "Institute of Social and Political Research" of the Russian Academy of Sciences, Moscow, Russia

R. M. Aliyev
Dagestan State Technical University, Makhachkala, Russia

G. B. Badavov
Institute for Geothermal Research of Dagestan SC RAS, Dagestan, Russia

© Springer Nature Switzerland AG 2019

V. M. Filippov et al. (eds.), *The Cyber Economy*, Contributions to Economics,
https://doi.org/10.1007/978-3-030-31566-5_17

1 Introduction

A key requirement for the formation of the cyber economy is training competent digital personnel, as they will enable the development of digital business, implementing breakthrough technologies and providing labor for the execution of routine business processes. However, the best process for training digital personnel remains unclear.

Firstly, there is no clear idea of the priorities for the structural transformation of the labor market. The training of digital personnel for the cyber economy could be conducted either by the re-training of digital specialists in the labor market or by training new personnel. The consequences for nondigital personnel are also an important issue.

Secondly, the optimal process for training digital personnel for the cyber economy is uncertain. What methods and which technologies should be used during theoretical and practical training? Thirdly, there is a high risk of unemployment among digital personnel due to the lack of a precise quantitative assessment (number of personnel) and qualitative assessment (specializations, level of qualification, set of competencies) of the economy's need for such personnel.

In the process of the digital modernization of economy, a hi-tech educational sector—EdTech—is formed which is to become the scientific and educational platform for training digital personnel. A current problem is the creation of conceptual foundations for this process to reduce uncertainty and accelerate practical implementation. The purpose of this chapter is to develop a conceptual model for hi-tech university based on EdTech and a scientific and educational platform to train digital personnel for the cyber economy.

2 Materials and Method

The subject of training digital personnel for the cyber economy has been studied in many recent works: Bogoviz (2019), Cominu (2018), Kissmer et al. (2018), Lampinen et al. (2018), Popkova (2019), Popkova and Sergi (2019), Popkova et al. (2019), Sukhodolov et al. (2018), and Wentrup et al. (2019). Scientific substantiation, perspectives on, and practical experience of the formation and development of EdTech are given in the works of Burch and Miglani (2018), Macgilchrist (2019), and Thomas and Nedeva (2018).

A specific feature of the existing studies and publications on the topic of training of digital personnel for the cyber economy is differentiation between the scientific and educational process. According to the existing scientific paradigm, R&D for the cyber economy and the training of digital personnel should be conducted separately within separate organizations (R&D institutes and universities).

This is the case in Russia where R&D is assigned to R&D institutes (e.g., departments of the Russian Academy of Sciences, and the Skolkovo Innovative

Center). Federal flagship universities are assigned with the function of training digital personnel.

The applied approach does not ensure either a high level of readiness for the cyber economy or the competitiveness of the Russian economy's digital competitiveness. Thus, in 2016, according to data from the World Economic Forum (2019), the networked readiness index in Russia constituted 4.5 points out of 7 (41st position among 139 countries in the rating). The scientific subindex (second pillar: Business and innovation environment) was assessed at 4.5 points out of 7 (57th position among 139 countries). The educational subindex (fifth pillar: Skills) was assessed at 5.4 points out of 7 (48th position in the world among 139 countries).

According to the IMD's digital competitiveness index (2019), in 2018 Russia was ranked overall 40th among 60 countries. In the scientific subindex (technology) it was 43rd and in the educational subindex (knowledge) it was 24th. Based on this statistical data, we deem it necessary to reconsider the existing conceptual ideas on the formation of a scientific and educational platform for training digital personnel in Russia.

3 Results

We propose to combine the functions of R&D for the creation of breakthrough digital technologies and the function of training digital personnel through the use of EdTech. As the digital modernization of the Russian economy is highly differentiated from region to region, hi-tech universities should be created throughout the country.

The current model for the creation of a scientific and educational platform to train digital personnel does not satisfy national needs and has not been adapted to the specific features of modern Russia. The country suffers from low labor mobility (training in a certain region leads to employment in the same region), labor migration to other regions of the country is treated with criticism, and differences in the production specializations of different regions leads to innovation focused on the current needs of a specific region in view of its sectoral specifics.

Ensuring that hi-tech universities exist in all of the regions of Russia will provide the following advantages:

- Well-balanced development and long-term balance in the labor and educational market: The location of a hi-tech university in the region's territory and its orientation toward the regional economy will allow for precise evaluations of the need for digital personnel and correspondence to the current needs of the labor market, offering much more flexibility than national universities that are not tied to regions.
- Targeting and accelerating the innovative process: An orientation of R&D in hi-tech toward the region will allow highly effective market research and targeted R&D with guaranteed commercialization of innovations, eliminating the need to

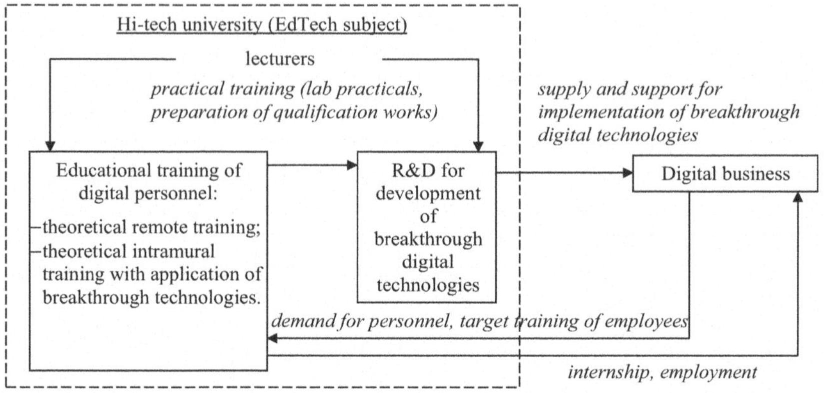

Fig. 1 The conceptual model for a hi-tech university using EdTech and a scientific and educational platform for training digital personnel for the cyber economy. Source: Compiled by the authors

adapt finished innovations to the needs of various potential users, as they will have been created for known customers and based on concluded agreements.

In order to gain these advantages, we recommend the creation of a scientific and educational platform to train digital personnel by transforming the federal flagship universities of Russia into hi-tech universities (transferring the sphere of science and education into the EdTech segment). This requires implementation of the following framework measures:

- Adoption of normative and legal provisions for the transformation of federal flagship universities of Russia into hi-tech universities (conditions, terms, necessary documents, and involved government bodies)
- Adoption of federal standards (requirements and norms) to the work of Russian hi-tech universities as a scientific and educational platform for training digital personnel
- Monitoring the effectiveness of hi-tech universities (with emphasis on both the quality and quantity of training for digital personnel).

We propose the following developed conceptual model for a hi-tech university based on EdTech and scientific and educational platform for training digital personnel (Fig. 1).

As is seen from Fig. 1, hi-tech university lecturers (academic and pedagogical staff) provide educational preparation for digital personnel and also conduct R&D for the development of breakthrough digital technologies. The hi-tech university cooperates closely with regional digital businesses that it supplies with breakthrough digital technologies (with informational and consultational support for their implementation).

To utilize such innovations, digital businesses must adapt, and require digital personnel that have competencies in using the technologies. They obtain such personnel from the hi-tech university, requesting target training for their employees (advanced training and retraining for mastering competencies in the usage of new technologies acquired by the business).

The educational training of digital personnel includes two components. The first of these is theoretical training. This could be conducted remotely—a popular form of delivery for working specialists—or within an institution by utilizing breakthrough educational technologies (e.g., technologies of virtual and alternate reality, quantum technologies, neurotechnologies, and AI).

The second component is practical training. This requires practical training (laboratory work, preparation of projects) on the basis of R&D that is conducted by the hi-tech university, i.e., by involving students in the research process. Practical training is also connected to work experience internships at the digital businesses with which the hi-tech university cooperates. This stimulates further employment opportunities for students with digital business partners.

4 Conclusion

As a result of the research it has been substantiated that the existing scientific and economic paradigm of training digital personnel for the cyber economy does not offer universal practical solutions. In particular, the generally accepted theory of differentiating between the scientific and educational functions of EdTech subjects does not conform to the specific requirements of modern Russia. Instead of stimulating digital modernization, the current system restrains it due to its low effectiveness.

The authors have specified the conceptual foundations for the formation of a hi-tech sector in the sphere of science and education, EdTech, which will be the foundation of a scientific and educational platform for training digital personnel. The developed conceptual model of a hi-tech university based on EdTech and a scientific and educational platform for training digital personnel will reduce uncertainty in this process, providing solutions to current scientific and practical problems.

According to this model, hi-tech universities should train new digital personnel, and re-train employees with skills that are in high demand in the labor market. It is recommended that breakthrough digital educational technologies are utilized in theoretical training (including remotely) and that cooperation with local digital businesses offers opportunities for work experience internships, future employment for graduates, and a more precise quantitative and qualitative determination of the current needs of the regional economy for digital personnel.

It should be concluded that these measures, which are necessary for the transformation of the federal flagship universities of Russia into hi-tech universities, are only considered generally. As these measures are of a legal nature, they go beyond the framework of this work. They should be further studied in more specialized multidisciplinary works at the juncture of economics and law.

References

Bogoviz AV (2019) Industry 4.0 as a new vector of growth and development of knowledge economy. Stud Syst Decis Control 169:85–91

Burch P, Miglani N (2018) Technocentrism and social fields in the Indian EdTech movement: formation, reproduction and resistance. J Educ Policy 33(5):590–616

Cominu S (2018) Are we all knowledge workers? Upskilling and deskilling at the time of digital | [Tutti knowledge worker? Ricchezza e impoverimento Dei lavori al tempo del digitale]. Sociologia del Lavoro 151:174–189

IMD (2019) World digital competitiveness rankings. https://www.imd.org/wcc/world-competitiveness-center-rankings/world-competitiveness-ranking-2018/. Accessed 01 March 2019

Kissmer T, Knoll J, Stieglitz S, Gross R (2018) Knowledge workers' expectations towards a digital workplace. Americas conference on information systems 2018: digital disruption, AMCIS 2018 2(1):28–34

Lampinen A, Lutz C, Newlands G, Light A, Immorlica N (2018) Power struggles in the digital economy: platforms, workers, and markets. In: Proceedings of the ACM conference on computer supported cooperative work, CSCW, pp 417–423

Macgilchrist F (2019) Cruel optimism in EdTech: when the digital data practices of educational technology providers inadvertently hinder educational equity. Learn Media Technol 44 (1):77–86

Popkova EG (2019) Preconditions of formation and development of industry 4.0 in the conditions of knowledge economy. Stud Syst Decis Control 169:65–72

Popkova EG, Sergi BS (2019) Will industry 4.0 and other innovations impact Russia's development? Exploring the future of Russia's economy and markets. Emerald, Bingley, pp 34–42

Popkova EG, Ragulina YV, Bogoviz AV (2019) Fundamental differences of transition to industry 4.0 from previous industrial revolutions. Stud Syst Decis Control 169:21–29

Sukhodolov AP, Popkova EG, Litvinova TN (2018) Models of modern information economy: conceptual contradictions and practical examples. Emerald, Bingley, UK, pp 1–38

Thomas DA, Nedeva M (2018) Broad online learning EdTech and USA universities: symbiotic relationships in a post-MOOC world. Stud High Educ 43(10):1730–1749

Wentrup R, Nakamura HR, Ström P (2019) Uberization in Paris – the issue of trust between a digital platform and digital workers. Crit Perspect Int Bus 15(1):20–41

World Economic Forum (2019) The global information technology report 2016. http://www3.weforum.org/docs/GITR2016/WEF_GITR_Full_Report.pdf. Accessed 01 March 2019

Embracing Artificial Intelligence and Digital Personnel to Create High-Performance Jobs in the Cyber Economy

Svetlana V. Lobova and Aleksei V. Bogoviz

Abstract *Purpose*: The purpose of the chapter is to study the process of creating highly efficient jobs in the cyber economy through the integration of AI and employees' mastering new digital competencies.

Methodology: Evolutional (historical) methods, analysis, synthesis, and algorithmization are used.

Conclusions: It is determined that the modern labor market is peculiar for the emergence of a new type of employee—AI. The management of labor efficiency in the cyber economy is oriented not at humans but at robots, which reduces production costs. Depending on the level of coding of operations, highly efficient jobs in the cyber economy are either fully replaced by AI or envisage effective interactions between humans and AI. In the latter case, human employees will need to continually improve and develop their cyber competencies. In order to measure the efficiency of a job working with AI, there has to be an integral indicator taking account of the usage of resources, involvement of employees, and work satisfaction.

Originality/value: The authors propose competencies that employees have to possess with the wide implementation of AI technologies. They reflect on the conditions in which highly efficient jobs could be created, and offer a vision for the transformation of jobs into highly efficient jobs within the cyber economy.

1 Introduction

Recently, certain researchers have announced a so-called AI revolution (Makridakis 2017). The wide distribution of AI is connected to technological opportunities and the need for new factors of sustainable economic growth as traditional sources have depleted. The IMF has stated that by 2022, the intensity of economic growth in the

S. V. Lobova (✉)
Altai State University, Barnaul, Russia

Ural State University of Economics, Ekaterinburg, Russia

A. V. Bogoviz
National Research University "Higher School of Economics", Moscow, Russia

© Springer Nature Switzerland AG 2019

V. M. Filippov et al. (eds.), *The Cyber Economy*, Contributions to Economics,
https://doi.org/10.1007/978-3-030-31566-5_18

USA, Japan, and certain developing countries is likely to slow (IMF 2017). One of the significant reasons for slow rates of economic growth is a reduction in the rates of labor efficiency in national economies. Experts and consultants to the White House say that in two recent decades 30 (out of 31) developed countries exhibited a reduction of labor efficiency (In 1995–2005 the average annual value in growth rates for labor efficiency in the USA constituted 2.5%; in the period 2005–2015, this had fallen to less than 1%) (White House 2016). To provide further growth in labor efficiency a new type of employee is needed—AI. In this case, AI is treated as a totality of the intelligent systems that are implemented at various stages of the economic reproduction process (production, distribution, turnover, and consumption) that can perform the labor and cognitive functions of a human worker, and thus replace him or her. Based on the results of their expert survey, Muller and Bostrom (2013) ventured that by 2022, AI will account for 10% of human cognition, and by 2040, as much as 50%. In 2075, the intellectual and thinking processes of robots will reach 90% of human capacity, thus becoming almost identical.

2 Background and Materials

The role of AI in stimulating economic growth is determined by a well-known thesis on its larger contribution to the formation of GDP as compared to other production factors, such as labor and capital. The work of Graetz and Michaels (2015), which contains the results of a study of robot application in 17 countries, shows that automatization and intellectualization of production allowed them in 1993–2007 to add 0.4% to the average annual growth of GDP. Growth of GDP by means of AI is explained by direct (the development of economic sectors that produce AI technologies) and indirect (the creation of highly efficient jobs at companies and organizations that use AI) influences. Highly efficient jobs are jobs with high labor efficiency where a large number of operations and production tasks are connected in end-to-end processes, per time period as compared to similar jobs.

Later research shows that the contribution of AI to GDP growth could be even more substantial. According to the specialists from the National Bureau of Economic Research, AI could stimulate the creation of endless income in a finite period of time (Aghion et al. 2018). According to PwC analysts, the contribution of AI to the world economy in 2030 will be USD 15.7 trillion (at 2016 prices), which will constitute 14% of total growth in global GDP (PwC 2017). This is more than the combined current volume of production of China and India. It should be noted that USD 6.6 trillion of this sum is likely to be obtained from increases in labor efficiency, i.e., the creation of highly efficient jobs. It is expected that such increases in labor efficiency will provide more than 55% of all GDP growth from the application of AI technologies in 2017–2030.

At present, leading economists treat AI as a potentially critical factor—together with labor and capital—to stimulate the growth of efficiency (White House 2016). A study by Dell Technologies shows that replacing human employees with robots may reduce expenses for labor by 90%, which is far more profitable than relocating production facilities to countries with cheap labor costs (generally saving about 65% of labor expenditures). AI could be treated as a "new type of employee" in the cyber economy, capable of constructing and reproducing similar employees and with large competitive advantages in efficiency over humans (Odegov and Pavlova 2018).

Of course, the consequences of such a competition between humans and robots, in terms of labor efficiency, causes debate between researchers regarding the future of the market labor. Manyika et al. (2013) and Wolfgang (2016) are sure that AI will soon lead to a large annual reduction of jobs. The World Economic Forum estimates that such reductions in industry will be 0.83% of the workforce (WEF 2016). Other works (Ford 2015; Vermeulen et al. 2018) state that the automatization of production will influence only routine work, which involve the simple execution of rules and operations, without providing substitutes for the cognitive processing of information, which is usually performed by employees with average wages. For roles where tasks and works are difficult to codify and require physical agility, creativity, improvisation, and social intellect, humans are currently very difficult to replace. Thus technological replacement of jobs by AI will primarily concern routine work. The report by Miller and Atkinson (2013) shows that high efficiency, ensured by robotization, is accompanied by low unemployment rates. In fact, automatization and intellectualization of production could be accelerators for the creation of new jobs due to growing production opportunities (Morris et al. 2017).

3 Results

The results of the integration of AI into the production sphere are as follows: replacement of routine human labor by robots; a reduction of the resource intensity of production due to an increase in its knowledge intensity; transformation of the labor market through (1) emergence of new professions and assigning current professions with new functions, (2) disappearance of obsolete routine and unskilled professions, which are not strategic or social and do not require creative thinking; necessity for continuous learning and development of an organization's personnel to obtain new competencies and transform to digital personnel.

The guarantee of employment in the cyber economy does not depend on a certain speciality, certain job, or certain employer. Employment in the cyber economy is ensured by the ability to continually adapt to the changing requirements for knowledge, skills, and abilities. The labor market will enter the "age of humanitarian talents" (Horx 2005), where importance is placed not on product, production, or capital, but ideas, knowledge, talent, creative potential, and innovative spirit.

The implementation of AI in order to increase labor efficiency requires new competencies for both managers and employees. Competencies—not university diplomas—are now the key currency for an employee. While a reboot of the content

Table 1 Competencies of personnel in highly efficient jobs in the cyber economy

Categories of employees		Competencies
Managers		Interpersonal communication and creative approach to solving problems and tasks
Employees	Creators	Vision of development of the cyber economy, possession of knowledge and creative abilities for the creation and improvement of technologies of AI
	Technical specialists	Specialists in knowledge technologies and presence of abilities for the implementation and servicing of AI
	Skilled users	Skills in using the technologies of AI in production, educational, everyday, and other activities

Source: Compiled by the authors

of professional education was performed 20–30 years ago, the implementation of AI should start a mechanism update courses of professional education, including additional professional education, in the next 2–3 years. Digital personnel need to be able to perform analytical work in conditions of uncertainty, independence, and improvisation.

The employees of the cyber economy have to possess competencies connected to the creation, servicing, management, effective usage, and control of AI. They must be ready for deep interactions with AI and open to the expansion of the possibilities of the human brain through the means of AI (Table 1).

An effective technology for the cybernetization of education and development of personnel is gamification. It is based on the principles of instantaneous feedback. During the usage of this tool, skills with AI technologies increase. Gamification ensures the formation of a stable system of knowledge and skills with the maximum involvement of the employee in the process.

The algorithm for the creation of highly efficient jobs in the cyber economy could have the following form (Fig. 1).

The efficiency of jobs that are based on the usage of AI has to be measured not by traditional methods—labor per unit of time or unit of expenditure—but by other methods. The efficiency of an AI job should be balanced with the human factor. This should be an integral indicator comprising the effectiveness of the usage of resources, involvement of employees, and work satisfaction. The two latter components represent the humanistic approach in the management of automatized production.

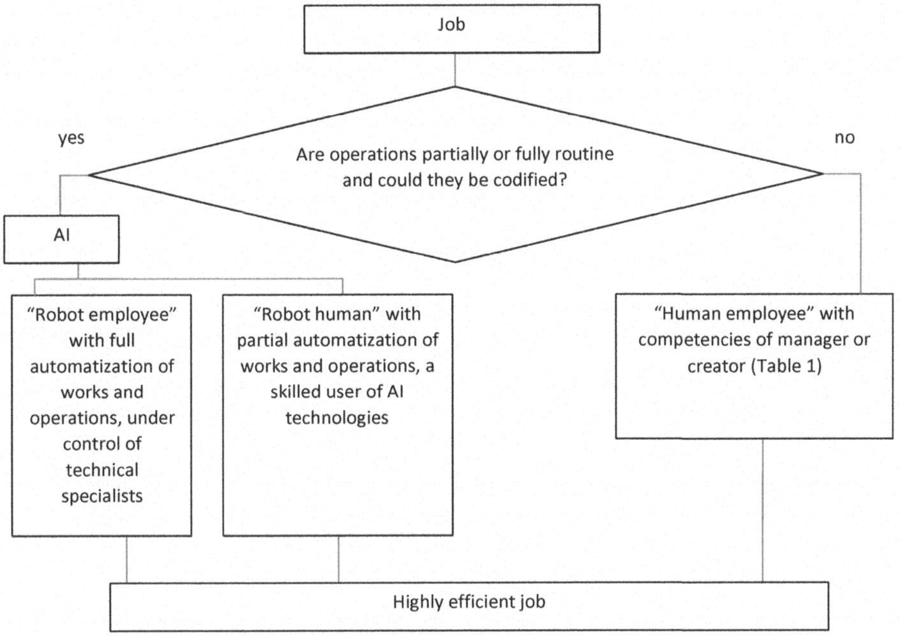

Fig. 1 The algorithm for the transformation of jobs into highly efficient jobs in the cyber economy. Source: Compiled by the authors

4 Conclusions

AI is a progressive technology, the implementation of which leads to a growth in labor efficiency. The creation of highly efficient jobs in any form of production is impossible without AI, which is a new type of employee, that allows for a large reduction in labor costs. However, the development of the cyber economy and growth of investment into the robotization and automatization of production processes is complicated by a deficit of personnel with digital competencies. For humans to remain a partner of AI in production processes, there is a need to master new knowledge and skills. Humans with the necessary competencies to interact with AI, controlling, correcting, subjecting, and directing robots, is an important precondition for the emergence of highly efficient jobs in the near future.

References

Aghion P, Jones BF, Jones CI (2018) Artificial intelligence and economic growth. The economics of artificial intelligence: an agenda from NBER. https://econpapers.repec.org/bookchap/nbrnberch/14015.htm. Accessed 04 March 2019

Ford M (2015) The rise of the robots: technology and the threat of mass unemployment. Oneworld, Oxford

Graetz G, Michaels G (2015) Robots at work. The London school of economic and political sciences: centre for economic performance (CEP). Discussion paper no 1335, March, p 53

Horx M (2005) Wie wir leben werden. Unsere Zukunft beginnt jetzt. Campus Verlag (Frankfurt). Auflage. 397 Seiten

IMF (2017) World economic outlook. April 2017: gaining momentum? https://www.imf.org/en/Publications/WEO/Issues/2017/04/04/world-economic-outlook-april-2017. Accessed 04 March 2019

Makridakis S (2017) The forthcoming artificial intelligence (AI) revolution: its impact on society and firms. Futures 90:46–60

Manyika J, Chui M, Bughin J, Dobbs R, Bisson P, Marrs A (2013) Disruptive technologies: advances that will transform life, business, and the global economy. McKinsey Global Institute, San Francisco, CA

Miller B, Atkinson RD (2013) "Are robots taking our jobs, or making them?" (information technology and innovation foundation, September 2013). https://itif.org/publications/2013/09/09/are-robots-taking-our-jobs-or-making-them. Accessed 04 March 2019

Morris KC, Schlenoff C, Srinivasan V (2017) A remarkable resurgence of artificial intelligence and its impact on automation and autonomy. IEEE Trans Autom Sci Eng 14(2):407–409

Muller VC, Bostrom N (2013) Future progress in artificial intelligence: a survey of expert opinion. Springer, Fundamental Issues of Artificial Intelligence, Synthese Library, Berlin

Odegov YG, Pavlova VV (2018) New technologies and their impact on the labour market. Living standards of Russian regions 2(208):60–70

PwC (2017) Sizing the prize. What's the real value of AI for your business and how can you capitalise? https://www.pwc.com/gx/en/issues/analytics/assets/pwc-ai-analysis-sizing-the-prize-report.pdf. Accessed 06 March 2019

Vermeulen B, Kesselhut J, Saviotti PP (2018) The impact of automation on employment: just the usual structural change? Sustainability 10:1661

WEF (2016) The future of jobs. Employment, skills and workforce strategy for the fourth industrial revolution. http://www3.weforum.org/docs/WEF_Future_of_Jobs.pdf. Accessed 06 March 2019

White House (2016) Artificial intelligence, automation, and the economy. https://obamawhitehouse.archives.gov/blog/2016/12/20/artificial-intelligence-automation-and-economy. Accessed 04 March 2019

Wolfgang M (2016) The robotics market – figures and forecasts. RoboBusiness, Boston Consulting Group, Boston, MA

Part IV
The Relationship Between Intelligent Machines and Digital Personnel in the Cyber Economy

Interactions Between Intelligent Machines and Digital Personnel in the Industrial Production of Industry 4.0 Under the Conditions of the Cyber Economy

Anna V. Bodiako

Abstract *Purpose*: This chapter considers the development of mechanisms for the interaction of intelligent machines and digital personnel in the industrial production process of Industry 4.0.

Design/methodology/approach: In order to evaluate the scale of potential interactions between intelligent machines and digital personnel, the author performs a structural, horizontal, and trend analysis of the current (2016–2018) and forecast (2019–2025) statistical data from the National Research University "Higher School of Economics" and PricewaterhouseCoopers (PwC).

Findings: It is determined that interactions between intelligent machines and digital personnel in the industrial production processes of Industry 4.0 will be based upon the mechanism of labor division. Routine functions will be performed by intelligent machines; AI and controlled robots, manipulators (possibly also controlled also humans), unmanned transport vehicles (also controlled by humans), and digital devices that are connected to the Internet of Things; while managerial functions in the cyber economy will be performed by digital personnel; AI engineers, digital marketing specialists, digital production managers, digital innovators, digital production engineers, and digital quality assurance specialists. This will increase labor efficiency and provide a balance between intelligent machines and digital personnel.

Originality/value: It is substantiated that due to the expected functional load of digital personnel and growth of demand for them in the industry of 2025 in the likelihood of social unrest due to mass unemployment of digital personnel is improbable. On the contrary, it is possible to expect growth in the quality of life of digital personnel who are involved in Industry 4.0.

A. V. Bodiako
Federal State-Funded Educational Institution of Higher Education "Financial University under the Government of the Russian Federation", Moscow, Russia

© Springer Nature Switzerland AG 2019

V. M. Filippov et al. (eds.), *The Cyber Economy*, Contributions to Economics,
https://doi.org/10.1007/978-3-030-31566-5_19

1 Introduction

The Fourth Industrial Revolution has started the process of digital modernization in all spheres of the economy. Industrial production is very susceptible to change, as it already has the largest level of automatization and minimum social interactions in its business processes. As of early 2019, the automatization of industry (on the basis of robotization) is happening around the world.

According to the calculations of the Russian export agency FB (2019), there are 70 robots per 10,000 employees on average in the world. The highest levels of the robotization of industry are observed in South Korea (631 robots per 10,000 employees), Singapore (488 robots per 10,000 employees), and Germany (309 robots per 10,000 employees). The highest rate of automatization of industry is observed in Asia (a 9% increase annually) and America (a 7% increase annually). Russia still has a very low level of industry robotization (1 robot per 10,000 employees).

The most well-known and successful examples of the automatization of industry (on the basis of robotization) are as follows AIN (2019):

- Using robots in metal production at *Canadian Metalworking* (Canada)
- Robotized metallurgical plants: *Teesside Beam Mill* (USA), *Corus Group Construction* (USA), and *Industrial Division* (USA)
- Robotized wood processing industry at *Willamette Valley Co.* (USA)
- Robotized packaging for industrial products at *Packaging World* (USA), *Yasakawa* (Japan), and *Robotics Tomorrow* (USA)
- Using robots in the paper industry for marking (sticking on labels) and wrapping at *Control Engineering* (USA) and *Pulp & Paper Canada* (Canada).

As is seen, the existing experience of automatization of industry is limited to certain countries (the USA, Canada, and Japan) and certain production business processes. The transition to the cyber economy theoretically requires the full automatization of industry covering all business processes. However, the scientific and theoretical basis for such a change has not yet been formed—there is no overall conceptual idea for the organization of automatized industrial production.

The most important problem in the context of developing the concept of automatized industrial production for Industry 4.0 is finding the right mechanism for the participation of an interaction between intelligent machines and digital personnel, which are the mandatory subjects of economic activities. This chapter seeks to develop such a mechanism.

2 Materials and Method

The advantages of the creation and implementation of intelligent machines are studied in detail in the works Date et al. (2019), Huang (2019), and Jaafari et al. (2019). Issues relating to the training and usage of digital personnel in the industrial

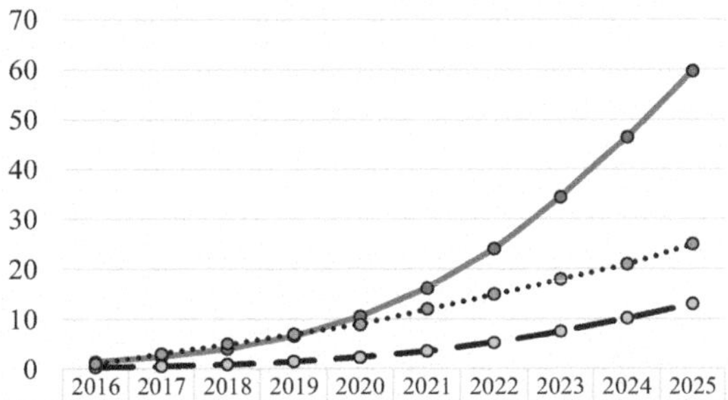

	2016	2017	2018	2019	2020	2021	2022	2023	2024	2025
Volume of the global market of AI, USD billion	1.4	2.4	4	6.6	10.5	16.2	24.1	34.4	46.5	59.7
Digital personnel interacting with AI, million people	0.31	0.53	0.89	1.46	2.30	3.55	5.28	7.54	10.19	13.08
Average global level of automatization (robotization) in the sphere of industry, %	1	3	5	7	9	12	15	18	21	25

Fig. 1 Forecast technological trends in the industrial production processes of Industry 4.0 under the conditions of the cyber economy until 2025. Source: Compiled by the authors based on the National Research University "Higher School of Economics" (2019)

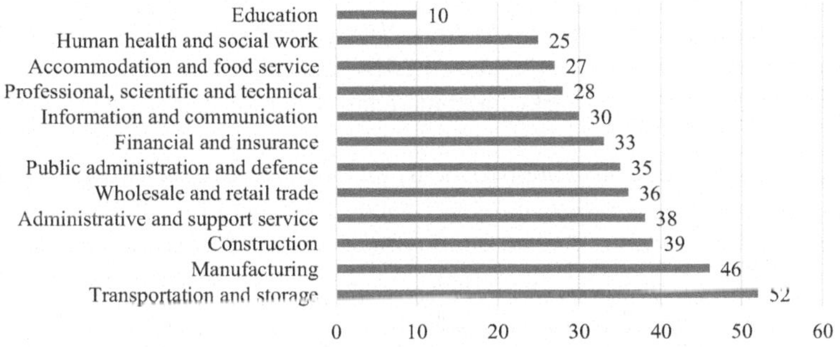

Fig. 2 Forecast levels of automatization in the economy by 2025. Source: Compiled by the authors based on PricewaterhouseCoopers (2019)

production processes of Industry 4.0 are studied thoroughly in the works Bogoviz (2019), Cominu (2018), Kissmer et al. (2018), Lampinen et al. (2018), Popkova (2019), Popkova and Sergi (2019), Popkova et al. (2019), Sukhodolov et al. (2018), and Wentrup et al. (2019).

However, the issue of interactions between intelligent machines and digital personnel is poorly studied. In order to evaluate the scale of such interactions, the author performs a structural, horizontal, and trend analysis of the current (2016–2018) and forecast (2019–2025) statistical data from the National Research University "Higher School of Economics" and PricewaterhouseCoopers (PwC). These are set out in Figs. 1, 2, and 3.

The data from Fig. 1 show that by 2025 the volume of the global market of AI will reach USD 59.7 billion, as compared to USD 6.6 billion as of early 2019, i.e., it will

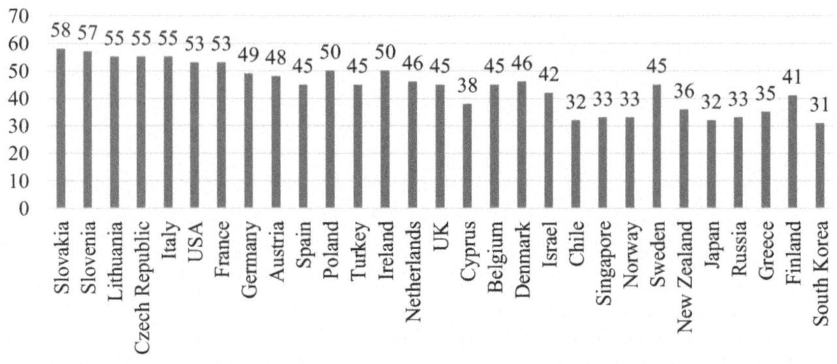

Fig. 3 Forecast level of automatization of industry by country in 2025. Source: Compiled by the authors based on PricewaterhouseCoopers (2019)

increase by 15 times. The average annual growth rate of this indicator for the period 2016–2025 constitutes 53%. By 2025, the average global level of automatization (robotization) in the sphere of industry will be 25% (compared to 5% in 2019). In 2025, more than 13 million digital personnel will be interacting with AI, having increased by 42 times as compared to early 2019 (0.31 million). The average annual growth rate of this indicator in the period 2016–2025 is 52%.

Figure 2 shows that the level of automatization of industry in 2025 will be very high—46%.

Figure 3 shows that the countries with the highest level of automatization of industry by 2025 will be in Slovakia (58%) and Slovenia (57%). In Russia, the level will reach 33%. Average global employment in the industrial sphere will be 14.4%—the highest among all spheres of economy (PricewaterhouseCoopers 2019). Therefore, although the automatization of industry will radically increase by 2025, it will not be accompanied by the mass ousting of humans from production processes but by an expansion in the interactions between digital personnel and intelligent machines.

3 Results

An analysis of the algorithm of industrial production processes in Industry 4.0 was made. The mechanism of interactions between intelligent machines and digital personnel, reflecting the specifics of each stage of this algorithm, is shown in Fig. 1.

As is seen from Fig. 4, an AI engineer conducts a preliminary (at the zero stage) and regular (at each following stage) setting. The first stage envisages the marketing of industrial products. AI interacts with the intelligent digital devices of consumers, and a digital marketing specialist interacts with consumers in the process of promotion (advertising, PR) and collection of orders (bulk and individual).

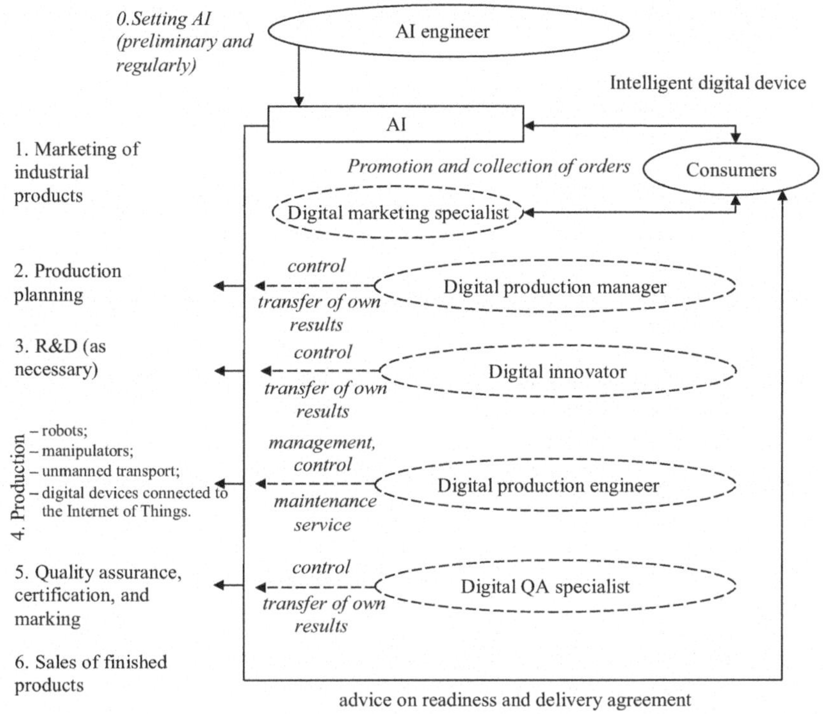

Fig. 4 The mechanism for interactions between intelligent machines and digital personnel in the industrial production processes of Industry 4.0 under the conditions of the cyber economy. Source: Compiled by the authors

The second stage envisages production planning, which is conducted by AI under control of a digital production manager who can correct its plans. The third stage includes R&D (As necessary, this is not a mandatory stage). A digital innovator controls the innovative activities of AI, conducts R&D, and transfers the results of AI. The fourth stage involves the production of industrial products. This process involves such intelligent machines as robots, manipulators, unmanned transport, and digital devices that are connected to the Internet of Things. A digital production engineer provides management, control, and maintenance services.

At the fifth stage, AI performs quality assurance (QA), certification, wrapping, and marking of finished industrial products under the control of digital QA specialist, who can also perform QA independently (product tests, etc.), passing results back to AI. The sixth stage envisages the collection of finished industrial products. AI informs consumers (or their intelligent digital devices) that their orders are ready and concludes delivery arrangements.

The competency-based characteristics of all identified digital personnel in the industrial production processes of Industry 4.0 are shown in Table 1, which also reflects the corresponding Russian specialities and standards of training for them (i.e., basic competencies), as well as additional digital competencies.

Table 1 Competency-based characteristics of digital personnel in the industrial production processes of Industry 4.0

Digital personnel	Correspondence of the modern nomenclature of specialities (federal educational standard of higher education of the Russian Federation, speciality)	Additional digital competencies	
AI specialist	090,000 Information and computing science (bachelor's and master's programs)	Technical device and AI programming	Knowledge of principles of work with AI (for interacting with intellectual machines)
Digital marketing specialist	380,000 Economics and management (bachelor's and master's programs)	Digital marketing	
Digital production manager	270,000 Management in technical systems (bachelor's and master's programs)	Using digital technologies of production planning	
Digital innovator	Sectorally specific—e.g., 290,000 Technologies of light industry (postgraduate program)	Using digital technologies of R&D	
Digital production manager	Sectorally specific—e.g., 290,000 Technologies of light industry (bachelor's and master's programs)	Using digital technologies of industrial production (equipment, manipulators, and unmanned transport)	
Digital QA specialist		Using digital technologies of QA	

Source: Compiled by the authors based on materials from the portal of Federal Educational Standards of Higher Education (2019)

Table 1 shows that apart from specific additional digital competencies, all-digital personnel will require knowledge of the principles of work with AI to enable interactions with intelligent machines. This presented competency-based set of characteristics for digital personnel is recommended for practical usage to modernize the federal educational standards of higher education of the Russian Federation in order to adapt them to the current needs of the developing cyber economy.

4 Conclusion

It was determined that interactions between intelligent machines and digital personnel in the industrial production processes of Industry 4.0 under the conditions of the cyber economy will be conducted through the mechanism of labor division. Routine functions will be performed by intelligent machines; AI and controlled robots, manipulators, unmanned transport vehicles, and digital devices that are connected to the Internet of Things.

Digital personnel—AI engineers, digital marketing specialists, production managers, digital innovators, digital production engineers, and digital QA specialists—will perform managerial functions. This will enable increasing labor efficiency while providing job satisfaction for digital personnel. Due to the functional load and expected demand for digital personnel in the sphere of industry by 2025, high levels of unemployment for such specialists are unlikely. On the contrary, it is possible to expect improvements to the quality of life that they will enjoy.

References

AIN (2019) Five examples of using robots in production. https://ain.ua/2017/10/16/5-primerov-ispolzovaniya-robotov-na-proizvodstve/. Accessed 01 March 2019

Bogoviz AV (2019) Industry 4.0 as a new vector of growth and development of knowledge economy. Stud Syst Decis Control 169:85–91

Cominu S (2018) Are we all knowledge workers? Upskilling and deskilling at the time of digital l [Tutti knowledge worker? Ricchezza e impoverimento dei lavori al tempo del digitale]. Sociologia del Lavoro 151:174–189

Date RC, Jesudasen SJ, Weng CY (2019) Applications of deep learning and artificial intelligence in Retina. Int Ophthalmol Clin 59(1):39–57

FB (2019) Robotization of production in the world: sphere of application, examples, pros and cons. http://fb.ru/article/406125/robotizatsiya-proizvodstva-v-mire-sfera-primeneniya-primeryi-plyusyi-i-minusyi. Accessed 01 March 2019

Huang A (2019) The era of artificial intelligence and big data provides knowledge services for the publishing industry in China. Publ Res Q 35(1):164–171

Jaafari A, Zenner EK, Panahi M, Shahabi H (2019) Hybrid artificial intelligence models based on a neuro-fuzzy system and metaheuristic optimization algorithms for spatial prediction of wildfire probability. Agric For Meteorol 266–267:198–207

Kissmer T, Knoll J, Stieglitz S, Gross R (2018) Knowledge workers' expectations towards a digital workplace. Americas conference on information systems 2018: digital disruption, AMCIS 2018 2(1):28–34

Lampinen A, Lutz C, Newlands G, Light A, Immorlica N (2018) Power struggles in the digital economy: platforms, workers, and markets. In: Proceedings of the ACM conference on computer supported cooperative work, CSCW, pp 417–423

National Research University "Higher School of Economics" (2019) Indicators of digital economy 2018: statistical bulletin. https://www.hse.ru/data/2018/08/20/1154812142/ICE2018.pdf.pdf. Accessed 01 March 2019

Popkova EG (2019) Preconditions of formation and development of industry 4.0 in the conditions of knowledge economy. Stud Syst Decis Control 169:65–72

Popkova EG, Sergi BS (2019) Will industry 4.0 and other innovations impact Russia's development? Exploring the future of Russia's economy and markets. Emerald, Bingley, UK, pp 34–42

Popkova EG, Ragulina YV, Bogoviz AV (2019) Fundamental differences of transition to industry 4.0 from previous industrial revolutions. Stud Syst Decis Control 169:21–29

PricewaterhouseCoopers (2019) Will robots really steal our jobs? An international analysis of the potential long term impact of automation. https://www.pwc.co.uk/economic-services/assets/international-impact-of-automation-feb-2018.pdf. Accessed 01 March 2019

Sukhodolov AP, Popkova EG, Litvinova TN (2018) Models of modern information economy: conceptual contradictions and practical examples. Emerald, Bingley, UK, pp 1–38

The Federal portal of federal educational standards of higher education (2019) Federal educational standards of higher education of the Russian Federation. http://fgosvo.ru/fgosvo/7/4/7. Accessed 02 March 2019

Wentrup R, Nakamura HR, Ström P (2019) Uberization in Paris – the issue of trust between a digital platform and digital workers. Crit Perspect Int Bus 15(1):20–41

Competition Between Intelligent Machines and Digital Personnel: The Coming Crisis in the Labor Market During the Transition to the Cyber Economy

Tatiana M. Rogulenko, Svetlana V. Ponomareva, and Taisiya I. Krishtaleva

Abstract *Purpose*: The purpose of the chapter is systemic study of the future labor market in the cyber economy in view of the influence of not only the demographic factor but also of the more important technological factor, which is connected to formation and increase of competition between intellectual machines and digital personnel.

Methodology: The authors determine the influence of the demographic and technological factors on the future of the Russian labor market. The authors perform analysis of statistical data for the Russian labor market, which allows forecasting further expansion of the spheres and popularization of automatization of the production and distribution processes in the Russian economy. Thus, the need for digital personnel will reduce, as their functions will be taken over by intelligent machines.

Results: It is determined that in modern Russia no efforts are made for assessment of the potential needs for digital personnel either at the government, university, or corporate levels. Training of digital personnel is announced as a strategic priority of the national program "Digital economy of the Russian Federation" dated July 28, 2017, No. 1632-r. In view of the determined highly probable negative influence of the technological factor (growth of competition of intelligent machines and digital personnel), it is possible to forecast a crisis of the Russian labor market in the future.

Conclusions: It is substantiated that a crisis is imminent in the Russian labor market: firstly, due to growth of competition of digital personnel under the influence of the increase of their number and, secondly, due to establishment and growth of

T. M. Rogulenko (✉)
Federal State Budgetary Educational Institution for Higher Professional Education "State University of Management", Moscow, Russia

S. V. Ponomareva
St. Petersburg State University of Economics (UNECON), St. Petersburg, Russia

T. I. Krishtaleva
Federal State-Funded Educational Institution of Higher Education "Financial University under the Government of the Russian Federation", Moscow, Russia

© Springer Nature Switzerland AG 2019
V. M. Filippov et al. (eds.), *The Cyber Economy*, Contributions to Economics,
https://doi.org/10.1007/978-3-030-31566-5_20

competition of intelligent machines and digital personnel. It is concluded that it is necessary to have state anti-crisis management of the Russian labor market.

1 Introduction

The future of the labor market in the conditions of the digital economy is influenced by two factors. First factor—demographic tendencies in the socioeconomic system, which determines the structure of digital personnel, their accessibility, and level of mastering of digital competencies. The population size of a country depends on the demographic state of its society, which is determined by external (exogenous) and internal (endogenous) factors. The forecast of the Federal State Statistics Service of the Russian Federation has various variants of the change of the total population and economically active population.

In the case of the most positive demographic development, the population of Russia will increase by 5.5 million by 2030, but there may still see a negative influence on the labor market in the form of a reduction of the number of economically active population by 3.1 million (the employed population will therefore decrease by 8.5 million, accordingly). This is due to a large increase in the elder share of the population. According to the forecast, both the economically active population and the number of people employed will reduce, negatively influencing the Russian labor market.

Such a decrease in the economically active population will lead to a decrease in offers in the labor market. The forecast of indicators for the employed population is also influenced by expected migration. Regardless of this forecasted migration, the number of the employed will total 3.6 million people by 2030. Based on the forecasted indicators, the number of the employed (without migration) in 2030 will decrease by 1.7 million people, as compared to 2020. If migration is included, it will grow by 0.9 million.

Given this data and in view of the forecasts, the number of people employed in the Russian labor market will decrease by 2030. In order to maintain the growth of economic indicators and be able to supply the labor market, it is necessary to preserve a stable flow of labor migration. It is necessary also to take into account the share and the level of qualification of digital personnel (representatives of various professions that could use the digital technologies) in the structure of economically active population, which, as of now, does not reach 1%.

Second factor—automatization of the production and distribution processes, which leads to a reduction of demand for digital personnel in the labor market due to competition between intelligent machines and digital personnel. Intelligent personnel will become an alternative (could replace) digital personnel in the future. The share of production and distribution processes that could be fully automatized—i.e., could be implemented without direct human participation (by intelligent machines)—and created advantages (e.g., higher precision and efficiency, as well as reduction of costs) will define the demand for digital personnel and opportunities of their employment in the future.

A gap in the existing research literature on the topic of studying the future labor market is separate consideration of two distinguished factors—which hinders the compilation of precise forecasts. This chapter seeks the goal of filling the gap and studying the future labor market in the cyber economy in view of the influence of not only the demographic factor but of the more important technological factor, which is connected to formation and increase of competition between intelligent machines and digital personnel. We offer a hypothesis that competition between intelligent machines and digital personnel could cause a crisis in the labor market during the transition to the cyber economy.

2 Materials and Method

The influence of the demographic factor in the future of the Russian labor market is moderately favorable. Sustainable economic development requires not only the formal filling of jobs but skilled employees who have the competencies for work in interdisciplinary areas, as the digital economy envisages hi-tech jobs. Education and qualifications are an important aspect of the modern requirements, so it is necessary to change to new employment policies and improvement mechanisms for the regulation of the labor market.

In order to prevent the emergence of social tension in the labor market, it is necessary to adopt legislation for the new emerging relationships of employment. A strategy for the development of the digital economy, to ensure the competitiveness and economic effectiveness of the country should stimulate economic well-being.

The implementation of new information technologies and "smart" labor tools means that only those who keep up with the times and even exceed them win (Slivina 2008). All countries are now engaged in a competitive struggle to benefit from the new opportunities offered by the digital economy. The UK claims leadership in the global hyperspace, which will allow it to raise socioeconomic parameters and potentially prosper. The UK believes that an increase of labor efficiency will lead to a large breakthrough in the market of labor resources, which will require people with high levels of competencies and will secure the full possibilities of the application of modern technologies. Strategic maneuvers of the UK include the usage of Big Data to develop systems for the statistical processing of information in the economy. New technologies enable an increasing level of trust in economic systems and the opening of new horizons on their application (Zavalko et al. 2018). Such intentions are clear, as the UK is also a leader in the application and usage of AI in the financial markets. Finance and cyberspace are now twins, and they cannot exist separately. It is impossible to now imagine banks or stock markets functioning without information technologies (Patapskaya 1997).

Singapore and the USA are the leading countries in the development of the digital economy. According to the global index of innovation (GII), Singapore is ranked sixth in the rating of innovative economies. Its government is striving to become "smart" nation, with the implementation of information technologies aimed at the improvement of the population's quality of life. The government is responsible for coordination of all actions in the application of the digital economy (Zavalko 2013). The presence of large venture capital and international financial corporations is a great competitive advantage for Singapore, which will stimulate the effective development, testing, and implementation of solutions in this direction.

China is ranked third in the production of hi-tech electronics, behind only the UK and Germany. In the aggregate turnover of the retail sector, China is ranked highly in e-commerce, with online sales accounting for 8.4% of all sales.

The Chinese government adopted a 10-year plan to address "economic imbalance" and sees the "smart" economy as a savior. By 2049, China aims to transform from the world's factory into the world's laboratory. The top-priority direction of development for the national IT industry is the provision of strategic security.

Russia is also making progress, despite its relatively low position of 41st in the international rating of readiness for the digital economy. Special attention in the Russian digital economy is paid to the legal regulation of relations and training of personnel for the digital economy. It aims to create at least ten leading companies in the sphere of digital technologies, able to compete in the global market. In the developed program one of the weaknesses is the absence of a strategic direction that determines the competitive advantage for leadership in one or several directions of the digital economy. President Putin set a completely new task: forming new markets by 2035 and creating conditions for the global technological leadership of Russia (Milner 2008).

Experts now call for constant progress in building Big Data, for the purpose of conquering new markets and obtaining leadership in this sphere. The program for the digital economy of the Russian Academy of Sciences supports the development of the end-to-end technology of Big Data, but has yet to find a common language that would unify science and technological development.

In view of the scale of growth of production and the complications of production interconnections in the Russian economy, increasing the volume of information that passes to top management makes it more difficult to process to make effective decisions. At the moment, the growth of labor expenses in servicing information processes is much faster than labor expenses in the real sector of economy. This system of management worked in the "old" regime, as managerial personnel dealt with document turnover (preparation of reports, etc.) (Zavalko and Ragulina 2013). However, this system simply stimulates the growth of erroneous information, which leads to bad decision-making.

Utilizing information technologies to automatize document turnover management is restrained by the growth of the number of managerial personnel. The chaotic growth of Big Data leads to high loads of personnel, additional paperwork, and an increase in the number of managerial personnel. In order to overcome this situation, it is necessary to implement the economic cyber system that would coordinate the activities of economic agents to achieve set goals in real time. Implementation of the economic cyber system will be seen as the start of managerial revolution (cyber revolution) (Matyunina et al. 2018).

In order to achieve Russia's set strategic goals with regard to the digital economy, a national program has been adopted by President Putin. Implementation of the program will stimulate the execution of strategic tasks until 2024. It is being enacted by the government programs "Information society," "Economic development and innovative economy," and in conjunction with sectoral government programs.

The program "National economy" includes the following aims:

- Formation of a new regulatory environment: "citizen–business–state"
- Creation of modern high-speed infrastructure for the storing, processing, and transfer of data
- Provision of security and sustainability for the functioning of the system
- A new system of personnel training
- Development of prospective digital technologies and projects for their implementation
- Effectiveness of state management and provision of state services through the implementation of digital technologies.

A federal project was developed for each aim of the program.

Let us consider in more detail the project, "Personnel for the digital economy."

The project envisages:

- Development of human potential
- Formation of an information space (based on citizens' needs for correct and authentic data)
- Development and usage of various educational technologies (remote and online teaching)
- Development and implementation of programs to partner Russian hi-tech organizations with higher education and their improvement
- Development of technologies for online interactions (between citizens, organizations, local administrations, etc.)
- Stimulation of Russian organizations to provide the conditions for remote employment
- Creation of systems to manage and monitor the populations public life, based on information and communication technologies.

The developed federal project "Personnel for the digital economy" is aimed at encouraging the development of the educational system, in which new modern infrastructure is created, personnel are trained, their advanced training and retraining are performed, and more effective mechanisms of management are created.

Increasing the digital literacy and competencies of citizens is based on a free online service, offering personal digital certificates. It aspires to obtain the following results:

- Ten million people will take online training programs for development of digital literacy (starting in 2019).

- At least 1 million people will undertake training in the government system for personal digital certificates for the development of competencies in the digital economy (starting in 2019).

The federal project envisages:

- Accepting 120,000 people for programs of higher education in IT-related subjects.
- Accepting 270,000 working specialists (managers of organizations, representatives of executive authorities) for training in competencies for the digital economy.
- Teaching 1 million people the competencies of the digital economy in the government system of personal digital certificates.
- Teaching 10 million people in online programs of development of digital literacy.
- Providing graduates of the system of professional education with key competencies for the digital economy.
- Providing support for 2000 projects for the development of educational technologies to support the digital economy.

The most important directions are as follows:

1. Supporting talented high school students and undergraduates in the sphere of informatics and mathematics.
2. Determining and supporting the best lecturers, postgraduates, and graduates of universities in the sphere of IT and mathematics.
3. Development and approbation of training simulators and virtual laboratories for studying informatics and mathematics.
4. Creation and functioning of a system of international scientific and methodological centers on the digital economy.

The necessity to compete in the new knowledge economy dictates new rules. It is necessary to increase the percentage of skilled personnel in the labor market. According to forecasts, there might be a large deficit of skilled personnel in Russia by 2025 (more than 10 million people). This deficit will include managers, doctors, engineers, and other specialists in various sectors; specialists with real knowledge, and competencies, who can conduct creative, analytical work and are able to make autonomous decisions (Ragulina and Zavalko 2013a, b).

Implementing such programs as “Russia 2025: from personnel to talents” shows that the only possibility for Russia to preserve a competitive position in the global economy is to perform a qualitative change in the labor market and to increase the percentage of skilled professionals through the implementation of the current scenario of rapid modernization.

Let us consider the system of the Danish researcher, J. Rasmussen, which is based on distributing all employees according to three categories: Rule, Skill, and Knowledge.

1. The "Rule" category includes people who perform manual labor.
2. The "Skill" category includes people who perform technical routine work and make decisions within certain rules (low-level managers, foremen, hotel administrators, ordinary economists, and lawyers, who are in abundance in Russia).
3. The "Knowledge" category includes people whose work consists mainly of analytical and creative tasks, improvisation, and the ability to take autonomous decisions.

According to the performed research, only 17% of working Russians belong to the 'Knowledge' category. According to this criterion, Russia is at the transitional stage between a resource economy and a knowledge economy (Metelev and Zavalko 2014). Japan, the USA, Germany, and Singapore are noted for high incomes, developed digital economies, and a high index of human development; the share of human resources in the "Knowledge" category in these countries exceeds 25%. This is one of the key indicators of any country's competitiveness.

Russia lags behind the leading countries. The reason is not a mass brain drain but the gap between skills (knowledge acquired at universities) and the real needs of the economy. According to the data of the performed research, 80% of the able-bodied population is not ready to work in modern markets. This is partially due to drawbacks of the educational system and partially due to personal qualities.

The primary task of Russia is the development of human capital, based on the criteria of education and personnel training.

The influence of the technological factor on the future of the Russian labor market is less favorable. This is connected to the already achieved high level of automatization of a lot of production and distribution processes in the Russian economy. Thus, according to the experts of the National Research University "Higher School of Economics" (2019), financial calculations in the electronic form are performed by 53.7% of Russian companies in 2019. Partial or full automatization of solution of organizational, managerial, and economic tasks is performed by 52.7% of Russian companies. 6.2% of Russian companies use RFID technologies during sales. On average, the annual growth of automatization of the production and distribution processes in Russia in 2019 constituted 15%, as compared to 2018.

The above statistical data allow forecasting further expansion of the spheres and popularization of automatization of the production and distribution processes in the Russian economy. Thus, the need for digital economy will be reducing, as their functions will be taken over by intelligent machines.

3 Results

Eight main steps for development of human capital in Russia are distinguished by the experts:

1. Creation of competitive offers for wages and labor conditions for professionals from the "Knowledge" category (employers with public participation).

2. Necessity for a reduction of the ineffective "social employment" program with redistribution of the salary fund in favor of the employees from the "Knowledge" category.
3. Implementation of a system to re-train dismissed personnel from other categories.
4. Creation of favorable conditions for doing business in Russia, including stimulating the development of innovative small companies.
5. Transformation of the educational system for training of employees of the "Knowledge" category.
6. Stimulation of talent in the sphere of education.
7. Reorientation of employees in professional training and development programs with a focus on lifelong learning.
8. Creation of a system to stimulate professional growth and obtain new knowledge.

The key direction in global competition for economic power and political influence is education.

Russia has been able to achieve significant success in this sphere, having set the task of turning the country into a respected member of global society. The President of the Russian Federation has introduced a large-scale systemic program to launch the digital economy, in which humans are the key element in the transition process. For Russians in the age of knowledge, there is a need for critical and creative thinking, activity, responsibility, adaptability, and innovativeness.

Digital competence is the confident and effective usage of information and communication technologies in all spheres of human activities: work, leisure, communication, etc. Initiative and entrepreneurial competencies are needed to turn ideas into action, the ability to plan and manage a project through creative thinking and an innovative approach while assessing risk.

The growth of digitization results in the need for better evaluation of efficiency and the effectiveness of human activities. The increasing usage of formalized regulations, procedures, and assessment processes; consultants and experts; and usage of automatized systems (the accumulation of large volumes of data for recording the activities of all members of an organization) are all responses to this.

Accumulated data on educational and professional activities and their evaluation form an individual's career digital history. It contains digital record books, diplomas, and certificates for attained educational levels, qualifications, recommendations, portfolios, a CV, and workbooks.

The digital economy also envisages an increase of quality of life, reductions in expenses for life necessities, the optimization of educational routes for citizens with handicaps, and usage of their human potential as a positive element of the digital economy.

In the educational sphere, the Program of training envisages unifying the following interconnected directions: formation of graduate's image, educational standards, programs, evaluation systems, methods and means of educational activities at all levels and in the whole structure of the educational process.

The competencies of the twenty-first century, including digital competence, form in the sphere of higher education, professional education, additional professional education, and in the process of professional and everyday activities. Refusal from application of digital technologies in certain elements of the educational process (applied in life in similar situations) will require special analysis and substantiation.

At the same time, in modern Russia there are no attempts to assess the future need for digital personnel at the government, university, or corporate levels. Training of digital personnel was proclaimed as a strategic priority of the national program "Digital economy of the Russian Federation" dated July 28, 2017, No. 1632-r. In view of the determined highly probable negative influence of the technological factor (growth of competition of intellectual machines and digital personnel), it is possible to forecast a crisis of the Russian labor market in the future.

The future number of digital personnel will not have enough time to return the investments into education (mastering of digital competencies) and will face the problem of low salary and unemployment. That is why there is a necessity for preventive measures of state support for employment of digital personnel, of which the most perspective is the conclusion of long-term (more than 15 years) labor contracts. This will allow reducing the future crisis of the Russian labor market.

4 Conclusion

As a result of the research, the offered hypothesis is proved. It is substantiated that a crisis could be expected in the Russian labor market—firstly, due to growth of competition among digital personnel under the influence of the growth of their number; secondly, due to establishment and growth of competition of intellectual machines and digital personnel. That is why there is a necessity for anti-crisis management of the Russian labor market, which is aimed at (1) informing the future digital personnel on the increasing competition in the labor market, (2) limiting (increase of current increasing) the future digital personnel—emphasis should be made not on their quantity but quality (level of mastering of digital competencies)—and (3) limiting the competition of intelligent machines and digital personnel.

References

Matyunina OE, Zavalko NA, Kozhina VO, Sokolov AA, Lebedeva OE (2018) Development of financial infrastructure in the system of state regulation of digital economy. Econ Entrep:26–29

Metelev SE, Zavalko NA (2014) Advancement in the aspect of regionalization of education. Life Sci J:129–132

Milner BZ (2008) "Knowledge economy" and new requirements to management. The issues of the theory and practice of management:108–120

National Research University "Higher School of Economics" (2019) Digital economy – 2019. Short statistical collection. https://www.hse.ru/data/2018/12/26/1143130930/ice2019kr.pdf. Accessed 25 July 2019

Patapskaya NA (1997) Economic aspects of development of the scientific and educational potential of higher school. Ural State Technical University, Omsk

Ragulina JV, Zavalko NA (2013a) Integration processes in the chain: science, higher vocational education and production, as a factor in increasing the competitiveness of the educational institution. Middle-East J Sci Res:161–166

Ragulina JV, Zavalko NA (2013b) Theoretical and methodical background of efficiency of educational services in the system of higher education. Life Sci J:199–204

Slivina TA (2008) Formation of a competitive personality of future specialist in the educational process of university, Krasnoyarsk, p 24

Zavalko NA (2013) Formation of qualitative aspects of higher professional education in the conditions of the market environment. Bull Acad:135–137

Zavalko NA, Ragulina YV (2013) Increase of effectiveness of interaction in the market of educational services. Bull Acad:126–128

Zavalko NA, Matyunina OE, Kozhina VO, Sokolov AA, Lebedev KA (2018) Digital economy and its influence on state and municipal management. Econ Entrep:101–104

The Development of the Agro-industrial Complex in the Cyber Economy

Irina A. Morozova and Tatiana N. Litvinova

Abstract *Purpose*: The purpose of the research is to determine the possible scenarios for the development of the agro-industrial complex (AIC) in the cyber economy of Russia and to determine the most optimal path forward from the perspective of the provision of national food security.

Design/methodology/approach: The authors use the method of scenario analysis, which allows a determination of the consequences for the national food security of Russia for various scenarios of development of the AIC. The forecasts are compiled for the period until 2024. The method of regression analysis is applied to determine the dependencies of key indicators for Russia's national food security—affordability, availability, quality, and safety—on the share of companies in the agro-industrial sector that performs innovations, and the cost volume of implemented fixed funds in this complex for the period 2009–2018 (the post-crisis period).

Findings: The authors determine the positive influence of innovative development (digital modernization) in the Russian AIC at the level of national food security. This leads to the conclusion that the most optimal scenario for the development of the AIC in the cyber economy of Russia is a transition to a cyber AIC, which envisages the highest level and systemic character of automatization and the use of the breakthrough digital technologies of Industry 4.0. Within the scenario that envisages a transition to a cyber AIC the maximum (100 points) value of the indicators of food security—price accessibility, guarantee of quality and security of food products, transparency of production and distribution, full-scale information support for interested parties, and free communication with manufacturers—will be achieved.

Originality/value: A conceptual model of cyber AIC is developed. It is recommended for practical application not only in modern Russia but also in other countries of the world.

I. A. Morozova (✉) · T. N. Litvinova
Volgograd State Technical University, Volgograd, Russia

© Springer Nature Switzerland AG 2019

V. M. Filippov et al. (eds.), *The Cyber Economy*, Contributions to Economics,
https://doi.org/10.1007/978-3-030-31566-5_21

1 Introduction

During the formation and development of the cyber economy it is necessary to pay close attention to the potential consequences of this process for key sectors of the economy, which include the agro-industrial complex (AIC), the functioning of which determines national food security. On the one hand, it is necessary to determine possible risks for the AIC in the cyber economy. These may include the risk that new technologies and innovative development through digitization may be difficult to implement. On the other hand, it is important to evaluate the possibilities for and potential advantages of the utilization of such new opportunities by the AIC. New digital technologies may stimulate the optimization of business processes of the AIC, thus increasing the effectiveness of entrepreneurial activities and ensuring food security, a central goal in the sphere of sustainable development. At the same time, it is necessary to take into account the national specifics of development of the AIC in the cyber economy, as large differences can be observed not only in the countries of different categories but also in different countries of the same category.

Thus, the current scientific and practical problem—and the aim of this chapter—is determining and comparing scenarios for the development of the AIC in modern economic systems. We offer the hypothesis that a positive scenario for such development in modern Russia is cyber AIC.

2 Materials and Method

Perspectives on the development of the AIC are thoroughly studied in the context of digital modernization and transition to Industry 4.0 in the works Altukhov et al. (2019), Bogoviz et al. (2019), Butorin and Bogoviz (2019), Popkova (2019), and Popkova and Sergi (2019). The scientific and practical recommendations for implementing certain digital technologies or the modernization of certain business processes in the AIC are offered in the works Huh and Kim (2018), Khaiturina et al. (2018), Kreneva et al. (2018), Matei et al. (2017), Pandithurai et al. (2018), and Weltzien (2016).

However, there is still no clear idea of the potential scenarios of the development of the AIC in the cyber economy, which complicates management decision-making and is a potential threat to food security.

The authors use the method of scenario analysis to study this problem. This tool allows us to evaluate the consequences for the national food security of Russia in various scenarios of the development of the AIC. Forecasts have been compiled up until 2024 (the planned year for the completion of digital modernization of the Russian economy according to the program "Digital economy of the Russian Federation").

Table 1 Dynamics of the indicators for the innovative development of the agro-industrial complex and Russian food security 2009–2018

	Percentage of companies of the AIC that implement innovations, %	Implementation of the fixed funds in the AIC, RUB million	Affordability, points 1–100	Availability, points 1–100	Quality and safety, points 1–100
Year	x_1	x_2	y_1	y_2	y_3
2009	8.3	282,736	50.5	43.7	53.8
2010	9.2	310,879	51.5	44.6	54.9
2011	11.2	380,133	53.6	46.4	57.2
2012	11.3	385,484	54.4	47.1	58.0
2013	12.5	424,285	59.9	51.8	63.9
2014	12.5	424,567	59.9	51.8	63.9
2015	12.2	449,408	61.8	53.4	65.9
2016	12.2	606,343	65.6	56.8	70.0
2017	13.2	657,792	69.1	59.8	73.7
2018	14.4	713,607	70.5	61.0	75.2

Source: Compiled by the authors based on Federal State Statistics Service of the Russian Federation (Rosstat 2019) and the Economist Intelligence Unit (2019)
AIC agro-industrial complex

Table 2 Regression dependence of the indicators of Russia's food security on the indicators of innovative development of the agro-industrial complex

Dependent variables	Models of multiple linear regression	Significances F of the models	Multiple R of the models
Affordability	$y_1 = 46.03 + 0.97*x_1 + 0.0004*x_2$	0.00001	0.9798
Availability	$y_1 = 39.85 + 0.84*x_1 + 0.0003*x_2$	0.00001	0.9599
Quality and safety	$y_1 = 49.10 + 1.04*x_1 + 0.0004*x_2$	0.00001	0.9485

Source: Calculated by the authors

The method of regression analysis is used to determine the dependencies of the indicators of Russia's national food security—affordability, availability, and quality and safety (as calculated by the Economist Intelligence Unit within the annual report 'The Global Food Security Index') on the percentage of companies in the AIC which implement innovations, and the cost volume of implemented fixed funds in this complex in the period 2009–2018 (the postcrisis period). The initial data for the regression analysis are given in Table 1, and results are provided in Table 2.

The data from Table 2 show that all compiled models of multiple linear regression are statistically significant at the level $\alpha = 0.05$, as significances F do not exceed 0.05, and multiple R exceed 0.90. This allows for these models to be used during scenario analysis.

3 Results

Based on the obtained regression models, we determined the characteristics for all distinguished scenarios of development of the AIC in the Russian cyber economy for the period until 2024:

- Scenario 1: preservation of the current technological mode of the AIC. Within this scenario, the percentage of companies that implement innovations and the cost volume of new fixed funds remains unchanged (at the 2018 level).
- Scenario 2: fragmentary digital modernization, which envisages growth in the innovative activity of some companies and the optimization of certain business processes on the basis of digital technologies (not necessarily breakthrough technologies). This could just involve a transition to better equipment and normal usage of the Internet, etc. Within this scenario, the percentage of companies that implement innovations will grow by 1.7 times, and the cost volume of new fixed funds will increase by 1.5 times.
- Scenario 3: transition to cyber AIC, which envisages the mass implementation of breakthrough digital technologies (blockchain, Internet of Things, AI, cloud technologies, etc.) and the creation of cyber-physical systems (Systemic digital modernization which covers all business processes). Within this scenario, the percentage of companies that implement innovations will grow by 2.7 times, and the cost volume of new fixed funds will grow by 3 times.

The results of the performed scenario analysis are given in Table 3.

Table 3 shows that scenario 3 provides the highest maximization of indicators for food security, through a full transition to cyber AIC. Let us consider an example of forecast evaluation of these advantages on the basis of affordability. In the model of multiple linear regression $y_1 = F(x_1,x_2)$, we put the percentage of companies of the AIC that implement innovations (40%) and the cost volume of new fixed funds (RUB 848,208 million). We then have $y_1 = 46.03 + 0.97*40 + 0.0004*848208 = 116.5$. The obtained value exceeds the maximum allowable level and is thus equaled to 100.

Scenario 3 will enable Russia to attain a sustainable growth of competitiveness for its AIC sector, achieve the goals of import substitution, increase of export of food, and maintain a high level of national food security. For successful practical implementation of this scenario, we developed the conceptual model of cyber AIC (Fig. 1), which should become a target landmark for Russian companies in the AIC sector and its state regulators.

Figure 1 shows that in cyber AIC, production is almost completely automatized. The intermediary food products constantly provide important information (e.g., temperature, growth, and chemical structure of soil at the stage of agricultural production; weight, volume, and nutritional value at the stage of production of food products in the food processing industry) to AI, as it is connected to ubiquitous computing and the Internet of Things.

AI controls unmanned vehicles (e.g., agricultural equipment and production equipment in the food industry), robots, and manipulators (though these could also

Table 3 Scenarios for the development of the AIC in the cyber economy of Russia until 2024

Characteristics of scenarios	Scenario 1 Preservation of the current technological mode of the AIC	Scenario 2 Fragmentary digital modernization of the AIC	Scenario 3 Cyber AIC
Production technology	Manual labor with some means of mechanization (machine equipment under human management)	Digital machine equipment	Cyber-physical systems (internet of things, ubiquitous computing, and AI)
Distribution technology		Manual labor with some means of mechanization	
Share of the AIC companies that implement innovations, %	14.4 (∗1)	25 (∗1.7)	40 (∗2.7)
Implementation of new fixed funds, RUB million	282,736 (∗1)	424,104 (∗1.5)	848,208 (∗3)
Affordability, points 1–100	70.5	86.1	Maximum: 100.0 (116.5)
Availability, points 1–100	61.0	74.6	Maximum: 100.0 (100.8)
Quality and safety, points 1–100	75.2	91.9	Maximum: 100.0 (124.3)
Qualitative treatment of competitiveness of the AIC	Critical reduction of competitiveness	Supporting competitiveness at the current level	Sustainable growth of competitiveness
Qualitative treatment of food security	Increase of dependence on imports, high risk of food crisis	Preservation of positive foreign trade balance, moderate risk of food crisis	Import substitution, increase of exports, high level of food security

Source: Calculated and compiled by the authors

be controlled by humans) in the production process. All information on food products is processed and sent to the proper digital node of the database of the AIC, which is organized on the basis of blockchain and cloud technologies.

All interested parties (intermediaries and consumers) have free access to the information database the possibility of highly effective processing of the information with the help of Big Data technologies. This enables full transparency of the production and distribution processes in cyber AIC and its control by the state regulators of economic activities in the cyber economy.

Interested parties can place orders for food products and leave feedback for the manufacturers. This ensures the supply of the required volume of food products at the required quality and with a guarantee of safety for the market. Thus, a high level of national food security is supported.

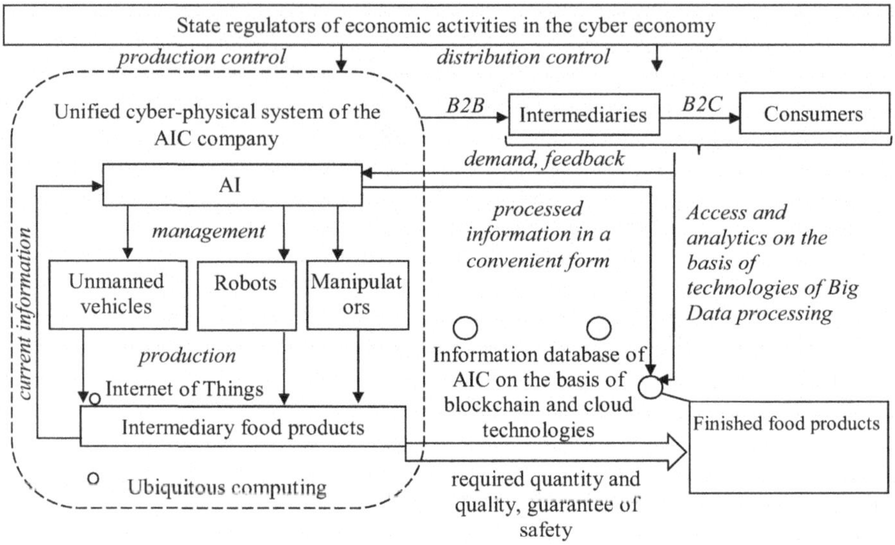

Fig. 1 The conceptual model of cyber AIC. Source: Compiled by the authors

4 Conclusion

The positive influence of innovative development (digital modernization) of the Russian AIC with regard to ensuring national food security has been determined. The most optimal scenario for the development of the AIC in the cyber economy of modern Russia is a transition to cyber AIC, which envisages the highest level and most systemic form of automatization and usage of the breakthrough digital technologies of Industry 4.0.

Within the scenario that envisages the transition to cyber AIC, the maximum (100 points) value of the indicators for food security will be achieved: price accessibility, a guarantee of quality and security of food products, as well as transparency of production and distribution and full-scale information support for interested parties and open communications with manufacturers. The developed conceptual model of cyber AIC is recommended for practical application in modern Russia and other countries.

References

Altukhov AI, Bogoviz AV, Kuznetsov IM (2019) Creation of an information system – a necessary condition of rational organization of agricultural production. Adv Intell Syst Comput 726:800–809

Bogoviz AV, Sandu IS, Demishkevich GM, Ryzhenkova NE (2019) Economic aspects of formation of organizational and economic mechanism of the innovative infrastructure of the EAEU countries' agro industrial complex. Adv Intell Syst Comput 726:108–117

Butorin SN, Bogoviz AV (2019) The innovative and production approach to management of economic subjects of the agrarian sector. Adv Intell Syst Comput 726:758–773

Federal State Statistics Services of the Russian Federation (Rosstat) (2019) Russia in numbers: statistical collection. http://www.gks.ru/wps/wcm/connect/rosstat_main/rosstat/ru/statistics/publications/catalog/doc_1135075100641. Accessed 22 March 2019

Huh J-H, Kim K-Y (2018) Time-based trend of carbon emissions in the composting process of swine manure in the context of agriculture 4.0. PRO 6(9):168

Khaiturina E, Kreneva S, Bakhtina T, Larionova T, Tsareva G (2018) Strategic benchmark of the digital economy in the region's agro-industrial complex. International Multidisciplinary Scientific GeoConference Surveying Geology and Mining Ecology Management, SGEM 18 (5.3):767–774

Kreneva S, Tsaregorodtsev E, Tereshina V, Sredina Y (2018) Agro-industrial complex in the conditions of development of digital society as the instrument of economic development of the region. International Multidisciplinary Scientific GeoConference Surveying Geology and Mining Ecology Management, SGEM 18(5.3):19–26

Matei O, Anton C, Bozga A, Pop P (2017) Multi-layered architecture for soil moisture prediction in agriculture 4.0. In: Proceedings of international conference on computers and industrial engineering, CIE, pp 65–79

Pandithurai O, Aishwarya S, Aparna B, Kavitha K (2018) Agro-tech: a digital model for monitoring soil and crops using internet of things (IOT). ICONSTEM 2017 – proceedings: 3rd IEEE international conference on science technology, engineering and management, 2018-January, pp 342–346

Popkova EG (2019) Preconditions of formation and development of industry 4.0 in the conditions of knowledge economy. Stud Syst Decis Control 169:65–72

Popkova EG, Sergi BS (2019) Will industry 4.0 and other innovations impact Russia's development? Exploring the future of Russia's economy and markets. Emerald, Bingley, UK, pp 34–42

The Economist Intelligence Unit (2019) The global food security index. https://foodsecurityindex.eiu.com. Accessed 22 March 2019

Weltzien C (2016) Digital agriculture – or why agriculture 4.0 still offers only modest returns. Landtechnik 71(2):66–68

Analysis and Forecasting of the Likely Development of the Digital Economy in Modern Russia

Nabi S. Ziyadullaev, Kobilzhon Kh. Zoidov, and Daler I. Usmanov

Abstract *Purpose*: The purpose of this chapter is to study socioeconomic problems and perspectives on the development of the cyber economy in modern Russia, as well as to present the results of research into the implementation of the program for the digital economy.

Design/methodology/approach: An analysis of data from a range of national and international reports, documents, and programs devoted to innovative development of the digital economy allowing an identification of the key vectors for the strategic development of socioeconomic processes of Russia.

Findings: The analysis shows that implementation of a complex program of digitization has serious obstacles to overcome, caused by factors that hinder the development of the key spheres of economy and a transition to the new technological mode (drawbacks in the regulatory and normative environment, low Internet coverage, insufficient implementation of digital technologies into the national system of education, low level of digitization in local administrations, growth of cybercrime rates, and insufficient effectiveness of scientific research connected to creation of prospective information technologies).

Originality/value: Requirements for the digitization of certain spheres of the economy are substantiated and characterized, and target indicators for implementing the program of the digital economy in Russia by 2024 are offered.

1 Introduction

According to the Federal program "Digital economy of the Russian Federation," the percentage of Russian citizens using broadband Internet was 18.77% in 2016. There were 159.95 cell phones per 100 people, and 71.29% of the population used mobile Internet. The average speed of the Internet in Russia increased by 29% (to 12.2 Mbit/s), and thus, according to this indicator, Russia is at the same level as France, Italy, and Greece. According to the Program, in 2017 the Russian market for commercial

N. S. Ziyadullaev (✉) · K. K. Zoidov · D. I. Usmanov
Market Economy Institute (MEI RAS), Moscow, Russia

© Springer Nature Switzerland AG 2019

V. M. Filippov et al. (eds.), *The Cyber Economy*, Contributions to Economics,
https://doi.org/10.1007/978-3-030-31566-5_22

centers for storing and processing data reached RUB 14.5 billion (an 11% increase as compared to 2016). This dynamic was largely caused by seven normative requirements on the storing of the personal data of Russian citizens. However, unlike most countries, Russia does not have standards of assessment at such centers and there is no objective possibility to evaluate the quality of provided services, or the volume of data stored. The market for cloud services is growing rapidly by around 40% annually.

The World Economic assesses readiness for the digital economy through the "Networked Readiness Index," last presented in their 2016 report, "Global information technologies." The improved index measures the level of economies' usage of the digital technologies for increasing the competitiveness and well-being of its citizens and evaluates the factors that influence the development of the digital economy.

According to this research, the Russian Federation is ranked 41st, lagging far behind the top 10 countries: Singapore, Finland, Sweden, Norway, the USA, the Netherlands, Switzerland, the UK, Luxembourg, and Japan. From the point of view of the economic and innovation gains from the usage of digital technologies, Russia is ranked 38th, again, far behind the leaders: Finland, Sweden, Israel, Singapore, the Netherlands, the USA, Norway, Luxembourg, and Germany (Alekseev 2018). Similar results are also noted in the World Bank's World Development Report (2016).

Such a large underrun in the development of the Russian digital economy can be explained by gaps in the normative basis for the digital economy and an insufficiently favorable environment for business and innovation. As a result, there is a low level of application of digital technologies by business structures.

The World Economic Forum's Global Competitiveness Report 2016–2017 emphasizes the special role investment in innovation plays in terms of the development of infrastructure, skills, and effective markets. Russia is ranked 43rd in the international rating, far behind the most competitive economies of the world: Switzerland, Singapore, the USA, the Netherlands, Germany, Sweden, the UK, Japan, Hong Kong, and Finland. The low level of innovation and underdevelopment of business, as well as insufficient development of state and private institutes and the financial markets are barriers to Russia's competitiveness in the global digital market.

2 Materials and Method

The theoretical and methodological basis of the research refers to the work of Gashenko et al. (2019), Sukhodolov et al. (2019), and Popkova and Ostrovskaya (2019). It uses the following methods: analysis, synthesis, comparison, statistical analysis of data on the share of the digital economy in the GDP of Russia and other countries, companies' investments into digitization, and graphic interpretation of data.

In order to analyze the development of the digital economy in the Russian Federation, as compared to the countries of the European Union and certain non-EU countries, it is possible to use the I-DESI index, published by the European Commission in 2016. The I-DESI index, developed from the DESI index for EU members, evaluates the effectiveness of the countries of the EU and of the EU as a whole, as compared to Australia, Brazil, Canada, Iceland, Israel, Japan, South Korea, Mexico, New Zealand, Norway, Russia, Switzerland, Turkey, and the USA. The I-DESI index uses data from various international sources: the OECD, the UN, the International Telecommunication Union and others.

The main components of the I-DESI index are communications, human capital, Internet usage, implementation of digital technologies in business, and digital services for the population. In terms of the development of the digital economy, The I-DESI index places Russia behind the EU, Australia, and Canada, but ahead of China, Turkey, Brazil, and Mexico. On the accessibility of fixed broadband Internet, Russia and the USA were ahead of the EU and other countries in 2016. In terms of human capital, Russia had a better position than the EU countries on average, Turkey, Mexico, and Brazil, but was behind Japan, South Korea, Sweden, Finland, the UK, and the leading countries of the EU. As to the frequency of Internet usage (daily and regularly, on average), Russia had low usage when compared to the EU, the USA, New Zealand, and Australia, but was ahead of China, Brazil, and Mexico. In the sphere of implementation of digital technologies by companies, Russia is far behind the EU and other countries and only slightly ahead of Turkey, China, and Mexico (Tsvetkov et al. 2018a, b).

The development of the digital economy in Russia lags behind the EU and the USA (Revolutionizing Business 2016), with the share of the digital economy as a percentage of the aggregate GDP of Russia currently constituting just 3.9% which is 2–3 lower than in the USA, China, the EU, and Brazil (The Future of Productivity 2015).

Table 1 shows that the digital expenditures of Russian households constitute 2.6% of Russia's GDP. Despite the fact that the contribution of the digital expenditures of households is significant as an indicator of the mastering of new technologies, figure is lower (on average) than leading countries (Shvab 2017).

Table 1 Contribution of the digital economy to Russia's GDP as compared to other countries, 2016 (Shvab 2017)

Country	share in GDP, %	Households' expenditures on digital products, %	Investments of companies in digitization, %	Government expenditures for digitization, %	Export of ICTs, %	Import of ICTs, %
USA	10.9	5.3	5.0	1.3	1.4	−2.1
China	10.0	4.8	1.8	0.4	5.8	−2.7
EU	8.2	3.7	3.9	1.0	2.5	−2.9
Brazil	6.2	2.7	3.6	0.8	0.1	−1.0
India	5.5	2.2	2.0	0.5	2.9	−2.1
Russia	3.9	2.6	2.2	0.5	0.5	−1.8

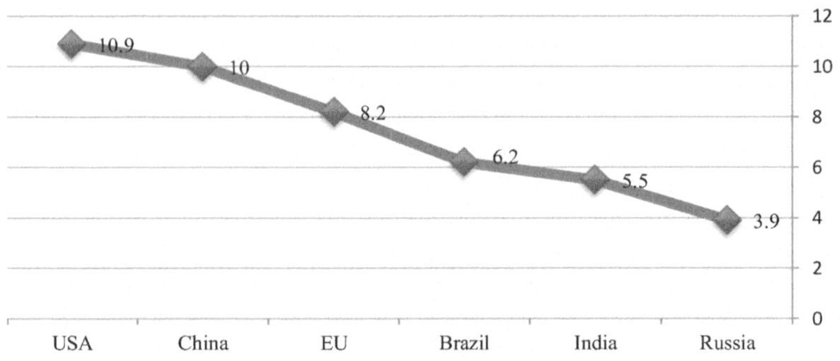

Fig. 1 Share of the digital economy as a percentage of GDP in Russia and other countries in 2016 (compiled by the authors based on Tsvetkov et al. 2018a, b)

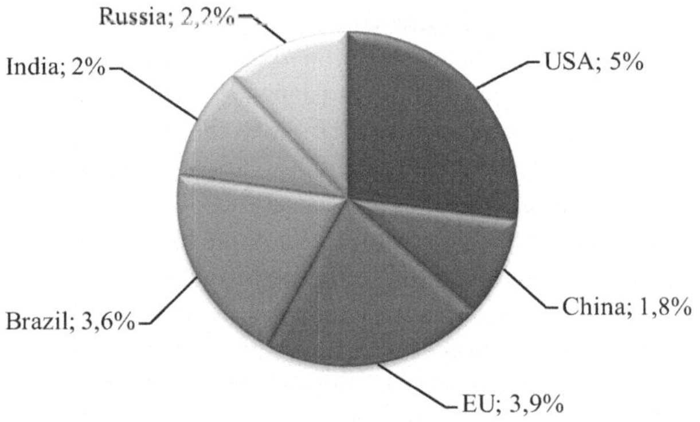

Fig. 2 Investments of companies in digitization in 2016, % (compiled by the authors based on Tsvetkov et al. 2018a, b)

The same could be said of the Russian business sector in terms of their use of digital technologies, investment into the usage of technology, increases in efficiency, and creation of new products and services (Fig. 1).

As we see from Fig. 2, in Russia, the volume of private companies' investments into digitization constitutes only 2.2% of GDP, while in the USA it is 5%, in Western Europe 3.9%, and in Brazil 3.6% (Coccia 2015).

This leads to reduction in the competitiveness of Russian companies in the global market, which is already at a low level due to the presence of a lot of foreign companies in the spheres of online trade, social networks, and search engines (Professionalnaya Nauka Publ 2018).

So, what problems could Russia face on its path to the digital economy? (Shomakhova 2017).

1. The low level of usage of information technologies in education
2. Absence of the necessary infrastructure for unique Russian products in the global marketplace, despite the fact that Russia has important innovations in the spheres of neurotechnologies, robototronics, and other areas of the digital economy

3. Undervaluation of current digital assets and their influence on the effectiveness of business growth as a whole, leading to low levels of application as compared to developed countries of the world.

In order to overcome these problems, it is necessary to create at the government level favorable conditions for the training and development of the young generation in the sphere of science, technology, and innovation, applying innovative forms of organization for educational, scientific, and research work.

The preconditions for the development of the digital economy in Russia include the following (Kungurov 2016):

- The traditional system of Russian education has a lot of opportunities for training creative specialists for the digital economy. This is very important, as in the conditions of the digital economy humans will be tasked with implementing the systemic organization of interactions with machines, who will perform only routine operations (Keshelava et al. 2017).
- There is a unique organizational and technological engineering opportunity for the development of a successful global infrastructure for industrial ecosystems in the digital economy (Gosbook 2016).
- Sanctions are a barrier to the appearance of new technologies and business models, created in the pre-digital era, in Russia.

Let us consider the forecast of the share of the digital economy as a percentage of Russia's GDP.

Figure 2 shows the positive dynamics of growth in the share of the digital economy in Russia's GDP; this tendency until 2020 could be described by the linear equation $y = 0.3859x - 0.9804$ with the approximation coefficient 0.9084—thus, if these dynamics are preserved, the share of the digital economy in Russia's GDP in 2020 will be at least 4.8% (Fig. 3).

Scenarios for the development of digitization in Russia are shown in Fig. 4.

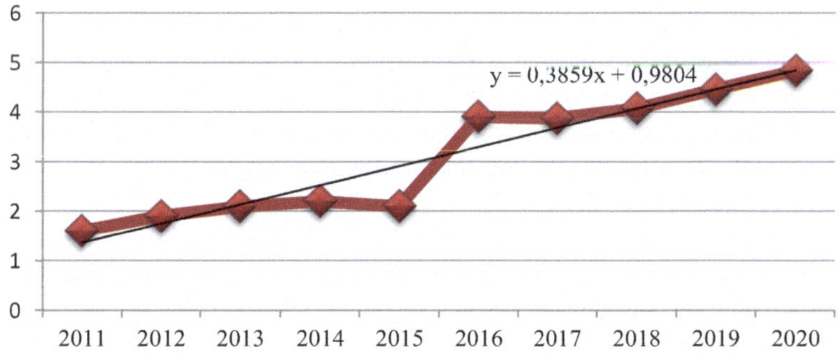

Fig. 3 The share of the digital economy in Russia's GDP in 2011–2016 and the forecast for the period up until 2020, %

Fig. 4 Scenarios for the development of digitization in Russia

Thus, Russia has the preconditions for the development of the digital economy, which will allow building high-quality niches for digital innovations, which can become leaders in the internal market and, with small expenditures, global leaders.

3 Results

The following factors hindering the digitization of Russian tasks of digitization are determined:

1. Drawbacks of the regulatory and normative environment. The program "Digital economy of the Russian Federation," adopted by the federal government in 2017, names the factors that hinder the digitization of Russia, including drawbacks in the regulatory and normative environment. In certain cases these create significant barriers to the formation of new institutes for the digital economy, the development of information and telecommunication technologies, and related types of economic activities.
2. Level of Internet usage in Russia. The level of usage of PC-based Internet in Russia is lower than in much of Europe; there is also a serious gap in digital skills between different population groups.
3. Insufficient implementation of digital technologies into the national system of education. In the Russian system of education the application of digital technologies is expanding. IT and information and communication technologies courses have been established in the programs of general education, and personnel for the digital economy are trained. However, the government program states that the

training of personnel and correspondence of educational programs to the needs of the digital economy is insufficient. There is also a serious deficit of personnel at all levels of education. The modern digital tools of educational activities are not used at a sufficient level in the procedures for final assessment.

4. Low level of digitization of local administrations. Serious problems can be seen in the application of information and telecommunication technologies at the level of local administration bodies. Only 10% of municipal entities conform to the requirements for digitization that are set out in the Russian laws.
5. Growth rate of cybercrimes. The rate of international cybercrime is increasing rapidly and requires urgent cyber security measures. There is insufficient scientific research into the creation of prospective information technologies to address this issue of low personnel provision in the sphere of information security.
6. The program for the digital economy in Russia. The federal program “Digital economy of the Russian Federation” was adopted by the Decree of the Government of the Russian Federation on July 28, 2017, No. 1632-r. This document determines the goals, tasks, directions, and terms of implementation of the main measures of the national policy on the creation of the necessary conditions for the formation of the digital economy.

According to Part I, the goals are as follows:

- Creating the ecosystem for the digital economy of the Russian Federation, in which data in the digital form are the key production factor in all spheres of socioeconomic activities and which ensures the effective, including transborder, interactions of business, the scientific and educational community, government, and citizens
- Creating the necessary and sufficient conditions of the institutional and infrastructural character, eliminating the existing obstacles and limitations for the creation and (or) development of hi-tech business, and preventing the emergence of new obstacles and limitations in the traditional spheres of economy and in new spheres and hi-tech markets
- Increasing the competitiveness in the global market of certain spheres of the Russian economy and the Russian economy as a whole.

The digital economy is presented as consisting of three levels, which, in their close interaction, influence the life of people and society as a whole:

- Markets and spheres of economy (spheres of activities), in which the interactions between specific subjects (suppliers and consumers of goods, works, and services) is conducted
- Platforms and technologies in which competencies for the development of markets and spheres of economy (spheres of activities) are formed
- An environment which creates the conditions for the development of platforms and technologies and effective interactions between market subjects and spheres of the economy (spheres of activities) and covers normative regulation, information infrastructure, personnel, and information security.

As effective development of markets and spheres (spheres of activities) in the digital economy is possible only with developed platforms, technologies, and an institutional and infrastructural environment, the government program focuses on two lower levels of the digital economy—the basic directions—determining the goals and tasks of development of:

- Key institutes within which the conditions for the development of the digital economy (normative regulation, personnel and education, formation of research competencies, and technological achievements) are created
- The main infrastructural elements of the digital economy (information infrastructure, information security).

In the government program, each direction of development of the digital environment and the key institutes takes into account support for the development of the existing conditions for the emergence of breakthrough and prospective end-to-end digital platforms and technologies and the creation of conditions for the emergence of new platforms and technologies. The main end-to-end digital technologies within the program are as follows: Big Data; neurotechnologies and AI; blockchain; quantum technologies; new production technologies; industrial Internet; components of robototronics and sensors; wireless technologies; and technologies of virtual and alternate realities. The list of these technologies is subject to change in the course of the emergence and development of other breakthroughs. These technologies and technological and sectoral projects are important from the point of view of the development of cooperation between Russian and foreign companies in the sphere of the digital economy (Tsvetkov et al. 2016).

Implementation of certain directions for economic spheres (spheres of activities), primarily in healthcare, the creation of "smart cities" and state management, including control and regulatory activities, will be conducted on the basis of supplementing the program "Digital economy" with corresponding plans and measures ("road maps") formed within the program.

Implementation of the program also requires the close interaction of the state, business sector, and science as the main result of its implementation should be the creation of at least ten leading national companies—hi-tech companies that develop end-to-end technologies and manage digital platforms which are competitive in the global market—and a system of start-ups, research groups, and sectoral companies that will ensure development of the digital economy.

Based on the performed analysis of the distinguished factors, the following perspective directions for the development of the digital economy in Russia are determined. In order to manage the development of the digital economy, the government program determines the goals and tasks for five basic directions in the Russian Federation until 2024. These basic directions are normative regulation, personnel and education, formation of research competencies and technical achievements, information infrastructure, and information security.

3.1 Normative Regulation

The main goal of the direction concerning normative regulation is the formation of a new regulatory environment that ensures a favorable legal regime for the emergence and development of modern technologies and for the implementation of economic activities that are related to their usage. The following measures are proposed:

- Creation of a regular mechanism for the management of change and competencies (knowledge) in the regulation of the digital economy
- Cancelling of key legal limitations and the creation of separate legal institutes aimed at solving the primary tasks for the formation of the digital economy
- Formation of a complex legislative regime for the regulation of new relationships that appear due to the development of digital economy
- Measures for the stimulation of economic activities that are connected to the use of modern technologies and the collection and usage of data
- Formation of a policy on the development of the digital economy within the territory of the Eurasian Economic Union (EEU), and harmonization of approaches to normative legal regulation that stimulate the development of the digital economy within the EEU
- Creation of the methodological basis for the development of competencies in the sphere of regulation of the digital economy.

There is a necessity for the normative and legal regulation of most of the measures that are to be implemented for the achievement of the set goals within the basic and applied directions for the development of the digital economy. The development and implementation of the concepts for primary, mid-term, and complex measures to improve the legal regulation of the digital economy within the direction for normative regulation makes it important to consider the proposals for the normative and legal regulation of other basic and applied directions, which envisage close interaction between created competencies with the center of competencies, to ensure effective monitoring and improvement of the legal regulation of the digital economy.

The main goals of the direction on personnel and education are as follows:

- Creation of the key conditions for the training of personnel for the digital economy
- Improvement of the system of education that has to provide the digital economy with competent personnel and provide the labor market with human resources that conform to the requirements of the digital economy
- Creation of a system of motivation for mastering the necessary competencies and participation of personnel in the development of the Russian digital economy.

3.2 Formation of Research Competencies and Technological Achievements

The main goal of the direction on the formation of research competencies and technological achievements is to create a system of support for research and applied research in the sphere of the digital economy (a research infrastructure for digital platforms), which ensures technological independence for each end-to-end digital technology that is competitive at the global level. The following measures are offered:

- Formation of an institutional environment for the development of R&D in the sphere of the digital economy
- Formation of technological achievements in the sphere of the digital economy
- Formation of competencies in the sphere of the digital economy.

3.3 Target Indicators for Implementing the Program for the Digital Economy in Russia by 2024

The planned characteristics of the Russian digital economy are to be achieved through the achievement of the following indicators by 2024.

The ecosystem of the digital economy:

- Successful functioning of at least ten leading companies that are competitive in global markets
- Successful functioning of at least 10 sectoral digital platforms for the main spheres of economy (including for digital healthcare, digital education, and "smart cities")
- Successful functioning of at least 500 small- and medium-sized companies in the sphere of creating digital technologies and platforms and provisions for digital services

Personnel and education:

- The number of graduates from higher educational organizations in subjects connected to information and telecommunication technologies will increase to 120,000 annually.
- The number of graduates from higher and secondary vocational education who possess competencies in the sphere of information technologies at the average global level will increase to 800,000 annually.
- The share of population with digital skills will increase to 40%.

Formation of research competencies and technological achievements:

- The number of implemented projects in the sphere of the digital economy (with a minimum value of RUB 1 billion) will be 30.
- The number of Russian organizations that participate in the implementation of large projects (with a value of USD 3 million or more) in top-priority directions of international scientific and technological cooperation in the sphere of the digital economy will be 10.

To manage the development of the digital economy, the government program has formed a "road map," which includes descriptions of the goals, key landmarks, and tasks to be completed for all directions. The "road map" will be the basis for the development of a plan containing description of all measures that are necessary to achieve specific landmarks in the federal program, with specifications of the responsible parties and sources and volumes of financing. The plan of measures will be adopted for an initial 3-year period, after which it will be updated annually. The "road map" envisages three main stages in the development of the directions of the digital economy, as a result of which the target state for each direction is to be reached.

In the government program, each direction for the development of the digital environment and key institutes takes into account support to improve existing conditions for the emergence of breakthrough and end-to-end digital platforms and technologies and the creation of conditions for the emergence of new platforms and technologies. As Russia has a competitive advantage in the defense and space industries, it is expedient to focus on developments for hi-tech production. There are successful examples already. Russian Space Systems has fully automatized its production: from initial concept to sales and utilization. Severstal uses innovative technologies at steel factories, implementing "smart" machines and information systems.

Russia should use the existing transitional period in the global economy to enter new socio-innovative and technological markets, in order to ensure a competitive position. Thus, as the performed research shows, the digital economy becomes an inseparable part of everyday life. One cannot imagine human activities today without electronic technologies. From communication and purchases to the issue of goods and corporate functions—everything relies on the digital environment (World Bank 2016).

The publications of the OECD (Organization for Economic Cooperation and Development) use the term "digital economy" for markets that function on the basis of information and communication technologies that are used for trading information and digital goods or providing services via the Internet (The Future of Productivity 2015). V. Ivanov gave the widest definition of the term: "...Digital economy is a virtual environment which supplements our reality" (RIA Novosti 2018). The formation of the digital economy requires supportive conditions for the creation of new digital technologies and the application of the leading innovative models for the organization of business, trade, logistics, and production (Billon et al. 2016).

4 Conclusion

Thus, the performed analysis and forecasting of the likely development of the digital economy in modern Russia shows that implementation of a complex program of digitization has serious obstacles to overcome, caused by factors that hinder the development of the key spheres of economy and a transition to the new technological mode (drawbacks in the regulatory and normative environment, low Internet coverage, insufficient implementation of digital technologies into the national system of education, low level of digitization in local administrations, growth of cybercrime rates, and insufficient effectiveness of scientific research connected to creation of prospective information technologies).

References

Alekseev I (2018) Digital economy: peculiarities and tendencies of development of online interaction. https://intelaktive-peus.ru. Accessed 04 March 2019

Billon M, Lera-Lopez F, Marco R (2016) ICT use by households and firms in the EU: links and determinants from a multivariate perspective. Rev World Econ:629–654

Coccia M (2015) General sources of general purpose technologies in complex societies: theory of global leadership-driven innovation, warfare and human development. Technol Soc:199–226

Gashenko IV, Zima YS, Davidyan AV (2019) Optimization of the taxation system: preconditions, tendencies and perspectives. https://link.springer.com/book/10.1007%2F978-3-030-01514-5. Accessed 22 June 2019

Gosbook (2016) Development of digital economy in Russia. http://gosbook.ru/node/94904. Accessed 04 March 2019

Keshelava AV, Budanov VG, Rumyantsev VY (2017) Introduction into digital economy. In: All-Russia research institute of geological, geophysical, and geochemical systems, p 28

Kungurov D (2016) Russians to face digital economy. Utro.ru. https://utro.ru/articles/2016/12/04/1307336.shtml. Accessed 04 March 2019

Nizhny Novgorod. Professionalnaya Nauka Publ (2018) Development of digital economy in Russia as the key factor of economic growth and increase of population's standards: monograph. Nizhny Novgorod. Professionalnaya Nauka Publ, p 230

Popkova EG, Ostrovskaya VN (2019) Perspectives on the use of new information and communication technology (ICT) in the modern economy. https://link.springer.com/book/10.1007%2F978-3-319-90835-9. Accessed 22 June 2019

Program (2017) "Digital economy of the Russian Federation". Decree of the government of the Russian Federation no. 1632-r dated July 28, 2017

Revolutionizing Business (2016) Harvard business review. International digital economy and society index (I-DESI). European Commission

RIA Novosti (2018). https://ria.ru/science/20170616/1496663946.html. Accessed 04 March 2019

Shomakhova ZA (2017) Digital economy – successful future. Volume: problems and perspectives of economic development of regions. Collection of articles of all-Russia scientific and practical conference devoted to 45th anniversary of the Institute of Economics and Finance, p 180

Shvab K (2017) The fourth industrial revolution. E Publ., Moscow, p 16

Sukhodolov AP, Popkova EG, Litvinova TN (2019) The main components of well-balanced information economy. https://www.emeraldinsight.com/doi/abs/10.1108/978-1-78756-287-520181022. Accessed 22 June 2019

The Future of Productivity (2015) Preliminary version. The new high-tech strategy. Innovations for Germany. Federal Ministry of Education

Tsvetkov VA, Stepnov IM, Kovalchuk YA, Zoidov KK (2016) Dynamics of development of economic systems. In: Tsvetkov VA (ed) Central Economic Mathematical Institute of the Russian Academy of Sciences/Institute of Market Issues of the Russian Academy of Sciences, p 380

Tsvetkov VA, Zuyadullaev NS, Zoidov KK, Yankauskas KS (2018a) Problems and perspectives of development of the digital economy in Russia. Strategic trends of transformation of socio-economic systems within the digital economy. In: Tsvetkov VA, Zoidov KK (ed) Proceedings of the international scientific and practical conference. February 27–28, 2018. Institute of Market Issues of the Russian Academy of Sciences, Moscow, pp 207–215

Tsvetkov VA, Loginov EL, Zoidov KK (2018b) Digitization in Russia. Research work report. Institute of Market Issues of the Russian Academy of Sciences, p 30

World Bank (2016) World development report 2016. "Digital dividends". https://openknowledge.worldbank.org/bitstream/handle/10986/23347/210. Accessed 04 March 2019

An Algorithm for the Crisis-Free Transition of Modern Socioeconomic Systems to the Cyber Economy

Arsen S. Abdulkadyrov and Irina Y. Eremina

Abstract *Purpose*: The purpose of the chapter is to develop an algorithm for the crisis-free transition of the modern socioeconomic systems to cyber economy.

Design/methodology/approach: The case method is used to review modern economic systems and to determine the need and readiness for starting the process of a transition to the cyber economy in developed and developing countries. The statistical data of the IMD, the World Bank, and the World Economic Forum as of early 2019 are used. In order to cover both developed and developing countries (ensuring the representativeness of the selection), the authors study the top 10 countries from the first half of the rating (1–10) and the top 10 countries from the second half of the rating (31–40) with regard to digital competitiveness.

Findings: It is substantiated that the process of transition of the modern socioeconomic systems to the cyber economy is largely determined by the national specifics. A universal algorithm of a crisis-free transition to the cyber economy is offered.

Originality/value: Recommendations are made in the sphere of crisis management for the cyber economy (at its formative stage and in its development and functioning), which conform to the current needs of both developed and developing countries.

1 Introduction

The cyber economy will be formed on the basis of the Fourth Industrial Revolution. However, the transition of the modern socioeconomic system to the cyber economy will cause a deep bifurcation and result in a high susceptibility to crises. From the position of the theory of economic cycles, even when the transitional period is

A. S. Abdulkadyrov (✉)
Federal State Institution of Science Institute of Social and Political Research of the Russian Academy of Sciences, Moscow, Russia

I. Y. Eremina
Gubkin Russian State University (NIU) of Oil and Gas, Moscow, Russia

© Springer Nature Switzerland AG 2019
V. M. Filippov et al. (eds.), *The Cyber Economy*, Contributions to Economics,
https://doi.org/10.1007/978-3-030-31566-5_23

completed, socioeconomic systems will likely remain prone to cyclic fluctuations and crises of a different character.

Firstly, economic crises that are connected to a reduction in the rate of economic growth as a result of a reduction of business activity are caused by an unfavorable market situation. It should be noted that in the conditions of the Fourth Industrial Revolution economic crises will influence not only economic systems that have transitioned to the cyber economy (developed countries) but also economic systems that have not digitally modernized and retain the previous technological mode (developing countries). However, such economic crises will manifest themselves differently. The reasons for economic crises in countries that have embraced the cyber economy could include the unprofitability of investments due to insufficient marketing support or high competition in the global markets for hi-tech (low market prices and the impossibility of influencing them), while in developing countries, the critical decline of competitiveness (low demand for domestic products in internal and external sectoral markets) may well be difficult to overcome.

Secondly, social crises as a result of opposition to the transformational processes that will take place due to the formation of the cyber economy will be a factor. The anticipated growth of unemployment and changes in the conditions for the purchase and consumption of goods and services are potential trigger points. It should be noted that in developed countries the potential scale of social crises is lower (due to the local character of unemployment and successive changes in the conditions for the purchase and consumption of goods and services) than in developing countries, where unemployment has a potentially massive impact (due to the total decline of business activity in economy), and the conditions for the purchase and consumption of goods and services will be changed rapidly and unexpectedly (without preliminary preparation) in the course of the appearance of foreign suppliers from developed countries in their domestic markets.

Thirdly, ecological crises, which consist of the critical aggravation of the state of the environment due to the depletion of natural and energy resources, are likely to proliferate. Developed countries might be the first to face such ecological crises. However, in the future, they will affect developing countries, that, due to the low competitiveness of domestic manufacturers of goods and services, will have to specialize in the supply of natural and energy resources to the global markets (bearing the highest ecological costs).

To support the stability of the cyber economy and its well-balanced and sustainable development in the long term, it is necessary to consider its crisis management. Therefore, an important task is to develop an algorithm for a crisis-free transition of the modern socioeconomic systems to the cyber economy.

2 Materials and Method

The potential for economic crises in the process of digital modernization is emphasized in the works of Curran (2018), Duhăneanu and Marin (2014), Ipcioglu (2015), and Murdock (2017). Certain issues related to the crisis management of modern economic systems in the process of digital modernization are offered in the publications of Bogoviz (2019), Popkova (2019), Popkova and Sergi (2019), Popkova et al. (2019), and Sukhodolov et al. (2018). Serious drawbacks in the research on this issue in the existing scientific literature are as follows:

- Crises and measures in the sphere of crisis management are limited by the stage of transition of modern economic systems to the cyber economy (the process of digital modernization).
- It is supposed that crises will influence only developed countries, which implement digital modernization, and the measures for crisis management are developed specifically for them.
- Studying crises and offering measures for crisis management are limited to the economic and social spheres, while the ecological sphere is poorly studied.

Therefore, there is a need for comprehensive research on crises, a substantiation of the perspectives covered, and the development of recommendations in the sphere of crisis management for the cyber economy that covers all stages, from its formation, to its development and functioning and incorporates the risks for both developed and developing countries.

The case method is used in this chapter to review modern economic systems and to determine the need and readiness for starting the process of a transition to the cyber economy in developed and developing countries. The statistical data of IMD, the World Bank, and the World Economic Forum as of early 2019 are used.

The data selected includes the countries with the highest level of digital competitiveness. However, in order to cover both developed and developing countries (and thereby ensuring the representativeness of the selection), the authors selected the top 10 countries from the first half of the rating (1–10) and the top 10 countries from the second half of the rating (31–40) of digital competitiveness. The results are presented in Table 1.

According to the data of Table 1, most of the countries from top 10 of the first half of the rating (1–10): Singapore, Sweden, Denmark, Switzerland, Norway, and the UK, have a moderate need for the cyber economy and a high readiness for it. Other developed countries with a high readiness for the cyber economy also have a high need for it: the USA (due to the high energy-output ratio of the economy—5.41 MJ/ $2011 PPP GDP), Finland (due to a high unemployment level—8.25% of work force, and a high energy-output ratio of the economy—6.37 MJ/$2011 PPP GDP), and Canada (due to a high energy-output ratio of the economy—7.34 MJ/$2011 PPP GDP).

Most of the developed countries from top 10 of the second half of the rating (31–40): Spain, Portugal, Czech Republic, Slovenia, Lithuania, Poland, and

Table 1 Results of a review of modern economic systems as to the need and readiness for the cyber economy as of early 2019

Country	Index of digital competitiveness, points 1–100	Index of global competitiveness, points 1–7	Unemployment level, % of work force	Energy intensity level of primary energy, MJ/$2011 PPP GDP	Total natural resources rents, % of GDP	Need for the cyber economy	Readiness for the cyber economy, type of country
USA	100.00	5.85	4.04	**5.41**	0.28	High	High, low performing
Singapore	99.422	5.71	1.84	2.39	0.00	Moderate	High, progressive
Sweden	97.453	5.52	6.32	4.27	0.41	Moderate	High, progressive
Denmark	96.764	5.39	5.36	2.61	0.50	Moderate	High, progressive
Switzerland	95.851	5.86	4.78	2.19	0.01	Moderate	High, progressive
Norway	95.724	5.40	3.89	3.75	5.81	Moderate	High, progressive
Finland	95.248	5.49	**8.25**	**6.37**	0.57	High	High, low performing
Canada	95.201	5.35	5.87	**7.34**	1.01	High	High, low performing
Netherlands	93.884	5.66	3.79	3.94	0.37	Moderate	High, progressive
UK	93.239	5.51	4.00	3.02	0.39	Moderate	High, progressive
Spain	74.272	4.70	**14.55**	3.33	0.06	High	Low, low performing
Portugal	73.441	4.57	**7.35**	3.34	0.26	High	Low, low performing
Czech Republic	71.499	4.77	2.07	5.51	0.12	Moderate	Low, progressive
Slovenia	71.427	4.48	6.22	4.58	0.26	Moderate	Low, progressive
Lithuania	69.172	4.58	6.92	3.86	0.38	Moderate	Low, progressive
Poland	68.557	4.59	4.36	4.15	0.82	Moderate	Low, progressive

Chile	68.377	4.71	7.01	3.78	**10.50**	High	Low, low performing
Kazakhstan	65.504	4.35	5.07	**7.92**	**15.04**	High	Low, low performing
Thailand	65.272	4.72	1.27	5.41	1.21	Moderate	Low, progressive
Russia	65.207	4.64	5.06	**8.41**	**11.46**	High	Low, low performing

Bold type denotes a critically low value for that indicator that shows a serious deficit of that country and their high need for the cyber economy
Source: Compiled by the authors based on IMD (2019), World Bank (2019), World Economic Forum (2019)

Thailand, have a moderate need for the cyber economy and a low readiness for it. Developing countries with a high need for the cyber economy but low readiness for it include Spain (due to its high unemployment level—14.55%), Portugal (due to its high unemployment level—7.35%), Chile (due to its specialization in minerals production, the rent of which constitutes 10.50% of GDP), Kazakhstan (due to the high energy-output ratio of the economy—7.92 MJ/$2011 PPP GDP—and specialization in minerals production, the rent of which constitutes 15.04% of GDP), and Russia (due to the high energy-output ratio of the economy—8.41 MJ/$2011 PPP GDP, and specialization in minerals extraction, the rent of which constitutes 11.46% of GDP).

3 Results

We developed a universal algorithm for the crisis-free transition of modern socio-economic systems to the cyber economy, which could be used by both developed and developing countries (Fig. 1).

As is seen from Fig. 1, each of the stages of the algorithm is preceded by monitoring of the current economic system (an example is given in Table 1). As a result of the monitoring, which precedes the first stage, the need for the cyber economy is determined (it conforms to the period of digital modernization of the economic system).

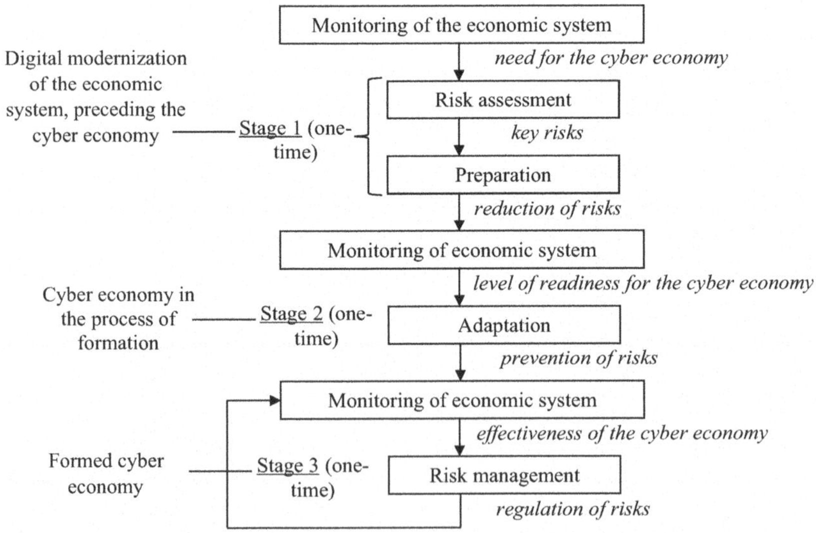

Fig. 1 The algorithm for the crisis-free transition of the modern socioeconomic system to the cyber economy. Source: Compiled by the authors

Table 2 shows the recommended framework measures for the crisis management of the transition to the cyber economy according to the economic system and in view of the stages of the algorithm for different types of countries.

As is seen from Table 2, the key economic risk for developed countries is the non-return of investment into digital modernization. Crisis management is connected to digital businesses gaining the "scale effect." Monitoring is aimed at determining the return on investment. Risk assessment involves strategic analysis of global demand for the products of a domestic digital business. Preparation is connected to the placement of government orders for the products of digital business. Adaptation envisages the stimulation of domestic and global demand (including international agreements on foreign economic activities at the government level) for the products of domestic digital business. Risk management in the formed cyber economy is connected to support for the transnationalization of domestic digital business.

The key economic risk for developing countries is the decline of competitiveness. Crisis management is connected to innovative development and starting the process of digital modernization. Monitoring is aimed at determining the level of global competitiveness of the economy. Risk assessment envisages determining the priorities for the innovative development of digital business. Preparation is connected to the stimulation of R&D into digital business. Adaptation envisages limiting foreign competition in the sphere of hi-tech. Risk management in the formed cyber economy is connected to the stimulation of innovative activity in domestic digital business.

The key social risks (for countries of both types) are unemployment and social protest. Crisis management is connected to the provision of social support for the cyber economy. Monitoring is aimed at determining unemployment levels and qualitative (sociological) analysis of the public mood. Risk assessment envisages strategic analysis of the labor educational markets. Preparation is connected to modernization of educational standards. Adaptation envisages social support (welfare benefits) and the stimulation of labor mobility (retraining, advanced training). Risk management of the formed cyber economy is connected to the stimulation of lifelong learning.

The key ecological risk (for countries of both types) is the environmental cost of socioeconomic growth and development of the cyber economy. Crisis management is connected to reduction of environmental costs. Monitoring is aimed at determining the value of environmental costs. Risk assessment envisages the strategic analysis of such costs. Preparation is connected to raising environmental standards. Adaptation envisages control over compliance of the adopted standards. Risk management in the formed cyber economy is connected to stimulation of green innovations.

Table 2 Crisis management measures for the transition to the cyber economy according to the economic system and in view of the stages of the algorithm for different types of countries

Stage of transition to the cyber economy	Stage of the algorithm of crisis management	Measures of crisis management as to the spheres of economic system			
		Economic		Social	Ecological
		Developed	Developing countries		
Key risk	Without any connection to the stage	Non-return of investments	Decline of competitiveness	Unemployment, social protest	Ecological costs of growth and development
Monitoring	Precedes each stage	Return of investments	Level of competitiveness	Unemployment level, public mood	Volume of ecological costs
Digital modernization of economic system, which precedes the cyber economy	Risk assessment	Strategic analysis of global demand	Determining the priorities of innovative development	Strategic analysis of the labor and educational markets	Strategic analysis of ecological costs
	Preparation	Government order	Stimulation of R&D	Modernization of educational standards	Increase of ecological standards
Cyber economy in the process of formation	Adaptation	Stimulation of demand	Limitation of foreign competition	Social support, stimulation of labor activities	Control over observation of ecological standards
Formed cyber economy	Risk management	Support for transnationalization of business	Stimulation of innovative activity	Stimulation of lifelong learning	Stimulation of green innovation

Source: Compiled by the authors

4 Conclusion

It is possible to conclude that the process of the transition to the cyber economy is unique to each country and largely predetermined by national specifics. However, the universal algorithm offered by the authors for the crisis-free transition of modern socioeconomic systems to the cyber economy aims to offer solutions. The authors provide framework recommendations in the sphere of crisis management, covering all spheres of the economic system, for the formation, development, and functioning of the cyber economy.

References

Bogoviz AV (2019) Industry 4.0 as a new vector of growth and development of knowledge economy. Stud Syst Decis Control 169:85–91

Curran D (2018) Risk, innovation, and democracy in the digital economy. Eur J Soc Theory 21 (2):207–226

Duhăneanu M, Marin F (2014) Digital agenda for Europe – risks and opportunities in a digital economy. Qual Access Success 15:57–66

IMD (2019) World digital competitiveness ranking 2018. https://www.imd.org/wcc/world-competitiveness-center-rankings/world-digital-competitiveness-rankings-2018/. Accessed 04 March 2019

Ipcioglu I (2015) A comparative analysis of knowledge management practices in times of crisis in the digital age: evidence from an emerging economy. Int J Soc Ecol Sustain Dev 6(1):1–16

Murdock G (2017) Communication, crisis and control: economies, ecologies and technologies of digital times. Medijska Istrazivanja 23(2):17–34

Popkova EG (2019) Preconditions of formation and development of industry 4.0 in the conditions of knowledge economy. Stud Syst Decis Control 169:65–72

Popkova EG, Sergi BS (2019) Will industry 4.0 and other innovations impact Russia's development? Exploring the future of Russia's economy and markets. Emerald, Bingley, pp 34–42

Popkova EG, Ragulina YV, Bogoviz AV (2019) Fundamental differences of transition to industry 4.0 from previous industrial revolutions. Stud Syst Decis Control 169:21–29

Sukhodolov AP, Popkova EG, Litvinova TN (2018) Models of modern information economy: conceptual contradictions and practical examples. Emerald, Bingley, pp 1–38

World Bank (2019) Indicators: environment. https://data.worldbank.org/topic/environment?view=chart. Accessed 04 March 2019

World Economic Forum (2019) The global competitiveness report 2017–2018. http://www3.weforum.org/docs/GCR2017-2018/05FullReport/TheGlobalCompetitivenessReport2017–2018.pdf. Accessed 04 March 2019

The Possibilities for Cyber Management Based on Cyber-Physical Systems in the Context of the Formation of a New Model of Development

Nikita A. Lebedev, Svetlana V. Zubkova, and Nataliya A. Stanik

Abstract *Purpose*: The purpose of the chapter is to examine the possibilities for cyber management based on cyber-physical systems in the context of the formation of a new model of development.

Design/methodology/approach: The research is performed with the help of regression analysis. The authors determine the regression dependence of the indicators for the competitiveness of the public (first pillar: Political and regulatory environment) and corporate (second pillar: Business and innovation environment) management of the indicators for the usage of new information and communication technologies in business (seventh pillar: Business usage), government (eighth pillar: Government usage), and the economy as a whole (ninth pillar: Economic impacts). The work is based on data and empirical materials in The Global Information Technology Report 2016, prepared by the World Economic Forum. The research objects are 20 countries, comprising the top 10 (1–10, developed countries) and the second (31–40, developing countries) in the World Digital Competitiveness Ranking for 2018, compiled by the IMD (63 countries in total are rated).

Findings: It is substantiated that the possibilities for cyber management based on cyber-physical systems in the context of the formation of a new model of development are substantial. The key directions for automatized state management are monitoring and control, statistical accounting, determining violations of the law, information and consultation support, and provision of state services. The key directions for automatized corporate management are economic accounting and reporting, production management, personnel management, and marketing management.

Originality/value: The developed structural and logical scheme of cyber management based on cyber-physical systems shows that such systems could be created at both the micro- and macro-levels using end-to-end (currently actively being developed) digital technologies of Industry 4.0: Internet of Things, AI, and

N. A. Lebedev (✉)
Institute of Economics of the Russian Academy of Sciences Moscow, Moscow, Russia

S. V. Zubkova · N. A. Stanik
Financial University under the Government of the Russian Federation, Moscow, Russia

© Springer Nature Switzerland AG 2019
V. M. Filippov et al. (eds.), *The Cyber Economy*, Contributions to Economics,
https://doi.org/10.1007/978-3-030-31566-5_24

Ubiquitous Computing. This could help to provide the expected advantages and support the announced principles of a new model of development: transparency, accessibility, and full openness of state management, as well as the effectiveness, flexibility, and integration of corporate management.

1 Introduction

In the modern postcrisis global economic system, the formation of a new model of development for socioeconomic systems is taking place, which conforms to the principles of sustainability—stable economic growth and increased attention on environmental issues—global competitiveness, social justice, and public well-being. This new model of development sets new priorities for the subjects of socioeconomic system management.

The priorities for state management are, firstly, transparency in the state regulation of economy. Decisions regarding the state management of socioeconomic systems should be based on general logic and conform with the interests of most interested parties, have full-scale information support, and be made only with a high level of stakeholder involvement. Secondly, state services should be widely accessible to all. They should be delivered with the minimum financial and time expenditure for the recipient, and offer convenience for all interested parties. Thirdly, state management should offer full coverage for its economic subjects, which requires systemic interactions between economic subjects and state regulators.

The priorities of corporate management are, firstly, the high effectiveness of entrepreneurial activities as a whole and within separate business processes in particular. This envisages optimizing the usage of resources. Secondly, corporations require high flexibility and adaptability to dynamically changing global market environments. Modern entrepreneurial structures have to be open and capable of transforming if necessary. Thirdly, there is a need for the integration of business processes and business systems. Internal and external communications in entrepreneurial structures have to be continuous.

Despite the general acknowledgment of the necessity for a transition to a new model of development of socioeconomic systems, a serious barrier to its practical implementation is the human factor (the source of irrational behavior by economic subjects damaging to their own interests, and public benefit), which predetermines the preservation of a large shadow sector of the economy, which cannot be controlled and which reduces the controllability of the system on the whole (to avoid the risk of an increase in the size of the shadow economy, the tax load is redistributed to other economic subjects, etc.).

An important scientific and practical problem is how to limit the influence of the human factor on the process of managing modern socioeconomic systems. Here we offer a working hypothesis that this problem could be solved by a transition to the cyber economy, which opens up the possibility of automatization (and, therefore, rationalization). The purpose of the chapter is to substantiate the possibilities for cyber management based on cyber-physical systems in the context of the formation of a new model of development.

2 Materials and Method

The essence and mechanisms for the functioning of cyber-physical systems are studied in detail in the works of Delicato et al. (2019), Leng et al. (2019), Li et al. (2019), Nikolakis et al. (2019), and Skowroński (2019). Based on a content analysis, cyber-physical systems here are defined as totalities of integrated physical objects (technical devices) and biological objects (e.g., plants, humans, and animals) with online databases under the control of AI as the basis of the means of electronic communication, the most popular mode of which is the Internet of Things.

The possibilities for the practical application of cyber-physical systems as part of Industry 4.0 are discussed in the works of Bogoviz (2019), Popkova (2019), Popkova et al. (2019), and Popkova and Sergi (2019). However, a comprehensive conceptual approach to the structure of cyber management based on cyber-physical systems is absent and predetermines the necessity for further research.

Our working hypothesis here is verified with the help of regression analysis. The authors determine the regression dependence of the indicators for the competitiveness of public (first pillar: Political and regulatory environment) and corporate (second pillar: Business and innovation environment) management on the indicators for the usage of new information and communication technologies in business (seventh pillar: Business usage), government (eighth pillar: Government usage), and the economy as a whole (ninth pillar: Economic impacts). The source of our data and empirical materials is The Global Information Technology Report 2016, prepared by the World Economic Forum.

The research objects are 20 countries from the top 10 (1–10, developed countries) and the second (31–40, developing countries) parts of the World Digital Competitiveness Ranking for 2018, compiled by the IMD (63 countries in total are rated). This ensures the representativeness of the selection (coverage of both developed and developing countries from different regions of the world). The initial data for analysis are given in Table 1, and the results are given in Tables 2 and 3.

Based on the data of Table 2, the authors compiled a model of multiple linear regression: $y_1 = 0.35 + 0.42*x_1 + 0.28*x_2 + 0.24*x_3$. According to this model, the competitiveness of state management grows by 0.42 points due to growth in the usage of information and communication technologies in business by 1 point, by 0.28 points due to growth in the usage of information and communication technologies in government; and by 0.24 points due to growth in the usage of information and communication technologies in the economy as a whole. Significance F and all r-values do not exceed 0.05—therefore, regression dependencies are correct at the significance level $\alpha = 0.05$. Multiple $R = 0.9578$—therefore, the change of the dependent variable by 95.78% is explained by the change of independent variables.

Based on the data of Table 3, a model of multiple linear regression is compiled $y_1 = 2.27 + 0.10*x_1 + 0.38*x_2 + 0.11*x_3$. According to this model, growth in the usage of information and communication technologies by business by 1 point leads to growth in the competitiveness of corporate management by 0.10 points; growth in the usage of information and communication technologies by government leads to

Table 1 Indicators on the use of information and communication technologies and the global competitiveness of management in selected developed and developing countries with the highest ratings of digital competitiveness in 2018

Category	Country	First pillar: Political and regulatory environment	Second pillar: Business and innovation environment	Seventh pillar: Business usage	Eighth pillar: Government usage	Ninth pillar: Economic impacts
		y_1	y_2	x_1	x_2	x_3
Digital competitiveness ranks 1–10	USA	5.2	5.5	5.9	5.4	5.8
	Singapore	5.9	6.0	5.4	6.3	5.9
	Sweden	5.5	5.2	6.0	5.0	6.1
	Denmark	5.3	5.3	5.7	4.7	5.1
	Switzerland	3.2	3.4	3.2	2.7	2.3
	Norway	5.7	5.4	5.5	5.2	5.4
	Finland	5.8	5.4	5.8	5.0	6.1
	Canada	5.4	5.5	4.9	5.1	5.2
	Netherlands	5.6	5.4	5.8	5.4	5.8
	UK	5.7	5.5	5.2	5.4	5.3
Digital competitiveness ranks 31–40	Spain	4.0	4.8	3.9	4.7	4.0
	Portugal	4.4	5.1	4.2	4.8	4.1
	Czech Republic	4.3	4.6	4.3	3.4	4.1
	Slovenia	3.8	4.9	4.3	3.6	4.1
	Latvia	4.2	5.0	4.1	4.3	4.0
	Poland	3.9	4.6	3.6	3.6	3.6
	Chile	4.3	5.2	3.9	4.6	3.5
	Kazakhstan	4.0	4.5	3.6	4.8	3.8
	Thailand	3.7	4.6	3.9	3.8	3.2
	Russia	3.6	4.5	3.6	4.4	3.7

Source: Compiled by the authors based on the IMD (2019)

Table 2 Regression dependence of the competitiveness of state management on the usage of information and communication technologies

Regression statistics						
Multiple R						0.9578
R-square						0.9173
Adjusted R-square						0.9018
Standard error						0.2759
Observations						20
Dispersion analysis						
	df	SS	MS	F	Significance F	
Regression	3	13.5193	4.5064	59.1878	7.00396E-09	
Residual	16	1.2182	0.0761			
Total	19	14.7375				
	Coefficients	Standard error	t stat	P-value	Lower 95%	Upper 95%
Intercept	0.3510	0.4872	0.7204	0.4817	−0.6819	1.3838
x_1	0.4239	0.2495	1.6992	0.0109	−0.1050	0.9528
x_2	0.2728	0.1385	1.9698	0.0066	−0.0208	0.5663
x_3	0.2414	0.2559	0.9432	0.0360	−0.3011	0.7839

Source: Calculated and compiled by the authors

Table 3 Regression dependence of the competitiveness of corporate management on the usage of information and communication technologies

Regression statistics						
Multiple R						0.9093
R-square						0.8268
Adjusted R-square						0.7944
Standard error						0.2547
Observations						20
Dispersion analysis						
	df	SS	MS	F	Significance F	
Regression	3	4.9544	1.6515	25.4647	2.48333E-06	
Residual	16	1.0376	0.0649			
Total	19	5.9920				
	Coefficients	Standard error	t stat	P-value	Lower 95%	Upper 95%
Intercept	2.2668	0.4496	5.0412	0.0001	1.3135	3.2200
x_1	0.1051	0.2302	0.4563	0.0065	−0.3830	0.5932
x_2	0.3832	0.1278	2.9981	0.0085	0.1122	0.6541
x_3	0.1096	0.2362	0.4640	0.0065	−0.3911	0.6103

Source: Calculated and compiled by the authors

growth in the competitiveness of corporate management by 0.38 points; and growth in the usage of information and communication technologies in the economy as a whole leads to growth in the competitiveness of corporate management by 0.11 points. Significance F and all r-values do not exceed 0.05—therefore, regression dependencies are correct at the significance level $\alpha = 0.05$. Multiple R = 0.9093—therefore, the change of the dependent variable by 90.93% is explained by the change of independent variables.

3 Results

The determined positive influence of new information and communication technologies on the competitiveness of management in the economy became the basis for developing a structural and logical scheme of cyber management based on cyber-physical systems (Fig. 1).

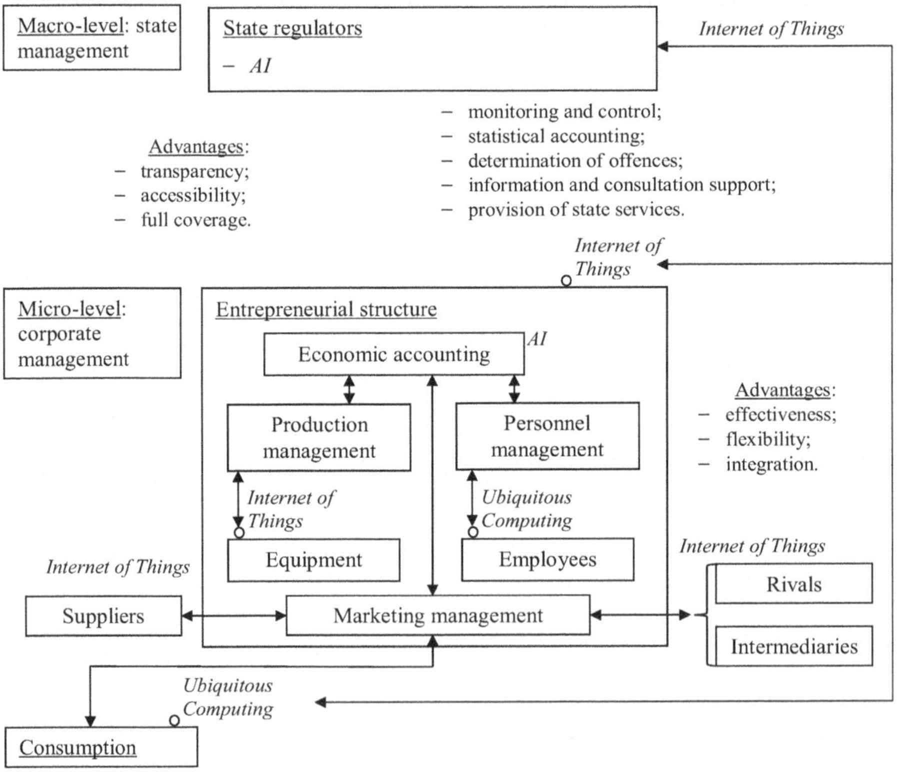

Fig. 1 A structural and logical scheme of cyber management based on cyber-physical systems (Source: Compiled by the authors)

Figure 1 shows that corporate management in the cyber economy (at the micro-level of the socioeconomic system) could be fully automatized. All production equipment could be connected to the Internet of Things, which would ensure automatized production management, which would in turn allow optimizing the spending of resources and determining equipment failures. The employees could be equipped with ubiquitous computing, which would ensure intellectual support for personnel management, to enable signs of decreases in labor efficiency (e.g., tiredness, aggravation of health, etc.) to be quickly identified. This could be useful in projects requiring teamwork or when using hazardous materials. Marketing management and communications and relations with consumers, suppliers, intermediaries, and rivals could also be also automatized through the use of Ubiquitous Computing and the Internet of Things. Financial accounting could be also automatized on the basis of AI.

State management (at the macro-level of a socio-economic system) could be automatized to a large extent. AI, the Internet of Things, and Ubiquitous Computing allow the formation of cyber-physical systems on a national scale able to conduct automatized state monitoring and control of the economy, statistical accounting, compliance with the law, and the provision of information and consultation support and government services.

4 Conclusion

It has been substantiated that the possibilities for cyber management based on cyber-physical systems in the context of the formation of a new model of development are substantial. The key directions for automatized state management are monitoring and control, statistical accounting, compliance with the law, information and consultation support, and provision of state services. The key directions of automatized corporate management are financial accounting and reporting, production management, personnel management, and marketing management.

Cyber-physical systems at both the micro- and macro-levels could be created using end-to-end digital technologies of Industry 4.0 (actively in development at the present time): the Internet of Things, AI, and Ubiquitous Computing, as shown by the developed structural and logical scheme for cyber management based on cyber-physical systems. This will provide the expected advantages and ensure that the proclaimed principles of the new model of development: transparency, accessibility, and full coverage of state management, as well as the effectiveness, flexibility, and integration of corporate management are achieved.

References

Bogoviz AV (2019) Industry 4.0 as a new vector of growth and development of knowledge economy. Stud Syst Decis Control 169:85–91

Delicato FC, Zhou X, Wang KI-K, Guo S (2019) Special issue: advances and trends on cognitive cyber-physical systems. Ad Hoc Netw 88:1–4

IMD (2019) World digital competitiveness ranking 2018. https://www1.imd.org/globalassets/wcc/docs/imd_world_digital_competitiveness_ranking_2018.pdf?MRK_CMPG_SOURCE=wcc. Accessed 15 March 2019

Leng J, Zhang H, Yan D et al (2019) Digital twin-driven manufacturing cyber-physical system for parallel controlling of smart workshop. J Ambient Intell Humaniz Comput 10(3):1155–1166

Li XX, He FZ, Li WD (2019) A cloud-terminal-based cyber-physical system architecture for energy efficient machining process optimization. J Ambient Intell Humaniz Comput 10(3):1049–1064

Nikolakis N, Maratos V, Makris S (2019) A cyber physical system (CPS) approach for safe human-robot collaboration in a shared workplace. Robot Comput Integr Manuf 56:233–243

Popkova EG (2019) Preconditions of formation and development of industry 4.0 in the conditions of knowledge economy. Stud Syst Decis Control 169:65–72

Popkova EG, Sergi BS (2019) Will industry 4.0 and other innovations impact Russia's development? Exploring the future of Russia's economy and markets. Emerald, Bingley, pp 34–42

Popkova EG, Ragulina YV, Bogoviz AV (2019) Fundamental differences of transition to Industry 4.0 from previous industrial revolutions. Stud Syst Decis Control 169:21–29

Skowroński R (2019) The open blockchain-aided multi-agent symbiotic cyber-physical systems. Futur Gener Comput Syst 94:430–443

The Methodology of Decision Support for the Entrepreneurial Sector in the Information Asymmetry of the Cyber Economy

Olga E. Akimova, Elena M. Vitalyeva, Natalia V. Ketko, Alexey F. Rogachev, and Natalia N. Skiter

Abstract *Purpose*: The authors interpret the cyber economy (digital economy) as business activities in which information becomes the primary factor of production, as well as that part of economic relations which is mediated by the development of the Internet and digital communication in the field of information.

Design/methodology/approach: The authors perform analysis of the factors of production in the cyber economy and determine the current problems for the business sector, which are connected to imperfection of governmental regulation in the cyber economy. Modeling of the behavior pattern of the market entity and information asymmetry in the goods and services market is performed.

Findings: The authors develop the scientific and methodological provision of the decision-making process in the cyber economy, which includes the algorithm of this process (which reflects its sequence and logical structure) and formulas for evaluating its efficiency at the corresponding stages.

Originality/value: The authors determine that information asymmetry will be present in any market. In the business sector, however, it should be minimized. This can be achieved through thorough control over information on the part of the state, nonprofit organizations, and people engaged in socially important areas of activities (in educational, medical organizations, etc.), as well as through the support of the decision-making process. It is difficult to reduce information asymmetry in the market economy, but the complexity is simplified in the course of transition to the cyber economy due to the large number of information transmission and dissemination channels.

O. E. Akimova (✉) · E. M. Vitalyeva · N. V. Ketko · A. F. Rogachev · N. N. Skiter
Volgograd State Technical University, Volgograd, Russia

© Springer Nature Switzerland AG 2019

V. M. Filippov et al. (eds.), *The Cyber Economy*, Contributions to Economics,
https://doi.org/10.1007/978-3-030-31566-5_25

1 Introduction

The authors interpret the cyber economy (digital economy) as business activities in which information becomes the primary factor of production, as well as that part of economic relations which is mediated by the development of the Internet, and digital communication in the information field. The key differences of the cyber economy from the customary economy are shown in Figs. 1 and 2, from the perspective of the economic factors of production.

The economic factors of production are replaceable. In classical economics, when the price of one factor of production increases it is replaced by another. This being said, a different picture can be observed in the cyber economy.

Business activities are carried out in the cyber economy by means of information, information and communication technologies, as well as scientific–technological progress, one of the factors for the development of which is the presence of entrepreneurial skills.

Entrepreneurship has been recognized as one of the driving forces of the digital economy, on a par with major corporations in developed Western countries, and the level of development of the business sector as such directly depends on realizing its potential. This "potential" has been called "entrepreneurial potential"; it has developed on the basis of labor potential, and it has long been perceived as a variety of it. However, the transition to the cyber economy, encouraged by the independent development of entrepreneurial potential, has shaped its characteristic features which depend on the nature of a particular type of activity and the specifics of the economic system, which makes it possible to subsume it under a separate economic category.

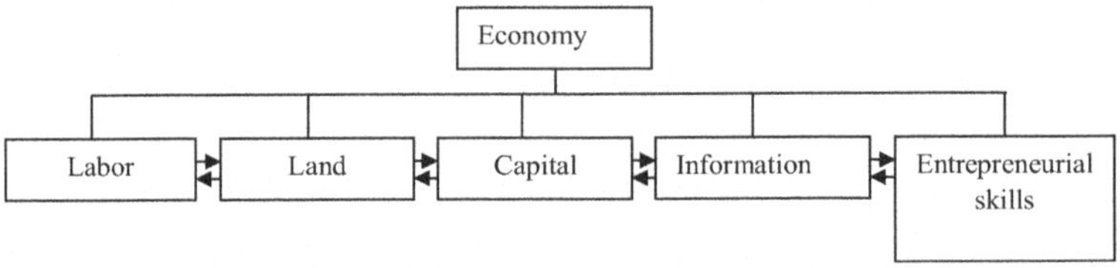

Fig. 1 Economic factors of production (Source: Compiled by the authors)

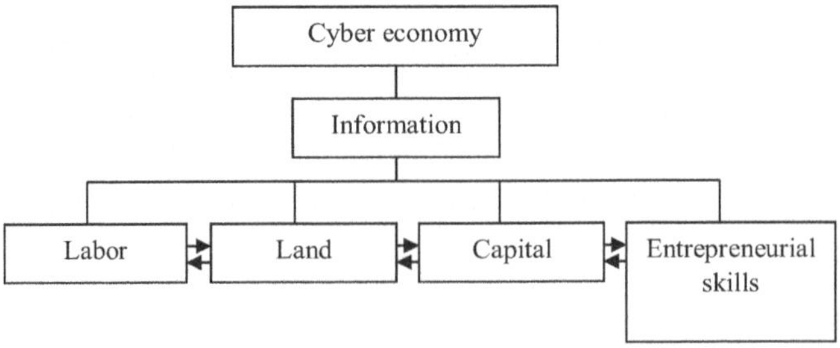

Fig. 2 Factors of production in the cyber economy (Source: Compiled by the authors)

2 Materials and Method

The practice of forming and developing entrepreneurial potential is mainly determined by a particular country's business environment. According to the studies of the World Bank, the fundamental problems of business in Russia in the digitization of economy are as follows:

1. Poor business infrastructure
2. Heavy burden of governmental regulation
3. Low investment attractiveness of the economy
4. Low level of competition and high level of monopolization of the markets
5. High level of differentiation of business conditions in various regions of the country
6. The lack of working finance, lending and risk insurance mechanisms in the business sector
7. Inconsistent taxation system
8. The lack of mechanisms that would ensure the accessibility of public and municipal property for the business sector
9. Poor cooperation ties between small businesses and big businesses
10. Complexity of the implementation of innovative projects and programs
11. The lack of an adequate information system for the support of the business sector, resulting in asymmetry of information flows
12. A sharp drop in the skill levels and professional competencies of personnel
13. Low quality of facilities and resources
14. A deficient legal framework regulating the activities of the business sector.

Since many transactions are carried out without intermediaries and governmental regulation in the cyber economy, the following problems for the business sector come to the fore:

1. Poor business infrastructure. Modern Russia is characterized by poor business infrastructure. This is due to the complexity of procedures for the registration and conduct of business, low accessibility of public services caused by the low quality of these services and low speed of their provision, low accessibility of lending resources which are mainly caused by economic volatility and significant inflation, nontransparency of legislation, including with regard to entrepreneurship, and its proneness to constant change, as well as a complex geopolitical situation and hampered export–import operations.
2. The investment attractiveness of the economy is determined by the degree of its openness, protection of investors' rights, as well as the presence of innovative technologies and innovation-oriented businesses. In connection with the accession of the Russian Federation to the WTO, the degree of openness of its economy has increased greatly, but investors still need a lot of time to adapt to new conditions.

   Investor rights in Russia are poorly protected due to the instability of legislation and the economy as a whole. As long as investors are not sure of the reliability of their investments, they will not enter Russian markets. Given the possible redistribution of property in the country that has been observed in the Russian economy over and over again, investors treat Russian businesses with caution. Innovation-oriented businesses are poorly represented in Russia. Innovative technologies are created, but investors would rather buy them than invest in them; this is why the flow of investment into the Russian economy is virtually nonexistent.

3. The level of competition determines the presence of market entry barriers for new businesses and the conditions of operation for existing businesses in the market. In Russia, there is a tendency for the monopolization of many markets due to imperfect legislation on competition that is not fully adequate for the actual state of things, the lack of effective work of the antimonopoly service, and the involvement of government institutions in business activities despite various restrictions and prohibitions.

   A high level of monopolization by big business in many market segments prevents the business sector as a whole from growing and developing. The problem of monopolization is even more exacerbated by government institutions which oblige small businesses to receive the so-called paid "services" from state supervision and oversight authorities, and do not allow any alternative obtainment of similar services from other organizations. This duty creates a supportive environment for government institutions (fire safety authorities, licensing authorities, public health authorities, etc.), which enables them to "force-feed" the level of prices and the quality of "service" without regard to the capabilities of the consumer.

4. High level of differentiation of business conditions in various regions of the country. This is due to both geographic features, primarily regional differences in the possession of natural resources, and political conditions—the desire to develop the central region to the detriment of other regions to raise the status of the capital as an image of modern Russia, taking into account the low probability of visits of foreigners to other regions.

5. The lack of working finance, lending and risk insurance mechanisms in the business sector. Not only bank loans, but leasing tools can be used as lending mechanisms for small businesses; moreover, tax concessions can be used not only in the form of reduced tax rates, but also in the form of accelerated depreciation. The state has currently prohibited small businesses to use accelerated depreciation. The conclusion of lease agreements is associated with big expenses that are backbreaking for small businesses; the law governing leasing relations is contrary to the provisions of the Civil Code of the Russian Federation.

   The development of entrepreneurial potential requires special conditions for its funding, investment, and lending; it requires the creation of organizations specializing specifically in lending to the business sector by attracting private domestic and foreign investments.

   The funds for the support of microentrepreneurship that have been established thus far with a view to providing concessional loans to emergent entrepreneurs are ineffective and are not performing their functions due to the low level of budgetary financing. The federal law that regulates business activities in the business sector is not coordinated with the tax code in terms of the taxation of funds for the support of microentrepreneurship.

6. Imperfection of the taxation system is one of fundamental problems that hampers the development of entrepreneurial potential in Russia. This is caused by frequent changes to tax legislation, a large number of taxes, and complex mechanisms for their calculation and payment.

   The state made several attempts to ease the tax burden through the creation of special tax environments, such as: simplified taxation, an accounting and reporting system, unified tax on imputed income, and unified agricultural tax. However, the introduction of these tax environments did not have the expected positive impact on the development of entrepreneurial potential due to the presence of internal conflicts in the taxation system.

   The tax burden on businesses in Russia is fairly high, and the introduction of simplified taxation, an accounting and reporting system, unified tax on imputed income, and unified agricultural tax did not reduce it, but only made accounting more complicated as a result of the contradictory nature of tax laws and regulations as well as their flaws at both the federal and regional levels.

   The tax concessions for small businesses are volatile. Punitive penalties exist for noncompliance that, in conditions of instability and confusion over tax rules, is particularly burdensome for small businesses and spells bankruptcy to many of them.

   A complex, unintelligible, and cumbersome accounting and tax system for small businesses forces them to commit significant expenditures on these procedures and diverts financial resources from the production process, thereby reducing production efficiency.

7. Poor cooperation between small businesses and big businesses. Cooperation between small and big businesses is one of the main sources of income as well as a potential business segment for the small business sector. The so-called cluster associations are a form of business organization that is specifically characteristic of the postindustrial period. Cluster processes consist of the improvement of cooperation between big and small businesses, due to a large business outsourcing its manufacturing needs for parts to smaller enterprises so that it can concentrate its efforts on strategic and operational procedures. This type of cooperation is widely used both throughout Europe and, to an even greater degree, throughout Asia. The German car manufacturer, BMW, serves as a striking example of mutually profitable cooperation between small and big business. In order to avoid tangible production costs, this company places orders for a variety of minor components (plastic parts, chassis parts, rubber parts, etc.) with outside focused facilities. Thus, management efforts can be focused on the main areas of production and development: on the development of new engines, the creation of improvements to existing safety systems, the creation of new bodies with optimized aerodynamic characteristics, on the modernization of the

braking system, etc. In turn, the small businesses acquire a strategic partner, which is a reliable and stable customer for their products.

For Russia, cooperation and interaction between large and small businesses is one of the most promising directions for the development of entrepreneurial potential, since the processes of improving competition of the economy and achieving financial and economic security in the current unstable conditions will make it possible to improve resource efficiency due to their cross-migration between businesses. The main reason for the current poor cooperation between big and small businesses is the poor quality of products manufactured by small businesses, which fail to meet the requirements of large manufacturers.

8. Complexity of the implementation of innovative projects and programs. High levels of risk for the innovative projects of entrepreneurs, associated with an underdeveloped system to ensure the implementation of such projects greatly hampers the development of knowledge-intensive business enterprises. However, it is small businesses that are better placed to implement academic innovations in the most effective way due to their potentially higher flexibility in reequipping and changing production methods. Inaccessibility of financing and investment hinders the critical need for equipment upgrades and acquisition of new and state-of-the-art technologies, greatly reducing the mobility of technical re-equipment of small businesses.
9. Underdevelopment of the system of informational support of small businesses. Currently, entrepreneurs are deprived of the opportunity to acquire unbiased information about the development of their business sector. Official sources are designed to collect, process, and store information that is of no worth for the sphere of small businesses. The fact that legislative and executive authorities do not have adequate and accurate information about the number of employees working in small businesses, the profit earned, amount of taxes collected, gross turnover, production output by different types of activity, life cycle of enterprises, and other factors, prevents them from developing and implementing truly effective government measures that make it possible to develop the small business sector. The insufficiency and partiality of information about the business area as a whole, and the role, place, and value of entrepreneurship in Russia makes it impossible to identify the most effective forms and methods for its support by government. The situation is further exacerbated by the so-called "information deprivation" of small businesses. There is a narrow range of marketing information about potential consumers in the information markets. The information about the opportunities for concessional lending, potential investors, new technologies, and new equipment is difficult to access.
10. Staffing problems. The lack of a differentiated system for the training of specialists that would meet the needs of employers and satisfy the requirements of business activities remains a problematic issue. There is a need to familiarize businesspeople and their employees with financial and legal issues that destabilize the business sector. The lack of professional knowledge in the field of economics and management in employees reduces their labor productivity and, as a result, the competitiveness of small businesses. The low occupational level

of civil servants who exercise the governmental regulation of small business activities reduces the effectiveness of government policies to support and develop small business in Russia.

The availability and the quality of labor resources also diverge widely in different regions of the country. Thus, the highest concentration of the most promising employees can be observed in the central region of Russia, whereas in other regions there is a deficiency in the regular labor force which is refilled by migration flows of low-skilled personnel, often not fluent in Russian, from the CIS countries. Another important aspect is the difference in the accessibility of public services that is much higher in the Central region of Russia and in St. Petersburg compared to other regions. There is also a difference in the degree of government support of businesses in various regions, which is due to the divergent orientation of policy in different regions.

11. Problems of material and resource provision for small and big businesses. Small businesses in the real sector of economy need high-quality raw materials for the practical approval and production of various innovations, and currently small businesses find it difficult to procure such materials and components at acceptable prices. Entrepreneurs are forced to buy raw materials from random suppliers, usually of low quality, which significantly reduces the quality of the output and complicates cooperation with big businesses. The quality of products is undermined not only by the lack of availability of quality raw materials but also by high levels of deterioration of equipment and the low qualifications of personnel.
12. Deficient legal framework regulating the activities of the business sector. Legislative instruments regulating the activities of small businesses are contradictory in nature. All applicable statutory provisions in the sphere of small business do not have a clear sophisticated implementation mechanism. The inaction of state authorities and the failure to obey the laws they themselves create generate uncertainty about the future and lead to a decrease in the entrepreneurial activity of the population.

    Complicated procedures for closing a business (compared to the opening of one) leads to the accumulation of a significant number of idle companies in the market, which have become unprofitable and noncompetitive. Under the circumstances, the state has a problem to remove such businesses from the market.

In addition to these numerous problems, the decision-making process (DMP) is complicated by a high level of information asymmetry.

Information plays a major role in the modern market economy. Under the conditions of continuously growing economic data, entities appear that have varying degrees of awareness of changing economic processes (entities should be understood as manufacturers, intermediaries, consumers, and competitors).

K. Arrow was one of the first researchers to describe such features of information and the mathematical model of a market with deficient information was developed by G. Akerlof.

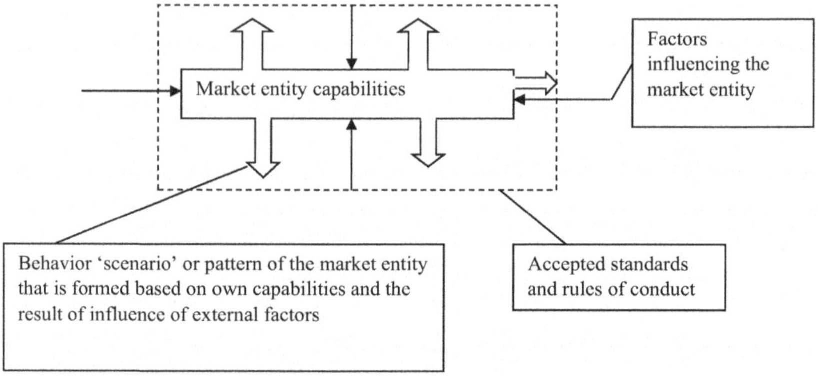

Fig. 3 Behavior pattern of the market entity (Source: Authors)

Society is aimed at systematizing market processes in order to perceive their nature and make forecasts for the future. All that is not subject to systematization is called the "exception to the rule, which confirms the rule once again." However, any action of a market entity is unpredictable and acts as a reaction to changes in existing conditions. The rate of reaction depends on the field and area of activities, time of operation in the market, location of the entity, impact factor leverage, etc.

This being said, a change in the factors that influence the market involves risks for market entities. The following risks can be identified:

- Financial risk
- Moral risk
- Production risk
- Risk of loss of time

In order to reduce risks, the market entity requires information about possible behavior patterns in this dynamic environment. The more information the entity has, the more alternatives it will be able to use.

Behavior "scenarios" or patterns of the market entity will be limited by the accepted standards and rules in the society (Fig. 3).

When there is perfect information awareness of all participants in the market process, then each economic entity is able to make a rational choice, which contributes to the optimal allocation of resources. However, the actual market economy does not correspond to these ideal conditions. Not every economic entity has the sufficient skills to correctly use necessary data and distinguish information that is important.

Information asymmetry exists virtually always; it enables the misuse of the lack of awareness of other participants in market relations. This problem arises due to unreliable, knowingly false or unfair information and results in poor decision-making by the market entity.

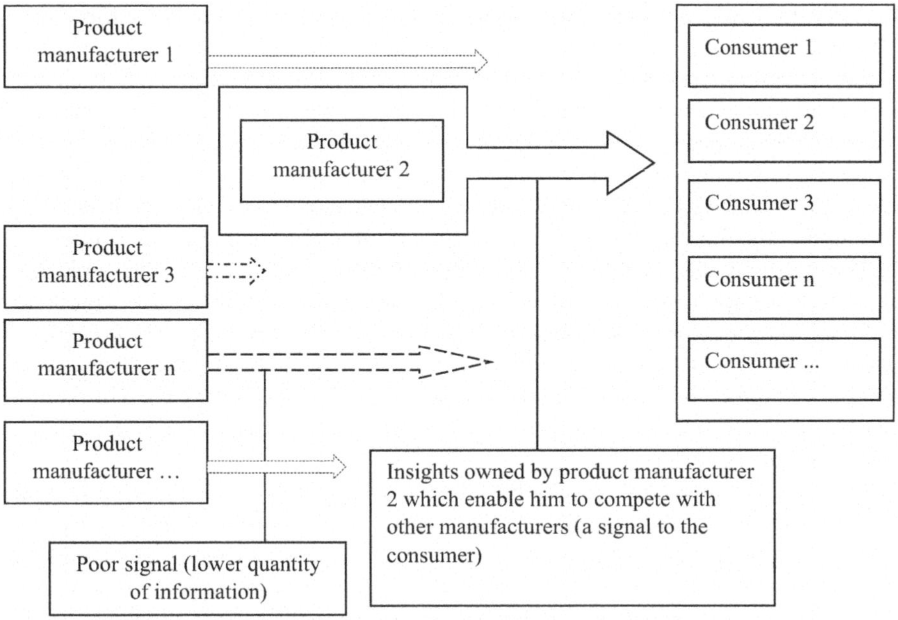

Fig. 4 Information asymmetry in the goods and services market (Source: Authors)

Information asymmetry gives rise to the following negative effects:

- Negative economic selection
- Consumer disappointment
- Opportunistic behavior of market entities
- Growth of the shadow economy.

Each market entity is aimed at having the insights for successful operation in the market (the more alternative outcomes the market entity can predict, the more competitive it is) (Popkova and Sergi 2018). Thus, when information is distributed unevenly, a competitive advantage is provided to a particular market entity. Hence, the constant presence of information asymmetry makes it impossible to develop market relations.

Information asymmetry is increased by the presence of various uncertainties resulting from a change in external factors: uncertainty of the future market environment in the country; uncertainties associated with cyclical fluctuations in the systems; uncertainties associated with events occurring in foreign countries and international organizations (Fig. 4).

The founder of information theory, C. Shannon, defined information as eliminated uncertainty. In other words, the acquisition of information is an essential prerequisite for the elimination of uncertainty.

It should be noted however that if one entity has a higher amount of information, it by no means always guarantees its competitive advantage. Competitive advantage is eliminated uncertainty that arises when the outcome of multiple events is clear.

Taking into account uncertainty is an important issue given the current stage of economic development. If there has been a high level of uncertainty in processes that cannot be quantified, then uncertainty is present in almost all processes of human activity at present. This is due to the accelerated rate of scientific and technical development and, accordingly, the development of all systems of human activity.

The most popular method for the elimination of uncertainty is the subjective opinion of an expert who determines his or her preference in how to solve a problem.

Every person makes decisions in the process of human activity; our life is indissolubly related to this process; and it serves as a basis for the management process. Voting is the simplest method of managerial decision-making. This simple method makes it possible to identify difficulties that adversely affect the relative objectivity of the result.

The first problem that should be taken into account in the decision-making process is the expert survey and estimation procedure. One should necessarily take into account the possibility of conformity with the opinion of the most established and reputable member of the work team or the opinion of the experts. One should clearly define each stage of the expert research, stage of discussions, from the decision-making stage to the stage when the final outcome should be implemented.

The second problem consists in conflicts due to areas of responsibility; it is important to determine the order of work to avoid conflict situations—that is, the area of responsibility of each person and the kind of decisions made by them.

An important stage of DMP is the choice of its method. First, the problem should be viewed as an entity, rather than broken down into separate questions. The author used such a systemic approach for these purposes in this research, as it makes it possible to present the problem in the form of an interrelated system of questions forming the problem. Besides, this also enables the usage of all available methods of modern applied mathematics in the decision-making process. Such methods are used for various purposes: for situation assessment; forecasting; for the generation of a variety of alternative decision options, and selection of the best of them.

The fourth problem in DMP is a need to take into account uncertainties. Various approaches are used for the description of uncertainties at present. To begin with, one should identify the units of measurement of various factors used in DMP. As can be seen from the above, in order to compare these factors, it is necessary to reduce them to single indices of quantitative or qualitative scales. Since it is the prerogative of the experts to select the scales, the estimation should be made with the use of a unified scale.

The authors suggest using the procedure for the support of DMP in the business sector as this will make it possible to reduce the level of information asymmetry through a reduction of the level of uncertainty.

3 Results

As can be seen in Fig. 5, estimation processes and DMPs can be conveniently classified into an initial stage, to set goals and establish an expert committee, a second stage for the assessment of alternative decisions and a third and final stage for the analysis of results for decision-making.

Stage 1—Setting the goal of the research and creation of the expert committee

The efficiency of any research primarily depends on intelligent goal setting. One should define the goal of the research before calling in the experts.

After goal setting and the identification of objectives, one may proceed to the creation of the expert committee. Competent specialists should be involved as experts; in other words, it is necessary to select people whose judgment will be most effective in the formation of results of the assessment, and which have a high degree of objectivity. The problem of the selection of experts is one of the most

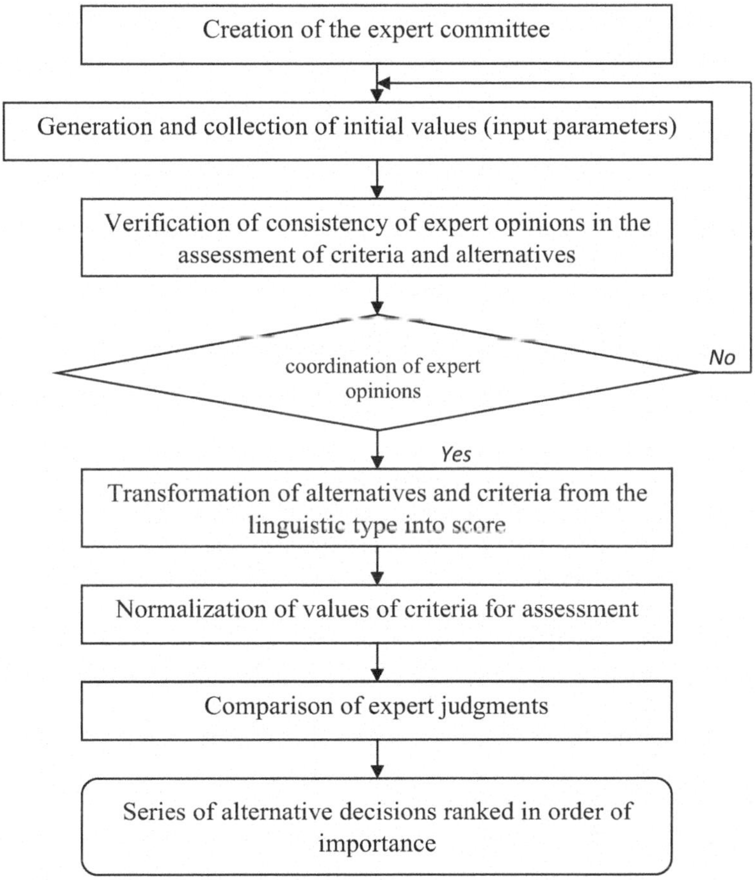

Fig. 5 Algorithm of support of the decision-making process

challenging in the theory and practice of expert research. This is due to the fact that they will fundamentally determine the certainty of results; hence, it is crucial that such people whose experience, knowledge, and qualifications will really help to make an adequate decision should be selected. In this regard, the obvious question that arises is how to identify such people.

The most important stages of expert assessment include:

- Formation of goals of the expert research: the information that is collected for the decision-maker according to the goals of research; the draft decision is prepared at a later stage.
- Creation of the expert committee: the objectivity of results depends on the composition of the team. The lists method, "snowball" method, self-assessment method, and mutual assessment method are all used in choosing an expert.
- Expert research management: the number of hours; expert survey procedures; method of accounting for expert opinions; management of the experts.

The proper implementation of each stage allows us to take into account the specifics of the expert research more accurately. Therefore, it is expedient to divide the first stage for the formation of the work team into the following substages:

Selection and Appointment of Participants of the Expert Committee First, the head of the team is selected. This person will manage the work of the experts and help the decision-makers to analyze the results of the research. The duties imposed on the head of the expert committee necessitate that it should be a person who is not a member of the expert group, which means a company should have an expert who is also able to conduct research.

The selection of experts is usually carried out as follows: A list of potential members of the expert committee is initially drawn up; then a selection of possible candidates is made according to the criterion of their competence. The "snowball" method is the most popular tool for the formation of the list of participants for the expert team. This method consists in the following: Each potential member of the expert committee is asked to name people who, in their opinion, are experts in the field under consideration. Every potential expert is interviewed in such a manner. According to the algorithm, this procedure is carried out until similar names cease to occur, which makes it possible to obtain an extensive long list of possible experts.

Assessing the competence of the experts is no less difficult than their selection. Such data as current position, academic degree and academic title, term of service, etc. can be used as auxiliary criteria for the assessment of expert competencies. However, it is not expedient to rely on such factors when making a final choice, since professionalism largely depends on the personal qualities of an expert.

Very common tools for assessing expert competence include self-assessment methods and methods of mutual assessment. When the self-assessment method is used, the expert independently describes their competence in various fields. The main drawback of this method is that the expert either overstates their actual professionalism and competence, or is overly critical when self-assessing their own capabilities.

The method of mutual assessment of experts makes it possible to coordinate the subjectivism of assessment; in this case, in addition to a more realistic definition of the capabilities of the experts, the experts' awareness of the capabilities of each other is determined. If the experts show familiarity, it is not advisable that they should work in the same team, since their opinions may be considerably similar.

In order to optimize the work of the expert committee, one should develop an estimation procedure, since the data generation procedure as such implies the face-to-face communication of participants. This is caused by a complex set of circumstances associated with the personal qualities of each expert. For example, an expert recognized as the "people person" by the team can bring the whole process to a standstill during joint communication. The work is destined for failure if there are antagonistic relations between participants in the expert group or their individual status is perceived as being very different.

In order to improve the quality of work of the expert committee, its ultimate composition may be influenced by the decision-maker. Particular experts could be added to the committee or others, seen as being inadequate, removed.

Development of Examination Procedure There are a great many methods for examination. Some options are if the work is individually carried out with each expert; or the expert is not notified of who else is a member of the expert group. This procedure makes it possible to prevent conformity with the majority opinion or with the opinion of more established participants in the expert group. Depending on the situation, the examination can be carried out by gathering the experts together for the generation of initial values required during the estimation. In this case, the experts elaborate their opinions during discussion with each other. Depending on the number of full-time employees, one can either fix the number of experts or increase this number, as is provided for by the "snowball" method.

The second important point in the management of the expert estimation procedure is the determination of the number of rounds. It is assumed that higher the number of rounds, the more objective the estimation will be; however, methods presented contain the algorithm for the assessment of consistency of expert opinions, which enable identifying the need for reassessment. A large number of tours may take a great amount of time, and since middle managers and (partly) top managers may be serving as experts, this can adversely affect the activities of the enterprise.

Goal Setting and the Identification of Objectives for the Experts The identification of objectives is an important element in the examination process. The expert group should provide systematized information to support the decision-making process or alternative projects of decision as such. The management of the work of the experts is helpful in this case, where the first expert voices his opinion on the problem under consideration in the first place.

In the case of estimation for the purposes of elaborating alternative projects that require decisions, it is more expedient to organize an individual expert survey, since an opinion that deviates greatly from the opinions of other experts can be eliminated in the course of discussion. However, based on the practical experience of the implementation of expert estimations, experts with opinions that deviate from the majority opinion are the most useful. In such a case, the expert voices an opinion not having any information about the opinions voiced by other experts, ensuring the complete independence of the opinion. In the case of such survey, however, there is a need to carry out the mandatory procedure of coordinating expert judgments. By managing the process in this way, only one tour of examination is held.

It is possible to manage anonymous correspondence communication, in which case the expert is offered the possibility to read the judgments of other experts, but remains unaware of the author of a particular judgment. A minimum of two tours are held using this management of examination. There is also another type of correspondence communication, which excludes anonymity; in this case, experts communicate openly with each other via the Internet. The advantage of correspondence examination is the lack of need to gather experts together physically, which frees the organizer from the need to agree on a convenient communication schedule and venue.

On-site examinations imply that the experts provide their judgments in person, not by presenting them in writing. Usually, when the examination is managed in this manner, experts manage to voice more judgments within the same period of time. On-site examination can be conducted with the imposition of limitations. In such a case, a strict examination procedure is developed, and should be strictly observed by all participants. In order to obtain more detailed judgments, on-site examination is conducted without time limitations, which implies that data will be generated during a normal discussion. All on-site examinations have the same drawback; they are associated with less established experts falling into line with the opinions of more established participants or with the majority opinion. Different types of management of examinations may be combined if necessary.

Competent specialists should be involved as experts. In other words, it is necessary to select people whose judgments will most help in the formation of coordinated decisions with a high degree of objectivity.

Elaboration and Approval of the Work Task for Examination At this stage, the time and the venue for the examination are clearly identified, the issue of payment for experts is resolved, and the necessary logistical support for the procedures is determined. The expert committee selects who will be engaged in the collection of information and the form of information collected; that is, a detailed scenario for the collection of expert judgments and estimations is formed. This procedure presents a detailed description of the particular kind of information that should be obtained from the experts, for example, words, sentences, cause-and-effect relations, or qualitative verbal valuations. It is also necessary to determine in what form the judgments should be presented. This could be verbally, with the judgments recorded, through written reports in hard copy, or via electronic forms sent for further processing. The three most popular modes of interaction between an expert and a knowledge specialist for expert methods of support for decision-making are: protocol analysis, interviews, and game simulations of professional activities.

Protocol analysis is a method of recording expert judgments during the discussion and finding alternate solutions in the subsequent analysis. However, this method has its drawbacks; for example, it is impossible to distinguish judgments of high importance from simple judgments during the processing. Besides, gaps can appear in reports when the expert stops the reasoning to think over a particular judgment. The gaps can only be corrected when the interview method is used.

In the game simulation method, the expert is placed in situation that has been simulated in accordance with their professional activity. A specialist who is observing the expert's behavior in various simulated situations forms a judgment of his or her expert knowledge. Any omissions in the course of the acquisition of knowledge are clarified with the expert in the interview mode.

The following interview methods are the most popular for expert estimations: staging, repertory grid, and confirmation of similarity. The staging method requires an expert to highlight the most important concepts in the area of interest. The algorithm of repertory grid strategy is the opposite of the staging method; its algorithm is designed to divide similar concepts. The procedure of confirmation of similarity consists of the identification of affiliations of two motives from the area of interest within the defined tolerance relation.

Creation of the Expert Committee At this stage, the list of experts is finally approved in accordance with their competencies. Subsequently, negotiations with experts are held with a view to obtaining their approval of the examination.

Stage 2—Generation of initial values (input parameters) required for the assessment of the significance of decisions

The knowledge acquisition process conventionally consists of three stages.

The first is the preparatory stage. It is designed to ensure that participants are thoroughly prepared for the knowledge acquisition procedure. To improve the efficiency of the procedure, it is desirable that the expert is morally or financially interested in achieving the set goal. This serves as an additional argument in favor of using middle managers as the experts. This stage defines the input and output parameters of assessment.

The second stage is the establishment of uniform categories for scores. This is necessary for the possibility of comparing objects belonging to different categories. A uniform vocabulary basis of assessment and a level of knowledge refinement are developed at this stage. This stage contributes to the development of rating scales in this procedure.

The third stage is gnoseological, which defines the patterns inherent in the area of interest and the conditions of reliability of expert judgments.

In accordance with the principal stages of acquisition of knowledge by the experts, the process for the generation of initial values is implemented in the following sequence.

Running a Process for the Generation of Alternatives The experts identify the maximum possible number of motives which will be represented by an unordered set of decisions: M1, M2, M3, ..., Mn, which will serve as alternatives at a later stage. This process is called the acquisition of knowledge. The experts' knowledge is revealed during their work for its subsequent conversion into a processable form.

In the process of the acquisition of knowledge one should take into account the importance of the field of knowledge, since it contains the basic concepts used by experts in describing the area of interest, its properties, and relations between the expressed concepts.

The experts generate an unordered set of decisions which serve as alternatives in the procedure and represent a group of linguistic variables. Linguistic variables were created for the elimination of bugs and preservation of data which produce fuzzy sets. Linguistic variables reflect fuzzy data in the form of real and whole numbers.

A linguistic variable is a variable which assumes values in the form of words and phrases of a natural or artificial language and the range of its values is specified on a certain quantitative scale. Fuzzy variables serve the purpose of describing linguistic variables. The category of linguistic variables and values assumed by them are intended for the possibility of estimation of nonnumerical objects with qualitative verbal descriptions. The linguistic variable and all of its qualitative values must necessarily be related to a particular quantitative scale. This scale is called the basic scale in the expert estimation procedure.

In order to increase the reliability of the scores, one should provide the experts with the opportunity to independently identify the synonyms of scores in the system of decision-making support, and identify the scale dimension.

Formation of the Basic Rating Scales The development of a point and factor scale is a separate substage in this method. Since the validity of this method mainly depends on elaborated scales, special attention must be paid to this process. After the scales have been developed, expert judgments are coordinated. Since decisions are assessed on the basis of cooperative decision-making, then one should coordinate expert judgments before the ranking procedure. Currently, the mathematical focus area of expert estimations contains a group of methods for the coordination of expert judgments: negotiations, weighted average score, ideal point method, Pareto ranking method, etc.

The experts independently identify the synonyms of the scores, establish correspondence between the scores of linguistic variables in the form of words or phrases of natural language and point values of the scale, and determine the dimension of the scale; this is due to the lack of motives and criteria for assessment of quantitative measurement with the experts, as well as the need to formalize the assessment process.

The graphic rating scale is used for the analysis of expert opinions. A separate paragraph called representative measurement theory deals with the issues of measurements in mathematics and it is this theory that serves as the basis for the theory of expert estimations.

The order scale is always used for linguistic variables and criteria for their assessment, which means that the experts can assess the alternatives as follows: judging from the "manufacturing quality level," "career advancement" is less preferable. The processing of expert judgments and estimations involves the ranking of alternatives by the preferability of their acceptance. Formally, ranks are represented as numbers 1, 2, 3, …, but even the simplest arithmetic operations cannot be performed with these numbers. Therefore, a theory was created for the analysis of qualitative data, providing the basis for studying, developing, and applying various calculation methods.

It should be noted that along with granted advantages of estimation, the use of the order scale gives rise to the following problems: setting the type of scale and searching for the data analysis algorithms which will not distort the result in case of any change of scale, which means that the result should be invariable in relation to a variation of the scale.

Selection of the type of measurement scale used during the mathematical simulation of any real-life situation is an important element of research, since the type of scale determines the possible mathematical transformations and operations; such transformations that do not have any impact and do not change the relations between the targets of research are acceptable.

There are two types of qualitative measurement scales: nominal scales and order scales. A nominal scale admits all possible one-to-one transformations. The numbers in it are used as a "marker"; their main purpose is to create the ability to distinguish objects.

The main purpose of the order scale consists in the arrangement of various objects. All steadily increasing transformations are considered to be admissible transformations in the order scale.

Expert estimations are only measured in the order scale; this is due to the possibility of answering comparative questions more correctly using qualitative classes. Hence, the nominal scale and the order scale form the basis of qualitative measurements. In other words, these are the scales of qualitative attributes; thus, in many studies where there is a high level of uncertainty, initial values and analytical results are treated as measurements on these scales.

The scales of quantitative attributes—interval scales, ratio scales, and difference scales—are also used in qualitative analysis. The interval scale is intended for the clusterization of a certain set of objects. To this end, their values should correspond to a particular range. Linear functions are admissible transformations in the interval scale.

Ratio scales are the most commonly encountered of quantitative scales. Zero is the point of reference in such scales, but there are no natural units of measurement; these scales are used for measurement of physical phenomena.

The difference scale is intended for the measurement of time (though the interval scale can also serve this purpose). Prime numbers result from the measurement of the absolute scale. The type of scale may change in the course of development of the relevant area of knowledge. For example, disagreements may arise between the participants in the expert group concerning the judgment measurement scale during the expert estimation procedure. This is why the selection and formation of the measurement scale by the experts was singled out as an individual substage of the research.

Since the invariance of conclusions with regard to admissible transformations of the scale is the basic requirement for the algorithms of comparison and analysis of linguistic variables through the use of representative measurement theory, and since the order scale is mainly used for measurement of qualitative data, the experts rely on this type of scale in this procedure as well.

Assessment of Alternative Decisions by the Experts The qualitative direct expert estimation of the generated unordered set of elements of alternative decisions are then assessed according to the developed basic rating scales and assignment of alternatives and relevant point scores to qualitative characteristics.

Stage 3—Coordination of expert judgments by the estimation of alternatives

After the expert assessment of alternative decisions it is necessary to coordinate these estimates through cooperative decision-making. Coordination of expert judgments is performed by the assessment of alternative decisions. Coordination is performed with the use of the following methods:

is the conduct of negotiations between the experts during which the values of qualitative characteristics are defined more precisely, for example, a "high degree of significance" may be assigned to a particular characteristic. More precise definitions of the qualitative parameters and the discussion of the significance of the expert decisions make it possible to strike a compromise about the scores.

Average score:

$$m_j = \overline{m}_{ij} / \sum_{j=1, i=1}^{N, K} \overline{m}_{ij},$$

where m_j is an average score of jth motive;

$\overline{m}_{ij}$ is a "weight" score of jth motive given by ith expert

is a weighted average score:

$$m_j = \sum_{i=1}^{N} m_{ij} * a_i / \sum_{i=1}^{N} m_{ij},$$

where m_j is a weighted average score of jth motive;

m_{ij} is a point value of score of jth motive by ith expert;
a_i is a weight which represents the significance of ith expert.

Stage 4—Ranking of alternatives

Expert judgments are compared at this stage without the involvement of the experts. The comparison of point scores for decisions is performed in accordance with the algorithm based on the method of fuzzy preference relations.

After alternatives have been ranked, the entrepreneur receives a series of decisions ranked in their order of importance. Decisions with the highest weight will be the most preferable.

4 Conclusion

It should be noted that information asymmetry will be present in any market. In the business sector, however, it should be minimized. This can be achieved through thorough control over information on the part of the state, nonprofit organizations, and people engaged in socially important areas of activities (in educational, medical organizations, etc.), as well as through the support of the decision-making process. It is difficult to reduce information asymmetry in the market economy, but the complexity is simplified in the course of transition to the cyber economy due to the large number of information transmission and dissemination channels.

Acknowledgments The chapter of the monograph has been prepared with financial support from the Russian Foundation for Basic Research, project No. 18-410-343004 "Generation of a strategy for the development of a regional infrastructure for technology entrepreneurship for the purposes of the sustainable development of territories (through the example of the Volgograd Region)," project No. 19-010-00018 "Formation of an adaptive methodology of regional development in the setting of transition to the 'smart city' concept."

Reference

Popkova EG, Sergi BS (2018) Will Industry 4.0 and other innovations impact Russia's development? In: Sergi BS (ed) Exploring the future of Russia's economy and markets: towards sustainable economic development. Emerald, Bingley, pp 51–68

Part V
Managing the Competitiveness of the Cyber Economy

Growth Vectors of the Cyber Economy and Perspectives on Their Activation

Vera I. Menshchikova, Margarita A. Aksenova, and Svetlana V. Vladimirova

Abstract *Purpose*: The purpose of the chapter is to determine the potential growth vectors of the cyber economy and to develop recommendations for their activation in modern economic systems.

Design/methodology/approach: To determine the potential growth vectors of the cyber economy the authors use the logical method and the method of proof by contradiction, which is based on the law of double negation. The authors also use the method of regression analysis for determining the influence of various potential growth vectors on development of the cyber economy. The information and empirical basis includes statistical materials from the World Bank and the IMD from 2018. The research objects are countries that show the highest level of development of the cyber economy as of 2018 (the highest share of medium-tech and hi-tech spheres in their gross added value).

Findings: It is determined that the main growth vectors in the cyber economy—internal hi-tech production, R&D, and education—do not have sufficient potential to stimulate the rapid development of the cyber economy. In order to fully realize the Fourth Industrial Revolution it is necessary to enable additional growth vectors for the cyber economy—hi-tech exports, energy, and telecommunications. At present, these additional growth vectors for the cyber economy are not sufficiently active due to incompletion of the process to institutionalize the practice of hi-tech exports (while preserving national competitive advantages) and attracting private investment into energy and telecommunications.

Originality/value: It is substantiated that the activation of additional growth vectors for the cyber economy is connected to the implementation of corresponding institutional measures from the state. A proprietary model is offered to illustrate this. Practical implementation of this model will ensure a systemic approach to support additional growth vectors for the cyber economy and the emergence of the synergetic effect—an acceleration of its development.

V. I. Menshchikova (✉)
Tambov State Technical University, Tambov, Russia

M. A. Aksenova · S. V. Vladimirova
Russian Presidential Academy of National Economy and Public Administration (Lipetsk branch), Lipetsk, Russia

© Springer Nature Switzerland AG 2019
V. M. Filippov et al. (eds.), *The Cyber Economy*, Contributions to Economics,
https://doi.org/10.1007/978-3-030-31566-5_26

1 Introduction

The cyber economy is the next evolutional form of the economic system. As with previous forms, it is based on certain vectors of growth. For example, the growth vector of the preindustrial (agrarian) economy was agriculture; the growth vector of industrial economy was industry; and the growth vector of the postindustrial economy was the service sector. The obvious growth vectors of the cyber economy are the spheres of hi-tech industry and the adjacent (complimentary) spheres of R&D and education.

However, unlike previous revolutions, the Fourth Industrial Revolution will not take place overnight. In 2012–2018, mixed results in the sphere of the digital modernization of economy, expressed through the partial automatization of business processes, were achieved. Forecasts for the massive robotization of industry and wide application of the Internet of Things and AI are reconsidered and recalculated annually.

However, in the postcrisis global economy we see an urgent need for rapid development of the cyber economy, to overcome the drawbacks of the postindustrial economy, due to its foundation and reliance of the real sector, and stimulate the activities of economic subjects. The importance of the search for the best means of managing the Fourth Industrial Revolution, which will create favorable conditions for development of the cyber economy, cannot be overstated.

The working hypothesis of this research is that there are additional growth vectors of the cyber economy—apart from hi-tech industry, R&D, and education—where potential has not yet been realized. This is delaying the onset of the Fourth Industrial Revolution and hindering the development of the cyber economy. The purpose of the chapter is to determine the key potential growth vectors of the cyber economy and to develop recommendations for their activation.

2 Materials and Method

The high demand for, but, at the same time, uncertainty around the completion of the Fourth Industrial Revolution and transition to Industry 4.0 are emphasized in the works of Bogoviz (2019), Griffiths and Ooi (2018), Loureiro (2018), Penker and Khoh (2019), Popkova (2019), Popkova et al. (2019), and Popkova and Sergi (2019). Growth vectors—as economic spheres that have a systemic influence on the cyber economy and accelerate its development—are discussed in the works of Barrell and Lemmens (2015), Chakpitak et al. (2018), Dyatlov et al. (2018), Martin-Shields and Bodanac (2018), and Pradhan et al. (2019).

In the above works, the growth vectors of the cyber economy are identified as being hi-tech industry, R&D, and industry. It should be noted that these growth vectors are distinguished on the basis of qualitative methods (logical analysis and expert evaluations), and the evidential basis for their systemic influence on the cyber economy is not sufficiently strong.

This causes the need for scientific studies of an empirical nature. Here, we use regression analysis to evaluate the influence of various potential growth vectors on the development of the cyber economy.

3 Results

In order to determine additional growth vectors (to those cited by other researchers) for the cyber economy the authors used the logical method and the method of proof by contradiction, which is based on the law of double negation. Three following vectors were determined:

1. Export of the products of hi-tech industry. If the products of hi-tech industry are a key direction for the specialization of internal industrial production in the cyber economy, they should also play an important role in external (export) specialization. The logical basis of this conclusion is based on a contradiction of the postindustrial economy: certain countries (e.g., Russia) were formally assigned to the category of postindustrial economies, and, while the share of the service sphere in the structure of GDP exceeded 50%, they also performed other key roles in the global economy (e.g., as a major exporter of the products derived from the extraction industry in Russia's case). To maximize the advantages that are gained from the cyber economy this contradiction should be excluded. The growth vectors should include the manufacture of hi-tech goods for both the internal and external markets.
2. Energy. The replacement of human labor with machines, support for the continuous communication of integrated digital devices on the basis of the Internet of Things and ubiquitous computing, and the highly efficient work of AI will increase the needs of economic systems for energy, primarily, electric energy. Unmanned transport, by AI, will be particularly energy intensive because of the need to support the work of sensors and programs. The production capacities of the modern energy sector will not be sufficient to satisfy the growing needs of business and society and entrepreneurship. There will be a need to accelerate the development sector, which will open new horizons for automatization.
3. Telecommunications. An inseparable part of the infrastructural provision for the cyber economy is the telecommunications sector (mobile communications, Internet, etc.). Cyber-physical systems cannot function if there are failures in the telecommunications network and therefore intensive development will be necessary.

The information and empirical basis for studying the influence of the main growth vectors on the development of the cyber economy are statistical data from the World Bank and the IMD for 2018 (Table 1). The research objects are the countries that show the highest levels of development in the cyber economy as of 2018 (the highest

Table 1 Initial data for regression analysis

Country	Medium- and hi-tech industry (including construction) (% manufacturing value added)	Digital competitiveness index, points 1–7	High-technology exports, USD thousand	Investment in energy with private participation USD thousand	Investment in telecoms with private participation, USD thousand
	y	x_1	x_2	x_3	x_4
Singapore	80.38	99.422	136,160,944.49	457,513.03	15,600,910.23
Qatar	66.87	78.873	33.29	0.58	19.92
South Korea	63.65	87.983	72,699,710.20	470,820.36	16,054,681.78
Switzerland	63.04	95.851	24,159,696.00	423,982.37	14,457,552.63
Germany	61.40	85.405	167,746,057.02	689,805.88	23,521,952.15
Ireland	61.02	84.285	25,727,976.92	306,604.92	10,455,037.28
Hungary	58.78	57.099	13,478,758.79	236,541.17	8,065,907.14
Japan	55.34	82.170	83,661,306.98	341,187.40	11,634,278.49
Denmark	53.38	96.764	7,467,358.20	131,046.02	4,468,587.86
Czech Republic	50.51	71.488	21,069,666.19	208,755.38	7,118,428.84
Belgium	49.47	82.165	30,703,539.07	216,821.96	7,393,494.10
France	49.38	80.753	98,688,797.22	926,907.55	31,606,971.57
Sweden	48.92	97.453	14,973,092.21	133,965.50	4,568,140.42
Slovenia	48.65	71.427	1,518,763.43	26,653.05	908,852.59
Netherlands	48.19	93.886	63,617,214.21	472,429.99	16,109,569.36
Russia	25.60	65.207	9,174,217.41	161,000.00	5,490,000.00

Source: Compiled by the authors based on World Bank (2019), IMD (2019)

share of medium-tech and hi-tech spheres in the structure of gross added value in industry).

Based on the data from Table 1, we built regression curves that reflect the influence of the main (Fig. 1) and additional (Fig. 2) growth vectors on development of the cyber economy in 2018.

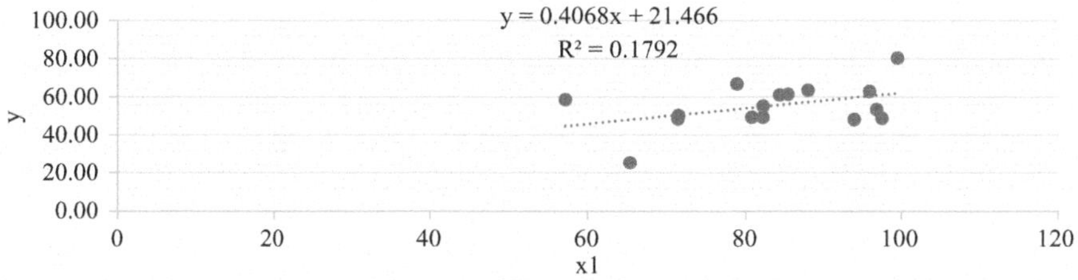

Fig. 1 Regression curve that reflects the influence of the main growth vectors on the development of the cyber economy in 2018 (Source: Compiled and built by the authors)

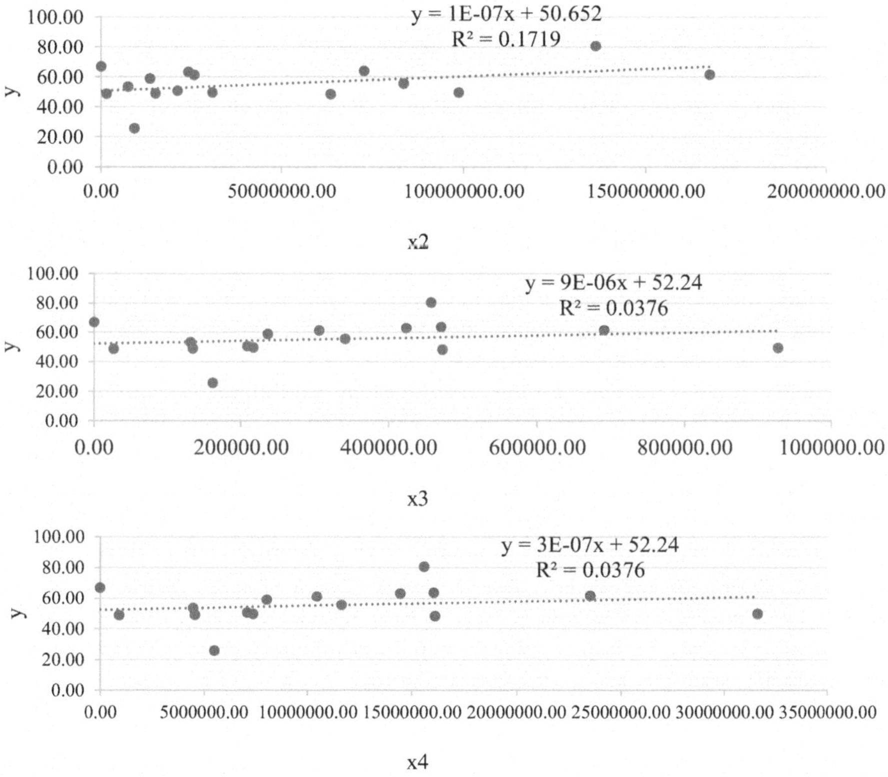

Fig. 2 Regression curve that reflects the influence of additional growth vectors on the development of the cyber economy in 2018 (Source: Calculated and compiled by the authors)

Figure 1 shows that an increase of digital competitiveness (through the development of hi-tech spheres, R&D and education) by 1 point leads to an increase of the share of medium-tech and hi-tech spheres in the structure of the gross added value in industry by 1%. The value of the determination coefficient is very low—17.92%. Therefore, these main growth vectors for the cyber economy do not reflect a substantial impact on growth and cannot be the only sources of development for the rapid uptake of the cyber economy.

Figure 2 shows that the influence of additional growth vectors we have identified on the development of the cyber economy is very low (low values of the estimate coefficients in the models of paired linear regression and low values of determination coefficients). Therefore, these additional growth vectors for the cyber economy are currently not being used due to the following reasons:

- The low share of hi-tech exports due to modern economic systems' striving to preserve the uniqueness of their competitive advantages (the focus is on the internal usage of hi-tech and products from the hi-tech spheres);
- Low volume of investment into the energy and telecommunications sectors due to assigning these spheres as infrastructural and there also being insufficient institutionalization of the inflow of private investment (high risk and limited opportunities for profit).

The determined perspectives and offered recommendations for the activation of these additional growth vectors for the cyber economy are shown in the following model (Fig. 3).

Figure 3 shows that in the offered model the activation of the determined additional growth vectors for the cyber economy can be ensured through the state management of two measures: firstly, the regulation of hi-tech exports. Exports that do not reduce the competitive advantage of the national economy should be stimulated, while limitations should be placed on exports that do have a derogatory effect on competitiveness. This will support the increase of the volume of hi-tech exports while preserving competitive advantages.

Secondly, there is the need for the creation of an institutional basis to implement investments and innovative projects in the spheres of energy and telecommunications through public–private partnerships. This will ensure the development of an alternative (ecologically safe) and innovative (highly efficient) energy sphere and the creation of an innovative and accessible telecommunications infrastructure.

Each of these economic spheres is notable in that the growth of business activity and creation of new highly efficient jobs will have a systemic influence on the development of the cyber economy and cause synergetic effects: an increase of the volume of hi-tech production and its share in the structure of gross added value, will accelerate the development of the cyber economy.

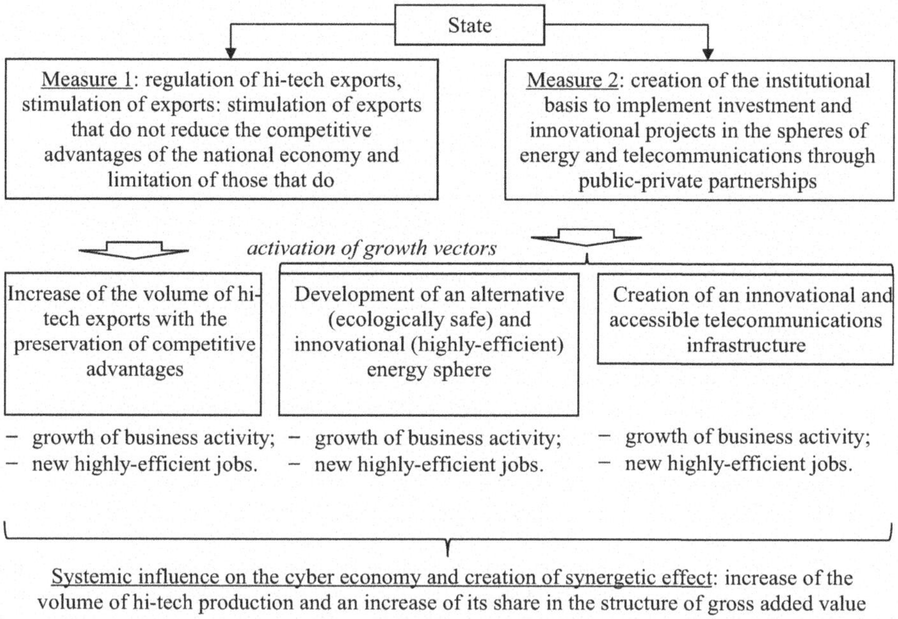

Fig. 3 The model for the activation of additional growth vectors for the cyber economy in the modern economic system (Source: Compiled by the authors)

4 Conclusion

It has been statistically shown that the main growth vectors of the cyber economy—domestic hi-tech production, R&D, and education—do not have sufficient potential to rapidly stimulate the development of the cyber economy. To accelerate the Fourth Industrial Revolution it is necessary to use additional growth vectors for the cyber economy—hi-tech exports, energy, and telecommunications.

At present, these additional growth vectors of the cyber economy are not sufficiently active, due to the incompletion of the process to institutionalize the practice of hi-tech export (while preserving national competitive advantages) and the failure to attract private investment into the energy and telecommunication sectors. In order to stimulate these additional growth vectors, corresponding institutional measures from the state are required, for which a proprietary model is offered. This will ensure the systemic influence of these additional growth vectors on the cyber economy and the emergence of a synergetic effect that will accelerate its development.

References

Barrell K, Lemmens W (2015) The future of digital services delivery embracing co-dependency for growth of the national digital economy. Aust J Telecommun Digit Econ 3(3):31–46

Bogoviz AV (2019) Industry 4.0 as a new vector of growth and development of knowledge economy. Stud Syst Decis Control 169:85–91

Chakpitak N, Maneejuk P, Chanaim S, Sriboonchitta S (2018) Thailand in the era of digital economy: how does digital technology promote economic growth? Stud Comput Intell 753:350–362

Dyatlov SA, Selishcheva TA, Feigin GF, Borodushko IV, Gilmanov DV (2018) The impact of network human capital on economic growth of supply chain in digital economy. Int J Supply Chain Manag 7(5):877–885

Griffiths F, Ooi M (2018) The fourth industrial revolution – Industry 4.0 and IoT [Trends in Future I and M]. IEEE Instrum Meas Mag 21(6), 8573590, 29–30

IMD (2019) World digital competitiveness ranking. https://www.imd.org/wcc/world-competitiveness-center-rankings/world-digital-competitiveness-rankings-2018/. Accessed 21 March 2019

Loureiro A (2018) There is a fourth industrial revolution: the digital revolution. Worldwide Hospitality Tourism Themes 10(6):740–744

Martin-Shields CP, Bodanac N (2018) Peacekeeping's digital economy: the role of communication technologies in post-conflict economic growth. Int Peacekeeping 25(3):420–445

Penker M, Khoh SB (2019) Cultivating growth and radical innovation success in the Fourth Industrial Revolution with big data analytics. In: IEEE international conference on industrial engineering and engineering management 607313, 526–530

Popkova EG (2019) Preconditions of formation and development of industry 4.0 in the conditions of knowledge economy. Stud Syst Decis Control 169:65–72

Popkova EG, Sergi BS (2019) Will Industry 4.0 and other innovations impact Russia's development? Exploring the future of Russia's economy and markets. Emerald Publishing, Bingley, pp 34–42

Popkova EG, Ragulina YV, Bogoviz AV (2019) Fundamental differences of transition to industry 4.0 from previous industrial revolutions. Stud Syst Decis Control 169:21–29

Pradhan RP, Arvin MB, Nair M, Bennett SE, Bahmani S (2019) Short-term and long-term dynamics of venture capital and economic growth in a digital economy: a study of European countries. Technol Soc 2(1):18–26

World Bank (2019) Indicators. https://data.worldbank.org/indicator. Accessed 21 March 2019

A Mechanism for Managing the Factors that Support the Development of the Cyber Economy

Marina I. Suganova, Natalia I. Riabinina, and Elena A. Sotnikova

Abstract *Purpose*: The purpose of this chapter is to determine the factors that influence the development of the cyber economy, to evaluate their strengths, and to develop a mechanism to manage them in both developed and developing countries.

Design/methodology/approach: The authors evaluate the influence of traditional (universal) factors of economic growth: institutional development, infrastructure, financial markets, and globalization. The resulting (dependent) variable is the digital competitiveness index. The influence of these factors is assessed with the help of the method of regression analysis based on the data of the IMD, KOF, and the World Economic Forum for late 2018/early 2019. The objects studied are the most developed economies (the G7) and the leading developing countries (BRICS).

Findings: It is determined that the cyber economy is, in general, strongly influenced by the traditional factors of economic growth. However, it is shown that the external factor (globalization) has only a small influence on the development of the cyber economy, while institutional provision is the most important. Developing countries have less mature and effective institutions and therefore less favorable conditions than developed countries for the development of the cyber economy. Developing countries also lag behind developed countries with regard to other factors.

Originality/value: In order to level the disproportionate development of the cyber economy in developed and developing countries, we developed a mechanism to manage the key factors that offers different recommendations for countries of both groups and reflects the general logic of managing the determined factors. The additional advantage of the developed mechanism is its potential for stimulating stability and active innovative development in the cyber economy.

M. I. Suganova (✉) · N. I. Riabinina
Orel State University, Orel, Russia

E. A. Sotnikova
Orel State University of Economics and Trade, Orel, Russia

© Springer Nature Switzerland AG 2019

V. M. Filippov et al. (eds.), *The Cyber Economy*, Contributions to Economics,
https://doi.org/10.1007/978-3-030-31566-5_27

1 Introduction

The cyber economy is the latest model for a socioeconomic system with high requirements. One of the key requirements is stability. The Fourth Industrial Revolution started after the 2008 global financial crisis, in order to overcome the drawbacks of the postindustrial model of development and its continuing instability caused by the creation of economic bubbles. Industry 4.0 is founded on intensive innovative development in the interests of reducing such cyclic fluctuations. The cyber economy also has a number of other requirements. One of these is the need to level the playing field between developed and developing economies in terms of reaping the economic benefits.

The simultaneous and full execution of the above requirements is a complex scientific and practical problem, as stability and innovation are antagonistic, and developed countries have already started the processes of digital modernization before developing countries. This problem can be solved through the determination and management of the factors that influence the development of the cyber economy to identify under what conditions these can conform to the stated requirements and the means for the creation of such conditions. This chapter will also identify key risks for the cyber economy and strategies for their reduction.

The authors offer a hypothesis that the cyber economy is subject to the influence of external factors, of which globalization is the most important. This hypothesis is based on the existing idea in modern economic science that a driving force for the formation and development of the cyber economy is global competition. One of the most authoritative metrics for measuring progress toward the cyber economy is the indicator of digital competitiveness—The Digital Competitiveness Index, developed by the IMD. In calculating the index, the IMD focuses on indicators of foreign economic activities (in particular, international experience, foreign highly skilled personnel, and net flow of international students).

The purpose of this chapter is to determine the factors that influence the development of the cyber economy, to evaluate their strength and influence on the cyber economy, and to develop a mechanism to manage these factors for both developed and developing countries.

2 Materials and Method

The direct process of studying the cyber economy has been led by international organizations under the guidance of the IMD. A methodological basis of indicative evaluation of the cyber economy was created and, based on this methodology the foundation of the theory of the cyber economy was established. Thus, the existing literature uses the components of the IMD's Digital Competitiveness Index to distinguish three factors that influence the development of the cyber economy: knowledge, technologies, and future readiness.

Examples that take this approach include publications by Azman et al. (2015), Bogoviz (2019), Masood and Egger (2019), Popkova (2019), Popkova et al. (2019), Popkova and Sergi (2019), Tolstykh et al. (2018), and Vegh (2018). We believe that the existing list of the factors that influence the development of the cyber economy is not complete. Also, it should be noted that despite the acknowledgment of the above factors, modern economic science does not offer a mechanism for their management and so it is difficult to use the accumulated knowledge in practice.

Contrary to the existing approach of determining the factors that influence the development of the cyber economy based on its specifics (high knowledge intensity, foundation of the breakthrough digital technologies of Industry 4.0), we use another approach; an assessment of influence on the development of the cyber economy of traditional (universal) factors of economic growth as defined by firstly, the World Bank in the framework for their annual "Global Competitiveness Report": institutional maturity (first pillar: Institutions), infrastructural development (second pillar: Infrastructure), and financial markets (eighth pillar: Financial market development), and secondly, by the KOF Swiss Economic Institute's "Index of Economic Globalization": globalization.

The resulting (dependent) variable is the digital competitiveness index. Influence is evaluated with application of the method of regression analysis based on the data of the IMD, KOF, and the World Economic Forum. The objects are major advanced economies (the G7) and leading developing countries (BRICS). The research is performed based on the data for late 2018–early 2019 (Table 1).

The results of a regression analysis of the data from Table 1 are presented in Table 2.

Based on the data from Table 2, we compiled a model of multiple linear regression: $y = -34.25 + 12.94{*}x_1 + 0.09{*}x_2 + 0.33{*}x_3 + 0.62{*}x_4$. According to this model, all selected factors have positive influence (direct connection) on the resulting variable. Digital competitiveness grows by 12.94 points due to an improvement of institutional provision by 1 point; it grows by 0.09 due to an improvement of infrastructural provision by 1 point; it grows by 0.32 points due to an improvement of financial provision by 1 point; and it grows by 0.62 points due to increase of globalization by 1 point.

Authenticity of the set regression dependencies is confirmed by the fact that significance F = 0.0018 (does not exceed 0.05)—the regression equation is statistically significant at the level $\alpha = 0.05$. All *p*-values do not exceed 0.05—all variables are included into the regression model. Multiple R = 0.9436—the change of the dependent variable by 94.36% is explained by the influence of the studied factors. Therefore, the most significant factor in the development of the cyber economy is institutional provision.

Table 1 The level of digital competitiveness and the potential factors that influence it in the G7 and BRICS in 2018

Country	Digital competitiveness index, points 1–100	First pillar: Institutions, points 1–7	Second pillar: Infrastructure, points 1–7	Eighth pillar: Financial market development, points 1–7	Index of economic globalization, points 1–100
	y	x_1	x_2	x_3	x_4
Major Advanced Economies (G7)					
Canada	95.201	5.4	5.7	5.4	84.38
France	80.753	4.8	6.1	4.5	87.20
Germany	85.405	5.3	6.0	5.0	88.17
Italy	64.958	3.5	5.4	3.1	82.59
Japan	82.170	5.4	6.3	4.9	78.37
UK	93.239	5.5	6.0	5.0	89.35
USA	100.00	5.3	6.0	5.7	82.10
BRICS					
Brazil	51.693	3.4	4.1	3.7	59.24
Russia	65.207	3.7	4.9	34	64.48
India	57.066	4.4	4.2	4.4	61.18
China	74.796	4.4	4.7	4.2	72.29
South Africa	56.876	3.8	4.3	4.4	69.89

Source: Compiled by the authors based on IMD (2019), KOF (2019), World Economic Forum (2019)

Table 2 Regression characteristics of the influence of the selected factors on the level of digital competitiveness in the economies of the G7 and BRICS in 2018

Regression statistics						
Multiple R	0.9436					
R-square	0.8905					
Adjusted R-square	0.8279					
Standard error	6.7876					
Observations	12					
Dispersion analysis						
	df	SS	MS	F	Significance F	
Regression	4	2621.6001	655.4000	14.2256	0.0018	
Residual	7	322.5026	46.0718			
Total	11	2944.1026				
	Coefficients	Standard error	t Stat	P value	Lower 95%	Upper 95%
Intercept	−34.2543	16.6832	−2.0532	0.0792	−73.7038	5.1952
x_1	12.9419	4.2077	3.0757	0.0179	2.9922	22.8916
x_2	0.0982	6.9433	0.0141	0.0099	−16.3202	16.5166
x_3	0.3265	0.2891	1.1296	0.0296	−0.3570	1.0100
x_4	0.6246	0.4668	1.3379	0.0223	−0.4793	1.7284

Source: Calculated and compiled by the authors

3 Results

Qualitative characteristics of the factors that influence the development of the cyber economy in both developed and developing countries are given in Table 3.

Table 3 shows that developed countries (direct average values are calculated on the basis of Table 1) have high values for all indicators. In view of their proven high direct influence on the development of the cyber economy, all factors have positive influence (they stimulate development). Developing countries have low values for all indicators. Thus, it is possible to state that all factors have a negative influence on the development of the cyber economy (they restrain development). In view of the different significances of the determined factors for the development of the cyber economy and the specifics of their influence on countries from different categories, we developed a mechanism to manage these factors (Fig. 1).

As is seen from Fig. 1, the subject of management in the offered mechanism is the state. The managerial tools include, according to the level of priority, firstly, the modernization of the normative and legal field and the strengthening of institutions for the cyber economy through support for the stability of the economy, and the protection of rights for the objects of intellectual property and investors. Secondly, stimulating the globalization of the cyber economy through the import of intellectual

Table 3 Qualitative characteristics of the factors that influence the development of the cyber economy

Characteristics	Factors that influence the development of the cyber economy			
	Institutional provision	Infrastructural provision	Financial provision	Globalization
	Significance * 92.50%	Significance * 0.70%	Significance * 2.33%	Significance * 4.46%
Influence of the factors in developed countries				
Average value	5.03	5.93	4.80	84.59
Qualitative treatment	High values that stimulate the development of the cyber economy			
Influence on the cyber economy	Legal protection of the subjects of the cyber economy	High demand, wide opportunities of automatization	Full-scale financial support	Free export and import of hi-tech
Influence of the factors in developing countries				
Average value	3.94	4.44	4.02	65.42
Qualitative treatment	Low values that restrain the development of the cyber economy			
Influence on the cyber economy	Legal uncertainty of the subjects of the cyber economy	Low demand, limited possibilities of automatization	Deficit of financial resources	Closed character of R&D, deficit of technologies

*Significance of each factor—percentage ratio of its estimate coefficient and the sum of all coefficients (12.94 + 0.09 + 0.33 + 0.62 = 13.99). For example, significance of institutional provision = 12.94*100%/13.99 = 92.50%

Source: Compiled by the authors

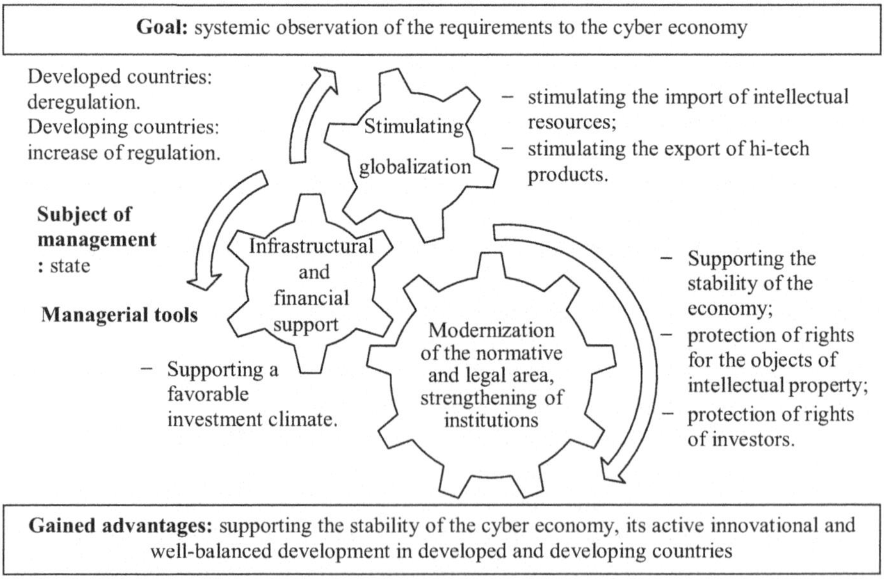

Fig. 1 The mechanism for managing the factors of development for the cyber economy (Source: Compiled by the authors)

resources and export of hi-tech products. Thirdly, infrastructural support is provided through support for a favorable investment climate.

In developed countries, in view of the already achieved results, it is recommended to conduct deregulation (a reduction of state interference into market processes), and in developing countries, in view of the currently insufficient government participation, it is recommended that regulation should be increased. The achieved advantages include supporting the stability of the cyber economy, its active innovative development, and a better balance between development in developed and developing countries.

4 Conclusions

Thus, it has been determined that apart from the influence of specific factors (knowledge, technologies, and readiness for their usage), the cyber economy is also affected by traditional factors of economic growth: institutional, infrastructural, financial provision, and globalization. The offered hypothesis was disproved, as it has been shown that the external factor (globalization) has a limited influence on the development of the cyber economy, while the most significant factor is institutional provision.

According to the indicator of institutional provision (first pillar: Institutions, Digital Competitiveness Report), developing countries (3.94 out of 7 points on average) exhibit unfavorable conditions for the development of the cyber economy, and lag far behind developed countries (5.03 out of 7 points on average). Developing countries also lag behind developed countries according to other indicators. In order to level these disproportions we developed a mechanism to manage the factors that influence the development of the cyber economy, offer recommendations for both developed and developing countries, and reflect on the general logic of managing these factors. The additional advantages of the developed mechanism are that it will stimulate stability and support the active innovative development of the cyber economy.

References

Azman H, Salman A, Razak NA, Hussin SB, Hasim MS, Sidin SM (2015) Determining critical success factors for ICT readiness in a digital economy: a study from user perspective. Adv Sci Lett 21(5):1367–1369

Bogoviz AV (2019) Industry 4.0 as a new vector of growth and development of knowledge economy. Stud Syst Decis Control 169:85–91

IMD (2019) World digital competitiveness ranking. https://www.imd.org/wcc/world-competitiveness-center-rankings/world-digital-competitiveness-rankings-2018/. Accessed 21 March 2019

KOF (2019) Globalisation index. https://www.kof.ethz.ch/en/forecasts-and-indicators/indicators/kof-globalisation-index.html. Accessed 21 March 2019

Masood T, Egger J (2019) Augmented reality in support of Industry 4.0—implementation challenges and success factors. Robot Comput Integr Manuf 58:181–195

Popkova EG (2019) Preconditions of formation and development of industry 4.0 in the conditions of knowledge economy. Stud Syst Decis Control 169:65–72

Popkova EG, Sergi BS (2019) Will Industry 4.0 and other innovations impact Russia's development? Exploring the future of Russia's economy and markets. Emerald Publishing, Bingley, pp 34–42

Popkova EG, Ragulina YV, Bogoviz AV (2019) Fundamental differences of transition to industry 4.0 from previous industrial revolutions. Stud Syst Decis Control 169:21–29

Tolstykh T, Shkarupeta E, Kostuhin Y, Zhaglovskaya A (2018) Key factors of manufacturing enterprises development in the context of industry 4.0. In: Proceedings of the 31st international business information management association conference, IBIMA 2018: innovation management and education excellence through vision 2020, pp 4747–4757

Vegh L (2018) Cyber-physical systems security through multi-factor authentication and data analytics. In: Proceedings of the IEEE international conference on industrial technology, pp 1369–1374

World Economic Forum (2019) The global competitiveness report 2017–2018. https://www.weforum.org/reports/the-global-competitiveness-report-2017-2018. Accessed 21 March 2019

International Economic Integration and Competitiveness in the Cyber Economy

Inna N. Rykova, Sergey V. Shkodinsky, and Andrei G. Nazarov

Abstract *Purpose*: The purpose of the chapter is to study how international economic integration can boost the competitiveness of the cyber economy.

Design/methodology/approach: The authors analyze the global turnover of the export of services for 2017–2018 and determine the future state of the cyber economy for certain countries. The potential growth of GDP indicators for the period 2025–2050 is studied, and perspectives on the global economic development of three groups of countries are considered. The share of expenditure for measures to support the cyber economy is determined for particular countries. The role of the cyber economy in Russia as a factor in international economic integration is also discussed. A SWOT analysis of the integrative activities of organizations for implementing the measures of the cyber economy is performed.

Findings: The calculations show that in 2020, the growth rate of GDP coordinated with the long-term balance of payments in Russia will reach 134%, and will continue to grow to 146.8% by 2025 and 154.4% by 2050. This growth is connected to the cyclic character of economic development in conjunction with the implementation of long-term, large-scale measures for the digitization of the Russian economy.

Originality/value: The formation of the cyber economy is subject to laws aimed far into the future, but it originated in the age of the birth of capitalism.

1 Introduction

Recent decades have been notable for high interest in the issues of international trade and economic integration. Regional trade integration has become one of the decisive factors in the development of international trade, and countries' participation in

I. N. Rykova (✉) · S. V. Shkodinsky
Federal State Budgetary Institution "Financial Research Institute of the Ministry of Finance of the Russian Federation", Moscow, Russia

A. G. Nazarov
All-Russian Public Organization "Business Russia", Moscow, Russia

© Springer Nature Switzerland AG 2019

V. M. Filippov et al. (eds.), *The Cyber Economy*, Contributions to Economics,
https://doi.org/10.1007/978-3-030-31566-5_28

global and regional integration processes positively influences their economic indicators. At the same time, the scientific community has focused on the problems of digital transformation and development of the cyber economy as a new sphere of economic theory and practice. Thus, the task of studying the effects of international economic integration on the competitiveness of the cyber economy has become very important. Despite a large number of works on integration processes, the level of elaboration on this problem is still insufficient. This is partly due to the recent emergence of the term “cyber economy.”

According to the Hungarian economist Béla Balassa (Kostyunina 2019), integration as a process means the implementation of measures to eliminate discrimination between national economies. According to the economist, N. Sadykov, the cyber economy is a complex system that provides optimal connections and interactions between the subjects and objects of economic relations during the production, exchange, and distribution of material goods. The cyber economy consists of systemic resources, which increase the effectiveness of economic processes through the optimal management of connection and interaction between the subsystems of the subjects and objects of economic relations (The Cyber Economy 2019).

International economic integration in its widest sense means the process of and approach to accretion in national economic systems. This envisages the liberalization of trade and investments, harmonization of legislatures in the sphere of economic regulation, and other measures. Of course, this is also directly connected to quality of digital transformation and usage of modern information and communication technologies in all spheres of economic life.

However, there is no need to rush the steps in a countries’ transition to the cyber economy, which envisages the development of the collection and ordering of economic information to solve planning “costs-issue” (Veduta 2019). The cyber economy in Russia is at the first stages of its formation. Its effective functioning requires the creation of a comprehensive sovereign information space and smart and successive steps in implementing the key tasks of digitizing society and the economy; and producing competitive digital technologies and platforms. The cyber economy is necessary for improving the quality of life, and it is interconnected with the tasks of international economic integration.

2 Materials and Method

The latest stage of globalization aims to unify people and companies via global information platforms, not through further trade and monetary unions. It is possible to observe the gradual transition from the trading of goods to trading services and technologies, while information is now the most valuable product (Nazarov et al. 2019). Twenty-seven countries of the OECD have already adopted national strategies to develop the digital economy.

In the European Union, the key priorities for the development of the digital economy are considered within the strategy of a unified digital market: “. . .market

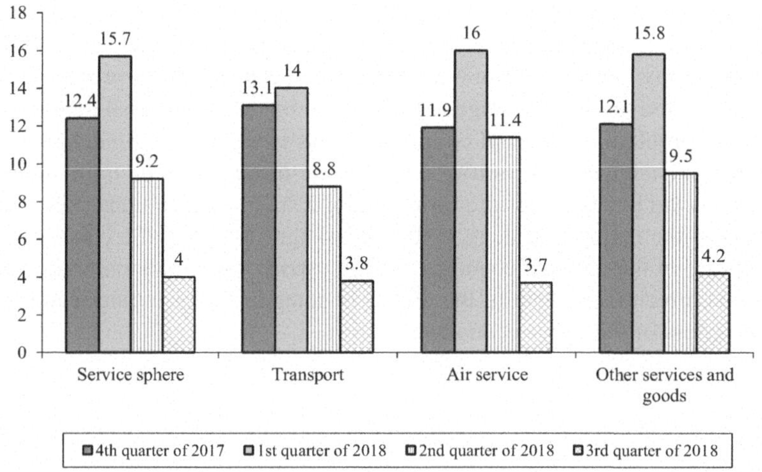

Fig. 1 Global turnover of the export of services in the conditions of the development of the cyber economy for 2017–2018, % based on the current rate of USD (Source: Compiled by the authors based on UNCTAD (2019))

with free movement of people, services and capital, where citizens and companies have free access and possibility to conduct online activities in the conditions of free competition and high level of protection of consumers' rights and personal data, regardless of their citizenship and residence location" (Aleksandrov et al. 2017).

Russia is currently ranked 35th in the world with regard to the quality of its infrastructure. In 2012–2017, the volume of investments into infrastructure constituted 3% of GDP, 1.8% of which came from budgetary investment, and 1.2% from private capital investment.

In the third quarter of 2018, the total volume of global services exported grew by 14%, which was largely caused by an increase of investor interest in the world market for the international exchange of services in the sphere of the digital economy (Fig. 1).

The global turnover of export of services in the third quarter of 2018 decreased as compared to the first quarter of 2018; the value of transport services reduced to 3.8% as compared to 8.8% in the same period of the past quarter.

Apart from the export of services, the most important indicator of the macroeconomic efficiency of integration is global GDP. Thus, global GDP grew by 3.1% in 2017 (increase by 0.7% as compared to 2016). This was the first time since 2011 that growth rates exceeded 3%. In 2018, growth rates of GDP dropped to 3%. At the same time, there are large differences in GDP per capita in the world. In 2017, average GDP per capita in developed countries constituted USD 30,000.

An important issue is the evaluation of participation in value-added chains, including an emphasis on the cyber economy and the digital aspects of inter-country interaction. The current processes of globalization and integration are notable for the fact that most goods (in our case, digital technologies and platforms) are manufactured in several economies with different technological levels and opportunities. In a certain sense, products are now made in the world (Klinov 2008); each separate economy does not assume the full cost of a product but produces only its added value at the production stage, which is conducted by national manufacturers.

Thus, the problem of national competitiveness is significant. Understanding the comparative advantages of countries and the role in international trade unions and agreements is the key issue for the formation of a smart foreign trade policy and for integration of the national strategy in the digital age. Absence of a clear idea of the role and place of the national economy in the system of international trade does not allow for a correct assessment of the effects of integration, including increasing the competitiveness of the cyber economy.

3 Results

The need for calculating volumes of trade in terms of added value, not in terms of gross product, arises from the problem of dual calculation and indirect supply, which might influence the value of gross exports by increasing them or redistributing them between trade partners. This influences the evaluation of economic effects from the processes of regional integration and is an important element during the formation of strategy integration.

The future outlook for the economies of foreign countries is described by the tendency of growth for most economic indicators, of which gross domestic product is the most important. Table 1 provides statistics for the indicators of the future development of the cyber economy in selected countries.

Under the conditions of the international integration of business processes and growth of the population by 35 million, the GDP of the USA will increase by USD 15.14 trillion, with GDP per capita increasing by USD 34,500 by 2050.

Table 1 The future state of the cyber economy in selected countries

	GDP, trillion USD		Population, millions		GDP per capita, USD thousand	
Country	2025	2050	2025	2050	2025	2050
USA	21.42	36.56	340	375	63.0	97.5
Japan	6.30	8.92	125	122	50.4	73.1
Germany	3.94	5.72	82.3	80.3	47.9	71.2
UK	3.11	4.82	61.7	63.3	50.4	76.1
France	3.06	4.61	62.3	63.9	49.1	72.2
Italy	2.86	4.24	60.4	62.0	47.3	68.3
Canada	1.85	2.97	36.8	40.6	50.4	73.1
All developed countries	54.33	86.63	940	990	57.8	87.5

Source: Compiled by the author based on Klinov (2008)

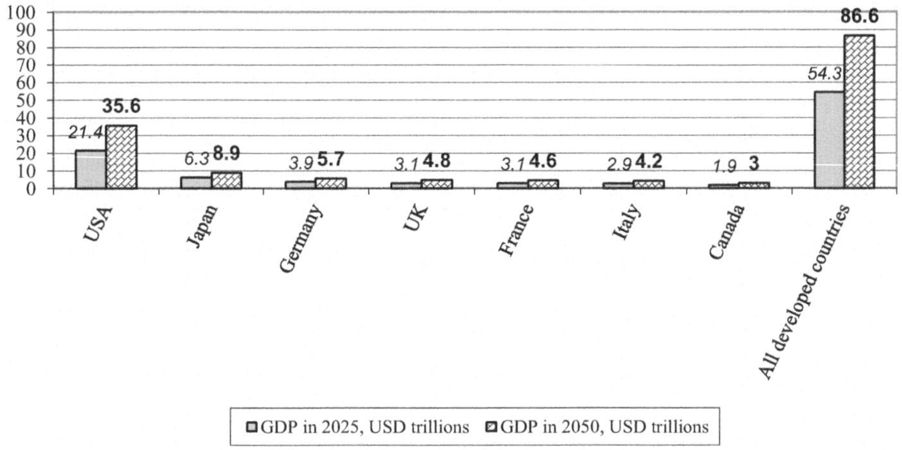

Fig. 2 Potential growth of indicators of GDP under the conditions of the development of the cyber economy in 2025–2050 (Source: Compiled by the authors)

In Japan, GDP per capita will increase by USD 22,700, as a result of the growth of Japan's GDP by USD 2.62 trillion. These results are the consequence of forecasting of insufficiently high business activity of the population and legal entities in the spheres of economic activities, comprehensive robotization of production and trade, and leadership of these countries in many aspects of the international integration of business processes.

All other analyzed countries of the world will also experience growth of GDP between 2025 and 2050 (Fig. 2).

In 2025 developed countries will have GDP per capita of USD 57,800, compared to USD 10,700 in developing countries.

Countries with transitional economies will be situated midway between developed and developing countries with GDP per capita of USD 22,000 (Table 2).

Positive changes in terms of GDP per capita for the period 2025–2050 can be observed in all categories of the analyzed countries.

It should be emphasized that the cyber economy is a science in the sphere of economic management, the initial item of planning for which is full employment, which involves the population in the processes of creation of money margin and commodity margin. The government has to stimulate these developments through strategic management to optimize the balance of payments. Economic cybernetics has to become a doctrine in the future state of the Russian economy.

Let us now study the potential of existing integration associations, taking into account the share of their expenditures for the purposes of developing the cyber economy (Table 3).

Our evaluation shows that the energy sector is the dominating internal factor in such unions as the EAEU (28.7%), the EU (29.1), and the OECD (28.9%); while the chemical industry dominates in the OECD (30.2%), the Shanghai Cooperation Organisation (24%), and NAFTA (22.9%) (Table 4).

Table 2 Perspectives on the global economic development for three groups of countries

Groups of countries	2025		2050		Changes in 2050 as compared to 2025, %	
	GDP per capita, USD thousand	population, millions	GDP per capita, USD thousand	population, millions	GDP per capita, USD thousand	population, millions
Developed countries	57.8	940	87.5	990	151.38	105.32
Developing countries	10.7	6390	22.4	7150	209.35	111.89
Countries with transitional economies	22.0	410	40.8	110	185.45	26.83
All countries	17.0	7740	30.8	8550	181.18	110.47

Source: Compiled by the authors based on Klinov (2008)

Table 3 Share of expenditures of the participants in international economic integration unions for measures to support the cyber economy

No.	Integration union	Share in the structure of gross expenditures (%)
1	Shanghai Cooperation Organisation	7.3
2	EAEU	8.4
3	OECD	12.7
4	Eurasian Customs Union	9.5
5	APEC	14.1
6	BRICS	15.8
7	Mercosur (Chile, Colombia, Bolivia, Peru, and Ecuador)	13.3
8	European Union	19.7
9	NAFTA	16.1

Source: Compiled by the authors

In view of the sectoral specializations of organizations aimed at international integration, Russia should choose the strategy of interacting with the Shanghai Cooperation Organisation and the EAEU in the course of expanding joint production in the sphere of petrochemistry and has industry.

Table 5 shows a SWOT analysis of the activities of organizations for economic integration in implementing measures for the cyber economy.

Thus, in relation to the development of the cyber economy it is possible to distinguish the following strengths of international associations for economic integration:

- High level of consumption
- Technological progress

Table 4 Key spheres of the cyber economy, %

Integration unions	Key spheres of the cyber economy							
	Metalworking production	Processing industry	Machine building	Chemical industry	Agro-industrial complex	Fuel and energy complex	Construction	Food industry
Shanghai Cooperation Organisation	10	5	12	24	34	28	17	14.2
EAEU	5	24	30.1	5.3	10	28.7	17.4	6.8
APEC	12	17	28.7	12	18.4	14.5	5.4	4.8
EU	24	36	19.8	11.8	19.7	29.1	3.2	7.3
NAFTA	34	12.7	29	22.9	20.5	7.8	22.5	7.1
Eurasian Customs Union	28	19	30.7	14.2	25.8	14.3	10.2	9.4
OECD	17	15.5	19.4	30.2	30.1	28.9	11.9	15.7

Source: Developed by the authors

Table 5 SWOT analysis of the activities of organizations for economic integration in implementing measures for the cyber economy

Integration association	Strengths	Weaknesses
Shanghai Cooperation Organisation	High level of consumption	Absence of centralized management of information systems
EAEU	Expansion of limits of digitization	"Shocks" (crises) in the cyber economy
OECD	Development of technological progress	High risk level of financial tools
Eurasian Customs Union	High level of socioeconomic development	Fluctuations during the emergence of inflation expectations
APEC	High level of specialization	Low participation in international division of labor
BRICS	High-quality oil with low sulfur and absence of bismuth	Growth of government loans through usage of obligations
Mercosur	Good geographic location	Low level of legal regime including violation of the rights of investors
EU	Low unemployment levels	Geographic distance between the leading economic districts
NAFTA	Development and sustainability of the market and the cyber economy on the whole	Growth of foreign trade debt
Integration association	**Opportunities**	**Threats**
Shanghai Cooperation Organisation	High level of environmental friendliness	Risks of digitization with absence of specialized ecological platforms
EAEU	Possibility to generate added value in global digital cooperation	Absence of the tools for the centralized management of digital technologies
OECD	High level of competitive advantage	Absence of the cyber security systems
Eurasian Customs Union	Large share of budget expenditure to support population's living standards	Problems of globalization
APEC	Aims for the full employment of population in the cyber economy	Deficit of skilled personnel
BRICS	Possibility to improve the system of planning and management of money margins	High dependence on inflation processes
Mercosur	High level of quality in the oil and gas industry	Limited food sector
EU	Increase in the levels of commodity margins	Demographic problems
NAFTA	Standardization of the processes for a unified information space	Environmental problems and risks of nature protection activities

Source: Compiled by the authors

Table 6 Unified markets as participants in international economic unions

No.	Integration union	Types of markets
1	Shanghai Cooperation Organisation	Energy market
2	EAEU	Labor market
3	OECD	Digital market
4	Eurasian Customs Union	Currency market
5	APEC	Insurance market
6	BRICS	Oil market
7	Mercosur (Chile, Colombia, Bolivia, Peru, and Ecuador)	Diamond market
8	EU	Medicines market
9	NAFTA	Financial market

Source: Developed by the authors

- High level of specialization
- Low unemployment rates
- High level of socioeconomic development.

The stages of development of the cyber economy during the optimization of international economic relations are:

1. Formation of flexible chains of added value at the global scale
2. Implementation of the strategies of portfolio players
3. Diversification of the offer of goods and technologies
4. Creation of additional demand for digital technologies
5. Development of "special" relationships with buyers
6. Adaptability and speed of digital transformation.

Table 6 shows unified markets as participants in international economic unions.

There are objective and subjective factors that influence the competitiveness of the cyber economy. These include the effects of internal policy on the management of digital assets and technologies, the practices related to balance of payments in integration unions, specialization of production, and the implementation of long-term strategic plans. A special role belongs to investments in the cyber economy at the scale of economic international integration (Table 7).

Thus, the total cost of capital that is attracted by the participants in integration unions for implementing the cyber economy will equal USD 8.13 per USD 1 of investments. In other words, the interest rate on the alternative price of capital will exceed 8.13%. This should be used as a discount price during the implementation of joint foreign trade projects, and with the rate above 8.13% it is expedient to evaluate discounted currency flows within the implementation of interstate investment programs.

Ultimately, the important role of studying this problem and the development of strategies and tactics for economic development under the conditions of the cyber economy lies with economic forecasting, as this allows—within a certain margin of error—forecasting the results of decisions, including those regarding the integration of national policy. Regardless of the political regime, the results of economic

Table 7 Average volume of investments in the cyber economy at the scale of economic international integration

No.	Integration union	Dominating source of financing	Share	USD price	USD cost
1	Shanghai Cooperation Organisation	Money margin	10	0.076	0.76
2	EAEU	Stock market tools	20	0.076	1.52
3	OECD	Special drawing rights	4	0.08	0.32
4	Eurasian Customs Union	Subsidies	1	0.02	0.02
5	APEC	Share issues	5	0.05	0.25
6	BRICS	Subsidized crediting	20	0.10	2.0
7	Mercosur (Chile, Colombia, Bolivia, Peru, and Ecuador)	Loans and credits	30	0.08	2.4
8	EU	Leasing	5	0.10	0.5
9	NAFTA	Infrastructural mortgage	5	0.04	2.0
10	Total	–	100	–	8.13

forecasts are used as the main argument to explain a decision on acceding to a particular integration union, including in the interests of digitizing the economies of the integrated countries. Economics has a range of methods and tools for forecasting, each of which has its advantages and disadvantages. Besides, the consequences of a country's participation in an integration union could influence dozens of economic indicators both positively and negatively. However, it is not possible to find a universal model to forecast all of these effects. Nevertheless, it is necessary to determine the key consequences of such a decision, and so the selection of forecasting tools is very important for any researcher.

Here we treat forecasting as the process of developing a conclusion on the future development and result of something (Ozhegov and Shvedova 1996). There are two different approaches to forecasting: search (genetic) forecasting and normative and target forecasting. In the first case, forecasting takes place on the basis of the current information, which is the starting point for the researcher who builds the forecast. In the second case, the starting point is the selection of target indicators that are to be achieved in the future.

The British economist David Hendry distinguishes the following types of macroeconomic forecasting (Hendry 2003):

- Guessing, "rules of thumb," "informal models"
- Expert judgments
- Extrapolation
- Leading indicators
- Surveys
- Time series models
- Econometric systems (Turuntseva 2011).

Table 8 Effectiveness of the Russian cyber economy according to the Thirlwall's Law for the period until 2050

No.	Indicators	2020	2025	2030	2035	2040	2050
1	Elasticity of demand for export for revenues €	0.35	0.51	0.54	0.57	0.72	0.79
2	Growth rate of revenues abroad (z)	1.11	1.18	1.22	1.05	1.14	1.27
3	Growth rate of demand for exports (x) p. 1 × p. 2	0.39	0.60	0.66	0.60	0.82	1.00
4.	Elasticity of demand for imports for domestic revenues (*П*)	0.29	0.41	0.48	0.33	0.64	0.65
5.	Growth rate of GDP, coordinated with long-term balance of payments (g_B), % p. 3 ÷ p. 4 × 100%	134.0	146.8	137.3	181.4	128.3	154.4

Source: Compiled by the authors based on the data on Russia's balance of payments

The latter two methods are essential for macroeconomic forecasting from the point of view of precision and for the possibility of explaining mistakes. The most popular methods in Russia are econometric models (including time series models), consensus forecasts, and leading indicators (Turuntseva 2011). According to the collective monograph of the Institute of World Economics and International Relations of the Russian Academy of Sciences, "The scientific and expert community came to their conclusions on the ineffectiveness of applying the mathematical methods of modeling. . .during forecasting of socio-economic and political processes" (Dynkin 2011).

Let us perform a forecast for the development of the cyber economy in view of its dynamic development in the international arena, according to Thirlwall's Law (Table 8):

$$g_e = e \times z \div P = x \div P \times 100\% \tag{1}$$

where:

g_B—growth rate of GDP, coordinated with long-term balance of payments
e—elasticity of demand for exports for revenue
z—growth rate of revenues abroad
P—elasticity of demand for imports for domestic revenues
x—growth rate of demand for export.

The calculations show that in 2020, the growth rate of GDP coordinated with the long-term balance of payments in Russia will reach 134%, growing until 2025, when its estimated value will reach 146.8%.

By 2050, the studied indicator of the cyber economy will grow to 154.4%, which is connected to the cyclic character of economic development and implementation of long-term, large-scale measures for the digitization of the economy in the Russian Federation.

4 Conclusions

It is possible to conclude that the formation of the cyber economy is subject to laws that aim into the far future, but the foundations for its development originated in the age of the birth of capitalism.

Of course, studying the problem of international economic integration in the context of the competitiveness of the cyber economy requires further scientific elaboration. In this chapter, we only outline the key positions and landmarks as a foundation for further research that should focus on the strategic consequences for business and government of the ubiquitous implementation of digital technologies and resources, including how they interact with the economic integration of countries.

References

Aleksandrov OV, Dobrolyubova EI, Talapina EV (2017) Development of the digital economy: the approaches of the OECD and priorities for Russia. The state and citizens in the electronic environment (1), 17

Dynkin AA (ed) (2011) Strategic global forecast 2030. Expanded variant. Institute of World Economy and International Relations of the Russian Academy of Sciences: Magistr, pp 17–18

Hendry DF (2003) How economists forecast, outstanding economic forecasts. MIT Press, Cambridge, p 24

Klinov V (2008) World economy: forecast until 2050. Issues Econ 5(1):62–79

Kostyunina GM (2019) International economic integration. Moscow State Institute of International Relations. https://docplayer.ru/29335077-Mezhdunarodnaya-ekonomicheskaya-integraciya-mgimo-universitet-m-id-rf-kostyunina-g-m.html. Accessed 19 February 2019

Nazarov VS, Lazaryan SS, Nikonov IV, Votinov AI (2019) International trade: search for the causes of the fall. Issues Econ 1(1):79–91

Ozhegov SI, Shvedova NY (1996) Dictionary of the Russian language. Az, Moscow

President of the Russian Federation (2019) Decree dated May 7, 2015, No. 204 "Concerning national goals and strategic tasks of development of the Russian Federation until 2024"

The Cyber Economy (2019) Web-site of Nodir Sadykov. http://cybereconomics.ru/cybereconomy/. Accessed 05 March 2019

Turuntseva MY (2011) Forecasts of foreign trade indicators: comparative analysis of qualitative features of various models. Russian Bull Foreign Econ (2), 35–45. http://www.rfej.ru/rvv/id/37D065/$file/35-45.pdf. Accessed 15 February 2019

UNCTAD (2019) Statistics 2018. Quarterly trade in services, 2018/Q3. https://unctadstat.unctad.org/EN/Infographics.html#&gid=2019&pid=Trade%20in%20services%2C%202018%20Q3. Accessed 12 February 2019

Veduta EN (2019) Economic cyber system – a necessary tool of sustainable development of the defense complex. http://iabrics.org/page559800.html. Accessed 22 February 2019

Integration of the Cyber Economy with Research and Development at the "University–Science–Industry–Market" Level

Anna A. Ostrovskaya , Nadezhda Ilieva, and Antonina Traykova Atanasova

Abstract The evolution of economic systems requires changes in the ways that they are managed and, therefore, dictates new approaches for the conduct of scientific research and the training of personnel.

The purpose of this chapter is to characterize the processes for the integration of universities, science, and industry with the needs of the cyber economy.

The research is divided into three main blocks: characteristics of the main directions of such integration, determining potential problems, and the development of proposals for its acceleration.

The research shows that in the modern conditions of widespread digitization, the rapid development of universities, scientific institutes, and industrial companies could and should be built on a close and systemic approach to integration processes and on the creation of a unified closed cyclic system, which satisfies the disparate needs of the digital economy: from the training of skilled personal to the implementation of applied R&D to industrial production through the application of modern digital technologies.

A. A. Ostrovskaya (✉)
RUDN University, Moscow, Russia
e-mail: ostrovskaya-aa@rudn.ru

N. Ilieva
National Institute of Geophysics, Geodesy and Geography, Bulgarian Academy of Sciences, Sofia, Bulgaria

A. T. Atanasova
Sofia University "St. Kliment Ohridski", National Institute for Geophysics, Geodesy and Geography, Bulgarian Academy of Sciences, Sofia, Bulgaria

© Springer Nature Switzerland AG 2019
V. M. Filippov et al. (eds.), *The Cyber Economy*, Contributions to Economics,
https://doi.org/10.1007/978-3-030-31566-5_29

1 Introduction

The paradigm for the development of a unified economic system envisaged the interaction between three key components: education, science, and production. The modern development of economic systems and the necessity for the commercialization of all types of activities introduced a fourth element into the equation—the market.

A systemic approach to the integration of the activities of educational establishments, scientific establishments, and industrial companies to satisfy consumer needs should ensure the optimality of the connections and interactions between the above subjects and objects of economic relations during the production, exchange, and distribution of material goods, which fully conform to the requirements of the cyber economy. The cyber economy consists of systemic resources, which increase the effectiveness of economic processes through the optimal management of connections and interactions between the subsystems of subjects and objects of economic relations.

The importance of a high level of interaction between the above subjects is because information carriers are often the same specialists who use the unified information environment. The integration processes between education, science, and industry have the potential to accelerate technological progress and allow for the rational usage of the intellectual potential of science and higher school of a separate country and the global community on the whole. Analysis and usage of such experience may bring large profits for all participants in the process (Borobov 2014).

The rapid development of information technologies in the last decade has charged the processes and technologies for processing big flows of data with a unique role in managing the economy and its competitiveness. Information and data in the modern world directly influence all spheres of economic activities, transforming into an international means of interaction between the integration processes of countries, spheres, companies, and even separate specialists (Zavarzin and Goev 2001).

The task of developing an economy based on the leading information technologies predetermines the importance of the formation of a unified information system able to interact between various economic subjects that conduct their activities in different spheres (industry, science, education, etc.). This system has to take into account the requirements that are set by the market for the results of analysis and forms of the provision of data.

It should be noted that more and more industrial companies, including those that are partly or wholly government owned, are using the model of open innovation, which allows for the commercialization not only of internal but also external ideas through the implementation of joint research projects with educational and scientific organizations, as well as with startups, teams, and individual scholars (Kashirin 2013).

Thus, the integration of education, science, and industrial production is a joint usage of potential for mutual benefit, primarily in the training and advanced training of personnel, joint scientific research, implementation of scientific developments,

Fig. 1 Evolution of concepts for managing the developmental role of universities

etc. These integration processes cover a wide range of various directions of activity and are expressed in diverse forms (Borobov 2014).

2 Materials and Method

Under modern economic conditions, any university that wants to assume a leading reputational position has to be active not only in the markets for educational services (University 1.0) and scientific research (University 2.0), but also must be an entrepreneurial university (University 3.0). Such a university will be oriented toward the competitive demands of the market, in the training of personnel, and with a focus on R&D in selected top-priority directions. University 3.0 is a new type of university that functions as the integrator of the main processes related to technological entrepreneurship and innovation, the development of new businesses, and the formation of new markets.[1]

The changing stages in the concept of the developmental role of universities are presented in Fig. 1.

While the Russian education system has sufficient experience of implementing the management of universities according to the concept of University 2.0, the issues surrounding a transition to University 3.0: implementing joint educational programs;

[1]University 3.0—a center of science, education, and technological entrepreneurship. http://inno.nsu.ru/facts/2016-05-30.htm

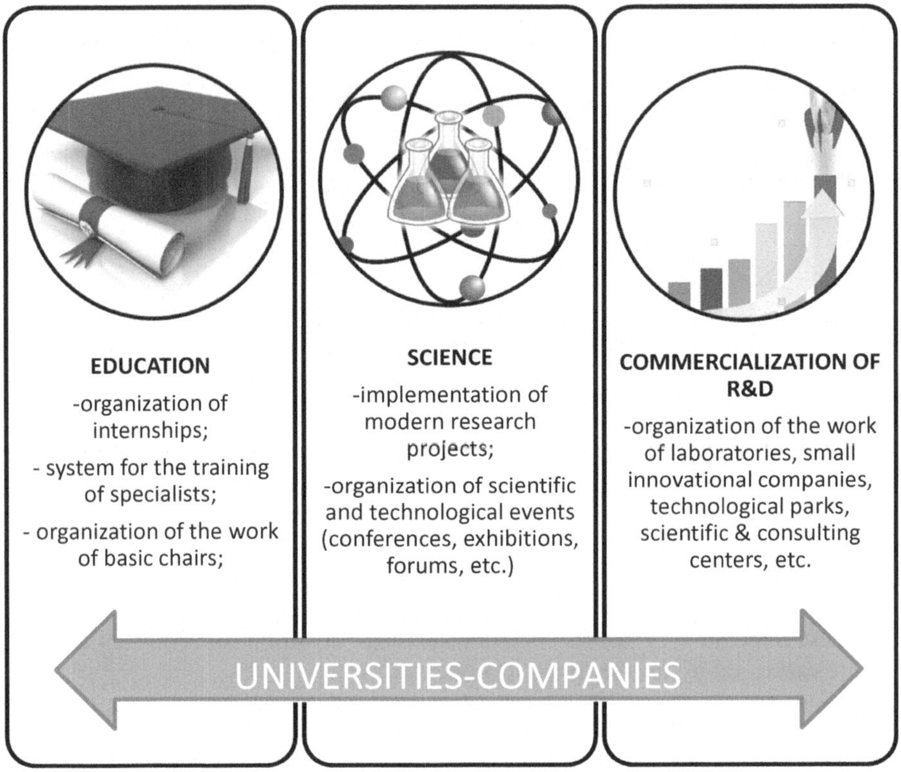

Fig. 2 The main directions of interaction between universities and companies

conducting R&D for industrial partners to produce new products and services for new markets; and the creation of innovative entrepreneurial ecosystems that utilize the mechanisms of the cyber economy are still unsolved.

For the purpose of formulating new approaches to accelerate the integration processes of the cyber economy in the sphere of "university, industry, markets," it seems expedient to divide the research into three parts:

- Distinguishing the main directions for interactions between universities, science, and companies in the Russian Federation
- Determining the existing problems that emerge during such interactions
- Formulating proposals on how to accelerate the integration processes between these subjects, in view of the decisive market factors.

Analysis of existing Russian practice allows us to distinguish three main areas where interactions between universities and companies are happening (Fig. 2).

A number of problems are apparent during the implementation of these directions of interaction.

1. Despite the theoretical effectiveness of trilateral target agreements on training (company, trainee, university), neither of the parties fully implements the potential of such agreements in practice. Companies have no influence on the quality or content of the education for which they pay in order to get a skilled specialist; the trainee is not aware of the company's specifics; and the competencies envisaged by educational standards and shaped by universities, do not conform to the professional competencies that the companies require. The organization of internships is an important form of interaction between universities and industry. Despite the fact that these are utilized in the Russian educational system during the last year of training, they are of a rather formal character, as undergraduates are not given specific applied tasks that would stimulate the practical application of competencies they have obtained at university. It should also be noted that companies do not show a lot of initiative in the organization of internships, underestimating the potential of such opportunities to select the best prospective personnel (Kokuytseva et al. 2016). This problem is caused by the fact that traditional technical education in higher school is based on providing a theoretical rather than practical scientific foundation. New knowledge and the practical scientific basis on Russian and most foreign universities are usually formed on the basis of experience and practice that are confirmed by their implementation in various spheres of economy. In hi-tech spheres of the economy, real practice influences the development of technology and equipment in the economy and in society on the whole. Such practical solutions are usually implemented in educational programs in the form of laboratory sessions, workshops, on-the-job training, etc. When training a specialist in the sphere of the design of complex technical systems (machine building, instrument engineering, new materials, microelectronics, control systems, etc.), real experience can only be gained after 3–5 years in a construction bureau or production company. In the practical conditions of working in a company, the specialist faces real technical tasks—technical conditions, technological limitations, equipment, design tools, CAD systems—and real economic issues—pricing limitations, difficult negotiations, financing, limitations of choice and components, sanctions, embargos, complex logistics, limitations of working with suppliers, and cooperation.
2. The implementation of joint research projects between companies and universities, and company support for such projects, expand the opportunities for exchanging competencies. However, currently the cooperation of companies and universities is largely limited to the creation of reports on performed research work without taking forward the joint implementation of developed innovations. A similar situation is observed in the commercialization of R&D. The government has implemented a policy to stimulate university science, moving financing from educational programs to scientific programs, which has allowed universities to open laboratories, educational and demonstration complexes, technological parks, consulting centers, etc. and to purchase expensive equipment. Due to these changes, universities have become more attractive to companies for joint research work. However, the results of such joint efforts rarely reach commercialization and industry still largely operates a closed innovation system (Kokuytseva et al. 2016).

3 Results

The necessity to accelerate the integration processes between economic objects in view of decisive market factors and the digitization of all processes is emphasized by German Gref, CEO of Sberbank, "We do not hire lawyers who do not know how to work with neural networks. If you care about your future, please take the corresponding training courses. Regardless of your specialty—manager, economist, lawyer, etc.—you will have to work with Big Data".[2] Of course, all participants in economic activities aim at reducing the time taken for the execution of a certain procedure, as time is a most valuable resource. The information age is becoming the digital age through the appearance of Big Data technology, which has allowed for the usage of an unlimited volume of unprocessed data from the Internet. Another breakthrough has been the advent of cloud technologies, which allow saving space on hard drives through storing data in a digital space, enabling instantaneous processing. The volume of data produced by digital devices grows constantly.

Given this digital revolution, the educational process cannot stay on the sidelines; it must also modernize. In terms of new technologies and the educational process, the enactment of the following measures is essential:

1. Implementation of the project approach in educational programs, especially at the second and third stages of education, which conforms to the requirements of students and companies: The project approach takes into account the current limitations and problems in the training of students in an integrative manner for the organizations of the hi-tech industry. The elements of such an approach include the adoption of end-to-end complex projects and the establishment of educational programs in specific, high-priority areas (e.g., design of technical complexes, radio electronic equipment, consumer electronics, modeling of complex technical systems, and machine building devices). Such programs are built on introducing all key stages of the company's product life cycle: its real technologies, standards, methodology and practice of project management, modeling, design, and production methods into educational practice. Students will be instructed on the whole path for the creation of a real product and master the implementation of production technologies. Such university/industry integration could be ensured through the new possibilities offered by digitization and the technologies of Industry 4.0 (tools for digital imitation modeling, cloud calculations, 3D and 4D printing, industrial Internet of Things, digital doubles of devices and processes, digital originals, centralized management of master data, etc.) (Chursin and Tyulin 2018). This will also add to the competitiveness of graduates entering the labor market as specialists (developers, engineers, economists, managers, etc.) as this is largely determined by their knowledge and skills in digital transformation in all spheres of the economy and ubiquitous implementation of

[2]Sberbank shall not hire lawyers without experience with neural network. https://ria.ru/20170723/1499009528.html

the technologies of Big Data processing and analysis, predictive analytics, the Internet of Things, new interfaces machine-human, technologies of location and geo-location, industrial autonomous robots, horizontal and vertical connection between information and cyber-physical systems, virtual and alternate reality, etc. Such advances in the integration of educational programs could be implemented by universities, in partnership with sectoral leaders and innovative technological companies. Implementation of joint educational and applied programs in technical and humanitarian sciences by universities and hi-tech companies will create new experts: "digital engineers," "research technologists," "data scientists," and "system economists." Such specialists will be able to perform a wide range of key tasks immediately after graduation.
2. Implementation of individual educational trajectories for students with the help of active usage of the mechanisms of the cyber economy and modern information and communication technologies: All accumulated data, i.e., the "digital trace," of each student should be stored in the unified cloud space for certain programs, and "digital avatar" for each student should be formed.
3. Creation and practical usage of joint centers of competencies (bringing together the University, Science, and Industry) through the creation of an information platform/ecosystem, that contains all relevant data in a unified form, using the possibilities of AI, which processes large arrays of data on the basis of neural networks to provide analytics for two key directions:

Educational Activities

- Formation of demand in the labor market, based on the portfolio of employees of state corporations, where the functions of each employee are assigned according to their competencies (an analog of the "digital employee profile")
- Formation of proposals for improving certain federal state educational standards and adding specific competencies to a subject on the basis of employer demands

Scientific Activities

- Joint applied scientific research in the sphere of technologies for the processing and usage of digital data, creation of digital doubles and digital avatars in order to produce joint modern service solutions, which will allow involving information on the object into the economic turnover.

One of the examples of an improvement to the integration processes between the economic objects "University—science—industry—market" is the interaction between *Russian Space Systems JSC* and the Center of Management of Industrial Spheres of the RUDN University in Big Data processing within the project "Digital Earth." The results of the project provide new opportunities and objective information regarding agriculture and forestry, mapping, cartography, regional management, control and prevention of emergencies. In short a digital double of the Earth was created. The educational integration component within the selected thematic sphere, Big Data processing was the creation of a joint master's program: "Big Data economy." The scientific component was the applied scientific research entitled

"Territory." A web application will be created, which will allow using neural network algorithms in the automatic regime in order to recognize various objects (buildings, object of forest fund, etc.) in satellite images with very high resolution. The results of this project are already in high demand in the market, which shows the effectiveness of well- implemented integration measures.

4 Conclusions

It is possible to conclude that in the modern conditions of digitization of all processes it is impossible to ensure the rapid development of such objects as universities, research institutes, and industrial companies without an integration component. Only a systemic approach to such interactions with the usage of advances in the sphere of AI can stimulate the formation of the unified closed cyclic system to satisfy the needs of the digital market economy, from the training of specialists to research into the production of competitive goods and services.

Acknowledgments The chapter was prepared with financial support from the Ministry of Education of the Russian Federation within the scientific project No. 14.575.21.0167 (identifier RFMEFI57517X0167).

References

Borobov V (2014) Integration of education, science, and production at the modern stage of development. Mod Sci Curr Issues Theory Pract (3–4). http://www.vipstd.ru/nauteh/index.php/%2D%2D-ep14-03/1177

Chursin A, Tyulin A (2018) Competence management and competitive product development: concept and implications for practice. Springer, Cham, p 241

Kashirin A (2013) Open innovations. The world practice and experience of corporation 'Rostekh'. Innovations 12(182):10–17

Kokuytseva T, Ostrovskaya A, Semenov A, Kychanov V (2016) Managing competencies in the Russian machine building sphere on the basis of development of interaction between universities and companies. Econ Entrep 9(74):1024–1029

Zavarzin V, Goev A (2001) Integration of education, science, and production. Russian Entrep 2 (4):48–56

A Strategy for Implementing the Technologies of Industry 4.0 and the Tools of Competency Management in the Digital Economy

Andrey E. Tyulin

Abstract This chapter studies the economic essence of Industry 4.0. The law of interconnection between competencies and the emergence of new markets is used to substantiate the dependence of demand for innovative products on the effective functioning of science-driven companies and on the development of fundamental science as a whole. A generalized list of internal resources and characteristics of a company, which influence its innovative potential, is given, and a mathematical evaluation of innovative potential is provided. The influence of the effective usage of a company's innovative potential on the competitiveness of the products that it produces is shown. A scheme for a self-reproducing process to improve competencies is presented, and the tools of competency management for a company implementing the technologies of Industry 4.0 are studied. Formulas for a mathematical description of innovative technology and its competitiveness are presented. An algorithm for the development of a strategy to implement the technologies of Industry 4.0 and the tools of competency management in digital industry are given.

1 Introduction

Industry 4.0 is anticipated to result in the creation of a digital economic system through the integration of all subjects of economic relations (consumers, investors, companies, etc.) in the process of value creation. Intelligent companies, comfortable with transformation and adaptation and able to use resources efficiently, will be dominant. The digital economy is oriented toward the individual desires of customers and is based on rapid technological development, which is achieved by means of the wide usage and intelligent analysis of Big Data from the global information space in real time.

In each industrial revolution (Fig. 1), the economic system offers its own tools and mechanisms for the implementation of technologies. In the Third Industrial

A. E. Tyulin
Joint Stock Company "Russian Space Systems", Moscow, Russian Federation
e-mail: tyulin_ae@rudn.ru

© Springer Nature Switzerland AG 2019
V. M. Filippov et al. (eds.), *The Cyber Economy*, Contributions to Economics,
https://doi.org/10.1007/978-3-030-31566-5_30

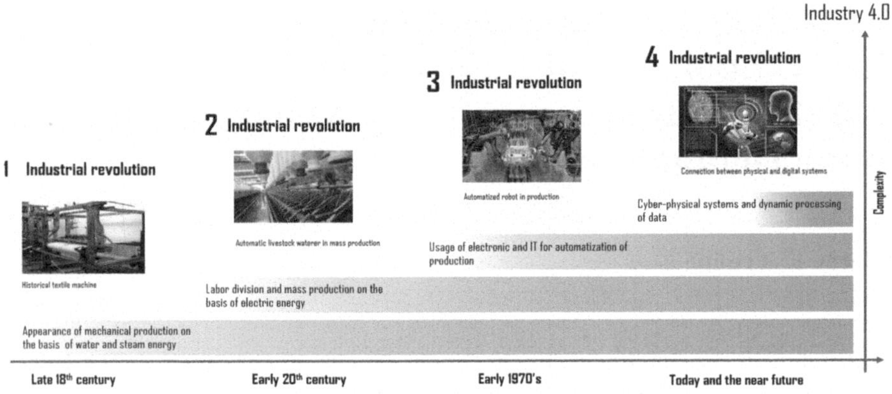

Fig. 1 The four industrial revolutions (Source: Shukalov et al. 2018)

Revolution, these tools included the establishment of programs for innovative development leading to new technologies and the formation of new key competencies (or their invention).

2 Materials and Method

Industry 4.0 requires the development of new strategic approaches to implementing technologies and forming competencies that are necessary for the development, production, and promotion of products in the market. The economic law on the interconnection between competencies and the emergence of new markets states that the creation of unique competencies increases resources in hi-tech companies, which leads to the rapid appearance of unique innovative technologies that are used in the creation of completely new products. Emergence of these products leads to an increase in the needs for yet more new benefits. The resultant growth of the economy stimulates further demand for yet more unique technologies. This law illustrates spiral turnover: "competencies–resources–products–needs–competencies" (Tyulin and Chursin 2016a, b).

The development of unique competencies ensures a large synergetic effect in the economy, which is manifested in industry and education—as the demand for new competencies and a high level of education creates demand for new educational services. The development of new competencies and the resultant emergence of new technologies also create conditions for the development of new consumer markets. Competition in the sphere of hi-tech and unique competencies also has other effects—unlike the traditional industry—as companies react to changes in their rivals' activities faster, guaranteeing rapid and effective changes to their behavior.

The effective functioning of science-driven companies creates demand for innovative products leading to a snowball effect and demand for key competencies in new spheres. Increase in this demand stimulates an increase in offers for key competencies. All of this stimulates the development of fundamental and applied science to provide applied inventions, which become the basis of innovative technologies, which then become new goods and services. Striving for the commercialization of innovative technologies encourages hi-tech companies to stimulate the creation of new markets for promoting their new products. The creation of new consumer markets for selling innovative products leads to growth in production and forms a large number of new key competencies, which, in turn, lead to the appearance of more new products and, eventually, new consumer markets.

The conceptual model “competencies, innovations, markets” therefore shows that an increase in the level of competencies stimulates the expansion of consumer markets by means of the emergence of new products, which satisfy new needs and become dominant in the market. Market mechanisms stimulate the growth of investments in breakthrough technologies, which are used for the manufacture of these products. According to the laws of the innovative economy, these investments stimulate the increase of competencies in the sphere. Of course, this growth takes place only for a certain period of time, when the expansion of consumer markets takes place, as, according to economic laws, any consumer markets have limits, expressed by the fact that over a period of time innovative technologies become ordinary. Further growth requires a constant stream of new innovative technologies, which prologue further growth of consumer markets and, accordingly, the growth of competencies. A nonmarket tool for managing a company’s economic development in the Fourth Industrial Revolution could be the strategy of implementing the modern technologies of Industry 4.0 along with the tools of competency management during the digital transformation of industry to the cyber economy.

The cyber economy will be founded on digital production. It represents a system of economic relations that functions in the conditions of the information space and ensures optimal ties and interactions between the subjects and objects of economic relations during the production, exchange, and distribution of material goods. The cyber economy offers—on the basis of the digital approach—a system for a company’s resource management—the basis for the development and implementation of new technologies. An important task of the cyber economy is managing the technological platform and production system of a company for manufacturing new products.

In order to facilitate this, one important tool is the evaluation of a company’s innovative potential. Thus, in order to implement the modern technologies of Industry 4.0 and use of the tools for competency management as the basis of this strategy, it is necessary to evaluate the innovative potential of the company. This is determined as a totality of various types of resources and factors, including production and technological, financial and economic, intellectual, research and development, and other resources, necessary for the implementation of innovative activities.

For an organization to achieve the necessary level of innovative potential, an innovative system must be developed and managed. Each component of innovative potential is based on a certain set of knowledge, which transforms into competencies for both the organization as a whole and its internal groups and teams.

Each of the distinguished types of resources and factors could have a different number of criteria that are determined by various sources. For an organization, such sources could include accounting documents, production reports, data produced by the HR department, results of employee surveys, etc. Attention should be focused only on the criteria that stimulate the growth of the organization's innovative activity. For each type of resource or factor, an integral index is set, the value of which indicates the high, medium, or low innovative potential of the organization for this type of resource or factor.

The innovative potential of an organization is determined primarily by internal resources and factors:

- Financial and economic resources
- Intellectual resources
- Organizational and managerial resources
- Research and development resources
- Production and technological resources
- Marketing factors
- Information and methodological factors.

The distinguished resources and factors make different contributions to the formation of the overall innovative potential of the organization.

As the methods for managing the organization's innovative potential envisages significant spending of resources, it is necessary to have tools that allow for assessment of the components of innovative potential.

For example, an assessment of the various components of innovative potential could be built on the basis of a certain system of criteria y_i (Chursin 2010).

The integral assessment (index) of the component of innovative potential *IP* is a weighted sum of assessment criteria:

$$IP = \sum_{i=1}^{n} w_i y_i,$$

$$\sum_{i=1}^{13} w_i = 1.$$

Such an assessment could also be obtained for other components of the innovative potential. According to the calculated indices, each component of the organization's innovative potential is assigned with the category:

- "High" level of the component of innovative potential with the value of the corresponding integral index [0,65; 1]
- "Medium" level of the component of innovative potential with the value of the corresponding integral index [0,5; 0,64]
- "Low" level of the component of innovative potential with the value of the corresponding integral index [0; 0,49].

With the known values of the components of innovative potential, integral assessment *IP* could also be a weighted sum of the components.

In practice, certain components of innovative potential could achieve a high level, and other components could be at the lower level. The areas where innovative potential is not sufficient require the formation and development of new competencies.

Through the effective usage of its innovative potential, the organization can support its competitiveness and the competitiveness of its issued products. The effect of the implementation of such innovations includes either the possibility to produce more products with the same volume of spent resources or the preservation of the existing volume of production with lower spent resources (Fig. 2).

In the language of production functions this means that an increase by means of growth of the technological coefficient A: $Y = A \cdot F(x_1, x_2, \ldots, x_n)$, where A—technological coefficient (growing as a result of the implementation of innovations), F—production function, $x_1, x_2, \ldots, x_n$—production functions.

Management of each component of the organization's innovative potential is connected to development of the corresponding competencies by means of the resources spent on this process. An organization that strives for domination in the market has to start a self-reproducing process of improving competencies (Fig. 3) and increasing the effectiveness of resource usage. The process of developing unique competencies should be oriented at the necessity for the evolution of the production line of the organization in order to preserve its dominant position in the market. This requires tools to increase the effectiveness of construction and technological and production processes using Industry 4.0 as the basis for the development of new competencies.

Let us consider the tools for competency management within the strategy of implementing the technologies of Industry 4.0 in digital industry. Assessment and

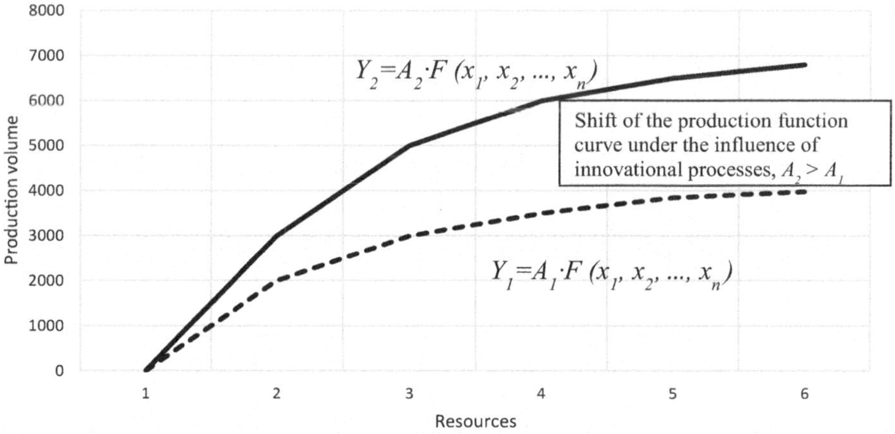

Fig. 2 Shift of the production function as a result of the effective usage of the innovative potential (Source: Compiled by the authors)

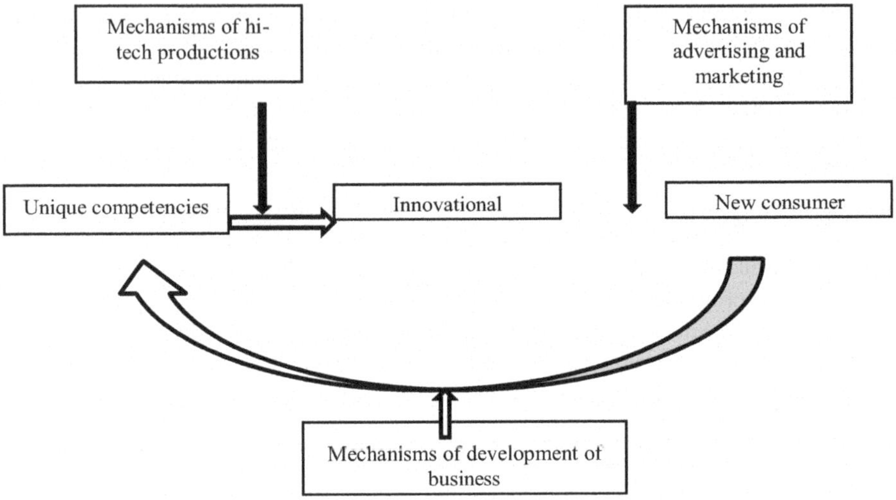

Fig. 3 Self-reproducing process for the improvement of competencies (Source: Compiled by the authors based on Shamin et al. 2017)

ranking of the key competencies are built according to the following scheme (Chursin and Tyulin 2018). The economic and mathematical model is used for calculating the aggregate value (index) that characterizes the importance of the competency based on a range of qualities that are distinguished according to the developed form of description of the key competence. Ranking of the key competencies is determined by their comparison on the basis of calculated scores.

Thus, the formation of an aggregate assessment requires quantitative expressions for each quality that corresponds to its specific features.

The formula for calculating the index of the key competency *EK* has the following form:

$$EK = \sum_{i=1}^{N} (w_i \cdot M_i(l_i - \alpha_i)^{\gamma_i}),$$

where *N*—number of characteristics that describe the key competency (e.g., professionally competent work groups with an effective research team and modern production facilities; a functional environment in which the work group performs its scientific and production activities; the level of maturity of technologies that are developed due to the considered competency; the ability to disseminate the key competencies in other spheres of industry; the presence of competing subjects—owners of similar key competencies; in the case of the presence of rivals—their advantages or disadvantages as compared to each other; the presence of a university/research center that undertakes work connected to the key competency; the presence of licenses, certificates, and awards (primarily with international acknowledgment); potential for the preservation of key competencies over the mid- and long-term);

w_i—weight coefficients that satisfy the ratio $\sum_{i=1}^{N} w_i = 1$, values of weight coefficients that characterize the relative contribution of the corresponding parameters of the key competencies into the general assessment *EK;*

l_i is the assessment of the corresponding feature according to the scale l: $0 \le l_i \le 1$;

M_i is the coefficient of the sustainability of the feature and expresses the level of the threat of the studied competency's elimination from the overall set of key competencies: $0 \le M_i \le 1$; in this sense, the coefficient of sustainability depends on the level of risk that is connected to the possible reduction of the feature's score;

α_i, has to conform to the conditions: $0 \le \alpha_i \le 1, i = 1, 2, \ldots, N$, the sense of these coefficients consists in the marginal valuation of the studied feature;

γ_i is the indicator of unique innovations. This indicator could take values from interval [0; 1]. The economic sense of this indicator consists in the measure of correspondence between the studied features with the notion of unique innovative characteristics.

Based on the assessment of unique competencies, it is possible to make a decision on whether to start development of the innovative technology that will be the basis for the creation of highly competitive products. Thus, when selecting innovative technologies for the creation of new products it is necessary to take into account their character and influence on the competitiveness of the products they will produce (Tyulin and Chursin 2017). Let us consider the following set of innovative technologies: I_1, I_2, I_N.

Each studied innovative technology has to improve the characteristics of the studied products in case of its successful implementation. As a rule, an innovative technology can improve several characteristics of a product. In order to denote this feature of the innovative technology we shall use the vector of characteristics (q) of products $Q(I_i) = \left(q_1, q_2, \ldots, q_{M_i}\right)$. We suppose that I_i technology improves M_i various characteristics of products. In different variations of the economic and mathematical model we shall use values q_i as fixed numbers or as random values. Each innovative technology is described by its cost of development and implementation. The value shall be described in the following way: $V = V(I_i)$.

In various options of application of the studied economic and mathematical model we shall be using the interval value as value V, as for hi-tech companies in modern economic conditions the cost of the development and implementation of an innovative technology could be greater than planned.

Usage of any technology—and especially an innovative technology—is connected to certain risks. The risk during the implementation phase consists in the fact that the anticipated effect could be much lower than expected. This risk shall be described by a random value $0 \le R(I_i) \le 1$.

A zero value of $R(I_i)$ means there is zero effect from the usage of an innovative technology, as value 1 means that expectations for the effectiveness of implementation were fully justified.

Thus, an innovative technology shall be described in the following way: $I_i = (Q_i, V_i, R_i)$.

Another object in the studied economic and mathematical model is the competitiveness of the developed product. As already noted, the notion of product competitiveness belongs to the complex category, which should include many factors. In the economic and mathematical model we shall consider product competitiveness as a vector consisting of a set of numerical indicators determined by the initial data for calculations.

Competitiveness shall be denoted in the following way: $CQ = (CQ_1, CQ_2, \ldots, CQ_K)$.

Thus, we consider K as the total of various indicators of competitiveness. We shall suppose that all of these indicators are brought down to the same numerical scale. Indicator $CQ_i(t')$ in the moment of time t' is better than this indicator in the moment of time t'' if the following inequality is true: $CQ(t') > CQ(t'')$.

It is only possible to compare the indicators of the same time. It is also only possible to implement partial order of the set of vectors of indicators for competitiveness, because not all vectors can be compared.

The general economic and mathematical model to evaluate the influence of innovative technologies on a products' competitiveness shall have the following form:

$$MQ = \max_{I_{i_1}, I_{i_2}, \ldots, I_{i_L}} \left(CQ\left(Q_{j_1}, Q_{j_2}, \ldots, Q_{j_s}\right)\right).$$

Model MQ has the indicator that shows the maximum effectiveness of innovative technologies for increasing a products' competitiveness.

The tool for assessing the competitiveness of hi-tech innovation companies in view of competitive advantages that are based on the formation of key competencies is an important element in the creation of innovative strategies.

Let us consider the mathematical model for the quantitative assessment of organizational competitiveness based on competitive advantages that appear as a result of the formation of competencies in the studied organizations. An organization's competitiveness shall be assessed with the help of the vector of numerical indicators of an organization's competitiveness. Let us consider N to denote the numerical indicators of an organizations' competitiveness, which are denoted as Q_i. These indicators are unified into the vector of competitiveness (1):

$$Q(t) = \begin{pmatrix} Q_1(t) \\ Q_2(t) \\ \vdots \\ Q_N(t) \end{pmatrix}. \tag{1}$$

As the task of assessing competitiveness in view of dynamic factors connected to the emergence of new competitive advantages, which appear as a result of an organization's acquisition of the corresponding competencies, is considered, the indicators of competitiveness are treated as the ones dependent on time. In the mathematical models, which describe the dynamic processes in economy, it is expedient to use differential equations. Usage of differential equations envisages consideration of the model with continuous time. This mathematical abstraction is allowable in this case, as the dynamics of competitiveness in science-driven organizations develop in longer time intervals.

The main dynamic Eq. (2) could be presented in the following form:

$$\frac{dQ(t)}{dt} = F(t, Q(t), G(t, Q(t))). \tag{2}$$

This formula uses function G to reflect the influence of external and internal factors on the dynamics of competitiveness. In particular, the formalism of this function helps to consider the influence of competencies on organizational activities. Let us consider the specific implementation of the main dynamic differential equation.

It is well known that dynamic models that describe the behavior of the indicators of competitiveness are susceptible to natural diffusion. This diffusion leads to a situation that, in the absence of external factors, the numeral indicators have a constant tendency to reduce.

The mathematical interpretation of this phenomenon is expressed in the following way:

$$\frac{dQ(t)}{dt} = A(t)Q(t) + G(t, Q(t)).$$

The offered dynamic models show that in order to obtain specific advantages organizations have to possess the key competencies. Acquisition of these competencies and their implementation requires a large commitment of financial and time resources. The factor of time has a decisive role in managing the competitiveness of science-driven organizations.

Another tool of competency management is the creation of a competencies exchange (Fig. 4) for obtaining feedback from the labor market on the competencies in demand and quick reactions from the market to an organization's search for current competencies.

3 Results

The following tools are the basis of the mechanism for the implementation of the modern technologies of Industry 4.0 in conjunction with effective competency management in digital industry:

Fig. 4 Competencies exchange (Source: Shukalov et al. 2018)

1. The tool to determine the direction of development and implementation of technologies of Industry 4.0 to increase the competitiveness of new products.
2. The tool to manage the product range to preserve the dominant position in the market.
3. The tool to evaluate innovative potential in order to achieve a dominant position in the market.
4. The tool to select innovative technologies to increase product competitiveness.
5. The tool to evaluate production and resource opportunities on the basis of an analysis of the innovative potential and competencies.
6. The tools to evaluate, rank, and select competencies for developing innovative technologies.
7. The tool to evaluate organizational competitiveness on the basis of competitive advantages that appear as a result of the emergence of new competencies.
8. The tool to evaluate the effectiveness of the implementation of the modern technologies of Industry 4.0 and the tools of competency management in view of the law of mutual influence on the level of financing for key competencies with the emergence of new consumer markets. This tool measures the emergence of organizational resources for developing new competencies as a result of new revenues from economic activities.
9. Tools of Industry 4.0: digital design, digital production, cyber-physical, and intelligent systems.

The methods for achieving a dominant position in the market, based on managing key competencies and adapted to Russian companies, could be systematized and divided into four groups: the institutional sphere, personnel management, the scientific and technical sphere, and the information and communication sphere. The unification of these methods into a single corporate platform promotes a synergetic effect through technology exchange and the attraction of key competencies from the labor market, which together increases scientific and technical potential.

International practice has shown that the main efforts in the development of innovation-active spheres should be concentrated on the provision of the right balance between market mechanisms for self-regulation and state stimulation. Large corporations are notable for having a wide range of competencies that ensure the effectiveness of all stages in the development and sales of products.

This approach is much more effective than the current Russian system, which connects all suppliers and contractors to the government as a customer and thus does not allow them to increase their competencies in the market usage of their technologies. If government orders are reduced in a certain sphere, these suppliers and contractors are left with large and often unique resources and assets, including in the realm of intellectual and human capital, but without the competencies that would allow them to use these resources effectively in the open market.

To implement the elements of the strategy for Industry 4.0 and benefit from the use the tools for competency management a service industrial platform (system), with the maximum integration of the physical and digital environment for all production and business processes is needed.

The key to this unifying concept is the creation of the geographically distributed factory of space instrumental engineering, that integrates all elements of product manufacture—from order to development to production—through the use of the technologies of Industry 4.0. This approach requires no verbal communication between the customer, developer, and manufacturer of certain items; the market participants all interact within the unified online space.

Such a model of interaction will reduce the period from development to implementation of a technology and will allow for the reshaping of the market to a more effective model for order distribution. In this system, small innovative companies and groups or small companies that have mastered a certain technological process will be able—without bureaucratic complications—to achieve a competitive position with large corporations in the production of complex and expensive equipment. This will provide new dynamics to the development of the whole Russian hi-tech sector. Based on improving the market mechanisms for competition, the outcome may be a very adaptive system for the selection of the best technological and production solutions. Such tools for the development of business ensure the reduction of costs, maximum differentiation of products, and quick reactions to changes in the market.

A cloud platform with all of the necessary software is a key tool for developers. All participants in a particular project will be able to access and use it, creating solutions in the unified digital space. In view of the fact that all calculation capacities and programs are in the "cloud," powerful and expensive hardware and software is not required—all developers will be able to work with any convenient devices from anywhere in the world.

This system will also feature "production items" with a set of characteristics of equipment and employee competencies. The term "production item" means a certain function—from individual job roles to computer numerical control (CNC). Each of these items obtains a technological digital passport—software defines all of its possibilities and technological allowances.

For example, if there is a machine that drills holes within the set parameters (diameter, speed, etc.), the digital passport will describe all of this information in a form that could be used for programming in the algorithm. The designer and production team will receive guaranteed quality and immediate access to all information without the need for verbal communication. All interactions will take place in the language of CAD systems. Tasks that used to take years in the past will be done very quickly in the near future.

The system automatically regulates all production actions according to the information it is provided with. It will be impossible to use materials of different quality, set incorrect distances between parts, or use different semiconductor items, etc. In the near future, the geographically distributed factory of space instrumental engineering will be able to provide information on the presence of spare parts and materials in storage facilities and the dates of their delivery. The developer will know how much time will be needed for production and will be able to reduce this through the replacement of certain spare parts with others that are more accessible.

This system is already being implemented. At the first stage it will unify several design centers and dozens of production platforms of six companies within the holding company. After development of these processes, the system will be open for all companies and individual developers in Russia. Due to the increase of competition between manufacturers, the system (platform) will stimulate the development, implementation, and distribution of such key elements of Industry 4.0 as robotization, print electronics, and additive technologies. The system should be able to stimulate the replacement of standard functions currently performed by humans, who will then focus only on creative work—design and programming.

The newly created geographically distributed production facility (factory) and industrial platform will interact with each other, creating a "competencies exchange." This will be a self-regulating system for order management. This system will form and implement a digital double of the product's life cycle and the whole route for the execution of orders. The functioning of the "competencies exchange" will require the full ontology of the product's life cycle. The effect could be large reductions in transaction costs (logistics, technological preparation of production, configuration, procurement, coordination of contracts and terms of deals, technical, technological, and economic assessment of the projects' implementation, etc.). Deals with a long negotiation and precontract cycle will be structured with the help of the adaptive algorithm or neural network, depending on the quantity and type of registered suppliers, manufacturers, developers, and other participants in the industrial platform, price, cost of components, season, specific offers, and market situation.

In concluding the study of the theoretical issues for the implementation of the modern technologies of Industry 4.0 and tools of competency management for digital industry it is possible to offer the following algorithm (Fig. 5).

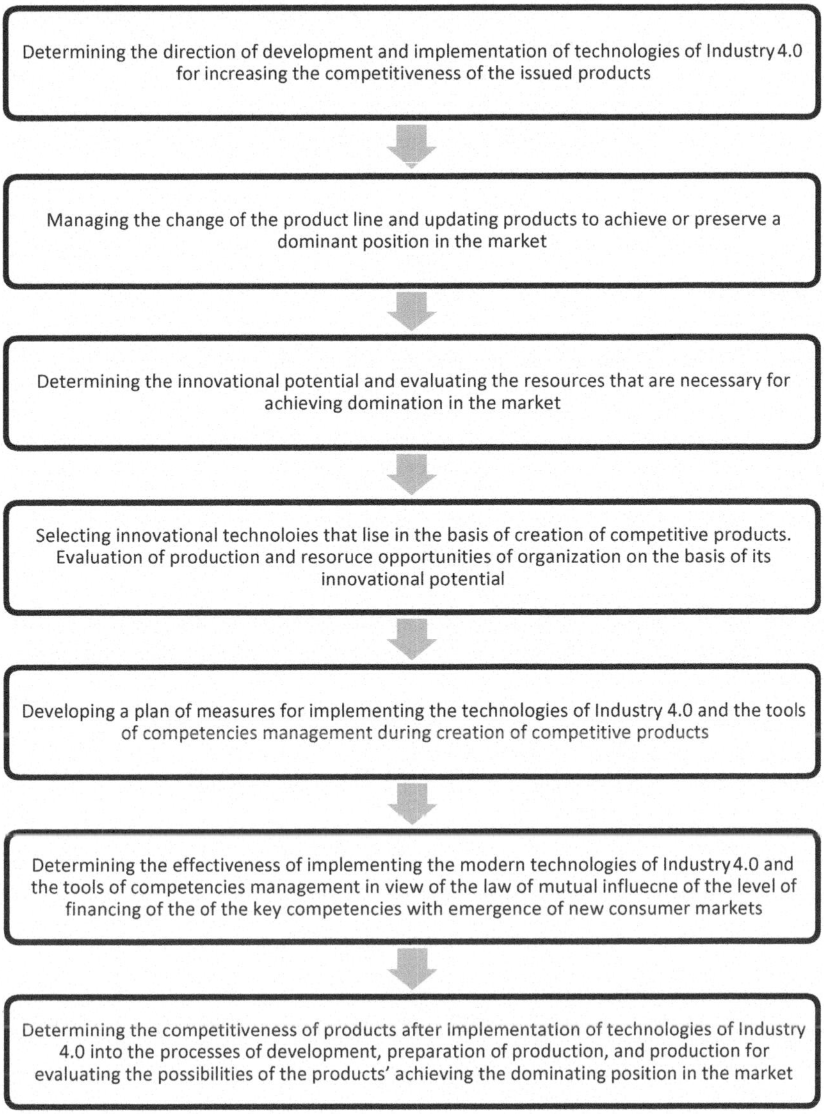

Fig. 5 The algorithm for the development of a strategy to implement the modern technologies of Industry 4.0 and tools of competency management in digital industry. (Source: Compiled by the authors)

4 Conclusions

In this chapter, the issue of the influence that key competencies have on the effectiveness of organizational activities under the conditions of Industry 4.0 has been considered. The main tools that are the basis for the implementation of the technologies of Industry 4.0 and the methods of competency management in digital industry have been discussed. The algorithm for developing a strategy to manage the implementation of the technologies of Industry 4.0 and tools of competency management in digital industry have been offered. Through the use of this strategy, an organization will be able to achieve a dominant market position through the issue of highly competitive products.

References

Chursin A (2010) Innovation and investment in the organization. Mashinostroenie, Moscow

Chursin A, Tyulin A (2018) Competence management and competitive product development: concept and implications for practice. Springer, Heidelberg

Shamin R, Chursin A, Fedorova L (2017) The mathematical model of the law on the correlation of unique competencies with the emergence of new consumer markets. Eur Res Stud J XX (3A):39–56

Shukalov A, Zakoldaev D, Zharinov I (2018) From industry 3.0 to industry 4.0: an overview of innovation, working paper, Defense Engineering Problems. Series 16: the technical means of combating terrorism, scientific and production association of special materials, Saint-Petersburg, 11–12(125–126), 153–159

Tyulin A, Chursin A (2016a) Economic and mathematical model for evaluating the efficiency of the use of budgetary resources in the space industry. Working paper, Microeconomics, Institute of microeconomics, Moscow, 5, 5–12

Tyulin A, Chursin A (2016b) An integrated approach to assessing the effectiveness of the resources allocated for space projects. Working paper, RISK: Resources, Information, Supply, Competition, Moscow, 4, 248–253

Tyulin A, Chursin A (2017) Fundamentals of management of innovative processes in high-tech industries (practice), Economy, Moscow

Environmental Resources Management and the Transition to the Cyber Economy

Alexander S. Tulupov

Abstract For Russia, a major producer of natural resources, digitization and implementation of the principles of Industry 4.0 into the sphere of environmental resources management is a strategic task. This will allow preserving and using natural resources effectively, as well as ensuring the ecological well-being of the country.

The purpose of this chapter is to identify improvements to the existing mechanism of environmental resources management for implementing the principles of Industry 4.0.

Methodology: The theoretical and methodological basis of the research is scientific work by both Russian and foreign scholars on the digitization of the economy, creation of Industry 4.0, rational use of natural resources and environment protection, and sustainable development.

A systemic approach was taken using a complex set of methods and methodologies that conform to the research tasks. The main scientific tools are economic analysis, including ecological and economic analysis, and various types of systemic analysis: conceptual content analysis, information modeling, theory of sets, and theory of multidimensional information spaces.

Results: It is shown that the formation of the cyber economy, in which all elements of the economic mechanism of environmental resources management interact with the help of information technologies on the basis of AI, requires a corresponding favorable environment. To achieve this, it is proposed that there should be a fundamental modernization of the economic mechanisms for natural resources management to harmonize the normative and legal foundation, add methodological provisions, provide organizational and economic support, and incorporate financial, technological, and social components. It is determined that the process of digitization and implementation of the principles of Industry 4.0 should be aimed at achieving the functioning of the national economic system so that the goals of economic development do not contradict ecological imperatives. Only through the strict observation of this criterion will well-balanced and sustainable socioecological and socioeconomic development of the national economy be able to provide competitiveness in the global markets.

A. S. Tulupov
Market Economy Institute of the Russian Academy of Sciences, Moscow, Russia

© Springer Nature Switzerland AG 2019

V. M. Filippov et al. (eds.), *The Cyber Economy*, Contributions to Economics,
https://doi.org/10.1007/978-3-030-31566-5_31

1 Introduction

The digitization of the economy on the basis of Industry 4.0 and formation of the cyber economy seeks to increase living standards. For the first time in the history of social development, special attention is being paid to the provision of the ecological well-being of the population, and, accordingly, to environmental protection within the parameters of the production process.

Digitization of the economic mechanisms for natural resources management in this chapter is treated as a process for the creation of optimal interactions between the subjects and objects of the system for rational environmental resources management through the usage of modern information systems. This includes the full digitization of a wide range of thematic databases, information exchanges, and automatization of document turnover.

The cyber mechanism for natural resources management is treated as an intellectual cluster hierarchical system for the storing and processing of information, which allows for the autonomous management and development of rational environmental resources management with minimum human participation.

Digitization and cybernetization of the economic mechanisms of natural resources management should be performed on the basis of the basic principles of Industry 4.0: industrial Internet of Things, alternate reality, Big Data, business analytics, cloud technologies, autonomous work, horizontal and vertical integration, information security, additive production, and digital modeling.

In Russia, the equivalent of the German program "Industrie 4.0" was the national technological initiative (http://www.nti2035.ru/nti), and digitization is performed according to the principles outlined within various iterations of it (Strategy 2016; Strategy 2017; Program 2017; Decree 2018). Unfortunately, on February 12, 2019 by the Decree of the Government of the Russian Federation (Decree 2019) the Program (Program 2017) was canceled and succeeded by the national program "Digital economy of the Russian Federation" (Passport 2018). In our opinion, the previous program (Program 2017) contains the general conceptual provisions for the digitization of the Russian economy and does not duplicate the new Digital Economy program (Passport 2018), which contains more specified goals, measures, and results of digitization for the corresponding responsible parties. Moreover, the previous program (Program 2017) is to be implemented by 2024.

It should be noted that researchers usually treat the formation of a "smart" society from the position of the digitization of a certain sphere of activities. We believe that it is necessary to deal with the contradictions in each sphere and to create the conditions for the most favorable implementation of the above principles of Industry 4.0.

The existing mechanisms for environmental resources management do not conform to the requirements of the new economic conditions. There is an urgent necessity for the complex modernization of the existing model of development and creation of the conditions that would stimulate the transition to new eco-friendly technological solutions according to the requirements of Industry 4.0.

2 Materials and Method

The theoretical and methodological basis of the research includes reference to the work of both Russian and foreign scholars on the digitization of the economy, the creation of Industry 4.0, the rational use of natural resources and environment protection, and sustainable development.

A systemic approach is taken to solving the set tasks through the application of methods and methodological tools including economic and ecological analysis and various types of systemic analysis (conceptual content analysis, information modeling, theory of sets, and theory of multidimensional information spaces).

The set tasks are solved with the help of scientific generalization, expert evaluations, aggregation, forecasting, and sociological and statistical analysis.

3 Results

Firstly, it is necessary to improve the normative and legal basis to coordinate the tasks for the formation of the cyber economy, Russian economic development goals, and the ecological priorities of sustainable development.

In 2017, Russia officially adopted the Strategy (Strategy of Economic 2017), which is the basis for the formation and implementation of the national policy in the sphere of the provision of national economic security. The Strategy determines the challenges and threats to economic security and formulates the goals, main directions, and tasks for national policy in providing economic security for the Russian Federation.

This document is necessary (in the strategic sense) for the development of the national economy but its contents illustrate (Strategy of Economic 2017) the current imbalance between economic and ecological policy goals. Certain provisions contradict the generally accepted global principles of sustainable development.

One of the priorities for a new technological mode and formation of the cyber economy in developed countries is boosting the eco-friendly sector of the energy sector (solar, wind, geothermal, biomass, and other types of energy), which has been developing very quickly in recent decades. In the German program, Industrie 4.0, energy and the creation of "smart" networks is one of the key directions. In the European countries as a whole, unconventional and renewable energy accounts for a large share of national energy balances. Thus, 40–85% (depending on the month) of electric energy is produced by renewable sources in Germany, with the aim of increasing this indicator to 100% by 2050. In the German *Energiekonzept* (Energy strategy until 2050) there is a clear tendency to reduce traditional carbon-based energy and even nuclear energy—all nuclear power plants are to be closed by 2022 (Energiekonzept 2010). In Denmark, due to successful implementation of the Strategy (Energy 2011), excessive energy from alternative power sources are sold to other countries. Unconventional energy is a strategic direction in the development of the global economy.

The official Russian Strategy (Strategy of Economic 2017) names the following main environmental-related threats and challenges to economic security: changes to the structure of the global demand for energy sources and the structure of their consumption, development of energy-saving technologies, reduction of materials consumption, and development of "green technologies." So, issues that are perceived as drivers of economic development by developed countries are treated as threats by the resource-dependent Russian economy.

When considering economic security in terms of protecting it from external and internal threats,[1] one such threat to the economic security of Russia is "setting excessive requirements in the sphere of ecological security, growth of expenditures for the provision of ecological standards of production and consumption." However, at the official level it is acknowledged that the 15% of Russian territory where "a large part of the population resides and a large part of production capacities and most productive agricultural lands are concentrated", is "disadvantaged according to the ecological parameters." This fact is reflected in the national Strategy of Ecological Security (Strategy of Ecological Security 2017), which was officially adopted in 2017. The Strategy of Ecological Security of the Russian Federation states that in Russian cities and adjacent territories, where 74% of the Russian population resides, the ecological situation is "subject to significant negative influence" from the effects of industry, the energy sector, transport, and construction: "17 million people, which is 17% of the urban population of Russia, reside in cities with a high or very high level of air pollution."

It is clear that there are contradictions in the economic and ecological strategies for development and a need to coordinate them with the tasks of digitization. Requirements for the provision of ecological security have to be raised, not assigned as dangers or threats to the economy. When considering this from the position of the cyber economy there is the necessity for the full exclusion of any negative consequences.

It is also necessary to pass a raft of laws that have been promised by Russian legislators for some time: first of all the law, "On ecological audit," which would allow for the tracking and observation of nature protection requirements related to existing technologies and new solutions developed on the basis of Industry 4.0, and second, the law, "On ecological insurance" the importance of which is shown in earlier work by this author (Tulupov 2001, 2017b), that would allow for the compensation and even prevention of economic losses from an increased negative load by economic subjects on the components of the environment. At present, the corresponding legal norms in Russian law are unfocused, and the implemented approach is based on insuring certain spheres of activities and types of objects

[1]The Strategy defines economic security as "state of protection of the national economy from external and internal threats at which economic sovereignty, integrity of economic space, and conditions for implementing the strategic national priorities of the Russian Federation are ensured."

(e.g., (FZ No. 225)). Ecological risks are not clearly defined and are considered only fragmentarily as components of the possible consequences of an insurance case (accident, disaster, etc.).

Digitization in the sphere of rational environmental resources management should be aimed primarily at the creation of widely classified and interconnected information resources on negative influences on the environment, accident rate statistics, selection of the best (and cleanest) accessible technologies depending on the specifics of particular production processes, and the methodological provision of assessments on the probabilities of accidents, disasters, damage from pollution, and other ecological risks.

A very important issue is the creation of a unified information and analytical system for monitoring the state of the environment, as even without wide application of digital methods in this sphere there is no comprehensive system for monitoring the number of necessary observation posts and the quality of the performed measuring work undertaken.

There are also no databases on accident rate statistics in Russia, though developed countries created such systems to track the consequences for the environment back in the 1980s. Thus, the UK created one of the first systems, MHIDAS (Major Hazard Incident Data Acquisition System). At present, the most popular databases are the Dutch FACTS and American NTSB. MARS (Major Accidents Reporting System), which functions under the control of the European Commission in the Joint Research Center in Ispra, Italy, is also widely used and consulted.

The existing data that Russia does have is formed with the information subjects of economic activities, and is characterized by low precision and incompleteness, as many companies are not interested in providing real information on the consequences of their actions on the environment. The Federal State Statistics Service of the Russian Federation does not collect statistical data from this sphere. In view of this, digitization is especially important.

In terms of evaluating damage from violations of environmental legislation, we developed an information and analytical system, which contains several hundred methodological documents developed during the last 50 years by the leading research groups and institutions (Vitukhin and Tulupov 2016). The system allows using a wide list of criteria to evaluate a certain incident related to the environment pollution caused. The system envisages integration with similar systems in a unified information and communication space.

The potential directions for the development of science-driven production in Russia are studied in several works (Bezdudnaya et al. 2018). At present, improving the economic mechanisms for natural resources management is performed within the projects of the Russian Fund for Fundamental Research (project No.17-02-00245-OGN, “Formalization and assessment of the factors and probabilities for damage during environment pollution” and project No. 19-010-00791-A, “Economic tools for providing ecological security during the handling of municipal solid waste”).

The normative and methodological blockage is restraining the implementation of the principles of digitization and this is the second area where there needs to be improvement.

There are different methodologies—some of which have been adopted at ministry-level—but no official unified methodology to evaluate the damage, probability, and risk of negative influences on the natural environment. Approaches vary depending on the typology of the economic subject and the type of negative influence (noise, vibration, electromagnetic, or chemical influence) (Tulupov 2017a; Porfiryev and Tulupov 2017; Tulupov and Petrov 2018). What is needed is a unified digital system of data collection and automatized assessment of the parametric characteristics of the negative influence of economic subjects on the environment.

The third area for improvement relates to organizational and economic systems. The existing system for the protection of the natural environment does not contain clear economic motivation for organizations to reduce their negative influences through payments or fines for emissions, ecological fees and taxes, payment for the usage of natural resources and ecological violations, a system of security deposits, a system for emissions trading, subsidies, stimulating taxes and payments, payments for the coverage of ecological costs, and civil responsibility for polluters, including economic mechanisms such as the insurance of ecological risks.

The system of mutual settlements, reduction of taxes for green technologies, payments for pollution during the conduct of nature protection measures, and support for the implementation of environmentally friendly technologies are very popular in Europe.

During the implementation of digitization it will be necessary to solve the problem of how to apply the optimal combination of economic regulations for each economic subject. On the one hand, it is necessary to develop such rules for their transformation to the digital basis. On the other hand, the process of digitization will help to develop models that regulate the orientation and behavior of economic subjects.

Ecological expertise should be restored in the initial form (now it is too simple). The new technologies and solutions for Industry 4.0 should be verified to ensure that they correspond with increased ecological requirements.

In order to improve the work of the economic mechanisms for environmental resources management and create the conditions for the formation of cyber-economic mechanisms for environmental management it is also necessary to increase financing.

At present, the financing of federal and regional ecological projects is insufficient, which influences the quality of the research projects, including experimental implementation of the methods for calculating the probability, damage, and risks of environmental damage which could be applied in the digital system for economic regulators of the environment.

It is also necessary to solve technological problems. In the case of the implementation of a new technology there is always an objective necessity for the technological transformation of many interconnected production facilities within one cluster.

Information support for digitization and implementing the principles of Industry 4.0 is very important, as the socioeconomic environment is not ready to a new direction of development.

The intensification of the principles of digitization and formation of cyber-economic mechanisms for rational environmental resources management requires a complex of measures aimed at leveling the internal and external restraining factors.

4 Conclusions

For Russia, digitization and implementation of the principles of Industry 4.0 into the sphere of environmental resources management is a strategic task. This will allow preserving and using natural resources effectively, as well as ensuring the ecological well-being of the country.

As the performed analysis has showed, the Russian economy is not yet ready to lead innovative development in this area on the basis of the principles of Industry 4.0. The actions that are taken with regard to the protection and preservation of the environment are ineffective. It is very difficult to digitize underdeveloped or absent components of the economic mechanism for natural resources management. Of course, digitization may intensify certain directions of development. However, it is necessary to eliminate the specified contractions and create the conditions for innovative development on the basis of digital technologies.

There is still time to create the right conditions for favorable digitization, as even leading developed countries are only now at the threshold of the formation of the cyber economy. Thus, Germany plans to move to production on the basis of Industry 4.0 by 2022, and China, by 2025.

It is necessary for Russia to understand the global situation and implement policy into the realm of global economic transformations. The increase of the importance of environmental concerns, including the growth of clean and energy-saving technologies, is evident. The generally accepted priorities of sustainable development should be coordinated and built into the Russian model of economic development at all levels.

At present, there is a need for a new model of development, based on a widely diversified digital economy, which takes into account the global development trends, including the increased influence of environmental factors, along with national interests, which are set in the Strategy of National Security of the Russian Federation (Strategy of National Security of the Russian Federation 2015).

Digitization and the implementation of the principles of Industry 4.0 should be aimed at achieving a state where the functioning of the national economic system and the goals of development do not contradict ecological imperatives. Only through the observation of this criterion can Russia ensure well-balanced sustainable socio-economic and eco-friendly development of the national economy.

Acknowledgments The work was prepared with financial support from the Department of the humanitarian and social sciences of the Russian Fund for Fundamental Research (Project No. 17-02-00245-OGN "Formalization and evaluation of the factors and probabilities for loss during environment pollution"; and Project No. 19-010-00791-A "Economic tools for the provision of ecological security during the handling of municipal solid waste").

References

Bezdudnaya AG, Ksenofontova TY, Rastova YI, Kraiukhin GA, Tulupov AS (2018) On the issue of the perspective directions of the science-driven production development in Russia. J Soc Sci Res 3:76–80. https://doi.org/10.32861/jssr.spi3.76.80

Decree of the Government of the Russian Federation dated February 12, 2019, No. 195-r "Concerning the annulment of the Decree of the Government of the Russian Federation dated July, 07, 2017, No. 1632-r"

Decree of the President of the Russian Federation dated May 7, 2018 No. 204 (edition dated July 19, 2018) Concerning national goals and strategic tasks of development of the Russian Federation until 2024

Energiekonzept fuer eine umweltschonende, zuverlaessige und bezahlbare Energieversorgung. 28 September 2010

Energy Strategy 2050 – from coal, oil and gas to green energy (Denmark), 2011

Federal law "Mandatory Civil Liability Insurance of the Owner of a Hazardous Facility for Damage Resulting from an Accident" No. 225-FZ dated July 27, 2010 (edition dated December 18, 2018)

National Technological Initiative. http://www.nti2035.ru/nti/. Accessed 05 March 2019

Passport of the National Program "Digital economy of the Russian Federation". Adopted by the Presidium of the Council with the President of the Russian Federation for strategic development and national projects, protocol dated December 24, 2018 г. No. 16

Porfiryev BN, Tulupov AS (2017) Environmental hazard assessment and forecast of economic damage from industrial accidents. Stud Russ Econ Dev 28(6):600–607

Program "Digital economy of the Russian Federation". Adopted by the Decree of the Government of the Russian Federation dated July 28, 2017, No. 1632-r

Strategy of Development of Information Society in the Russian Federation for 2017–2030. Adopted by the Decree of the President of the Russian Federation dated May 9, 2017, No. 203

Strategy of Ecological Security of the Russian Federation until 2025. Adopted by the Decree of the President of the Russian Federation No. 176 dated April 19, 2017

Strategy of Economic Security of the Russian Federation until 2030. Adopted by the Decree of the President of the Russian Federation No. 208 dated MY 13, 2017

Strategy of National Security of the Russian Federation. Adopted by the Decree of the President of the Russian Federation dated December 31, 2015, No. 683

Strategy of Technological Development of the Russian Federation. Adopted by the Decree of the President of the Russian Federation No. 642 dated December 1, 2016

Tulupov AS (2001) Ecological insurance in provision of the systemic security, PhD thesis. State University of Management, Moscow, 186 p

Tulupov AS (2017a) Compensation for ecological damage in the economy of mining production. J Mining 8:61–65

Tulupov AS (2017b) Insurance in management of natural resources. State University of Management Publ., Moscow, 160 p

Tulupov AS, Petrov IV (2018) Fuel and energy complex and methods for assessing the harm from air pollution. In: International scientific conference "Knowledge-based technologies in

development and utilization of mineral resources". IOP conference series. https://doi.org/10.1088/1755-1315/206/1/012054
Vitukhin AD, Tulupov AS (2016) Information and analytical system of methodological provision of assessment of damage from violation of environmental legislation. In: Materials of the 5th International forum "Russia in the 21st century: global challenges and perspectives of development", Central Economic Mathematical Institute of the Russian Academy of Sciences, Moscow, 267–274

A Model for Sustainable Development in the Cyber Economy: The Creation and Implementation of Green Innovations

Elena S. Kutukova

Abstract *Purpose*: The purpose of this chapter is to develop a model for the sustainable development of the cyber economy based on the creation and implementation of "green" innovations.

Design/methodology/approach: In order to study the issue of sustainable development of the cyber economy based on "green" innovations the author uses the method of regression analysis. The author determined the influence of the values of the indices of digital competitiveness, calculated by the IMD, on the values of indices for the green economy, calculated by Dual Citizen LLC in early 2019 (based on data from late 2018). The countries selected for the research are those with the highest values in the green economy index (Top 33). To logically explain the determined regression dependence the author performs a SWOT analysis of sustainable development for the cyber economy based on the creation and implementation of "green" innovations.

Findings: It is determined that the formation of the cyber economy may stimulate the achievement of global goals in the sphere of sustainable development. Potential environmental risks, which appear or increase with the cyber economy, could be prevented or reduced through the adoption of the offered model for sustainable development of the cyber economy. The model is based on the circular mechanism of industrial production, tax stimulation of R&D, and responsible consumption.

Originality/value: Practical implementation of the developed model will support the high ecological effectiveness of the cyber economy through a reduction in the consumption of natural and energy resources.

1 Introduction

The cyber economy as a prospective concept for the organization of modern economic systems requires complex critical analysis, not only with regard to the economic and social implications but also the environmental risks. At present, the level of environmental risk associated with economic growth and development is

E. S. Kutukova
Financial University under the Government of the Russian Federation, Moscow, Russia

© Springer Nature Switzerland AG 2019
V. M. Filippov et al. (eds.), *The Cyber Economy*, Contributions to Economics,
https://doi.org/10.1007/978-3-030-31566-5_32

very high due to the depletion of natural resources. Some countries continue to extract mineral resources (metals, ores, and timber) and even specialize in their export (e.g., Saudi Arabia, Russia, and the countries of Central Asia).

Other countries have already depleted their natural resources (e.g., Japan) and have deficits (an example is the deficit of water resources in many countries of Africa and Europe). The intensive increase in the global consumption of natural resources leads to large increases in the volume of waste from industrial production, which has widespread ecological consequences (e.g., reduction of soil fertility, pollution of water, destruction of the ozone layer, and air pollution).

The ecological risks of economic growth are also caused by the insatiable needs for new energy resources. Only a few countries of the world (for example, Russia) can satisfy their own needs for energy resources through environmentally safe production methods (e.g., hydroelectric). However, even this has ecological costs (e.g., reduction of fish in the case of hydroelectric power stations).

Most other countries (e.g., countries of Europe and Japan) have had to develop nuclear power. The consequences of accidents at such power plants are ecologically disastrous as can be seen from Chernobyl or more recently, Fukushima. Alternative energy sources such as solar, wind, or tidal develop very slowly and have low effectiveness due to the need for large investment resources, as well as low and unstable (due to their susceptibility to geographical factors) efficiency.

Due to the above reasons, the management of ecological risks on the basis of the creation and implementation of "green" innovations is one of the global goals in the sphere of sustainable development for the United Nations (2019). Thus, a current task for modern science is to determine the potential for sustainable development based on the advent of the cyber economy; and the advantages and drawbacks of "green" innovations in terms of ecological effectiveness. The purpose of this chapter is to develop a model of sustainable development for the cyber economy based on the creation and implementation of "green" innovations.

2 Materials and Method

A number of fundamental and applied issues related to sustainable development and the creation and implementation of "green" innovations in view of the accumulated experience of different countries are studied in detail in the works of Bogoviz and Sergi (2018), Chen (2019), Karimi and Nabavi Chashmi (2019), Le Van et al. (2019), Morozova et al. (2019), Popescu (2019), Popkova et al. (2018a, b), and Wang et al. (2019). Certain aspects of the relationship between sustainable development of the cyber economy and the influence of the processes of digital modernization on "green" innovations are studied in the works of Bechtsis et al. (2018), Ciocoiu (2011), Jabłoński (2018), and Linkov et al. (2018).

However, sustainable development of the cyber economy based on the creation and implementation of "green" innovations is not sufficiently studied in the existing economic literature. Here, the method of regression analysis is used to determine the influence of the indices of digital competitiveness, calculated by the IMD, on the indices for the green economy, calculated by Dual Citizen LLC in early 2019 (based on data from late 2018). The countries selected for this research are the leaders in the green economy index (Top 33). The initial data is given in Table 1.

A regression analysis based on the data in Table 1 is shown in Table 2.

As is seen from Table 2, growth of the value of the digital competitiveness index by 1 point leads to an increase of the value of the green economy index by 0.0028 points. Significance F (0.0001) does not exceed 0.05;therefore, the regression dependence is correct at the significance level $\alpha = 0.05$. The determination coefficient $R^2 = 0.3668$. This means that the change of the dependent variable by 36.68% is explained by the change of independent variable. The obtained results show that digital modernization, which precedes the formation of the cyber economy, positively influences the process for the formation of the green economy.

Table 1 Indices of the green economy and digital competitiveness in the countries of the world as of early 2019

Country	Index of green economy, points 0–1 (y)	Index of digital competitiveness, points 1–100 (x)	Country	Index of green economy, points 0–1 (y)	Index of digital competitiveness, points 1–100 (x)
Sweden	0.7608	97.453	Japan	0.5927	82.170
Switzerland	0.7594	95.851	Belgium	0.5737	82.165
Iceland	0.7129	82.654	Italy	0.5606	64.958
Norway	0.7031	95.724	South Korea	0.5591	87.983
Finland	0.6997	95.248	Thailand	0.5551	65.272
Germany	0.6890	85.405	China	0.5531	74.796
Denmark	0.6800	96.764	Peru	0.5526	48.056
Taiwan	0.6669	86.190	Greece	0.5485	56.207
Austria	0.6479	90.226	United States	0.5471	100.00
France	0.6405	80.753	Hungary	0.5419	57.099
United Kingdom	0.6230	93.239	Brazil	0.5417	51.693
Colombia	0.6188	48.825	Spain	0.5411	74.272
Singapore	0.6154	99.422	Portugal	0.5405	73.441
Ireland	0.5993	84.285	India	0.5398	57.066
Canada	0.5966	95.201	Chile	0.5395	68.377
Netherlands	0.5937	93.886	Mexico	0.5263	56.685
New Zealand	0.5928	84.534	Russian Federation	0.4115	65.207

Source: Compiled by the authors based on Dual Citizen LLC (2019), IMD (2019)

Table 2 Results of a regression analysis on the dependence of the index of green economy on the index of digital competitiveness as of early 2019

Regression dependence						
Multiple R	0.6057					
R-square	0.3668					
Adjusted R-square	0.3471					
Standard error	0.0607					
Observations	34					
Dispersion analysis						
	df	SS	MS	F	Significance F	
Regression	1	0.0684	0.0684	18.5402	0.0001	
Residual	32	0.1180	0.0037			
Total	33	0.1864				
	Coefficients	Standard error	t Stat	P-Value	Lower 95%	Upper 95%
Intercept	0.3813	0.0520	7.3315	0.0000	0.2754	0.4873
x	0.0028	0.0006	4.3058	0.0001	0.0015	0.0041

Source: Calculated and compiled by the authors

3 Results

For a detailed logical explanation of the determined regression dependence (Table 2), we performed a SWOT analysis of sustainable development for the cyber economy based on the creation and implementation of "green" innovations (Table 3).

Table 3 shows that the cyber economy provides the preconditions for sustainable development in modern economic systems; these are connected to an increase in the transparency and controllability of economic activities (which allows better observation of environmental standards) and the high precision of production processes (which reduces resource intensity). At the same time, additional problems are created through the high-energy intensity of automatized production and growth in the usage of natural resources for the production of machines.

Opportunities to further sustainable development within the cyber economy consist of the creation of new production technologies and the work of machines, which may reduce the energy and resource intensity of production process and allow for more widespread recycling of materials for the production of machines. On the other hand, sustainable development may be threatened by a deficit of investment into the creation and implementation of "green innovations" and low demand for the products of green digital business.

Table 3 SWOT analysis of sustainable development for the cyber economy based on the creation and implementation of "green" innovations

S	Preconditions and strengths of the cyber economy to support sustainable development	– transparency and controllability of economic activities; – high precision of production, which reduces resource intensity.
W	Weaknesses of the cyber economy to support sustainable development	– high energy intensity of automatized production; – growth in the usage of natural resources for production.
O	Opportunities for the sustainable development of the cyber economy	– creation of new technologies of production and the work of machines, which allows reducing the energy and resource intensity of the process; – recycling of materials for the production of machines.
T	Threats to sustainable development from the cyber economy	– deficit of investments into the creation and implementation of "green" innovations; – low demand for the products of digital business, which create "green" innovations due to high ecological costs (low pricing competitiveness).

Source: Compiled by the authors

To address these issues we developed a model for the sustainable development of the cyber economy based on the creation and implementation of "green" innovations (Fig. 1).

As is seen from Fig. 1, the recycling of raw materials from which machines (robots, digital devices, etc.) are made as a result of their moral and physical wear is shown as mandatory (institutionalized) economic practice, which has no alternatives. This will result in the highly effective use of natural resources and prevent depletion. Together with active R&D this will also support the crisis-free functioning and development of the cyber economy until the creation of new construction materials the usage of which will not lead to the depletion of natural resources.

R&D that is aimed at the creation and implementation of "green" innovations will reduce the consumption of energy. Problems with low demand for industrial products that are manufactured with the application of "green" innovations due to a lack of price competitiveness could be prevented through state support for R&D on the basis of tax stimuli (which will support the cost at the previous level due to the reduction of tax expenditures). The state can also stimulate the environmental responsibility of consumers of industrial products, through raising demand for products that are manufactured with the help of "green" innovations, even if they have a higher price.

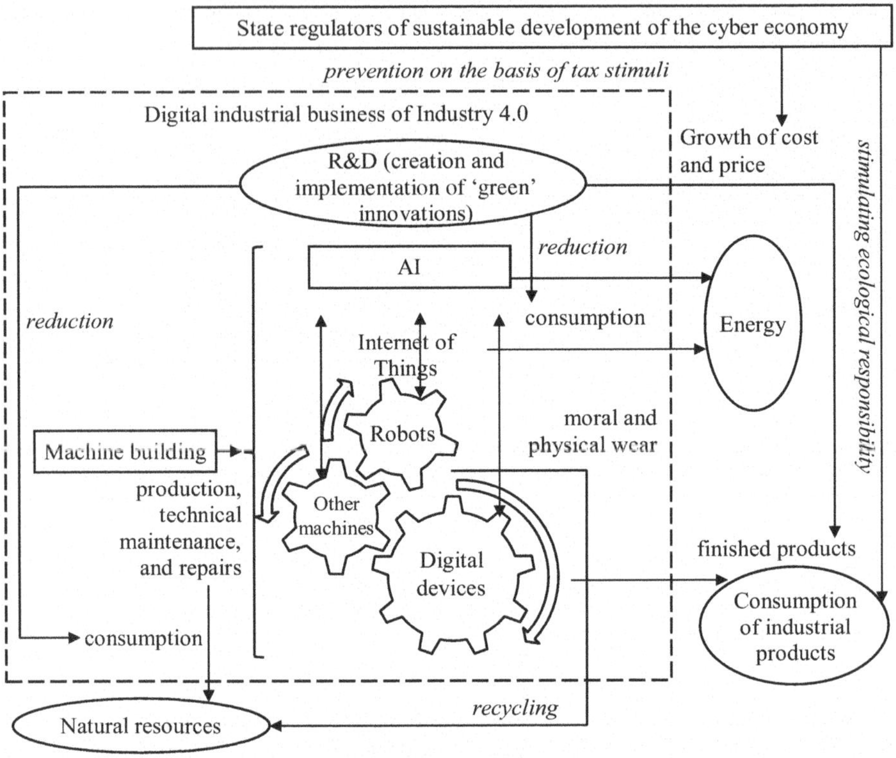

Fig. 1 The model for the sustainable development of the cyber economy based on the creation and implementation of "green" innovations (Source: Compiled by the authors)

4 Conclusion

It has been determined that the formation of the cyber economy could stimulate the achievement of the global goals in the sphere of sustainable development. The potential ecological threats and risks, which emerge or increase in the cyber economy, could be reduced or prevented by the adoption of the model for the sustainable development of the cyber economy based on the creation and implementation of "green" innovations. This model is based on the circular mechanism of industrial production, tax stimulation of R&D, and responsible consumption. The practical implementation of the developed model will guarantee the high ecological effectiveness of the cyber economy due to the low consumption of natural and energy resources.

References

Bechtsis D, Tsolakis N, Vlachos D, Srai JS (2018) Intelligent autonomous vehicles in digital supply chains: a framework for integrating innovations towards sustainable value networks. J Clean Prod 181:60–71

Bogoviz AV, Sergi BS (2018) The circular economy in modern Russia. In: Exploring the future of Russia's economy and markets. Emerald, Bingley, West Yorkshire

Chen S-Y (2019) True sustainable development of green technology: the influencers and risked moderation of sustainable motivational behavior. Sustain Dev 27(1):69–83

Ciocoiu CN (2011) Integrating digital economy and green economy: opportunities for sustainable development. Theor Empirical Res Urban Manag 6(2):33–43

Dual Citizen LLC (2019) The global green economy index 2018. https://dualcitizeninc.com/global-green-economy-index/. Accessed 03 March 2019

IMD (2019) World digital competitiveness ranking 2018. https://www.imd.org/wcc/world-competitiveness-center-rankings/world-digital-competitiveness-rankings-2018/. Accessed 03 March 2019

Jabłoński M (2018) Value migration to the sustainable business models of digital economy companies on the capital market. Sustainability (Switzerland) 10(9):31–43

Karimi RF, Nabavi Chashmi SA (2019) Designing green entrepreneurship model in sustainable development consistent with the performance of Tehran Industrial Towns. J Bus Bus Market 26 (1):95–102

Le Van Q, Viet Nguyen T, Nguyen MH (2019) Sustainable development and environmental policy: the engagement of stakeholders in green products in Vietnam. Bus Strategy Environ 2(1):18–26

Linkov I, Trump BD, Poinsatte-Jones K, Florin M-V (2018) Governance strategies for a sustainable digital world. Sustainability (Switzerland) 10(2):440

Morozova IA, Popkova EG, Litvinova TN (2019) Sustainable development of global entrepreneurship: infrastructure and perspectives. Int Entrep Manag J 15(2):589–597

Popescu DI (2019) Social responsibility and business ethics: IX. Green management and sustainable development of the firm. Qual Access Success 20(168):135–138

Popkova EG, Bogoviz AV, Ragulina JV (2018a) Technological parks, "green economy," and sustainable development in Russia. In: Exploring the future of Russia's economy and markets. Emerald, Bingley, West Yorkshire

Popkova EG, Popova EV, Sergi BS (2018b) Clusters and innovative networks toward sustainable growth. In: Exploring the future of Russia's economy and markets. Emerald, Bingley, West Yorkshire

United Nations (2019) Sustainable development goals. https://www.un.org/sustainabledevelopment/ru/sustainable-development-goals/. Accessed 03 March 2019

Wang M, Zhao X, Gong Q, Ji Z (2019) Measurement of regional green economy sustainable development ability based on entropy weight-topsis-coupling coordination degree—a case study in Shandong Province, China. Sustainability (Switzerland) 11(2):280

Government Control of the Cyber Economy Based on the Technologies of Industry 4.0

Mikhail A. Kovazhenkov, Gilyan V. Fedotova, Ruslan H. Ilyasov, Yury A. Nikitin, and Natalia E. Buletova

Abstract *Purpose*: The purpose of this chapter is to evaluate the effectiveness of the application of government tools to manage the current digitization of Russian society. We analyze the specific measures that are implemented in a number of countries for the market subjects of digital tools and analyze the existing normative documents on the implementation of the philosophy of Industry 4.0 in Russia.

Government control of the transition to the cyber economy is impossible without a normative and legal basis for the interactions in this sphere. In this chapter, the authors focus on the list of adopted documents, purposes and tasks of implementation, and the indicators of target planning on informatization.

An adequately selected list of target indicators will determine future government policy for the process of informatization in all spheres of the national economy. The indicators for government measures that are set at the planning stage should correspond with the final results.

Methodology: The following methods are used: comparative analysis of data, dynamic assessment, comparison, analogy, and systematization.

Results: Through the study of the main normative and legal documents of government control that determine the possibilities and potential directions for the informatization of the Russian economic system an assessment of the achieved

---

M. A. Kovazhenkov (✉)
Volgograd State Technical University, Volgograd, Russia

G. V. Fedotova
Volga Region Research Institute of Production and Processing of Meat and Dairy Products, Volgograd State Technical University, Volgograd, Russia

R. H. Ilyasov
Chechen State University, Grozny, Russia

Y. A. Nikitin
General A.V. Khrulev Military Academy of Material and Technical Provision, St. Petersburg, Russian Federation

N. E. Buletova
Volgograd Institute of Management the Branch of the Russian Academy of National Economy and Public Administration, Volgograd, Russia

© Springer Nature Switzerland AG 2019
V. M. Filippov et al. (eds.), *The Cyber Economy*, Contributions to Economics,
https://doi.org/10.1007/978-3-030-31566-5_33

results of informatization in certain spheres of the socioeconomic environment is performed. The main target indicators for digitization and the future landscape of the Russian cyber economy are considered; achievements in the transition to Industry 4.0 are studied; and conclusions on the possible successes in various spheres of public and economic life in Russia are made.

Recommendations: The current tools for government control over the processes for the informatization of Russian society should be reconsidered in respect to certain tasks and target indicators for the future transition to full digitization of all spheres of the national economy.

1 Introduction

The main actors in the development of Industry 4.0 are states and supranational organizations such as the UN, the EU, the BRICS, and other trading blocs.

Countries that act as global players due to their multiple ties in trade, diplomacy, and participation in international organizations (including monetary, sports, and cultural), have huge influence, regardless of the differences between them.

The German initiative, presented in 2013 as the main subject of the Hannover Messe and entitled "Integrated industry" (later updated to 'Industrie 4.0'), quickly spread to the other main global players: the USA, the EU, China, Japan, and South Korea.

Two key pillars of the concept of Industry 4.0 are the Internet of Things and cyber-physical systems, which allow the various components of production systems to interact with each other without human participation, via the Internet.

The German Plattform Industrie 4.0 now acts as the main hub for the adaptation of the German economy to the Fourth Industrial Revolution. The German government performs the functions of a coordinator, unifying all interested market participants and determining the main standards in this sphere. The government also represents German business in relations with other government actors within Industry 4.0.

The USA also presented its vision for the development of Industry 4.0 in 2015 and called it "The Industrial Internet of Things (IIoT)." The largest American corporations: AT&T, Cisco, General Electric, IBM, and Intel unified their efforts, creating the Industrial Internet Consortium (IIC), the main function of which was to bring together large corporations, innovative companies, educational establishments, and the government to accelerate the dissemination, development, and adaptation to the IIoT.

The IIC defines its mission in the following way: the provision of reliable infrastructure for the IIoT in which global systems and devices are connected securely and are controlled for provision of the results of transformation (*transition to the Internet economy*).

The IIC is treated as a private initiative but the American government has also initiated the program "Manufacturing USA," within which public–private partnerships create and promote production innovations, including the IIoT.

Within the "Manufacturing USA" program, promotion of the IIoT includes the following:

- America Makes: The USA is described as a national accelerator and leading partner in the sphere of technological research, inventions, creation, and innovations in adaptive production and 3D printing.
- ARM (Advanced Robotics Manufacturing): The mission of the ARM Institute consists of the creation and further implementation of robotized technologies by integrating a diverse set of sectoral practices and institutional knowledge in many disciplines—sensor technologies, development of final elements, software and AI, materials engineering, modeling of human and machine behavior, and quality assurance—to implement the promises of a reliable and innovative production ecosystem.
- CESMII (Clean Energy Smart Manufacturing Innovation Institute): "Intelligent production" stimulates the development of intelligent sensors and digital means of managing technological processes, which can raise the effectiveness of production in the USA.
- DMDII (Digital Manufacturing and Design Innovation Institute): DMDII stimulates plants and factories around the USA to implement the technologies of digital production and design, so that these plants and factories can become more effective and competitive.
- IACMI (Institute for Advanced Composites Manufacturing Innovation): IACMI strives to accelerate the development and implementation of the leading production technologies for cheap and energy-efficient production of modern polymer composites for transport vehicles, wind turbines, and gas storage tanks.

Within the 10-year plan "Made in China 2025" (MIC 2025), adopted in 2015, China strives to turn the country from the "world's factory" to an advanced industrial state by 2049. To achieve this, the Chinese government proposes technological advances in nine main directions: adoption of a new generation of IT; CNC machines and hi-tech robots; aerospace equipment; maritime engineering equipment and hi-tech vessels; leading equipment for railroad transport; energy saving and cars based on new sources of energy; electric energy equipment; agricultural machine building; new materials; biopharmaceuticals; and medical equipment with outstanding characteristics.

The first stage of the plan (2015–2020) envisages the implementation of digital network technologies into the production sphere at companies. The second stage (2020–2025) envisages the integration of network technologies and further intellectualization of production processes, in full accordance with the concept of Industry 4.0.

It should be noted that the specifics of state management in China (single-party system, state planning of economic development, government initiation, and support for the creation of new spheres of economy) has allowed the country to increase investments into R&D, IT, and the further automatization of production processes very quickly. Such rapid Chinese progress toward the cyber economy has caused certain worries with the leading countries of the West, particularly the USA, which considers China to be its main rival for the near future. The Chinese Ministry of Trade has even had to announce that MIC 2025 is not a threat to the technological domination of the USA. According to analysts, the US–China trade war, which was started in 2018 by the USA, is a consequence of America's analysis of the "over-ambitious" MIC 2025 and the rapid rates of its realization.

Japan, which is a recognized leader in the sphere of robototronics and implementation of the IoT into the everyday life of society, is also ready for the Fourth Industrial Revolution. In 2016, the Ministry of Economy, Trade and Industry of Japan organized a study on the implementation of the mechanisms of Industry 4.0 in different spheres of business: finance, logistics, trade, etc.

The IoT Acceleration Consortium (ITAC), created with the participation of the Ministry of Economy, Trade and Industry, sees its main goal as creating an environment for the attraction of investment into the future of the Internet of Things, through collaboration with the government and private business. The ITAC's concept is based on large changes to the existing structure of production and society as a whole through development of the Internet of Things (IoT), Big Data, and AI.

Moreover, Japan also considers the consequences of the Fourth Industrial Revolution for society, through the implementation of the concept of Society 5.0. The concept of Society 5.0 not only influences production (Industry 4.0) but also finance, logistics, construction, medicine, etc. Society 5.0 envisages a super-intelligent society, which uses Big Data in the process of its development. The concept appears to be a modern reinterpretation of the concept of the "Information society," which appeared in Japan in the 1960s.

2 Materials and Method

In the course of this research, the authors used the leading theoretical and applied works devoted to the issues of the formation of the digital economy in modern Russia: Sukhodolov et al. (2018), Kravets et al. (2013), Kuznetsov et al. (2016), Popova et al. (2015), Vertakova et al. (2016), Sibirskaya and Shestaeva (2016), Plotnokov et al. (2015), Fedotova et al. (2018), Romanova et al. (2017), Kovazhenkov et al. (2018).

The focus of modern economic policy on digital transformation and strategic options for delivering it result in the setting of new tasks, which we aim to solve with reference to successful international experience to assist in the effective digitization of the Russian economic system and transition to the cyber economy.

3 Results

The Russian Federation is striving to not fall behind the global leaders in the implementation of Industry 4.0. A lesson for implementing the elements of Industry 4.0 in Russia may be found in the attempts at digitizing the Russian economy and implementing new information technologies into state management, made by the Russian Government back in 2002. The Russian Government adopted the Federal Target Program "Digital Russia" for 2002–2010 (Decree of the Government of the Russian Federation dated January 28, 2002, No. 65).

The main goals of the Program were as follows:

- Increase of quality of interrelations between government and society
- Increase of effectiveness of inter-departmental interactions and the internal organization of the activities of public authorities
- Increase the effectiveness of state management.

Unfortunately, these goals were not fully achieved. However, certain elements of digital state management were created through the implementation of the Program. In particular, the website Gosuslugi.ru was established, and now has 86 million users.

The goals of the Russian Government in establishing this information resource were openness in the provision of information on the activities of executive authorities and local administrations, as well as increasing the quality and accessibility of the provided state and municipal services. At present, Gosuslugi.ru is the 12th most popular website in the country (according to Alexa.com).

After the unsatisfactory results of implementation of the program "Digital Russia," the Decree of the Russian Government dated October 20, 2010, No. 1815-r adopted a new national program "Information society," the main goals of which were to increase the population's living standards and quality of work, improve the conditions of organizations' activities, and develop the economic potential of Russia on the basis of usage of information and telecommunication technologies.

Within this program the government dealt with making information more transparent for citizens, providing openness in state management, and ensuring feedback. The concept of open federal public authorities was adopted through the "Open Government" program.

Within the activities of "Open Government," standards for the openness of government bodies were formed and information resources were implemented which ensured open data on government services (gossluzhba.gov.ru), the openness and competitive character of government purchases (zakupki.gov.ru), and openness in the sale of government property (torgi.gov.ru). Also, the digital environment "LegalTech" based on the information resources of the courts (kad.arbitr.ru, automatized system "Pravosudie") and service companies in the sphere of jurisprudence (ConsultantPlus, Garant, Pravo.ru, etc.) were formed.

These elements in the digital infrastructure of Russian state management are very similar to the Japanese concept of Society 5.0, which, in our opinion, considers the information environment, the Internet of Things, and cyber-physical systems as the elements in a more global way than Industry 4.0.

As the transition to the new technological mode and the Fourth Industrial Revolution progressed around the world, the President of the Russian Federation adopted in 2017 the "Strategy for the Development of the Information Society of the Russian Federation for 2017–2030."

The purpose of this "Strategy" is the creation of conditions for the formation of the knowledge society in the Russian Federation. The strategy should stimulate the provision of Russia's national interests, in particular:

- Development of human potential
- Provision of security for citizens and the state
- Increase of Russia's role in the global humanitarian and cultural environment
- Development of free, sustainable, and secure interactions between citizens and organizations, public authorities and local administrations
- Increase of the effectiveness of state management, development of the economy and the social sphere
- Formation of the digital economy.

The Decree of the Russian Government dated July 28, 2017, No. 1632-r adopted the program "Digital economy of the Russian Federation," the main goals of which are as follows:

- Creation of the ecosystem for the digital economy of the Russian Federation
- Creation of necessary and sufficient conditions for the institutional and infrastructural character
- Increasing competitiveness in the global market of the individual spheres of the Russian economy and of the Russian economy as a whole.

The main "end-to-end" digital technologies within this program are as follows:

- Big Data
- Neurotechnologies and AI
- Blockchain
- Quantum technologies
- New production technologies
- Industrial Internet
- Components of robototronics and sensors
- Wireless technologies
- Technologies of virtual and alternate realities.

The main result of this program, according to the Russian Government, will be the creation of at least ten national leading companies—hi-tech companies that develop "end-to-end" technologies and control digital platforms that work in the global market and form a system of "startups," research groups, and sectoral enterprises, which ensure the development of the digital economy.

Management of the development of the digital economy, according to the program "Digital economy of the Russian Federation," should include representatives of all interested parties in its development: government bodies, business, civil society, and the scientific and educational community. The activities in the management of the development of the digital economy should be transparent and controllable, built on the basis of the project approach, and should include three levels of management: strategic, operative, and tactical.

By 2024, implementation of this program should provide the following results:

(a) An ecosystem for the digital economy:

- Successful functioning of at least ten leading companies (ecosystem operators), that are competitive global markets
- Successful functioning of at least ten sectoral (industrial) digital platforms for the main subject areas of the economy (including for digital healthcare, digital education, and "smart cities")
- Successful functioning of at least 500 small- and medium-sized companies in the sphere of the creation of digital technologies and platforms and provision of digital services

(b) Personnel and education:

- The number of graduates of educational organizations for higher education in specialities within the field of information and telecommunication technologies should be 120,000 annually.
- The number of graduates of higher and vocational professional education with competencies in the sphere of information technologies should reach the average global level of 800,000 annually.
- The share of the population with digital skills should reach 40%.

(c) The formation of research competencies and technological skills:

- The number of implemented projects in the sphere of the digital economy (with a minimum value of RUB 100 million) should be at least 30.
- The number of Russian organizations that participate in the implementation of large projects ($US 3 million) in the top-priority directions of international technological cooperation in the digital economy should be at least 10.

(d) Information infrastructure:

- The share of households with broadband Internet (100 Mb/s) as a percentage of the total number of households should be 97%.
- In all large cities (1 million people and more) there should be stable 5G coverage.

(e) Information security:

- The percentage of subjects that use standards for secure information interaction between public and private institutes should be 75%.

– The share of internal traffic of the Russian segment of the Internet that goes through foreign servers should be 5%.

The Agency for Strategic Initiatives, created in 2011 by the Decree of the Russian Government as a non-profit organization, supports the development of projects for the preparation and implementation of ideas and technologies related to Industry 4.0. One such project is the National Technological Initiative (NTI), a program of measures for the formation of completely new markets and creation of conditions for the global technological leadership of Russia by 2035.

Within the NTI, the Agency for Strategic Initiatives suggests focusing on nine key markets:

- AeroNet—development of unmanned flying vehicles
- AutoNet—development of unmanned cars and intelligent transport systems
- EnergyNet—development of renewable energy and smart energy supply systems
- FinNet—development of distributed financial systems and cryptocurrencies
- FoodNet—development of systems of personal production and delivery of food and water
- HealthNet—development of personal medicine and healthcare
- MariNet—development of distributed systems for unmanned sea transport
- NeuroNet—development of distributed artificial components of consciousness and psychology
- SafeNet—development of personal security systems.

On February 14, 2017, the Council for the Modernization of the Economy and Innovative Development of the Russian Federation adopted the road map "TechNet," NTI's plan for the development of cross-market/cross-sectoral measures in "Leading production technologies," to ensure the competitiveness of Russian companies in the above directions listed above and in the hi-tech spheres of industry.

The Ministry of Industry and Trade of the Russian Federation is responsible for the implementation of "TechNet." The plan has been formulated up until 2035 and consists of three stages:

- First stage (2017–2019): creation of the initial infrastructure and start-up of the first test platforms (TestBeds); creation of a first generation of "factories of the future," etc.
- Second stage (2020–2025): development and testing of new technological solutions for the provision of global competitiveness for Russian companies in the hi-tech spheres of industry and in the markets of the future (NTI markets); development of an infrastructure for test platforms (TestBeds), centers (bodies or laboratories) for certification and educational centers (learning factories) for the development of competencies at the global level, which are required for digital, "smart," and virtual factories.
- Third stage (2026–2035): replication and customization of technological solutions for hi-tech spheres and the markets of the future; creation of the third generation of "Factories of the future"; creation of the global distributed network

for "Factories of the future" (digital, "smart,", and virtual), and scaling Russian presence in the global markets for hi-tech products.

The key component of "TechNet" is the "Factory of the future," a system of complex technological solutions (integrated technological chains), which ensures the design and production of a new generation of globally competitive products. The "Factory of the future" is generated on the basis of test platforms (TestBeds). The developers of "TechNet" think that "Factory of the future" will be the first stage on the path to the "Virtual factory"—a union of digital and (or) "smart" factories into one network or as part of a global supply chain (supply ⇒ production ⇒ distribution and logistics ⇒ sales and service maintenance), or as distributed production assets. The "Virtual factory" is the virtual model of all organizational, technological, and logistical processes of territorially distributed "digital" and "smart" production that are presented to the user as one object. The general effects of the implementation of the "Virtual factory" as compared to traditional models of production and design have been assessed as being: a growth of predictability by 204 times; reduction of expenditures by 40%; reduction of the number of equipment units by 7–15% (determined empirically during the implementation of a comparable leading project, GE Brilliant Factory).

According to the developers, the implementation of "TechNet" has to lead to a growth of labor efficiency, a significant increase in exports of Russian hi-tech products, Russian entry into the global hi-tech markets, development of non-resource exports, import substitution, replacement of fixed assets, reduction of dependence on imported technologies, mastering of new competencies, and growth of patent activity and revenues from licensed technologies and solutions.

The Russian Government's initiatives in the last 10 years have established a number of research centers and institutes that are helping to form the image of Industry 4.0 in Russia: Skolkovo Innovative Center near Moscow, the special economic area Innopolis, and Innopolis University in the Republic of Tatarstan. Private business is also striving to conform to the global and national trends and to implement the elements of Industry 4.0: automatized systems of management, cloud technologies, Big Data analysis, and industrial IoT. In particular, the Association for the Stimulation of Development and Standardization of Management Systems was created in 2017 on the basis of IIoT and the National Platform of Industrial Automatization was created on the basis of cooperation between the *InfoWatch* group of companies, *Eltex*, and *Tornado Module Systems*.

These and other examples show the complexity and uniqueness of the task of implementing the key elements of the cyber economy within Industry 4.0 in Russia. However, the forecast for change within the Russian economy is, on the whole, positive, as Russia has sufficient resources to implement the transition to the new technological mode, despite the fact that it currently lags well behind the leaders.

4 Conclusion

Given the above discussion, it is necessary to note the following important characteristics of the role of government in the transition to the new technological mode within the Fourth Industrial Revolution:

- Business initiatives to implement Industry 4.0 cannot be realized without support from the government. In all of the countries that are leaders in Industry 4.0 initiatives are promoted and developed by the efforts of government bodies, in collaboration with private business and the scientific community.
- The government, through normative regulation, financial participation, and direct participation in the creation of various institutes and projects that are aimed at realizing elements of Industry 4.0, forms the necessary environment and context in which the priorities for the development of the digital economy are determined.
- Governments assess the potential for the development of the economy in the process of implementing Industry 4.0 realistically, but they do not always realistically assess the requirements for joining this global trend.
- Russia has developed and achieved success with digital services for the general population but it lags far behind the leaders in the spheres of IIoT, robotization, Big Data, and additive technologies.
- The Russian approach to the cyber economy and Industry 4.0 is based on the concept of the "Information society"—i.e., the knowledge society, which is similar to the Japanese concept, Society 5.0.

Acknowledgments The reported study was funded by RFBR according to the research project No. 18-010-00103 A.

References

Fedotova GV, Kulikova NN, Perekrestova LV, Kozenko YA (2018) Target indicators of implementing the measures on formation of the model of information economy. In: Sukhodolov AP (ed) Models of modern information economy: conceptual contradictions and practical examples. Emerald Publishing Limited, London, pp 255–263

Kovazhenkov MA, Fedotova GV, Kurbanov TK, Uchurova EO, Tserenova BI (2018) Verification of state programs of geographically-distributed economic systems. In: Popkova EG (ed) The future of the global financial system: downfall or harmony: [materials of conference (Limassol, Cyprus, April 13–14, 2018)], Lecture notes in networks and systems, vol 57. Springer, Cham, pp 1043–1053

Kravets AG, Gurtjakov AS, Darmanian AP (2013) Enterprise intellectual capital management by social learning environment implementation. World Appl Sci J 23(7):956–964

Kuznetsov SY, Tereliansky PV, Shuvaev AV, Natsubize AS, Vasilyev IA (2016) Analysis of innovate solutions based on combinatorial approaches. ARPN J Eng Appl Sci 11 (17):10222–10230

Plotnokov V, Fedotova GV, Popkova EG, Kastyrina AA (2015) Harmonization of strategic planning indicators of territories' socioeconomic growth. Reg Sect Econ Stud 15-2:105–114

Popova L, Litvinova T, Ioda E, Suleimanova L, Chirkina M (2015) Perspectives of the growth of economic security by clustering of small innovative enterprises. Eur Res Stud J 18(Special Issue):163–172
Romanova TF, Andreeva OV, Meliksetyan SN, Otrishko MO (2017) Increasing of cost efficiency as a trend of public law entities' activity intensification in a public administration sector. Eur Res Stud J 20(1):155–161
Sibirskaya EV, Shestaeva KA (2016) The contents of innovative in the Russian economy. In: Paweł L, Tomasz R (eds) Knowledge-economy-society: contemporary aspects of economic transformation. Cracow University of Economics, Krakow, Poland, pp 27–37
Sukhodolov AP, Popkova EG, Kuzlaeva IM (2018) Internet economy: existence from the point of view of micro-economic aspect. Stud Comput Intell 714:11–21
Vertakova Y, Plotnikov V, Fedotova G (2016) The system of indicators for indicative management of a region and its clusters. Procedia Econ Financ 39:184–191

Conclusions

Vladimir M. Filippov, Alexander A. Chursin, Julia V. Ragulina, and Elena G. Popkova

Abstract It is possible to conclude that the term "cyber economy" has found its place in the modern scientific lexicon and it fully and precisely describes the new type of economic system that will form in the process of the Fourth Industrial Revolution. Formation of the cyber economy starts deep transformation processes at all levels of economic activity. The organization of production and distribution, based on the breakthrough technologies of Industry 4.0 and digital business, continues to become more popular. The diversification of consumption and modernization of state management are moving ahead apace.

It is possible to conclude that the term "cyber economy" has found its place in the modern scientific lexicon and it fully and precisely describes the new type of economic system that will form in the process of the Fourth Industrial Revolution. Formation of the cyber economy starts deep transformation processes at all levels of economic activity. The organization of production and distribution, based on the breakthrough technologies of Industry 4.0 and digital business, continues to become more popular. The diversification of consumption and modernization of state management are moving ahead apace.

Intelligent machines occupy a central place in the cyber economy, performing the functions of intelligent decision support and ensuring the functioning of automatized production and distribution systems. At the same time, the possibilities for their autonomous economic activities are limited to interactions with other machines, as their interactions with humans (employees and consumers) require human control.

The implementation and technical maintenance of intelligent machines, as well as the execution of functions that they cannot perform (e.g., intellectual activities and provision of services) require digital personnel—employees with digital

V. M. Filippov · A. A. Chursin · J. V. Ragulina
Peoples' Friendship University of Russia, Moscow, Russia
e-mail: rector@rudn.ru; chursin-aa@rudn.ru; ragulina-yuv@rudn.ru

E. G. Popkova (✉)
Plekhanov Russian University of Economics, Moscow, Russia

© Springer Nature Switzerland AG 2019

V. M. Filippov et al. (eds.), *The Cyber Economy*, Contributions to Economics,
https://doi.org/10.1007/978-3-030-31566-5_34

competencies and the ability to use intelligent machines. In the cyber economy, digital competence will become the basis of an employee's competitiveness in the labor market. The training of digital personnel is a serious challenge for the modern system of science and education, as this requires new educational programs and new methodologies and technologies for training. The adaptation of breakthrough technologies to the current needs of science and education is being performed in its hi-tech segment (EdTech).

Interactions between intelligent machines and digital personnel in the cyber economy could take a number of different forms. One of them is the competitive form. The production and distribution functions that are traditionally performed by humans are subject to automatization in the cyber economy. The possibility of intelligent machines becoming rivals that take human jobs and increase unemployment causes justified societal criticism and employee protests opposing their implementation.

Another form of interaction between intelligent machines and digital personnel in the cyber economy is their joint roles in the industrial production systems of Industry 4.0. In this case, automatization is full. However, the functions of digital personnel are not reduced simply to the technical maintenance of intelligent machines—an equal distribution of human and machine labor is possible. Therefore, there is scope for some harmony in the coming transition to the cyber economy.

The third form of interaction is the management of intelligent machines, which is performed by digital personnel. This revolutionary practice of management requires new managerial tools, far different from those used for human resource management. Rather, such tools should aim to take a hybrid form, marrying together management, training, and programming competencies. Mastering this practice will create highly efficient jobs, but also some challenges for digital personnel.

The fourth form of possible interaction is the management of digital personnel by intelligent machines. This is a new type of relationship, which is now being formed but which faces determined opposition from those that argue that it will lead to machine domination of humans.

Application of intelligent machines in the cyber economy is not limited to the spheres of production and distribution; they could also be applied more actively in the sphere of consumption. Examples include "smart" household appliances (e.g., remotely controlled ovens or washing machines), "smart homes," and "smart cities." The development of e-government envisages a constant increase in the digital literacy of the population. Thus, the problems of the social adaptation of the population to the conditions of the cyber economy appear.

Managing the competitiveness of the cyber economy requires the application of new approaches, as it envisages, firstly, supporting its stability through overcoming the opposition between digital personnel and intelligent machines, and, secondly, its foundation on digital business and new hi-tech spheres (HighTech and DigiTech) during the selection of priority areas for domestic and international production specialization.

An important role in supporting the competitiveness of the cyber economy lies with integration processes, which require targeted management. On the one hand, there is the need for international economic integration to support the openness of the cyber economy to new knowledge and technologies and to strengthen domestic digital entrepreneurship in the global markets of hi-tech and hi-tech products. On the other hand, internal integration of the cyber economy through better interaction and integration between universities, industry, science, and the market is necessary.

For effective management of the competitiveness of the cyber economy a strategy for implementing the modern technologies of Industry 4.0 along with the tools of competency management into digital industry is critical. Innovations of all types are required, not least to encourage the growth of green innovation to support the aims of sustainable development.

It should be concluded that the cyber economy is likely to develop very quickly, ensuring new opportunities to accelerate the growth of modern economic systems. This will be achieved on the basis of an increase in labor efficiency and the development and production of innovative goods and services, which fully satisfy consumer needs. However, the coming transition will also create new challenges and threats for business, society, and the state. Most of these challenges have a national character and are predetermined by the specifics of the cyber economy in each country. They can also be solved at the national level through the modernization of organizational and managerial practices based on breakthrough technologies.

Some challenges will be common for the whole global community and thus they could and should be solved at the level of international organizations. A new international institute for the cyber economy might be the optimal solution. This should specialize in the development of a methodology for evaluating the progress of economic systems in establishing the cyber economy and comparative analysis, as the existing and currently used methods are based on standard statistical indicators, which do not take into account the specifics of the digital economy.

A new international organization should also focus on the issues of stimulation and support for the transition of developing countries to the cyber economy to boost their rates of their growth, increase their global competitiveness, and ensure their sustainable development. Such international activities are not studied in this book but are important directions for future scientific research.

Many of the issues connected to the creation and training of intelligent machines and the normative and legal provisions necessary for the cyber economy are studied in this book, but some remain unsolved. These issues require further multidisciplinary research by scholars from the economic, legal, and social sciences.

The manufacturer's authorised representative in the EU is Springer Nature Customer Service Centre GmbH, Europaplatz 3, 69115 Heidelberg, Germany. If you have any concerns regarding our products, please contact ProductSafety@springernature.com

Printed and bound by CPI Group (UK) Ltd, Croydon, CR0 4YY
30/09/2026
02225657-0006